THE VERY RICH

A HISTORY OF WEALTH

THE
VERY RICH

A HISTORY OF WEALTH

BY JOSEPH J. THORNDIKE, JR.

AMERICAN HERITAGE PUBLISHING CO., INC.
BONANZA BOOKS
NEW YORK

This edition published by Bonanza Books, distributed by Crown
Publishers, Inc. by arrangement with American Heritage Publishing
Co., Inc.

h g f e d c b a

BONANZA EDITION 1981

Library of Congress Cataloging in Publication Data

Thorndike, Joseph Jacob, 1913-
    The very rich.

    Includes index.
    1. Wealth.   2. Millionaires—Biography.
I. Title.
HC79.W4T5 1981   305.5'2   81-18083
ISBN 0-517-36234-1   AACR2

CONTENTS

1 **PRIVATE FORTUNES**   4

    A PORTFOLIO: WEALTH IN HISTORY   25

2 **WEALTH FROM LAND**   36

    A PORTFOLIO: THE ENGLISH LANDED GENTRY   63

3 **WEALTH FROM NATURAL RESOURCES**   74

    A PORTFOLIO: WHAT A WAY TO GO!   103

4 **WEALTH FROM TRADE**   118

    A PORTFOLIO: THE GOOD LIFE OF THE DUTCH   141

5 **WEALTH FROM FINANCE**   148

    A PORTFOLIO: THE WEALTHY PATRONS   181

6 **WEALTH FROM TALENT** by Peter Andrews   192

    A PORTFOLIO: SOME WHIMS OF THE VERY RICH   223

7 **WEALTH FROM THE INDUSTRIAL REVOLUTION**   236

    A PORTFOLIO: THE GILDED AGE   269

8 **WEALTH FROM MODERN INDUSTRY** by Ralph Andrist   282

    A PORTFOLIO: THE AFFLUENT LIFE   313

9 **WEALTH & SOCIETY**   328

    ACKNOWLEDGMENTS & INDEX   344

1. PRIVATE FORTUNES

A PARADE OF FORTUNE

Imagine yourself a very old croupier at a roulette table in the casino at Monte Carlo. When you first went to work at the casino in the early years of this century, many of the seats around the table were occupied by titled aristocrats from the countries of Europe, especially England and Russia. Scattered among them were a few nouveaux-riches industrialists from Germany, France, and Belgium, an occasional maharajah, and always the Aga Khan. At times there might be an American such as James Gordon Bennett, Jr., the free-spending heir of a newspaper fortune, or Charles M. Schwab, the ebullient new president of United States Steel. With the Revolution of 1917 the Russian nobles disappeared, and after World War I there were fewer princes of the European royal houses. In the 1930's you began to see celebrities of the entertainment world such as Noel Coward, Maurice Chevalier, and Charlie Chaplin. After World War II the English milords were suddenly among the missing, but Hollywood moguls like Jack Warner and Darryl Zanuck had taken their places, as well as South American playboys with names like Bebe and Coco. By the 1950's oil millionaires from Texas were trying to break the bank. By the sixties the biggest yachts in the harbor below the casino belonged to Greeks, and one of them had actually bought the casino. Now, in the 1970's, you, the ancient croupier, look about you at a new set of faces: the princes and oil sheiks of Arabia.

Watching this parade of spenders, you would probably conclude that wealth is a transitory thing indeed. Certainly it is true that in the twentieth century the historic enemies of money—war, revolution, confiscation, and ruinous taxes—have laid waste the ancient, hoarded wealth of Europe and Asia. There are no landed aristocrats to succeed the Stroganovs in Russia, the Esterhazys in Hungary, the Radziwills in Poland. The princes of India have lost their cellars full of jewels, along with their lands and their powers, to Indira Gandhi's government. The noble lords of England huddle in single wings of ancestral palaces now filled with tourists and owned by the National Trust.

Yet the flow of wealth in the last quarter century has not been uniformly away from private hands. Where the free-enterprise system survives, new for-

tunes have been built to replace, and in some cases surpass, the old. The success story of Akio Morita and Masaru Ibuka, who built the Sony electronics empire in postwar Japan, has been matched in England, France, Germany, and Italy.

Meanwhile, the United States has remained, throughout this turbulent century, the best place to make or keep a fortune. While taxes have bitten deeply into the income of the corporate executive who gets a high salary, they have fallen lightly on the entrepreneur who builds up his own business and takes his reward in the form of capital gains. And the net of government regulations, while exercising a drag on all private enterprises, has been felt less strongly on the business frontier, where new industries are born and new fortunes made. In 1972, according to the estimates of James Smith, an economist at Pennsylvania State University, there were 133,400 millionaires in the United States—an increase of one hundred forty-four per cent since 1962. Even allowing for inflation, this is a remarkable increase in ten years and a testimony to the persistence of economic opportunity in the United States.

WEALTH AND POWER

Though individual fortunes have come and gone, the sources from which they sprang have remained much the same over the centuries, with only one major addition—manufacturing—in modern times. The earliest source of wealth was political power. It was the power of the tribal chief or later the king or great prince. It took the form of control over territory and over people—followers, clansmen, slaves, or serfs. Sometimes the chief could use the wealth of the tribe or nation to build a castle for himself and his family or, like the pharaohs, could divert the labor of a kingdom to build his own tomb. But because it was not private wealth in the modern sense, his control over it was limited. Most importantly, he could not dispose of it freely on his death. It passed to his successor—sometimes a dynastic or chosen successor but sometimes not.

Such political wealth was possessed in its purest form by the late Emperor Haile Selassie of Ethiopia, the Lion of Judah, who enjoyed it for fifty years until he was deposed in 1975. It is held today by such rulers as the shah of Iran and the king of Saudi Arabia. But it is strictly a concomitant of rule. The throne of Iran was seized by the present shah's father from another ruling dynasty. The kingdom of Saudi Arabia was carved out by the grandfather of

---

◄ PRECEDING PAGES: **This is the Neptune pool, of Carrara marble, at William Randolph Hearst's San Simeon.**
RENE BURRI, MAGNUM

the present king, and its last two rulers have been chosen by a council of the Saud family. During the lifetime of the present monarchs, their royal brothers of Egypt, Iraq, and Libya have been stripped of their wealth along with their thrones.

In rare cases, where the monarchy has been constitutionalized and the monarch's power is more formal than real, the ruler may be allowed by law or tradition to hold personal wealth. The two notable examples at present are the queens of England and the Netherlands. Queen Elizabeth's private property includes the estates of Sandringham and Balmoral, along with personal investments. The late Queen Wilhelmina of the Netherlands still appears in the *Guinness Book of World Records* as the richest of rulers, with an estimated personal wealth of over five hundred million dollars. But during the early 1960's she had to sell some of her family treasures to pay her

The Aga Khan, spiritual leader of twenty million Ismaili Moslems, was weighed against gold, diamonds, and platinum at an annual conclave of the faithful. Here he sits (at left) on one side of the scale while an attendant piles boxes of treasure on the other side to tip the scale at 234-1/2 pounds. The money was raised from his followers, and the Aga, who was already immensely rich, used it for charities. Since his death in 1957, the ceremony has been discontinued by his grandson, the present Aga, possibly because of the threat it posed to his waistline.

expenses, and today it is impossible to guess how great a fortune her daughter, Queen Juliana, possesses since the financial affairs of the house of Orange are not public.

Perhaps the last Europeans to exercise absolute power, combined with private wealth, were the White Rajahs of Sarawak. The founder of the

7

dynasty was a young Englishman named James Brooke, who used his family inheritance to equip a private naval vessel and sail it to the Southwest Pacific in 1838. On the northwest coast of Borneo he found a scattering of native, pagan tribes, some of them head-hunters, many of them at war with each other, and all of them restive under the nominal rule of the Malay sultan. By waging war first against the rebels and then against the sultanate, Brooke established his own rule and assumed the title of rajah, which was eventually recognized by the British government. Not only did Rajah Brooke thus fulfill the familiar boyhood dream of carving out one's own island kingdom, he ruled it for the rest of his life. He established order, put down occasional risings, abolished piracy and head-hunting, maintained a proper British court, and handed down his imperium to his nephew and grand-nephew. The third and last rajah was Sir Charles Vyner Brooke, who had no son but three beautiful daughters. Eligible bachelors being in short supply in Sarawak, the daughters removed to London, where the popular press of the 1930's gave rapt attention to their search for mates and their eventual marriages: Princess Gold to the Earl of Inchcape, Princess Pearl to Harry Roy, a jazz band leader, and Princess Baba to Bob Gregory, a prize fighter. It came as rather an anticlimax to this romantic saga that the Japanese occupied Sarawak in World War II. When they departed in 1945, they left affairs in such chaos that Rajah Brooke relinquished his title and his rule to the British government, which in due course granted Sarawak independence as part of the new country of Malaysia.

Even in our democratic society political power played a significant part in many financial success stories. Among the less savory fortunes piled up in the late nineteenth and early twentieth centuries were those of the big-city "traction kings." William C. Whitney was one of the richest and certainly the grandest of them. Arriving in New York from a small New England town by way of Yale, he got his start as a reform politician by chasing a greedy crew known as the "boodle aldermen" out of City Hall. But then he turned around and began acquiring franchises for New York City trolley lines. With

Thomas Fortune Ryan, he formed the Metropolitan Street Railway Company, which they called their "great tin box" and from which they drew many millions of dollars. During his years of accumulation he also served as Secretary of the Navy in President Cleveland's Cabinet. No one in the Gilded Age cut a more handsome figure in New York ballrooms or at the Saratoga race track.

The use of political influence as a steppingstone to wealth does not, of course, necessarily involve corruption. Lyndon Johnson arrived in Washington as a young Congressman with forty-seven dollars and left the White House with a fortune, in his own name and his wife's, that was estimated at about twenty million. Much of the money was made after 1943, when the Federal Communications Commission awarded to Lady Bird Johnson the franchise for television station KTBC in Austin, Texas.

OTHER SOURCES OF WEALTH

Next to political power the most ancient source of wealth is land. In the beginning the great landed estates of the European nobility were themselves founded on political power, having sometimes been long held by independent lords and sometimes conferred on royal favorites. But over the centuries they were held and handed down, bought, sold, and developed, as private property. Though most of these noble landed estates have been lost or greatly reduced, they were for centuries one of the stablest forms of wealth. Some survive, especially in Spain, where as late as 1976 the convulsions of the twentieth century had not yet touched the property of such grandees as the Duchess of Alba, who has nine titles of duchess, sixteen of marchioness, and twenty-two of countess. Her estates, inherited through many lines of descent, make her probably the wealthiest landowner in Spain and one of the wealthiest in Europe.

In the countries of the Old World it was common practice for "new men," who had acquired their fortunes in other ways, to invest them in landed estates, which carried status and frequently led to titles of nobility. Something of the same sort occurred in this country, but for reasons of investment and speculation. Thus real estate and its development have been responsible in large measure for such oddly assorted fortunes as those of John Jacob Astor, the Duke of Westminster, Marshall Field, Joseph P. Kennedy, and Bob Hope.

What lies beneath the land—the geological

resources of the earth—became an important source of wealth when men began to use iron for weapons and gems for decoration, and even more important when they began to fuel locomotives with coal and motor cars with oil. In most countries of the Old World mineral resources belonged to the state, but occasionally rulers granted mining rights to favored subjects. Long ago such grants played a major role in the spectacular rise of moneymen like Jacques Coeur in France and Jakob Fugger in Austria. In the twentieth century, by far the greatest beneficiaries of underground riches have been Americans. Of the four recent fortunes that have been generally estimated in the billion-dollar range, two were made by oilmen, J. Paul Getty and H. L. Hunt, while the other two had important connections to the oil industry. One of them belongs to Daniel K. Ludwig, who made most of his money by operating tankers. The other was that of Howard Hughes, who owed his original fortune to the oil drill invented by his father.

Trade, with its handmaiden finance, has been an avenue to wealth for enterprising men since civilization began. Yet it has been subject in many societies to a strange discrimination. In ancient Rome senators measured their wealth in land and slaves but considered trade beneath them. Cicero, more broadminded than most, could just bring himself to give it this guarded approval:

Trade, if it is on a small scale, is to be considered vulgar; but if wholesale and on a large scale, importing large quantities from all parts of the world and distributing to many without misrepresentation, it is not to be greatly disparaged. On the contrary, it even seems to deserve high respect if those who are engaged in its pursuit, satiated or rather I should say satisfied with the fortunes they have won, make their way from the port to a country estate, as they have often made it from the sea into port.

The English could hardly scorn trade, since it was the foundation of their empire, but those who made their fortunes from oceangoing commerce commonly hastened to provide themselves with estates and, if possible, titles to match those of the older aristocracy. Then they, too, could look down upon the newer fortunes being made in manufacture.

Henry Ford plays the part of a Western badman during an outing about 1923. Perhaps with the same mischievous sense of humor—or perhaps not—he supposedly once advised William Randolph Hearst to put aside two or three hundred million dollars for a rainy day.

In America the possessors of early fortunes made in land and trade were never so firmly entrenched as to look down upon millowners. The Industrial Revolution, which occurred in England at about the same time as the American Revolution, was slow to reach this country. But when it arrived, none were so quick to join it as the canny merchants of New England. Manufacture is the one wholly new source of wealth in the modern world, and the one that seems most characteristically American. It not only brought an explosion of wealth without precedent in the history of the human race but made popular heroes out of such captains of industry as Andrew Carnegie and Henry Ford. Calvin Coolidge spoke for his generation when he said in 1925, "The business of America is business." It is hard to think of any other country in which the head of state would have made such a remark.

OLD FORTUNES AND NEW

There has long been a notion abroad that American families of wealth typically go "from shirt-sleeves to shirt-sleeves in three generations." And indeed there are plenty of examples in the history of American fortunes to show that money is a hard thing to hold on to. If you confine your researches to the pages of the *New York Social Register*, you will find the traces of almost as many lost fortunes as you would find in the *Almanach de Gotha*. Where are the van Rensselaers, Beekmans, and Stuyvesants, where the Belmonts and Stotesburys, where even the Astors and Vanderbilts, where the Singers and Ryans and Goulds? The answer, financially speaking, is: not much of anywhere.

The enemies of private wealth in other parts of the world claimed only a few of these once-great fortunes. Revolution and confiscation wiped out some families who took the Tory side in 1776. Civil war cost Southern planters their acres and slaves. But throughout American history private fortunes have been more often founded than destroyed in wars.

No, the vanished fortunes of the American past have disappeared for other reasons. One is the absence in this country of the system of primogeniture, whereby European estates were handed down intact

BOB LANDRY, TIME LIFE PICTURE AGENCY © TIME INC.

William Randolph Hearst rides a merry-go-round at Marion Davies' beach house in California in 1937. In his conversation with Ford, the fun-loving, prodigal Hearst had to admit that the money he made—some twelve million dollars a year—went out as fast as it came in.

ROCKEFELLER   **FORD**   **GULBENKIAN**   **MELLON**   **NIZAM OF HYDERABAD**   **HUNT**

to eldest sons. The founders of American fortunes have generally split them up, as William Rockefeller, brother of John, did when he wrote a will that in time made fifty members of his family millionaires. Such fortunes have not gone out of existence but have been reduced to small units and have often passed to heirs with other family names.

A companion to primogeniture as a bulwark of inherited wealth was the system of entail, as permitted in England and the American colonies but severely restricted in all American states. Under the laws of entail a fortune could be so tied up that the heirs in any generation could not touch the principal. Entail was the great protection against family fools and wastrels. Freed of its restrictions, the Goulds, the Belmonts, and the Guggenheims have all lent substance to the "shirt-sleeves-to-shirt-sleeves" tradition.

A third peril to inherited wealth in the United States has been the tendency of fortune builders to give their money away. This practice, often recommended in the New Testament but strange and bewildering to the wealthy classes of the rest of the world, has removed from the ranks of the very rich such families as the Peabodys, the Carnegies, the Sages, the Rosenwalds, and the Astors. But while such philanthropy has scattered the wealth of the givers, it has also done much to preserve a social climate in which new fortunes could spring up to replace them.

Despite various perils to American wealth, the fact is that while some old fortunes have vanished from sight, many others have survived. Mellons, Du Ponts, Rockefellers, and Fords still appear in the top bracket of any roster of current multimillionaires. In his recent book, *Generating Inequality*, Lester C. Thurow, professor of economics at the Massachusetts Institute of Technology, estimated that roughly one-half of the greatest American fortunes are inherited fortunes. The greatest of them date from the period of economic expansion and unfettered free enterprise between the Civil War and the turn of the century. They are the legacy of the captains of in-

dustry—or robber barons, depending on who is describing them.

The other half of the great American fortunes now in existence were therefore made by persons still living at the time the figures were gathered, and most of them must have been made since the great depression of the 1930's. While the biggest of all were made in oil, the most numerous came from manufacture. Some were made in the electronics industry by men who got their start as military suppliers during World War II and managed the successful conversion to peacetime industry. Others were created, as if by magic, in conglomerates put together by such men as Royal Little of Textron, Charles Bluhdorn of Gulf and Western, and Harold Geneen of ITT. Later, during the stock-market boom of the 1960's, multimillionaires were popping up like crocuses on a spring lawn. But many of these were multimillionaires only because the market had priced their holdings at dizzy multiples—Electronic Data Processing at three hundred eighty four times earnings. Many of the "instant millionaires," such as Jimmy Ling of Ling-Temco-Vought, were shriveled by the cold blast of the stock-market drop in the 1970's.

The old-time captains of industry would have been surprised to see where some of the most recent solid fortunes have been made. Arthur Louis, who charts the rise and fall of multimillionaires for *Fortune*, found in 1973 that among those who had made the biggest fortunes in the preceding five years were Leonard Stern, who built Hartz Mountain Pet Foods, Roy J. Carver, who developed the Bandag process for retreading tires, and Milton J. Petrie, who runs a chain of clothing stores. If some of the fields that have proved so lucrative seem like peripheral areas of the economic structure, it is doubtless because so many of the basic industries are dominated by great corporations, which offer little scope for individual fortune builders. The significant fact is that ambitious men who found doors closing to them in industries that enriched the Vanderbilts and Mellons have found new avenues to great wealth.

HUGHES JOHNSON OPPENHEIMER MACARTHUR LUDWIG GETTY

HOW RICH IS RICH?

Most of the persons mentioned in the previous paragraphs are multimillionaires. Before going further, it may be well to consider for a moment just how rich is rich. At one point in his career, during the latter part of the nineteenth century, John W. Mackay said, "The fellow who has $200,000 and tries to make more is only borrowing trouble." Subsequently, Mackay went on to make about a hundred million dollars and to become known as a silver king. But the first figure was hit upon also by H. L. Hunt, the oil driller of the 1950's who said, "A man who has $200,000 is about as well off, for all practical purposes, as I am." Hunt's view may be discounted in light of the fact that he was the kind of billionaire who drove an old car and took his lunch to work in a paper bag. But Mackay was speaking of a sum that would buy in his day about what a million dollars will buy today. A million dollars is still a good, round symbolic figure, and perhaps it will serve as the base line for wealth in the present day. If there are 133,400 millionaires, as estimated, it hardly denotes an exclusive company.

How many millions does it take to qualify a man for recognition as one of the "big-rich"? It is a constantly escalating figure, as evidenced by the successive studies conducted by *Fortune*. In the first such survey in 1957, it identified one hundred fifty-five multimillionaires in categories ranging from one billion dollars downward to fifty million. In its 1968 survey it raised the cut-off point to a hundred million and still identified one hundred fifty-three individuals above that line.

The richest of the rich have their own special viewpoint on such matters. The late Gene Fowler claimed to have been present at a dinner at which Henry Ford asked William Randolph Hearst:

"Mr. Hearst, have you got any money?"

"I never have any money, Mr. Ford," replied Hearst. "I always spend any money that I am to receive before I get it."

The "billionaires' club" has included most of these men. Rockefeller, Hunt, and Getty made their fortunes in oil, Ludwig in shipping, Oppenheimer in diamonds, Mellon and Hughes in various fields. John D. MacArthur owns insurance companies; Robert Wood Johnson was the Band-Aid king. Included also are two who were habitually labeled billionaires by the press but probably never were: Calouste Gulbenkian, the Armenian oilman, and the Nizam of Hyderabad, who reputedly had cellars full of jewels. There are almost surely others—both Americans who have not surfaced yet and foreigners who manage to keep their financial affairs private. Missing is the only man who is known to have made a billion and lost a billion: H. Ross Perot, whose electronics company stock rose in the bull market of the 1960's and fell in the bear market of the 1970's.

"That's a darned shame," said Ford. "You ought to get yourself two or three hundred million dollars together and tuck it away."

It may be suspected that, if this conversation ever took place, Ford was putting the prodigal Hearst on. But there was nothing jocular about Andrew Carnegie's reaction to the news that J. P. Morgan had left an estate of sixty-eight million dollars (plus about fifty-million-dollars' worth of art). "And to think," exclaimed Carnegie, recalling Morgan's vast financial power, "he was not a rich man!"

WHO GETS RICH?

Perhaps the most common characteristic of those who acquire great wealth is their dedication to that single goal. This goes beyond the dedication of the corporate executive who regularly works a twelve-hour day, takes home a bulging briefcase, and puts his career ahead of his private life. The driving spirit of the true empire builder is something more than that rather drudging concentration on getting ahead. It is a fierce purpose, which may not take the form of regular hours or piles of paper or even a concern for money as such but which makes all other activities seem dull in comparison.

13

Such dedication often appears at a young age. When he was fourteen years old, Henry Huddleston Rogers was a newsboy in Fairhaven, near New Bedford, Massachusetts, at that time the greatest of whaling ports. One day as he was picking up his papers young Rogers noticed a story that a whaler with a heavy cargo of sperm oil had been lost at sea. The news, he knew, would cause a rise in the price of oil. Instead of delivering the papers to his regular customers, he took the whole load to one of the leading merchants and offered it to him for two hundred dollars, thus giving the merchant a beat on the news. The merchant paid the sum and presumably made a tidy profit by buying oil. As for Rogers, he went on to become one of John D. Rockefeller's partners in the early days of Standard Oil and make a personal fortune of something over a hundred million dollars.

The same dedication to the pursuit of wealth continues through life. In his book *The Proper Bostonians*, Cleveland Amory quotes an entry from the diary of William Appleton, a Boston merchant, who possessed one of the city's biggest fortunes: "I am quite eaten up with business; while in Church, my mind with all the exertion I endeavoured to make, was flying from City to City, from Ship to Ship and from Speculation to Speculation."

The late Lord Beaverbrook, who began his career in the Canadian lumber business before he moved to London and became a great newspaper publisher, knew what it takes to make a fortune: "A man must feel those early deals right down to the pit of his stomach if he is going to be a great man of business. They must shake the very fiber of his being as the conception of a great picture shakes the artist."

Often the fortune builders pay a high price in their personal and family lives for their dedication. When Judge Thomas Mellon, the founder of the Mellon fortune, decided that it was time for him to marry, he made an inventory of available prospects in his hometown, selected a bride, and stated his prospects to her. "The transaction was completed today," he wrote in his diary after she accepted, adding that if she had not accepted, he would not have been greatly troubled but "only annoyed at the loss of time."

To their wives the fortune builders were often cold, preoccupied husbands. To their children, they were often strangers. And sometimes the deprivation suffered by their families was more than emotional. During the brief uranium boom of the 1950's, one of the spectacular success stories was that of Charles A. Steen, a young oil geologist who took his wife and four children to live in a shack in the country near Moab, Utah. Month after month Steen roamed the barren plateau with his Geiger counter, certain that he knew where to look for ore. Summer turned to winter. His money ran out. The day came when the baby was fed sugared tea for lack of milk. Steen kept on with his search, and at last he struck a vein of pure uranium that became the Mi Vida mine and eventually made him a multimillionaire.

Another common characteristic of the fortune builders is that, with few exceptions, they worked for themselves. Men who rise through the ranks of great publicly owned corporations may draw salaries in the upper reaches of six figures, together with stock options, pensions, and the like. But from it all they are unlikely to keep more than a few million. In recent times the U.S. Department of Defense has been headed by an ex-president of General Motors (Charles E. Wilson) and an ex-president of Ford (Robert McNamara), both of whom enjoyed about as high rewards as the corporate world affords. But they were not even in the league with a recent Deputy Secretary of Defense, David Packard, who built his own electronics company (Hewlett-Packard) and went to the Pentagon with a fortune of three hundred million dollars.

Historically one may find exceptions to this rule. Several of John D. Rockefeller's partners ended up with fortunes in excess of a hundred million dollars apiece, and although some of them had owned businesses before they joined him, others like Henry M. Flagler made their entire fortunes from Standard Oil. Andrew Carnegie's executives were also well rewarded. When he sold out his steel company to J.P.Morgan, he created thirty instant millionaires, who launched on a spree of mansion building and high living that created something of a scandal in Pittsburgh, much to the dismay of the prudent, sober Carnegie.

It is no less true today that in order to make a great fortune you must be your own boss. Lists of recent multimillionaires do not contain the name of a single individual who got rich by working for someone else.

In any case, the type of man most likely to make a fortune is not the type most likely to rise to the top of an established enterprise. Going back further, he is not likely to be the boy with the highest grades in school or the one voted Most Likely to Succeed by his college classmates. It is a common experience at college reunions for members of the twenty-five-year class to find among their number one who has made it really big and to ask in some surprise, "Who was he?" He may well have been a dropout.

Though the big winners include all personality types, many of them are rather abrasive characters. One such was Samuel Zemurray, who did not go to college at all but worked his way up on the banana docks in Alabama. The banana business had been for years almost a private fief of the United Fruit Company, which, for all its evil reputation in Latin America, had the most proper of Boston managements. It was in Sam Zemurray's way, and since it had been doing poorly, it was open to attack. Zemurray began accumulating proxies until he had enough to take control. In 1932, in one of the memorable scenes of American business history, he walked into the annual meeting of its largely Brahmin board of directors, headed by T. Jefferson Coolidge, and announced, "You've been ----ing up this business long enough. I'm going to straighten it out." And so he did, with considerable success, for the next nineteen years.

Personnel directors of large corporations have a sixth sense for spotting such rough diamonds—not as future captains of industry, however, but as likely troublemakers in the corporate hierarchy. Usually such job applicants do not get past the initial interview. One who put this common observation to the test was Jeno Paulucci, the founder and president of Chung King Foods. Some time before he sold his interest in the company for sixty-three million dollars, he took a psychological test given to job applicants, submitting it under an assumed name. Sure enough, he was rejected as unfit for a responsible position.

A common experience of those who make it big seems to be that they suffered some hardship or met some unusual challenges during childhood. As might be expected, many were only children or eldest sons—a circumstance that seems to breed overachievers in every field. More puzzling is the fact that many were the children of broken homes.

In gathering material for his book *The Very Very Rich and How They Got That Way*, Max Gunther was struck by the fact that more than half of the men whose lives he studied had lost a parent early in life through death or divorce. It may be, he suggests, that such a loss breeds a feeling of insecurity that drives the person to pile up wealth as a protection against further blows. Or, having survived such a deprivation, he may gain confidence in his own ability to go it alone. At any rate, the prevalence of parental death and divorce in the personal histories of successful men was confirmed in a study of one hundred ten company founders made for the Small

Business Administration in 1960 by Professors David Moore of Cornell, and Orvis Collins and Darab Unwalla of Michigan State. In the book *The Enterprising Man*, they report: "The picture that comes through from the interviews is one of the lonely child, grubby fists in tear-filled eyes, accepting the loss and facing a dangerous future."

One inescapable element in the rise to riches is luck. It was partly luck that won Mike Bendum the title "King of the Wildcatters." His chauffeur was even luckier because, just by keeping his ears open, he picked up enough good tips on oil plays to pile up a tidy fortune of seventeen million dollars.

It was lucky for Henry Phipps that as a boy in Allegheny City, Pennsylvania, he lived near Andrew Carnegie and thereby became Carnegie's lifelong friend and partner. Of course, luck runs both ways. At a time when he was short of funds, Cyrus McCormick offered a quarter interest in his new reaper to a man who was trying to collect a bill for seventy-one dollars. The creditor refused, thus missing his chance to become one of the richest men of his time.

In a larger sense it can be argued, as Ralph Henry Gabriel did, that all the American captains of industry owed their success not so much to their own genius as to the fact that they "had stumbled upon

To build a fine house has always been one of the first impulses of the rich. Elizabeth, Countess of Shrewsbury in Tudor England, inherited fortunes from four husbands and used the money to build Hardwick Hall (to sixteenth-century eyes, "more glass than wall").

15

Rock stars are among the biggest spenders of the present-day plutocracy. Here Elton John emerges from Cartier's jewelry store in London, loaded with $7,000 worth of presents for members of his band and staff. His Rolls-Royce Phantom is waiting at the curb.

easy money in a terrain well protected by nature from foreign brigands." Certainly it is true that they were lucky in being born at a time and place and under a political system that allowed ambitious men to make and keep great fortunes.

In the American gospel of wealth the two prophets most commonly cited are probably Benjamin Franklin and Horatio Alger. What Franklin's counsel boiled down to was: work hard. What Horatio Alger kept repeating in his dozens of moralistic novels was that if a boy cultivated all the traditional virtues, he would surely rise to riches. But it did not escape notice that in fact all of Alger's heroes made it to the top by such strokes of luck as marrying the boss' daughter or receiving favor from a benevolent man of wealth. For those for whom it is already too late to arrange to have a boyhood home near Andrew Carnegie's, or to experience some family trauma, perhaps a combination of Franklin's forthright advice and Alger's unacknowledged daydreams may still yield the best formula for getting rich: work hard and be lucky.

THE BIG SPENDERS

It has been remarked that many of those who acquire great wealth seem to be temperamentally the least likely to enjoy it. This assumes, of course, that the enjoyment of wealth lies in the spending of it. But for many, if not most, of the fortune builders whom we shall meet in this book, the satisfaction came mainly in the getting of it. They sought wealth as other men have climbed mountains or gone on Crusades or run for political office—for the love of the game and the joy of winning.

There are plenty of others, however, who did enjoy the fruits of victory—men like J. P. Morgan and William Randolph Hearst, who lived as much like princes as it is possible to live in a country that offers no titles or crowns. And in cases where the men who made the money lacked the instinct for big spending, their wives and heirs commonly made up the deficiency.

About the first thing that most people have done when they have come into a good deal of money has been to get themselves a better place to live. For an ancient Roman this could have meant a marble villa on the Bay of Naples. For a great noble at the court of France it had to be a chateau in the Loire Valley, within easy reach of the greatest of all houses, the royal palace at Versailles. In the United States, in the great mansion-building period between the Civil War and World War I, the premier showplace of the new multimillionaires was Fifth Avenue, stretching from 50th Street, where the houses of the older families ended, to 90th Street. Since New York City was no place to spend the summer, the man of wealth had a place at Newport or Bar Harbor or the north shore of Long Island for July and August. By the 1890's he might also be building a place at Palm Beach for the winter.

Few of the owners of these vast houses took much personal interest in building them. They—or more often their wives—wanted homes that would advertise their wealth, serve as the settings of dinner parties and balls, and establish their place at the top of the social structure. The houses are not the creations of the owners but of their architects—some of them very talented architects like Stanford White and Richard Morris Hunt. The buildings show it. It is easy to imagine giving a great party at the Breakers in Newport. It is almost impossible to imagine living there.

One financier who built to please himself was J.P. Morgan. If his brownstone mansion included the most magnificent private library in the United States (see pages 184–85), it was because that was the kind of room in which Morgan liked to work. Likewise, William Randolph Hearst embodied his expensive whims in the fanciful pleasure dome he built at San Simeon. Its architecture was a mixture of Spanish, Moorish, Roman, Gothic, Romanesque, and California roadside, but to Hearst it was still "the Ranch," where, on a long oaken table from a convent in northern Italy, he provided his guests with ketchup and paper napkins.

Such personal palaces were built by men of great affairs in moments of recreation. In order to see the result that can be achieved by total dedication to building, we may look at the work of Elizabeth Hardwick, a contemporary of Queen Elizabeth I. Born into a family of some gentility but little money, she was married at fourteen to a wealthy boy of fifteen who died the next year of consumption, leaving her his money. Next she married William Cavendish, and together they built Chatsworth, one of England's finest country houses. It was hardly a cozy home but was not without advantages. Prime Minister Harold Macmillan, who spent Christmases there with his Cavendish wife in this century, noted that its huge halls and long corridors made it a perfect place for the children to rollerskate.

Even for its builder, Chatsworth was more of a family seat than a personal dwelling. After Cavendish died, Bess lived there, off and on, through two subsequent marriages, first to Lord St. Loe, a courtier of the queen, and then to the wealthy Earl of Shrewsbury. By the time she had outlived four husbands, inheriting fortunes from each, she was accounted the richest woman in England, save only the queen. It was then that she began work on her masterpiece. She was almost seventy when she sat down on a stool before a big tilted table and began to sketch with her own trained hand the walls and windows and stairways and towers of Hardwick Hall. Three hundred seventy-five men were set to work, year in and year out. When it was so cold that mortar froze in the mixing, Bess ordered kettles of warm beer to replace the water the masons used. Story by story, the house rose, with each story containing bigger windows and less stone than the one below, until someone observing it coined the jingle: "Hardwick Hall/ More glass than wall." Bess' great joy was to walk back and forth the length of the tapestry gallery on the top floor, lifting her face to the sun that streamed through the great windows or the rain and snow that beat upon them. Though her masterpiece was finished, Bess went on building, in country and city, perhaps half believing what others said—that as long as she kept on building, Bess of Hardwick would never die. On a wintry night in 1608, legend says, the workmen stopped their work and "Building" Bess died.

GETTING AROUND IN STYLE

After a place to live in, came a vehicle to get around in. For all the centuries of European civilization, from the late Middle Ages to the nineteenth century, the rich man's answer was the carriage. From kings in their golden coaches of state to country squires in their gigs, men of wealth displayed their standing by the fineness of their equipage. They had a very bumpy ride until good springs were first used in the middle of the eighteenth century; but if their backs were jolted, their dignities were inflated. Colonial Bostonians who saw the rich merchant John Hancock ride out in his gleaming green coach with a pair of matching grays, a coachman, and two footmen, might shake their heads at such wanton display, but they never forgot the sight.

Because the owners spent so much time in their carriages, they outfitted them almost like traveling homes and carried on nearly as many activities. Meals were served and drinks poured. Dr. Erasmus Darwin, the grandfather of Charles, wrote his didactic poems of natural history while riding between house calls. Mademoiselle de Coigny, who was studying anatomy, kept a corpse in her coach for dissection en route. Noble gentlemen made love to ladies in their carriages, just as teenagers do in automobiles—uncomfortably.

In the second half of the nineteenth century the art of carriage-making reached its peak. If you were lucky enough to get one made for you by Brewster of New York, it came with at least fourteen coats of paint and your coat of arms on the door. You could order your chariot in an eye-boggling variety of styles from the graceful two-wheeled curricle to the *grande daumont de visite*. Perhaps the grandest turnout of all in the Gilded Age was the tallyho, in which fine parties of twelve or more rode out to the races.

Only one other means of getting around the country ever surpassed the carriage as a symbol of wealth, and that was the private railroad car. It even surpassed the yacht, for no matter what J. P. Morgan might say to an impertinent questioner, you

STEPHANIE DINKINS, PHOTO RESEARCHERS

did not have to be big-rich to own a yacht. Yacht is a flexible term and yachts come in all sizes. But private Pullmans came in only one size (big) and one price (high). Leaving aside the presidents of railroads, who got them as perquisites of office, the list of private-car owners reads like a directory of captains of industry: Whitney, Belmont, Mills, Widener, Schwab, Reynolds, Ryan, Busch, Gates, Frick, and so on. There was only one thing grander than a private Pullman, and that was a whole train of them. You really had to be Commodore Vanderbilt or Jay Gould to enjoy that.

When the automobile was new and was being denounced by Woodrow Wilson as a plaything of the rich, it briefly approached the carriage as a status symbol. As early as 1899 Mrs. Oliver H. P. Belmont was holding on her lawn at Newport a *concours d'élégance* in which such entrants as Mrs. Hermann Oelrichs and Mrs. Stuyvesant Fish drove flower-decked cars over an obstacle course. The heyday of the automobile, socially speaking, came in 1904 when William K. Vanderbilt sponsored the Vanderbilt Cup Races, held on a thirty-mile private highway that he and his fellow car buffs acquired on Long Island.

Luxury in ancient Rome was Hadrian's Villa at Tivoli, where the emperor recreated the places that had pleased him in his lifetime of travels. The establishment covered as much ground as Disneyworld and was not entirely dissimilar. Above is Hadrian's reproduction of the pool at Canopus in Egypt, sanctuary of the god Serapis. Today, once again, luxury is a pool with colonnades and statues, as seen on the opposite page at the winter home of Douglas Cooper, the Philadelphia jeweler, in Jamaica.

For many years the Rolls-Royce appealed to the noveaux riches as about the cheapest way to claim a social status befitting their net worth. It was equaled in distinction only by the "royal" Daimler, so-called because its body was made high enough for a monarch to enter without stooping. Lady Docker, the brash wife of an English industrialist, sought to go royalty one better by having her Daimler plated in gold. But even she could not match the quiet one-upmanship of Andrew Mellon, who had a car custom-built entirely of raw materials produced by companies under Mellon family control.

The private plane is the true modern equivalent of the private railroad car, but hardly in the same class of opulence. They all look alike on the outside, with

the notable exception of Hugh Hefner's "Big Bunny," and the interiors reflect the taste of commercial decorators rather than of the owners.

RAIMENT FOR THE RICH

At various periods in history, though certainly not in the present, a man of wealth could be recognized by his raiment. Berry Wall, who set the pace as a boulevardier at the turn of the last century, was said to have had five hundred outfits to choose from. At Saratoga, on a bet, he once made his appearance during a single day in forty changes of costume.

In jewelers' terms the American sartorial champion of the Gilded Age was Diamond Jim Brady, the flamboyant salesman of railroad equipment. Taking Lucius Beebe's appraisal, Brady owned thirty sets of jewelry, valued at more than two million dollars. The most famous of them was the "transportation set" of studs, cufflinks, buttons, and stickpins in the shape of locomotives, Pullman cars, tank cars, automobiles, bicycles, and an airplane. This set alone contained 2,637 diamonds and twenty-one rubies, set in platinum, for a total value of $87,315.

Since Brady's time, masculine adornment has gone steadily downhill. Not so long ago it was still possible to behold an Indian maharajah wearing a million-dollar jewel in his turban, and as late as 1975 General Idi Amin of Uganda showed up at the United Nations with a chestful of hardware that Hermann Goering would have envied. But to see a truly impressive show of raiment, it is necessary to visit the back country of Ghana, where the asantahene, the chief of the Ashanti tribe, goes clad all in gold to ceremonies of state.

In the Western world, generally, women have far outshone men, mainly because they can carry more jewels. The all-time champion was probably Queen Elizabeth I, who had her dresses sewn with so many pearls, diamonds, rubies, and golden baubles that a courtier was kept busy recording in the royal wardrobe book the jewels "lost from Her Majesty's back." Undoubtedly, the present champion is the queen of Iran, who can draw upon the Iranian royal jewel hoard, which is valued at almost four billion dollars and which, in addition to adorning the queen and her husband on ceremonial occasions, provides the backing for the Iranian currency.

Leaving jewels aside, no American women have come close to the monetary level of dress reached by

BROWN BROTHERS

MUSEUM OF THE CITY OF NEW YORK, BYRON COLLECTION

BOTH: BROWN BROTHERS

The ultimate glory that an American heiress could bring her family—or so some mothers thought—was to marry into the European nobility. Directly above are May Goelet and her husband the Duke of Roxburghe, in 1903; the photograph was taken at a ball where she appeared in the costume, if not the manner, of Cleopatra. The most famous of all the heiress weddings was that of Consuelo Vanderbilt, daughter of Mr. and Mrs. William K. Vanderbilt, to the Duke of Marlborough in 1895. At top are coachmen standing outside St. Thomas Episcopal Church on Fifth Avenue during the ceremony. At right above is the wistful new duchess herself a while later, dressed for the coronation of King Edward VII.

European aristocrats of past centuries, although such ladies as Mrs. Harrison Williams and Mrs. William Paley have been financial mainstays of the *haute couture.* The most carefully itemized budget of recent years has been that of Mrs. Jacqueline Onassis, whose annual bill for clothes has been reliably reported to be at least thirty thousand dollars. This was the gross, not the net, cost of dressing Mrs. Onassis, however, because after she had worn the clothes, many of them found their way to Encore, a fancy New York secondhand outlet.

Of all the luxuries available to the rich, perhaps the one that has made the most difference has been service. When Otto Kahn built his house at Woodbury, Long Island, in the 1920's, he provided for a staff of one hundred twenty-five servants. Even a simple millionaire would expect to have eight or ten in help.

Service is, of course, the great lost luxury of the big-rich in the United States. As a lady of moderate affluence said, remembering the house of her grandmother, "all the vacuum cleaners and freezers and frozen foods cannot take the place of a Bridget or a Helga in the kitchen." Even the households of multimillionaires get along with a cleaning lady by the day and caterers for parties. By the standards of Mrs. Edward T. Stotesbury or Mrs. Stuyvesant Fish, the wives of the modern super-rich can only be regarded as deprived.

LESS TANGIBLE REWARDS

Beyond the tangible luxuries that comfort the rich in their material lives, there are other, intangible goods

20

that raise their spirits and gratify their egos. One of these, sought sometimes by the fortune builders but more often by their wives, is social position. For every Mrs. Cornelius Vanderbilt I, who hated to budge beyond her own parlor, there was a Laura Corrigan, widow of a Cleveland steel magnate, who stormed the court circles of Edwardian England. The husbands of such socially redoubtable ladies most often accepted their roles as social consorts with grudging grace, but others found refuge on their yachts, in their clubs, at the races, or with their mistresses. Sometimes, indeed, it seemed as if the Vanderbilts and the Astors kept yachts for the sole purpose of getting away from their wives' parties.

In some cases the builders of the family fortunes paid a price other than monetary for their wives' social aspirations. John W. Mackay, the silver king, spent thirty years living in hotel suites in San Francisco and New York while his wife carried on her social career as a hostess in Paris and London. And it was evidently not the fault of the Lowells that they acquired the reputation of speaking only, at one remove, to God. In their native Newburyport, according to Colonel Henry Lee, the Boston merchant, they were amiable, social fellows until they came down to Boston "and got some Cabot women that shut them up."

American millionaires, probably more than most, have lavished their wealth on their wives. But mistresses too have lived in style, and none more grandly than Lillian Russell, the music-hall queen and the favorite of Diamond Jim Brady. For their bicycle jaunts around Central Park and the resort of Saratoga, he presented her with a gold-plated bicycle, inset with diamonds, rubies, emeralds, and pearls.

An even more expensive companion was Marion Davies. To display her limited talents William Randolph Hearst financed her long string of movies. Some of those productions posed a problem to the entertainment editors of Hearst newspapers across the country, who searched hard for kind things to say about them, frequently falling back on the noncommittal encomium: "Marion never looked lovelier." Hearst never begrudged the cost, but when some naive financial adviser once suggested, "Mr. Hearst, there is money in movies," he answered shortly: "Yes, mine."

In the decades before European aristocracy fell upon hard times, it became the ambition of some of the very richest American ladies to acquire titles of nobility for their marriageable daughters. For-

tunately, this ambition coincided with the beginnings of a severe pinch on European—and especially British—noble incomes. As European aristocratic resources declined and American industrial assets ballooned, international marriages at the highest levels of society and finance reached flood tide in the Gilded Age. May Goelet was married to the Duke of Roxburghe, Ethel Field to Earl Beatty, Mary Leiter to Lord Curzon, and Anna Gould successively to Count Boni de Castellane and his cousin, the Duc de Talleyrand-Périgord. The heartache that one such marriage caused has been poignantly described by Consuelo Vanderbilt, who was married, much against her will, to the Duke of Marlborough. The marriage had been planned by her indomitable mother, who had just finished divorcing Consuelo's father to marry Oliver H. P. Belmont. The financial terms had been settled by an English solicitor dispatched by the Marlboroughs for the declared purpose of "profiting the illustrious family." In *The Glitter and the Gold* the bride wrote of her wedding day:

I spent the morning of my wedding day in tears and alone, no one came near me. A footman had been posted at the door of my apartment and not even my governess was admitted. Like an automaton I donned the lovely lingerie with its real lace and the white silk stockings and shoes. My maid helped me into the beautiful dress, its tiers of Brussels lace cascading over white satin. It had a high collar and long tight sleeves. The court train, embroidered with seed pearls and silver, fell from my shoulders in folds of billowing whiteness. My maid fitted the tulle veil to my head with a wreath of orange blossoms; it fell over my face to my knees. A bouquet of orchids that was to come from Blenheim did not arrive in time. I felt cold and numb as I went down to meet my father and the bridesmaids who were waiting for me. My mother had decreed that my father should accompany me to the church to give me away. After that he was to disappear. We were twenty minutes late, for my eyes, swollen with the tears I had wept, required copious sponging before I could face the curious stares that always greet a bride.

THE RICH AND PUBLIC WEAL

If the American super-rich have sometimes presented a rather frivolous and irresponsible image to the world, it is perhaps because they have not known what to do with themselves. Had Horace Dodge, the automobile manufacturer, been an Englishman, he would have been made Sir Horace Dodge and possibly Baron Dodge of Michigan. Thus elevated to the old aristocracy, and the House of Lords, Dodge would have found himself playing a role in political life and his children would perhaps have had something other than parties, jewels, and spending-sprees to claim their time.

Lacking any such automatic entree into the world of public affairs, some American fortune builders have used their wealth to acquire it by more or less democratic means. The United States Senate has been a particularly attractive target. Among the senators who gave it the name of "the millionaires' club" in the latter part of the nineteenth century were four from Nevada whose fortunes derived from the Comstock Lode alone: William Sharon, William Morris Stewart, James G. Fair, and John Percival Jones. The efforts of the robber barons to obtain seats in the Senate reached a peak of blatancy in 1884 when Henry B. Payne was running in Ohio. During his campaign his son, Oliver H. Payne, then treasurer of Standard Oil, sat at a desk in a Columbus hotel with a stack of bills in front of him, paying for the votes of the state legislators who at that time elected senators.

Another political honor held in great esteem by the very rich is an ambassadorship, and most especially the ambassadorship to the Court of St. James's. The list of U.S. ambassadors to London includes the following men of wealth: Whitelaw Reid (newspaper publishing), Walter Hines Page (book publishing), Charles G. Dawes (banking), Joseph P. Kennedy, Lewis W. Douglas (mining and banking), Walter S. Gifford (AT&T), Winthrop W. Aldrich (banking), John Hay Whitney (investments), Walter Annenberg (publishing), and Elliot Richardson. The present ambassador, Mrs. Anne Armstrong, is married to a Texas rancher with an eighteen-square-mile spread but insists, rather surprisingly, that "we're not millionaires." They can hardly be expected to keep up with the Annenbergs, who had spent a million dollars of their own money in refurnishing the embassy.

In one field of public service the record of the American rich is unique. That is in the giving of vast fortunes for charitable purposes. Other times and other countries have produced public benefactors, some of whom, such as Francisco Datini and Cecil Rhodes, will be met in this book. But in sheer mass there has never been anything like the great outpouring of American wealth for good works, and nothing to match the American foundation as an instrumentality for putting the money to use.

In a more informal way private fortunes, in the U.S. and elsewhere, have served smaller causes, some important, some frivolous, some eccentric, but all dear to the hearts of the respective benefactors. Thus, Robert Owen, the English millowner, used some of his money to found the utopian colony of New Harmony in Indiana. (It shortly failed.) In 1915 Henry Ford chartered a peace ship on which a collection of pacifists and social reformers sailed forth to stop World War I. (That too was a failure.) And Percival Lowell devoted his personal wealth to supporting an observatory in which he sighted "canals" on Mars and postulated the existence of the planet Pluto. (The canals were an illusion, but Pluto was real.)

VERY PERSONAL SATISFACTIONS

Great wealth also allows its possessors to act upon common human impulses, which less fortunate mortals are normally obliged to suppress. When James Gordon Bennett, Jr. was refused a table at his favorite restaurant in Monte Carlo, he bought the restaurant on the spot. When Jay Gould was excluded from the select company of boxholders at the old New York Opera, he organized a group of similarly disgruntled social climbers and founded a bigger and better opera, the Metropolitan. After Charles Steen struck it rich in uranium, he bought the bank in Dove Creek, Colorado, which had refused him a two-hundred-fifty-dollar loan. And when James Marion West, the Texas oilman, got into a fight with the Houston electric light department over his home electric bill, he built his own private power plant. All these gestures may be classed as expressions of the "So, there!" or "Nuts to you!" reaction. Judging by the number of wealthy persons about whom similar stories are told, such gestures must have a most exhilarating effect on the ego.

Even the laws of the land will sometimes bend to meet the personal requirements of the really rich. When Henry M. Flagler wanted to divorce his first wife, who was confined to an asylum, the Florida legislature had an opportunity to show its gratitude for all the money that the Rockefeller partner had poured into the development of that state. It passed a law adding insanity to the grounds for divorce. This was referred to as "Flagler's law" and was repealed soon after it had served Flagler's purpose.

If the rich seem to include an uncommon number of eccentrics, it is probably because wealth gives its possessors the opportunity to indulge whims that might otherwise never find fulfillment. There was, for instance, the colonial merchant in Newburyport, Massachusetts, who styled himself "Lord" Timothy Dexter. Both self-made and self-enobled, Dexter was a man of scant education but native wit. People thought him dotty when he shipped a cargo of New England bed-warming pans to the West Indies, but the pans found a ready market as ladles in the sugar cane refineries. With the fruits of his enterprise, Dexter bought a mansion and adorned its grounds with statues of such American heroes as Benjamin Franklin and George Washington, along with Adam and Eve, Indian chiefs, and classical goddesses. Undeterred by his lack of grammatical education, he wrote a book called *A Pickle for the Knowing Ones*, which omitted all punctuation and, instead, ran a page of periods, commas, question marks, and the like, with instructions to readers to "peper and solt it as they plese." Some of Lord Timothy Dexter's blood brothers and sisters appear in the portfolio on Whims, which begins on page 223.

The whims that can be indulged if money is no object are indeed limited only by the human imagination. If you were the ancient Roman general Crassus, you could celebrate an election victory by entertaining the entire population of Pompeii at ten thousand tables. If you were the mistress of Samuel Bernard, the eighteenth-century French financier, you could eat a five-hundred-thousand-franc bill. If you were J. P. Morgan, you could keep a tailor in residence at your Scottish lodge in the grouse season to make a complete set of shooting clothes for every guest. If you were O. H. P. Belmont, you could stable horses in the ground floor of your home and provide linen sheets for them to sleep on. If you were Aristotle Onassis and wanted to provide your bride with a private flight on your airline, you could throw ninety paying passengers off an Olympic Airways plane just before takeoff.

In the display of unlimited wealth, the Rothschilds had perhaps the most subtle finesse. Where others might have gold faucets in the bathroom and gold plates on the dinner table, the Rothschilds kept private vineyards, private zoos, and private symphony orchestras. But even these amenities paled

Mrs. Stuyvesant Fish makes her entrance at a garden party in the 1890's. All appearances to the contrary, Mamie Fish was the liveliest of Newport's social queens. She usually served champagne with dinner, explaining, "You have to liven these people up. Wine just makes them sleepy."

before the ultimate refinement of tea at the house of Baron Alfred de Rothschild. A guest would first be asked: "Milk or lemon, sir?" If the answer was milk, he would then be asked: "Jersey, Hereford or shorthorn, sir?"

DOES WEALTH BRING HAPPINESS?

Among those who have made big money, there have been a few who scorned and rejected it. One such was Amadeo Peter Gianini, the Italian immigrant who built the Bank of America into the biggest bank in the country. "To avoid being rich," he once said, "was one of the hardest things I tried to do."

Those who did accumulate large sums of money have exhibited toward it very different attitudes. At one extreme was Russell Sage, the railroad manipulator who could be seen haggling over the price of an apple with a street vender at a time when his income was something like five million dollars a year. No one who knew Russell Sage could believe that his fortune made him happy, but there is no reason to believe that he would have been happier without it. At the other extreme were the big spenders like Jim Fisk and William Randolph Hearst, who would probably have found happiness without great wealth but who enjoyed every million of it.

Perhaps because they were so wrapped up in the acquisition of money, few of the great fortune builders have left any record that they were unhappy about the possession of it. The complaints have come, rather, from the inheritors of wealth. John Jacob Astor III spoke for some of them when he said: "Money brings me nothing but a certain dull anxiety." The reason for his dissatisfaction is not far to seek. The laws laid down by his father for the perpetuation of the family fortune made William and all his line nothing more than glorified rent collectors.

Marshall Field II was a classic example of the weak-willed son of a strong-willed father. When he committed suicide, his widow lamented, "American wealth is too often a curse." But Marshall Field III exorcized the curse and used his money to build a publishing empire, which his son and grandson have carried on.

On a lower level of misery Doris Duke complained as a teen-age heiress: "I wish I could go into a store and shop for things just as a girl!" She and Barbara Hutton, the other "richest girl in the world," drew many crocodile tears from the tabloid press for their presumably futile quest for happiness through many

marriages and many divorces. No doubt their sad experiences gave some comfort to the readers of those papers, who had never enjoyed such opportunities for unhappiness.

Marjorie Merriweather Post, who was richer than either of them, never complained about her possession of a vast fortune. Thanks to her father, Charlie Post, the cereal king, who took her to board meetings when she was a girl of ten, she grew up with a grasp of great affairs that she put to use both as a director of General Foods and for a time as mistress of the United States embassy in the Soviet Union. At the same time she developed a personal life style that has seldom been matched in recent times for its opulence without ostentation.

Perhaps the only conclusion to draw is that great wealth may give its possessors a more than normal opportunity to become either happy or unhappy, depending on their own natures. The record shows that very few of those who have found wealth within their grasp have actually spurned it. Society itself seems inclined to permit a rich man almost any whim except disrespect for money itself. Once in a while, when a son of wealth has stood on the street and handed out hundred-dollar bills, he has been quickly committed by indignant relatives or shocked judges. In the view of most ordinary citizens, we must conclude that Joe E. Lewis had it right when he said: "I've been rich and I've been poor, and believe me, rich is better."

The common wisdom is expressed by Tevya, the hard-working dairyman in *Fiddler on the Roof*, when the young socialist tells him that money is the world's curse. Raising his eyes to heaven, Tevya implores: "May the Lord smite me with it! And may I never recover!"

The larger question is whether the acquisition and possession of great wealth have served the purposes of society at large. In older times the question was not much asked because most wealth had been in the same hands forever, or so it seemed, and there was not much, short of revolution, that anyone could do about it. But as the new industrial fortunes piled up in the late nineteenth century, people began to ask if such enormous rewards to a few individuals were really the necessary mainspring of the capitalist system. Even after all the taxes and regulations of this century, the question still remains. We shall return to it in the last chapter of this book. Meanwhile, in the following chapters we shall look at the ways in which fortunes have been built and the uses to which they have been put.

WEALTH BELONGED FIRST TO CHIEFTAINS, LORDS, AND KINGS. IN THE PORTFOLIO THAT BEGINS ON THIS PAGE, WE SEE SOME OF THE FORMS IT TOOK THROUGH THE AGES. THE THRONE ABOVE WAS FOUND IN THE TOMB OF PHARAOH TUTANKHAMEN, WHO RULED EGYPT IN THE THIRD MILLENNIUM BEFORE CHRIST.

HERMITAGE MUSEUM, LENINGRAD—LEE BOLTIN

Left: To the wild Scythian horsemen of the first millennium B.C. gold was a sacred metal. After they settled down near the Black Sea, their rulers coveted gold ornaments that the neighboring Greeks offered in exchange for grain. This pendant, bearing the head of Athena, is derived from the statue by Phidias that stood in the Parthenon. It was found in the grave of a Scythian noble at Kul Oba.

Opposite page: This wide-eyed princeling is Marcantonio Colonna, photographed by *Life* in 1949 in the art gallery of his family palace in Rome. With fifteen cardinals in their history, the Colonnas are generally ranked at the top of the papal aristocracy. The palace was begun by a Colonna pope, Martin V, in the fifteenth century. The ceiling frescoes commemorate the victory of a Colonna general, Marcantonio the Triumpher, at Lepanto in 1571.

OVERLEAF (pages 28-29): Royal power in the modern world reaches a peak of splendor in the person of the asantahene, chief of the Ashanti tribe in Ghana. Until 1970 he was a London-educated barrister who went by the name of J. Matthew Poku. For his coronation he assumed the title of Nana Opoku Ware II and donned the gorgeous raiment in which he is being borne through the streets of his capital city, Kumasi. Charms, talismans, and plates of golden armor cover his person. In his hand he carries a flintlock rifle to symbolize military prowess. Hidden from view is the Golden Stool, which, according to tribal tradition, descended from heaven to become the sacred repository of the Ashanti spirit.

JOHN READER, TIME-LIFE PICTURE AGENCY © TIME, INC.

The jewels and pearls worn by Queen Elizabeth I of England on a single costume were counted in the many hundreds.

Jewels have proclaimed the wealth of royal and noble families in different cultures all over the world. Below, from left are: Infanta Maria Ludovica of Spain; Maharajah Gulab Singh, a nineteenth-century ruler of the Punjab in India; and the wife of a high dignitary in China during the Ming dynasty.

The Mogul emperors of India ruled with barbari
cruelty but surrounded themselves with objects o
exquisite refinement. Seated beneath a ceremonial par
asol above is Humayun, the second Mogul ruler. A
left is the Taj Mahal, built by the fifth Mogul, Sha
Jehan, as a memorial to his beloved wife, Mumta
Mahal. The mausoleum, built of pure white Makran
marble, stands on a plinth from whose corners rise fou
slim marble minarets. After his wife died in 1631 th
shah had summoned architects from India, Persia, and
distant lands to design the loveliest building on earth

Peter the Great opened Russia to Western influence, Western trade, and Western ideas of what a fountain should look like. These golden statues, jets, pools, and a grand cascade set off his palace, the Peterhof, which he built in his new capital city of St. Petersburg (now Leningrad). The Romanov czardom, which Peter raised to a peak of power in the early eighteenth century, ended with Nicholas II, seen above in a photograph with his family: from left to right, Princesses Olga and Maria, the czar, Czarina Alexandra, Princess Anastasia, Czarevitch Alexei, and Princess Tatiana. They were murdered by the Communists in July, 1918.

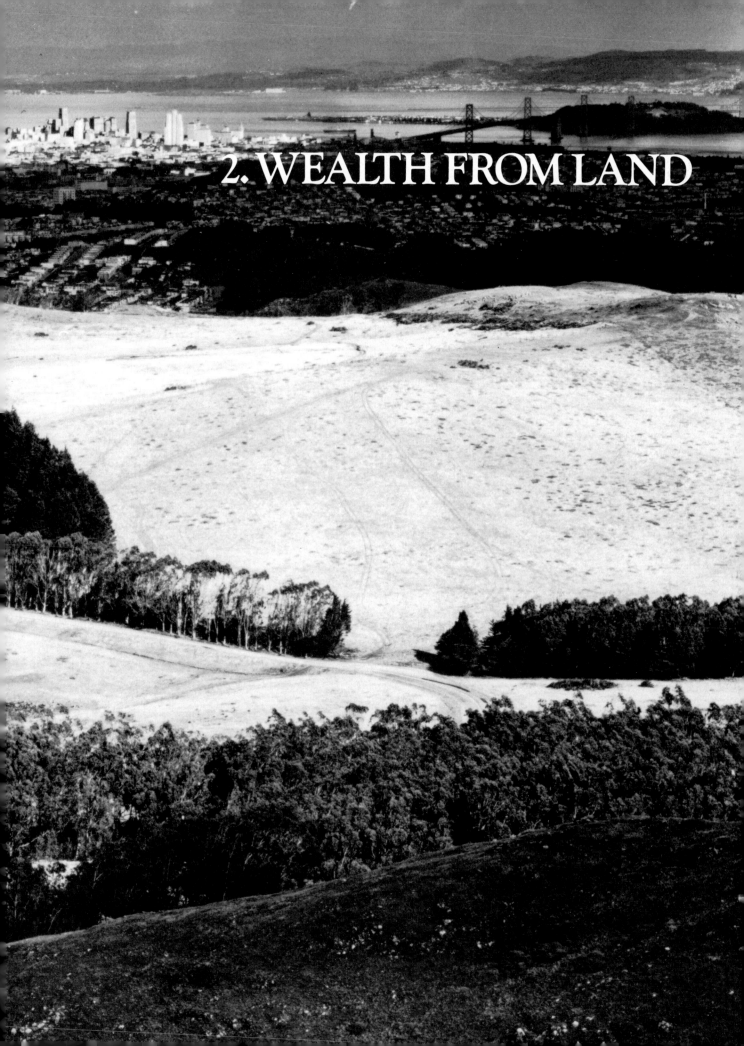

2. WEALTH FROM LAND

THE LANDED ARISTOCRATS

It has generally been assumed that the Dutch traders who bought Manhattan Island from the Indians for twenty-four-dollars' worth of trinkets got a bargain. But in fact the Indians may have gone away gloating over their skill in relieving their visitors of good trinkets in return for something that no one owned. Perhaps, they may have hoped, the Dutchmen would be back later to buy the sunlight or the fresh air.

To the American Indian, as to primitive peoples almost everywhere, there was no such thing as private property in land. As a Mohawk chieftain explained to George Washington, in refusing an offer for a tract in the Ohio Valley: "The Great Being above allowed it to be a place of residence to us." A piece of territory might be won in warfare between one tribe and another, but then it belonged to the victorious tribe, not to any individual owner.

In some parts of the world, as tribes settled down and built cities, and submitted to the rule of kings, land came to be viewed as the property of the king. He might assign certain portions of it to his chief supporters and public officials, but they held it only as long as they continued in office or in royal favor. Even when their positions became heriditary, as in Sumeria and Egypt, their landholdings were perquisites of office rather than private property in the modern sense. For that matter, the king's realm was his for only as long as he and his heirs retained the kingship.

From the earliest beginnings of Republican government in Greece and Rome, peasants held their land as private property. But not until the third century B.C. do we find record of great estates in the hands of absentee owners. In the last years of the Republic, Cicero describes at length the estates that, though far from the largest in Italy, demanded his close attention as landlord. During the Empire the latifundia expanded over most of the best agricultural land in Italy, driving the small farmers into the cities, where many of them existed on the dole. In North Africa, the principal granary of Rome, estates were even larger. In the second century A.D., according to Pliny the Younger, six great landowners possessed half of the cultivated land of that province.

The feudal system of land tenure that evolved in

Europe during the early Middle Ages was derived in part from that of Rome and in part from that of the Teutonic tribes that had overrun the western Empire. Its central principle was formulated thus in French law: "No lord without land, no land without a lord." The great nobles held their domains as vassals of the king and awarded tracts to their own vassals. Part of the land was parceled out to the serfs for cultivation, while the lords held the rest as forest or as "common land" for pasturage. By tradition the serfs acquired the right to keep their land and to pass it on to their sons, so long as they fulfilled their obligations to the lord in produce, labor, and military service. As the Middle Ages came to an end, however, the two-way obligations between lord and serf weakened. The serfs won their freedom to buy and sell their fields and even to leave the land, although normally at the cost of losing it, while the lords asserted their right to enclose as their own personal property the land that had been the peasants' "commons."

When Duke William of Normandy conquered England in 1066, he rewarded his chief retainers and allies with grants of land over which they exercised full feudal rights. Their names and estates, along with the names and properties of other nobles, squires, and yeomen, were recorded in the Domesday Book, a listing of all the landholdings in England compiled by order of the Conqueror in 1086. The names that appear in the Domesday Book are not, however, the names that appear among the great landowners of recent times. When the English government made another count of landholdings in 1873, it revealed that only one piece of property still belonged to the family that had held it in 1086. All the great holdings had passed out of the hands of the early holders. Some were lost because the families chose the wrong political side, especially in the bitter Wars of the Roses. Others disappeared because families ran out, or sold their lands for cash, or split them up among heirs.

The "New Domesday Survey" of 1873 had been ordered by Lord Derby, the prime minister, because he was tired of hearing that England was owned by its noble families and wanted to disprove the charge. But the survey did not serve his purpose. What it proved was that, after eight centuries, half the land of England still belonged to aristocratic families and that one acre in every eight belonged to a duke. As old families had disappeared from the list of great property owners, new ones had appeared. After the original Norman grants, the greatest distribution was made by Henry VIII, who had confiscated the lands of the monasteries. From that bonanza date such great holdings as those of the Cecil family and of the dukes of Bedford and the marquesses of Bath. Still other estates and accompanying titles were awarded by later rulers to their political supporters, their sons, their relatives, and even their mistresses. Four dukes hold their titles and estates by descent from the mistresses of Charles II: St. Albans (from Nell Gwynn), Grafton (from the Duchess of Cleveland), Richmond (from the Duchess of Portsmouth), and Buccleuch (from Lucy Walters). Many of the greatest landholdings were put together from smaller estates by well-planned marriages.

Throughout English history, land has been the basis of the aristocracy. As F.M.L. Townsend observed in 1865 in *The Great Governing Families of England*: "Aristocracy is only another word for the great owners of land." The status of an aristocrat depended directly on the land, which allowed him not only to live in a great house and entertain extensively but also to receive due homage from his tenants, control local politics, and speak for the local interest in affairs of the nation. Even in recent times, when new men made their money in trade or banking or manufacture, the first thing they did with it was to set themselves up with landed estates. Titles to match the estates were seldom long in coming.

The institutions of primogeniture and entail, permitted by law and hallowed by custom, made it possible for the peers and landed gentry to pass on their estates intact to their eldest sons and to prevent spendthrift heirs in one generation from wasting the patrimony of the next. To sell the family land was scarcely thinkable. When the sixth Duke of Devonshire toyed with the idea of raising some money that way to pay off his debts, his friend the third Earl Fitzwilliam expressed his shock in forceful terms:

But what do you lose in order to gain this small proportionate addition to your disposable income? Why, you lose greatly in station. You are now, taking all circumstances into consideration, the first gentleman in the East Riding of Yorkshire . . . the alienation of one of the great masses of your landed property . . . cannot fail to make a sensible inroad upon the position which you hold in the great national community.

The American Indian had no conception of private property in land. He believed, with primitive peoples elsewhere, that the country belonged in common to the members of the tribe that lived on it.

The wealth of a medieval lord was measured by his land. The French peasants in this scene from a Book of Hours are harvesting grapes outside the Chateau de Saumur.

Even before the time of crushing death duties, English land itself has seldom been the most profitable of investments. One calculation shows that for most of the nine hundred years since the Norman Conquest, the value of land in England, allowing for the general rise in prices, stayed almost at the same level. Even in the nineteenth century, when the growth of population and the demand for food drove land prices upward, they rose only 29 per cent between 1814 and 1868 as compared to a 169-per-cent rise in the value of all real property, including buildings and railways. The few great killings were made by landowners who found coal and iron beneath their property or had cities built upon it. The others, more often than not, were perpetually strapped for ready money. "Land gives one position," said Oscar Wilde's Lady Bracknell in *The Importance of Being Earnest*, "and prevents one from keeping it up."

Nevertheless, there is a permanence in landed wealth that has never been matched by any other kind of property. Fortunes have been made much faster in trade or banking or manufacture, but they have also been lost much faster. Politics, taxes, and revolution are perils to landed wealth as they are to

all wealth. In times of trouble the land cannot be spirited away in a jewel pouch or deposited safely in a Swiss bank. But with average luck and average intelligence a landed fortune can be handed down from one generation to the next with less risk than most forms of wealth. And because of this relative permanence, it affords its owner a greater chance of reaping a windfall by owning property in the right place at the right time.

A LEVIATHAN OF WEALTH

The effect of time, place, and luck on the growth of landed wealth may be seen in the history of one of England's oldest noble families, the Grosvenors. It was founded by Gilbert le Gros Veneur (Gilbert the Chief Huntsman), a nephew of Hugh Lupus, Earl of Chester, who was himself a nephew of William the Conqueror. Over the centuries the Grosvenors managed to choose the right political sides and to earn the gratitude of their kings, fighting with Edward II in the Scottish wars, with the Black Prince in France, and with the Stuarts against Cromwell. At the same time they gradually increased their estates in Cheshire through purchase and marriage. But the event that raised the Grosvenors from affluence to great wealth was the marriage in 1677 of the third baronet, Sir Thomas Grosvenor, to one Mary Davies, who had inherited a tract of four hundred thirty acres in what later became part of London's West End. With shrewd business sense and the help of the best eighteenth-century architects, Sir Thomas' heirs built Grosvenor, Belgrave, and Eaton squares. On the tide of its new fortune the family rose to a barony in 1761 and an earldom in 1784. The third earl was not only the richest man in England but a model Victorian nobleman who served as Privy Councillor and Master of Horse and pleased his queen by heavy contributions to her favorite charities. In 1874 she made him Duke of Westminster, the last nonroyal duke created in England.

While the Grosvenors had the luck to acquire the most valuable piece of property, many other families owned more territory. At the time of the "New Domesday Survey" in 1873 the greatest landowner of all was the Duke of Sutherland with 1,358,000 acres, mostly in the far north of Scotland. This bleak land, which only the Norsemen could have named "Sudreland" (Southland), had been the domain of the duke's ancestors since the thirteenth century. Until the time of the duke's grandfather it had been

London owes much of its charm to the squares that were built in the eighteenth century by large landowners. This fashionable promenade was depicted by William Harvey in 1827.

home to hardy Highland crofters who scraped a bare living from its hilly, rocky soil. Poor peasants make a poor lord, and the Sutherlands, for all their acreage, had never been rich in money. But in the second decade of the nineteenth century, the first duke discovered something that multiplied his revenues twentyfold and helped make him, in the words of the diarist Charles Greville, "a leviathan of wealth." This discovery was the Great Cheviot Sheep, which could provide mutton for the rapidly growing English population and wool for the English mills. By turning their land over to sheep-runs Sutherland and lesser Highland lords were able to make two shillings on an acre that returned only two pence as farmland.

But first the land had to be cleared of tenants. Beginning in 1807 the duke's agents began removing the crofters to the coast, giving them the beggar's choice of trying to make a living as fishermen or emigrating to the New World. The Sutherlands called this process "Improvement," but the Highlanders saw it as cruel eviction from lands that had been their home since anyone remembered. By the time the duke's agents had removed the families and put their cottages to the torch, there were forty sheepherders on land where ten thousand tenants had lived.

To the Sutherlands, as to other noble families, the event brought an excess of wealth that enabled them to live in more than ducal splendor. ("I have come from my mansion," said Queen Victoria, "to your palace.") But within a century English death duties had drained away much of the gain. The family seat, Dunrobin Castle, was turned into a school in 1965, and the duke's home near London, Sutton Place, was sold to J. Paul Getty, the American oilman.

The effects on the tenants and on the United States, to which most of them emigrated, was greater and more long-lasting. In the new country the vivid memory of the Scottish expulsions was joined to the memories of earlier emigrants whose ancestors had lost their lands through the lords' enclosure of the "commons" in England and Europe. This combined folk-memory gave impetus to passage of the great land laws of the nineteenth century, culminating in the Homestead Act with its noble promise of free land for free men. In the opinion of Roger Starr, the Housing Administrator of the City of New York, it is this folk-memory that, late in the twentieth century, still underlies the fanatic opposition to any infringement of private-property rights for the purpose of creating more livable and attractive cities and suburbs. Thus the memory of the expulsions and enclosures, though it may have outlived its social purpose, haunts American land policy to this day.

PATROONS ON THE HUDSON

Nothing could have been further from the minds of those who controlled the first white settlement of the New World than the idea of free land for free farmers. In their first approach to the question of American settlement, the monarchs and nobles of Europe attempted to follow the policies that had served them so well in the Old World. But the vast size of the new lands, as compared with the little states of Europe, and the nearly total ignorance of American geography, led the monarchs into follies of generosity. When the Sieur de Monts reported to Louis XIII in 1604 that he had founded a colony at the mouth of the St. Croix River in Quebec, that monarch responded by giving him title to the land of America from the present site of Philadelphia to Newfoundland. As it turned out, the king of France did not have most of that territory to give to anyone. But James I of England was no less willing to divide his American dominions between two companies of adventurers, one of which established Jamestown and the other, Plymouth Colony.

The Dutch, who went at it with hard business sense, were somewhat more precise. In 1629 the Dutch West India Company made this offer: to anyone who would transport fifty persons to New Netherland and establish a colony there, it would grant a tract stretching sixteen miles along any seashore or the banks of a navigable river (or eight miles on each side of a river) and as far inland as the owner could establish his domain. Along with the territory went the right of patroonship, which empowered him not only to collect rents but to make laws, appoint magistrates, and impose sentences.

One of those who took up the offer was a director of the company, Kiliaen van Rensselaer, an Amsterdam pearl merchant who established his estate on the Hudson near what is now Albany. Other Dutch merchants took out patents of patroonship, but only Van Rensselaer transported enough settlers to make a go of it. Though he never set foot in the New World, Van Rensselaer kept a tight rein on his managers and tenants. He kept his accounts to himself, saying, "I would not like to have my people get too wise and figure out their master's profit." Rensselaerswyck prospered, and the founder's son, Stephen, established the family in America. When the British took over New Netherland, they not only left Rensselaerswyck alone but created their own patroons on the same model, under the name of lords of the manor. Thus Robert Livingston became lord of

The Van Rensselaers, who bore this coat of arms, were the most durable of patroon families. Not until sixty years after the Revolution did they lose their manor.

two hundred fifty square miles stretching from the Hudson River to the Massachusetts border, Frederick Philipse got Philipsburgh in what is now Westchester County, Lewis Morris acquired Morrisania, and the Pells, Pelham.

The DeLanceys and the Philipses and the Pells lost their estates because they chose the wrong side in the Revolution, but the Livingstons, the Schuylers, and the Van Rensselaers, having supported the patriot cause, came into the new Republic in full possession of their manorial properties. Only when New York State abolished entail, thus making it impossible to pass the estates intact from one generation to the next, were they gradually broken up. The last of the Hudson Valley estates to go was Rensselaerswyck. It took a series of armed uprisings by the tenants in the 1830's and 1840's to break the hold of the last feudal Van Rensselaer, but by 1855 all of their seven hundred thousand acres had passed into other hands.

THE LAST LORD OF THE MANOR

Of the lordly manors granted in the New World by the governments of the Netherlands and Britain, one alone has survived into the fourth quarter of the twentieth century. It is Gardiners Island, off the eastern tip of Long Island, granted in 1639 to Lion Gardiner, a military engineer who helped fortify Boston against the Dutch and built Say-brooke fort in Indian country at the mouth of the Connecticut River. When he was ready to settle down, Gardiner bought the 3,300-acre island from the Montauk Indians, paying them "ten coates of trading cloath," one large black dog, a gun and ammunition, and some rum—the whole worth about twenty dollars. Just to be safe in his title he also bought a deed to the property from the Earl of Stirling, who held a vague grant from James I. In 1686 the first English governor recognized "the Lordshipp and Mannor of Gardiners' Island."

Later Gardiner bought much more land on Long Island, but most of this was sold off by succeeding proprietors. Gardiners Island remained in the family's hands and the manorial rights went unchallenged, possibly because the Gardiners had no tenants there to tax and no permanent residents whose heads they might have been tempted to cut

The Southern plantation produced most of its owner's needs as well as a cash crop for export. In this primitive painting we see the great house, slave cabins, barns, warehouses, a water mill, and in the foreground a tobacco ship with sails up.

off. Succeeding lords were shrewd about keeping in with the political powers on the mainland. The third lord, who was a friend of Captain William Kidd in his privateering days, was careful to keep his distance after Kidd went over the line into piracy. Before he was brought to trial, Kidd buried a chestful of treasure on Gardiners Island, but after his conviction Gardiner dug it up and turned it over to the British colonial governor in Boston. (It is the only part of Captain Kidd's treasure that has ever been recovered.) During the Revolution, Nathaniel Gardiner joined the Continental Army while his father, Abraham, hedged the family's bet by playing host to Tories.

Lion Gardiner left his domain and his title to his son, David, who left it to "John, my son, and his eldest heir, male, to the end of time." The present, and sixteenth, lord of the manor is Robert David Lion Gardiner, who has kept the island undeveloped while increasing his fortune by building a shopping

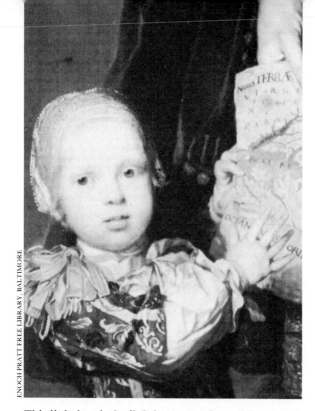

This little boy is Cecil Calvert, grandson of the second Lord Baltimore. In a detail from a portrait of his grandfather, he is clutching a map of the Maryland proprietorship granted to his family by King Charles I.

center on some of the remaining Gardiner land on Long Island. He takes pride in the fact that the manor has outlasted that of the Morrises ("that's the Bronx now") and the Livingstons ("that's Grossinger's"). He scarcely accepts the Du Ponts ("not even a colonial family") and thinks of the Rockefellers as still the nouveaux riches.

There is one peril that even the shrewdest estate management has not been able to avert. The present proprietor is sixty-five and has no direct male heir. The federal government has shown interest in one day acquiring Gardiners Island, which has among other assets the largest osprey colony in North America and the oldest untouched white oak forest in the world. It could be that Gardiner will be the last American lord of the manor.

THE GREAT PROPRIETORS

In the other northern colonies royal grants proved to be elusive properties. When the Plymouth Colony surrendered its charter, King James I issued a grant to the Council for New England for all the land between the 40th and 48th parallels (roughly from Philadelphia to Halifax), extending from the Atlantic Ocean to "the South Sea," whatever that might prove to be. The chief promoter of this grant was Sir Ferdinando Gorges, who proposed to divide it up among proprietors enjoying feudal rights. For himself he kept most of the settled coast of Maine, from the Piscataqua to the Kennebec rivers, which

Robert David Lion Gardiner, sixteenth lord of the manor, stands on a wind-blown, sandy cliff on Gardiners Island. His ancestor acquired the land from the Montauk Indians and his title from Charles I in 1639.

he named New Somersetshire. Captain John Mason got the territory immediately south, between the Piscataqua and the Merrimack, which became New Hampshire. For their respective efforts Gorges won a place in the history books as the "founder" of Maine and Mason as the "founder" of New Hampshire, but neither became an effective feudal lord and neither got rich. The settlements that grew up along the Atlantic shore looked to themselves and to the Massachusetts Bay Colony, rather than to the official proprietors, for protection. In 1677 Massachusetts paid Gorges' heirs £1250 for the nuisance value of their claims.

In the middle and southern colonies royal grants had more substance. The colony of Maryland, bestowed on George Calvert, Lord Baltimore, by King James I, was handed on to five succeeding proprietors. The entire Northern Neck of Virginia, between the Potomac and the Rappahannock River, was rather nonchalantly awarded by Charles II, first to seven of his followers and later to two special favorites, finally ending up in the hands of Lord Fairfax as sole proprietor. Other and sometimes conflicting grants were made by the colonial government. But the landed families of Virginia were founded mainly by men who put together their holdings by shrewd purchases and strategic marriages. Of these the most enterprising was Robert "King" Carter, who inherited one thousand acres from his father, John, "The Immigrant," and left his four sons 330,000 acres. The plantations of the first families—the Lees, Harrisons, Byrds, Shirleys, Randolphs, and others—stretched along the Tidewater rivers, each with its great house, its rich fields, and its slave quarters. Without ever having very much ready cash, the Virginia aristocrats created a life style as much as possible like that of the English gentry. The ships that took cotton, rice, and tobacco from their riverside landings brought back fine English furniture, fabrics, and carriages, while slave labor, inside and outside the plantation house, provided almost everything else that was needed for a bountiful life.

GEORGE WASHINGTON, SPECULATOR

Royal and colonial grants remained a nuisance to both settlers and speculators until after the Revolu-

tion. By the middle of the eighteenth century the Atlantic seaboard was filling up, and colonists were looking beyond the Appalachians for new land. No one had more ambitious plans than George Washington, who had gained knowledge of the western lands through his work as surveyor to the proprietor, Lord Fairfax, and later as colonel of the Virginia militia in the French and Indian wars. When in 1763 King George issued a proclamation forbidding further taking of Indian lands, Washington's response was simply to ignore the order and to instruct his agent to "keep this whole matter a profound secret . . . because I might be censured for the opinion I have given in respect to the King's proclamation."

Washington had his eye on the rich bottom land at the junction of the Ohio and Great Kanawha rivers. In 1770 he made a ten-day canoe trip down the Ohio to mark the land and eventually, after the king's ban was lifted, got title to thirty thousand acres, which he hoped to settle with tenants.

Washington was not the only great American who caught land fever in the years before the Revolution. Patrick Henry was busy negotiating with the Cherokee tribe, also in violation of the royal edict, and Benjamin Franklin found time, while representing the colony of Pennsylvania in London, to solicit sup-

port in the British government for a new colony of "Vandalia," which his son wanted to plant in the Illinois country. History caught up with the colonial land speculations of all these Founding Fathers. In the turmoil of the Revolution, Washington's land claims died of neglect, and remained only as a burden on his estate.

In the young Republic land speculation became a national fever. One of the grievances catalogued in the Declaration of Independence was that the king had tried to "prevent the population of these States" by "obstructing the laws for the naturalization of foreigners; refusing to pass others to encourage their emigrations hither, and raising the conditions of new appropriations of lands." Now the Congress was determined to throw open the western lands to settlement. But on what terms? Jefferson wanted to offer it in small lots, at a price they could afford, to settlers who would till it, improve it, and live on it. But the government also wanted to raise money from the sale of the public domain, and the speculators, who included many members of Congress, wanted

Charles Dickens, who got fleeced in an Illinois land promotion, had his revenge when he wrote *Martin Chuzzlewit*. These illustrations by "Phiz" show Chuzzlewit investing in the dream city (at left) and at the real site.

it sold in larger pieces. The early land acts of the Republic represented a compromise between these different aims. The price of one dollar and then two dollars an acre, in lots of a minimum six hundred forty acres, put it beyond the range of many settlers. In some areas they simply moved onto unclaimed land and made it theirs, proving Jefferson right when he warned, "They will settle in spite of everybody." But the squatter lived with the knowledge that when the government surveyors got around to his area, there might be an auction and he might lose the land, along with the work he had put into it and the buildings he had raised on it, to a higher bidder.

Some of the speculators got hold of large tracts through special grants from Congress, for scrip worth nine or ten cents an acre, and some of the congressmen were cut in on those grants. The land-office agents were overworked, sometimes inefficient, and not always above corruption. Nevertheless, over the long run the land laws accomplished their purpose. Though speculators reaped windfall profits, most of the land ended up in the hands of farmers who worked it. After 1834 even the squatters were confirmed in their possession, providing they could prove they had lived on the land and developed it. Finally, in 1862, the Homestead Act provided that thenceforth, so long as it lasted (and the poorest of it lasted until 1935), the public domain be given away, in lots of one hundred sixty acres, to anyone who asked for it.

The most venturesome of the speculators were out for a quick profit, and they had their eyes on the sites of future cities. One of the most flamboyant promotions of that period was for the city of Cairo, Illinois, at the junction of the Ohio and Mississippi rivers. Its imaginative promoter was a notorious town-jobber named Darius B. Holbrook. Though Cairo did not yet exist and was, in fact, a triangular tract of low land where the rivers meet, Holbrook had it portrayed as a thriving metropolis, queen city of the two rivers, in the lithographs he sent to likely investors, preferably in faraway places. In London alone he raised two million dollars from investors who included Charles Dickens. When Cairo failed to spring forth as promised, most of the investors swallowed their losses in silence, but Dickens, when he visited the United States some years later, made a point of inspecting Cairo. In his subsequent book, *Martin Chuzzlewit*, he got his revenge:

On ground so flat and low and marshy that at certain seasons of the year it is inundated to the housetops lies a breeding place of fever, ague and death, vaunted in England as a mine of Golden Hope, and speculated in, on the faith of monstrous representations, to many people's ruin. A dismal swamp, on which the half-built houses rot away; teeming with rank unwholesome vegetation, in whose baleful shade the wretched wanderers who are tempted hither, droop and die and lay their bones; the hateful Mississippi circling and eddying before it, and turning off upon its southern course, a slimy monster hideous to behold; a hotbed of disease, an ugly sepulchre, a grave uncheered by any gleam of promise; a place without one single quality, in earth or air or water, to commend it; such is this dismal Cairo.

Like many other victims of slick promoters, Dickens had made the mistake of looking at his property after he bought it instead of before. But at least he had grasped one basic truth about real-estate speculation, especially in the United States and especially in the nineteenth century: the money was to be made where the cities grew.

THE ASTOR FORTUNE

In 1847 the publisher of the New York *Sun* listed the richest men in the city, including twenty-five millionaires. A. T. Stewart, the department-store owner, had two million dollars; the Goelets among them had two million; Cornelius Vanderbilt had one and a half million. The one man who could buy and sell any twelve of the others was John Jacob Astor, with twenty million.

Where had it all come from? To most people of that time the name Astor meant the fur trade, and to those who had read Washington Irving's *Astoria* it meant the epic race between Astor's men and the Canadians to seize and control the fur trade of the Pacific Northwest. In old age John Jacob looked back upon that exploit as his finest moment; Irving wrote its story at Astor's invitation and largely at Astor's expense. Yet so far as the records show, this was the only undertaking, in a long and acquisitive life, that did not yield a profit. The Astorians beat the Canadians to the Oregon Territory, but under threat of attack by a British fleet in the War of 1812 they abandoned their post and sold their furs at a loss.

Astor was the son of the butcher in the small town of Walldorf, Germany. At twenty he arrived in New York, peddled cakes for a while, and then got a job with a fur merchant, beating the skins to get the dust and bugs out. Within a few years he was in business for himself, going into the forests up the Hudson with a backpack of trinkets, tobacco, and cloth to exchange for the Indians' beaver pelts. In a few more years he was hiring agents to go into the forests while he and his wife ran the business from a little shop on lower Broadway, living on the second floor above the piles of stinking furs. By 1820 his American Fur Company had a virtual monopoly of the fur trade east of the Rockies. Astor owned not only the furs but the ships that carried them to England and around the Horn to China, where they might sell for ten times what Astor had paid for them.

He was already a rich man when he bought his first piece of real estate. On Sundays he used to walk around the lower part of Manhattan, threading his way through the narrow streets, counting the new buildings, looking thoughtfully at the farms that began just north of what is now Greenwich Village. He began buying lots on Broadway for two hundred and three hundred dollars apiece. In 1801 he paid twenty-five thousand dollars for the Eden Farm, which extended from what is now Times Square west to the Hudson; by the time he died, it was worth twenty million dollars. As the city grew northward, Astor was always a few steps ahead of it, picking up a farm or an estate, watching the foreclosure notices for bargains, listening for gossip of landowners in trouble. He picked up most of the Clinton estate when that old family needed money, and Aaron

Burr's holdings when Burr had to flee after killing Alexander Hamilton in a duel. He kept a keen eye on the shallow waters around the edges of the island, which could be bought for a few dollars (with perhaps a few more to the right city officials) and then filled in for building lots. By the time he died, he owned about half the land on either side of Broadway from the Bowery to 46th Street as well as large tracts on the West Side and almost all of the Lower East Side. No man in modern history, it was said, ever owned so much of a great city.

He knew exactly what he owned, who rented the land from him, and how much the rent was, and when it was due. Even when he was too old to walk and had to be tossed in a blanket to get his circulation going, he demanded daily reports from his rental agent. His biographer, James Parton, tells of one such occasion:

"Has she paid yet?" he gasped.

"She can't," replied the agent. "She simply doesn't have the money."

"She must pay!"

The agent went to Astor's son and asked for advice. William Backhouse calmly counted out the money for the poor woman's rent and told the agent to bring the receipt to his father.

John Jacob was elated. "I knew you could get it, if only you went about it in the right way."

In the course of his career Astor formulated two rules, which he impressed so firmly on his descendants that they were held sacred in the family for five generations. The first was: Buy the acre; sell the lot. The second was: Leave the land alone; let someone else develop it. These rules would not have worked well in all places at all times, but they proved to be a magic formula for Manhattan Island during the following hundred years. One of the results was that the Astors became the greatest owners of land on which slums were built. As the wave of immigration reached its flood in the late nineteenth century, tenements on the Lower East Side that were built for three or four families came to house fifteen or twenty. Of course, as the Astors always said when confronted with the appalling statistics of death and disease in the East Side slums, they did not own the buildings—only the land.

CONTINUED ON PAGE 52

NEW-YORK HISTORICAL SOCIETY

John Jacob Astor (left), the butcher's son who founded the family fortune, would hardly have been at home in the ballroom of his grandson's wife. In the illustration from *Harper's Weekly* (opposite), Mrs. William B. Astor, Jr., in black, receives guests at her annual ball.

These members of the family of William Backhouse Astor, Jr. were painted in the ballroom of their Fifth Avenue house. Left to right: daughter Charlotte Augusta; John Jacob Astor IV, the only son; Mrs. Caroline Schermerhorn Astor; and daughter Caroline.

John Jacob Astor IV, who also appears with his mother and two sisters in the family painting at right, is seen above with his son Vincent at about the beginning of the century. He went down on the *Titanic* in 1912, after helping his pregnant second wife into a lifeboat. Vincent, the son of his first wife, Ava Willing, inherited most of the family fortune. Only a few million were left for the child born four months later to his second wife, Madeline Force. This unfortunate heir, the present John Jacob, is seen at right at an early age pulling a toy duck.

50

Ava Willing of Philadelphia (above) was one of the great beauties in American society when she married John Jacob Astor IV in 1891. It was the marriage of a selfish, willful woman who loved to dazzle society and a painfully shy husband who liked to tinker with bicycles. After ten stormy years she divorced him and moved to England, where she became Lady Ribblesdale.

The English branch of the family was headed by Lord Astor, the second viscount, seen at the races with his wife, left. Lady Astor, who had been Nancy Langhorne of Virginia, was the first woman elected to Parliament and a lively figure in British public life for a quarter century.

CONTINUED FROM PAGE 48

Another result of John Jacob's rules for success in real estate was that his descendants had a pretty dull time of it. Their lot in life was to sit in a little office on Prince Street and keep their eyes firmly fixed on the rent rolls. Not for them the adventure of running a railroad, like Commodore Vanderbilt's son, or expanding an industrial empire, like the Du Ponts. Not for them the satisfaction of giving their millions away, like the Rockefellers. "My money," said John Jacob's son, William Backhouse Astor, "brings me nothing but a certain dull anxiety."

Socially, as Mrs. John King Van Rensselaer said of the Astors, "Their wives made them." Even before he had any money, old John Jacob Astor, the founder, married Sarah Todd, the daughter of his impoverished landlady but also a cousin of the social Brevoorts. The Brevoort connection was helpful to a rising businessman who spoke with a thick German accent, ate his peas with a knife, and on one recorded occasion wiped his fingers on the sleeve of his dinner hostess, the fastidious Mrs. Albert Gallatin. In the second generation William Backhouse Astor took another step up the social ladder by marrying Rebecca Armstrong, whose father and grandfather were Revolutionary generals and whose family tree included both Beekmans and Livingstons. In the third generation William Backhouse, Jr. reached the top rung by marrying Caroline Webster Schermerhorn.

It was this Mrs. Astor who, in her Fifth Avenue mansion and her palatial Newport cottage, presided over "the Four Hundred." Why four hundred? "Because," her court chamberlain, Ward McAllister, explained, "when you get above that number you get into people who do not feel at ease in a ballroom or make others feel not at ease."

If the leader of an exclusive society is judged by the people she has the power to exclude, Mrs. Astor had no peer. Among the "outs" were not only the distasteful Goulds but the impeccable Stewarts, Harrimans, and although he hardly noticed, J. P. Morgan. Even after the William Kissam Vanderbilts built Marble House at Newport, they went unnoticed by Mrs. Astor until one day in 1883. Mrs. Vanderbilt had issued invitations to a housewarming ball at her new Fifth Avenue mansion, which had been modeled, at a cost of three million dollars, on Louis XII's Chateau de Blois. The debutantes of the season, one of whom was Mrs. Astor's daughter Carrie, undertook to put on a "star quadrille" for the occasion. Apprised of the plan, Mrs. Vanderbilt explained to the young people that unfortunately Carrie Astor could not be invited because her mother had never received the Vanderbilts. When this news was brought to Mrs. Astor by a tearful Carrie, she displayed the perfect sense of social *realpolitik* that always marked her reign. "I think," she said, "that the time has come for the Vanderbilts." Whereupon she put on her hat with the white egret feathers, summoned her carriage, and went to leave her card at the Vanderbilts' new house.

Mrs. Astor's husband, like his father before him and his son and grandson after him, was bored by high society. He spent much of his time on his yacht, the *Nourmahal*, not without female companionship. Sometimes at one of the great balls an indiscreet guest would ask Mrs. Astor about her absent husband. "The sea air is so good for him," she would answer. "It's a great pity I am such a poor sailor, for I should so much enjoy accompanying him."

By the 1880's Mrs. Astor had long since dropped her husband's middle name, Backhouse, as not genteel. Now, in the most preposterous act of her career, she decided to drop the first name, William, as su-

perfluous. Henceforth, she instructed her friends and the U.S. Post Office, she would be addressed simply as "Mrs. Astor." Her sister-in-law, Mrs. John Jacob Astor III, was merely amused by Caroline's pretensions, but her humorless nephew, William Waldorf, was so incensed that he tried to seize the name "Mrs. Astor" for his own young wife and, failing in the attempt, removed to England. Caroline, having thus achieved the social annihilation of her own relatives, remained *the* Mrs. Astor to the end of her days. Lloyd Morris has recorded the memory of her in those later years, after her mind had given way, standing alone in her diamond tiara and diamond stomacher at the door of her ballroom, "greeting imaginary guests long dead, exchanging pleasantries with ghosts of the utmost social distinction."

By the third generation the Astor fortune had grown until it reached two hundred million dollars, and was seemingly impervious to any perils presented by softhearted or profligate heirs. Old John Jacob, trusting no man, had seen to that. One half of his fortune he left in trust for his grandchildren; the other half he left to his son, but with strict instructions that William should leave his half to *his* grandchildren, and so on with each generation, thus circumventing the laws against entail, and leapfrogging any possible spendthrifts. Some of the Astor income was spent on lavish living, but hardly any was given away; so long as the founder's rules were followed, the family fortune was safe.

The William Waldorf Astor who moved to England—because America in his judgment was "not a fit place for a gentleman"—ended up as Viscount Astor. His son Waldorf became the husband of the famous Lady Astor, who enlivened the House of Commons for a quater of a century and who

These glum faces belong to men of the Astor line. From left on the opposite page, they are: William Backhouse Astor I, known as "the landlord of New York"; John Jacob II, his brother, who was mentally unstable; John Jacob III, who complained that his fortune brought him only "a certain dull anxiety"; William Waldorf, who found America "not a fit place for a gentleman" and moved to England, where he became a viscount; and John Jacob VI, who lost out when his half brother inherited most of the family fortune.

owned the estate of Cliveden, where, in the years before World War II, supporters of the Chamberlain government foregathered on weekends to manage the strategy of appeasing Adolf Hitler. It was also at Cliveden in the time of the third viscount that Minister of War John Profumo frolicked with Christine Keeler, the call girl who brought that politician to his downfall.

John Jacob Astor V, younger brother of the second viscount, owned the London *Times* and had his own title, Baron Astor of Hever Castle. Although most of his fortune was invested in American real estate, he faced the prospect that, if he died in England, almost all his estate would be claimed by the very heavy British death duties. Mindful of the Astor tradition in money matters, he moved to the south of France, where he died in 1959. As a consequence, the British Astors still appear to enjoy a substantial fortune.

Not so with the American branch as represented by the present John Jacob Astor. After William Waldorf moved to England, his cousin remained as sole possessor of the American fortune. It was this fourth John Jacob who went down with the *Titanic*, leaving a will that departed for the first time from the pattern prescribed by the family founder. He had one son by his first wife, and his young second wife was

CONTINUED ON PAGE 56

This is the mansion that Mrs. William Backhouse Astor, Jr.—*the* Mrs. Astor—built in 1895 on Fifth Avenue at 65th Street. Before that she had lived at 34th Street in the house with the ballroom where she had entertained the Four Hundred. Her nephew, William Waldorf Astor, had lived in the house next door until he lost a battle for social precedence with her and moved, in a fit of anger, to England. Supposedly to spite his aunt, he ordered a hotel —the first Waldorf—built on his property. But Mrs. Astor was already finding her house too small and was glad to move.

The white marble house at 65th Street, designed by Richard Morris Hunt, was a double mansion, with one half for Mrs. Astor and the other for her son, John Jacob IV. Between the two was a ballroom big enough for 1,200 guests, and the grand staircase seen above. It was at the top of this staircase, they say, that Mrs. Astor stood in her later years, when her mind had faded, greeting imaginary guests. The house remained in the family until 1925. Temple Emanu-el now stands on the site.

55

CONTINUED FROM PAGE 53

carrying an unborn child when he helped her into the lifeboat. To the first son, Vincent, then in his teens, the will left sixty-nine million dollars. The unborn second son, another John Jacob (the sixth, since the British cousin was the fifth), inherited a mere three million. Vincent Astor grew up to be a yachtsman, a friend of Franklin Roosevelt, and the possessor of a most un-Astor-like attribute, a social conscience. When he died childless in 1959 he left most of his fortune to a charitable trust. His hapless half brother, John Jacob Astor VI ("Jackims" to the tabloid chroniclers of his many marriages and divorces), manages to get by on the last scraps of the Astor fortune, but his son, another William Backhouse Astor, went to work for a living on Wall Street. The present head of the family, brooding on his half brother's giveaway, can only say: "That was not the way my great-great-grandfather would have wanted it." He is surely right about that.

A GARDEN FOR TOBEY

The Astor fortune was not the only one solidly founded on the bedrock of Manhattan Island. The Goelets, the Rhinelanders, the Schermerhorns, the Beekmans, the Lorillards all got their starts in trade, but all made their great killings in New York real estate. No family ever followed this route to wealth with more singleminded devotion than the Wendels. John Wendel worked as a porter for John Jacob Astor and took to heart his employer's advice to invest his savings in land. With unwavering trust in this ancestral wisdom, the family held on to their real estate until in the twentieth century it was valued at one hundred million dollars. The last of their line were two spinster sisters, Miss Ella and Miss Rebecca, who for fifty years seldom ventured outside their brownstone, huddled amid the stores and office buildings at the corner of 39th Street and Fifth Avenue. According to Lucius Beebe, they resisted offers of five million dollars and up because their succession of dogs, each named Tobey, liked the garden to run in. Once when they could not reach a veterinary, the current Tobey was taken to Flower Memorial Hospital, where a kindly doctor treated him. The Misses Wendel did not forget, and in 1931, when Miss Ella died, leaving the family estate to charities, sixteen million dollars of it went to Flower Hospital.

Virtually every American city has its legends of men who got in on the start of a land boom and rode it to great wealth. In Cincinnati it was Nicholas Longworth I, who arrived there as a law student in

UPI

Ella Wendel (above) shared with her sister Rebecca a mansion on Fifth Avenue, a hundred-million-dollar fortune, and a succession of dogs named Tobey.

1803 when the place had only eight hundred inhabitants. One of his clients was a man accused as a horse thief. Having no money, the man offered Longworth two copper kettles, used for distilling whiskey, which were in the possession of a friend. Longworth went to pick up the kettles but found that the friend also had a lot of several acres near the city and took that instead. The "kettle land" was valued in 1856 at two million dollars and became the cornerstone of a fortune that reached fifteen million at the time of Longworth's death.

One of the odd things about real-estate fortunes is that their possessors are often better known to the public for other wealth-producing activities. The name of Marshall Field is usually associated with the Chicago store, and this was, to be sure, the foundation of his fortune, but its increase from a fortune counted in the millions to one in excess of a hundred million was due mostly to real-estate investments. When he began putting his profits from the store into real estate, the value of a quarter acre in the heart of the city was on an escalator that took it from $20 in 1830 to $1,250,000 in 1894. His merchandising fortune in his own lifetime and that of his descendants was multiplied many times over. Even his philanthropies enriched him. When he gave millions of dollars to the University of Chicago and the Field Museum of Natural History, he held onto adjoining land, which fared well in the upward spiral of real-estate values.

Another famous fortune that owed its great bulk to real estate was that of Joseph P. Kennedy. The founding father of the Kennedy family got his start as a brash young speculator on Wall Street in the boom years of the 1920's (and was one of the few who got out before the crash). He increased it in the movie business and later, very substantially, by getting the franchise for English liquors just before the repeal of Prohibition. Meanwhile, he was making a political career as a backer of Franklin D. Roosevelt, chairman of the S.E.C., and ambassador to Great Britain. But during the 1940's, between the end of his own political career and the beginning of his sons', he began playing around, almost casually at first, with real estate. By the end of that decade, according to the agent who handled his transactions, he had made over one hundred million dollars from such deals. His greatest single asset was the Chicago Merchandise Mart, which he got for thirteen million dollars in 1945, but which, before he died, was producing annual rentals in excess of that amount.

THE FLORIDA BOOM

In the first quarter of the twentieth century many people thought they saw a chance to get rich even faster in residential real estate. No one had to go to Florida in the early 1920's to get in on the boom. Salesmen were knocking on doors all over the Northeast and Middle West with the message: "Don't wait until next month. Prices will be double by then." In Massachusetts so many depositors withdrew their savings to buy Florida lots that several banks went under.

Those who did go to Florida to see what they were buying found a twenty-four-hour carnival of salesmanship in progress. At Miami Beach dealers were doing business in hotel lobbies, warehouses, tents, and makeshift shanties or milling about in a kind of open-air market on the sidewalks. Every evening charabancs rolled through the streets, loaded with realtors shouting their offers over the sound of trombones and saxophones.

Prices were rising too fast to keep track of. A New York bank clerk who came down for his vacation with a thousand dollars went back three weeks later with one hundred seventy-five thousand. Many lots changed hands for a ten-per-cent binder that promised an additional payment in thirty days or so. The "binder boys" sold their deeds to other buyers, who in turn became "binder boys" and sold to other buyers, very much as if it were all a great chain letter. A northerner who tried to get his hair cut found that the barber had quit, "because he's a millionaire now." The city of Miami had trouble maintaining a police force because so many patrolmen turned to real estate.

Of all the developments of the 1920's the most grandiose was Coral Gables, the brainchild of George E. Merrick, who bought a tract of land outside Miami as the site of an "American Venice," complete with arched bridges and gondolas. Merrick invented many of the lures and gimmicks that have served developers ever since. He hired three thousand salesmen and brought prospects in buses from New York, Boston, and Chicago. Coral Gables promised not only homesites but golf courses, a clubhouse, and a marina, all on canals dredged out of the sand, and a new University of Miami.

Merrick was an experienced real-estate man and made a good start at delivering what he promised. Others were less responsible. Charles Ort, a developer who bought a tract in the Keys without inspecting it very carefully, found that much of it consisted of an abandoned quarry—but never mind, he renamed it "Sunken Gardens" and doubled the price for the lots with the deepest holes. Another, according to Kenneth Roberts in the *Saturday Evening Post*, ordered a sign reading, "A Million Dollar Hotel Will Be Erected Here"; but he could not raise the eighteen dollars to pay the sign painter. A journalist who visited "Okeechobee Highlands" reported that it rose twenty-four inches above the surrounding country.

The most richly imaginative promoters of all were Addison and Wilson Mizner. Addison was the self-taught, unlicensed architect who had built palaces for the Palm Beach millionaires in what his biographer, Alva Johnston, described as the "Bastard-Spanish - Moorish - Romanesque - Gothic - Renaissance-Bull-Market-Damn-the-Expense Style." His brother Wilson was a famous wit, raconteur, cardsharp, and bon vivant. Between them they launched Boca Raton, billed as "the Bride of the Gulf Stream," the "Anteroom of Heaven." Boca

FLORIDA STATE PHOTOGRAPHIC ARCHIVES

Raton was approached by the "World's Widest Highway," twenty lanes abreast with a Grand Canal in the center. It was also the shortest highway, running less than half a mile before it ended in the pine woods. Boca Raton, the Mizners proclaimed, was for "the best people . . . smart society," a sales pitch that was privately refined as, "Get the big snobs and the little snobs will follow." When the crash came, Wilson Mizner took it with a shrug: "The good people went in for a gamble. Now they are mad because they lost." He knew. He was one of them.

The first clouds had begun to appear in 1925. A lot that had sold for fifty thousand dollars in Miami Beach went for only twenty-five thousand. General T. Coleman Du Pont pulled out of Boca Raton, charging that the Mizners had used his name without permission. (Wilson got even by having a floozy of his acquaintance inform the General: "Sir, you are the father of my baby!") At the height of the

Palm trees sway and a band plays as couples dance at Tahiti Beach in Coral Gables in 1926. Coral Gables was the real-estate dream come true of George Merrick, who built this Florida subdivision during the land boom of the twenties.

winter season in 1926 the *New York Times* reported that the tourists were headed north in "a strangely quiet exodus."

The final blow was a hurricane that struck the Florida coast in September of that year, completely inundating Miami Beach. Suddenly there was no bottom to the market. Lytle Hull, a New York socialite who had refused an offer for fifty thousand dollars for some land, could only get two hundred dollars for it. A hotel almost completed by Paris Singer at Palm Beach remained a shell, and another hostelry at Miami was turned into a giant coop for 165,000 chickens. The concrete frame rising at Coral Gables to house the University of Miami was left

58

open to the winds, while a benefactor who had subscribed a million dollars to its construction was found waiting on tables in a restaurant. Yet all those Florida mirages of the twenties—with names like Coral Gables and Boca Raton—have since taken solid form as thriving communities and have enriched their subsequent owners in the vaster, longer-lasting boom of the mid-century.

MONEY IN THE SUBURBS

Meanwhile, as the cities grew too big for comfortable living, a less frenzied opportunity for fortune building appeared in the development of suburbs. Some of the older cities had preserved residential enclaves, like Boston's Brookline, and elsewhere the rich had established their own colonies outside the city, as Pierre Lorillard and his friends did at Tuxedo Park on the Jersey side of the Hudson. The classic pattern of the upper middle-class residential suburb was set in the 1920's by Mantis J. and Oris P. Van Sweringen in the development of Shaker Heights as a suburb of Cleveland. The bachelor brothers paid two hundred fifty thousand dollars for a tract that had belonged to a Shaker community, but instead of selling it off in rectangular lots, as was common practice, they laid out a plan for a community with large lots, winding roads, reserved parks, and houses that had to conform to a size and style approved by the developers. Social recluses themselves, the Van Sweringens promoted their suburb as a haven for the social and financial elite.

In order to provide transportation to downtown Cleveland, the Van Sweringens had sought to buy the right of way of the old Nickel Plate Railroad and ended up buying the whole railroad. They bought it on credit, thus making the heady discovery that they could acquire large properties without putting up any money of their own. This led them into the building of a railroad empire that came to include the Baltimore & Ohio and the Missouri Pacific. They were on the verge of completing a transcontinental system when the first cold breath of Depression toppled their pyramid of holding companies. The Van Sweringens lost their money, but Shaker Heights had already passed eighty million dollars in assessed valuation and become the model for other suburban developments across the country.

A more recent pattern of development is that of the mixed total community—residential, commercial, industrial, and recreational. On the California coast James Irvine owned a ranch of one hundred thirty-eight square miles made up of old Spanish grants acquired by his grandfather after the gold rush. As recently as 1932 an authority on land values could bracket him with William Randolph Hearst and E. L. Doheny as men who carried great estates as financial burdens for "the glory of being great landed proprietors." But during the last decades of Irvine's life the urban area of Los Angeles grew rapidly southward—and stopped short at the fences of the Irvine Ranch. In the early 1960's, under prodding from Irvine's strong-willed granddaughter, Joan, who did not like the one-per-cent return on her property, the trustees of the Irvine estate had a master plan drawn up for developing the ranch into a group of communities including one that was donated free for a new campus of the University of California. In 1963 *Fortune* estimated the value of the ranch, when fully developed, at something like one billion dollars.

THE KING RANCH

In Texas the King Ranch remains the greatest of the cattle baronies. It was put together by a riverboat captain named Richard King, who began buying land for a song from Spanish families driven out of Texas during the Mexican War. For the rest of his long life he kept on buying tracts of land until, at the time of his death in 1885, the longhorns that bore his Running W brand had a range of over half a million acres.

Over the years the King Ranch came to seem more and more like a private fiefdom. It was one of the first ranges in Texas to be fenced, and the fences were guarded by armed patrols. Under Captain King's successor, his son-in-law Robert Justus Kleberg, the ranch fought hard to keep a state highway from running through its land. The legend of the walled kingdom was given national circulation in 1936 when two hunters (the ranch said, poachers) ventured onto King property and were never seen again. The resulting uproar, with the threat of state interference, was not lost on the new young boss of the ranch, Robert Kleberg, Jr. Meanwhile, two other forces were working to break down the policy of isolation. One was the discovery of oil under the grazing land. The other was the development by the ranch of the Santa Gertrudis breed of cattle.

The merit of the old Texas longhorn was that it could stand the rigors of the thousand-mile drives from southeast Texas to the railhead at Abilene. As the rails reached down toward the Rio Grande,

CONTINUED ON PAGE 62

On the King Ranch in Texas, cowboys sort a herd of Santa Gertrudis cattle, selecting the best cows for breeding. The ranch is a family enterprise owned and managed by the descendants of Captain Richard King and his son-in-law, Robert Justus Kleberg. The horseman below is Bob Kleberg, Jr., who ran the ranch for fifty years and developed the Santa Gertrudis breed. His nephew Richard M. Kleberg, Jr., is now boss of the ranch.

CONTINUED FROM PAGE 59

ranchers began bringing in English stock, which carried more weight and yielded more tender steaks. But experience showed that for all their prize meat qualities, the Hereford and short-horn cattle, which had been developed in the gentle pastures of England, were ill-suited to withstand the perils of weather and disease on the dry Texas range. Looking for a more resilient strain, Bob Kleberg found the gray, hump-backed Brahman cattle of India, lean and stringy in their native land but resistant to heat, insects, and disease. By four successive crossbreeds of Hereford and Brahman cattle the King Ranch developed the cherry-red Santa Gertrudis breed—the first and only new breed of cattle established and recognized in this country.

The Santa Gertrudis not only proved itself in the American West, it opened up the prospect of cattle ranching in areas of the world where no one had ever dared attempt it before. Such an enterprise would take a lot of cash, which few ranchers have, but the discovery of oil under the King lands came as a timely windfall. By 1952 oil revenue exceeded livestock income on the books of the ranch, and as fast as it came in it was used to finance foreign ventures. The first was in Australia, where Santa Gertrudis cattle were successfully raised on the vast, sun-parched stretches of the outback that make east Texas look lush by comparison. From this super-dry country Kleberg next turned to the rain forests of South America and proved that, after the land was cleared by huge American earth-moving machines, the Santa Gertrudis could thrive even there. The demonstration that these inhospitable lands can be used for cattle raising has opened up the prospects of great new meat supplies for many backward countries. And meanwhile it has given the King Ranch, in partnership with local interests, control of more than thirteen million acres of land around the world.

The King Ranch is still owned by the heirs of Captain Richard King, and as some of them have chosen to pull out of the family enterprise, the size of the Texas holdings has shrunk from about 1,200,000 acres at its peak to 960,000—still bigger than Rhode Island. Bob Kleberg, who made it into a worldwide enterprise, was a tough son-of-the-range who felt more at home on a horse than at a desk and ran his business with all the freewheeling confidence of a man who has been his own boss for fifty years. Although he had his own fleet of airplanes, raced thoroughbred horses in Kentucky, and was said, at the time of his death in 1974, to be worth at least a hundred million dollars, he still liked to get up at dawn and rope steers with his cowhands. To those who said that the King Ranch floated on oil, he replied: "We operated the ranch for eighty-five years without oil. When the oil money came in we put it all back into cattle. Cattle-raising is our business and it will be our business long after the oil is gone."

THE OWNING OF LAND

The great fortunes made in land have aroused reformers at least since the elder Pliny complained that "the latifundia have ruined Italy." One of the most eloquent was Henry George, who preached that "the equal right of all men to the use of land is as clear as their equal right to breathe the air. It is a right proclaimed by the fact of their existence. For we cannot suppose that some men have a right to be in the world and others no right." It was George's notion in 1879 that if all land were confiscated by the state, a "single tax" upon its use would pay all the expenses of the government. Without going so far, John Stuart Mill proposed that the state take all land, with fair compensation for its present value, and keep all future increase in value as "belonging to society by natural right." Even that great champion of laissez-faire economics, Herbert Spencer, thought it wrong that men should grow rich by simply holding on to land.

Yet few articles of economic faith are held more sacred in this country than the right to private property in land. Whether it springs from the traumatic folk-memory of the European enclosures or from the satisfied hopes of the millions who streamed out of Europe to claim their own farmsteads in the New World, it enjoys the highest credentials in American history. "The small landowner," Thomas Jefferson pronounced, "is the most precious part of the state." Those reformers who have tried to dispossess private owners to make way for public parks and beaches or to repeal the special break accorded to the holders of home mortgages on line 18, Schedule A, of the federal income tax, soon realize that they are taking on something as untouchable as the public schools or the secret ballot. No matter how cogent the arguments against the windfall profits reaped by speculators in land, they weigh lightly against the emotion expressed by Henry Ward Beecher: "When a parcel of ground is deeded to you and you walk over it, and call it your own, it seems as if you had come into partnership with the Original Proprietor of the Earth."

NO LANDED SOCIETY EVER MADE A MORE AGREEABLE LIFE FOR IT-
SELF THAN THE ENGLISH WEALTHY CLASS OF THE EIGHTEENTH
CENTURY. ITS MEMBERS LIKED SPACIOUS HOUSES, VAST ESTATES,
FINE HORSES, AND MANY SERVANTS. THE YOUNG PEOPLE WHO
APPEAR ABOVE IN A "CONVERSATION PIECE" BY GEORGE STUBBS
ARE CHILDREN OF JOSIAH WEDGWOOD, THE ILLUSTRIOUS POTTER.

Longleat, seen through its massive gate on the opposite page, is the seat of the marquesses of Bath. The house, including such rooftop adornments as the one at left, was built by Sir John Thynne, founder of the family, in the sixteenth century; the grounds were laid out by the famous landscape architect Lancelot "Capability" Brown in the eighteenth century. It has been opened to the public by the present marquess who, in his eagerness to attract tourists, has gone so far as to stock the park with tame lions.

The grounds of Easton Neston, in Northamptonshire, have likewise been shaped through the centuries. In the view from the house (below), the eye is carried across a modern garden to the canal and park designed in the eighteenth century by Nicholas Hawksmoor.

Eighteenth-century England was a heyday for wealthy dilettantes. Some, like the members of the Cowper and Gore families (below), made their own music. Others found excitement in the new wonders of science (as illustrated in the satiric engraving at right of a lady looking through the wrong end of a telescope). Still others fancied such elegant artifacts as the jeweled chest below, which held powders, perfumes, needles, and the like. But when it came time for a couple like Mr. and Mrs. Thomas Coltman to be immortalized in paint by Joseph Wright of Derby (opposite page), they wanted the portrait to include their horses and dogs.

Some of the delights of English life in the eighteenth century are portrayed on this folding screen. The upper panels depict, from left to right: fox hunting, cock fighting, shooting, and fishing. The bottom panels include card playing, riding, dicing, and bathing.

English collectors found pleasure in filling their houses with objects made by the finest foreign craftsmen. The vase below, from the French royal porcelain factory at Sèvres, was bought by Edward, Viscount Lascelles, for his family's vast Harewood House in Yorkshire.

Owners of great houses had a taste for ornate furnishings. The room on the opposite page, with its heroic marble fireplace and its sixteenth-century tapestries, is the salon, or drawing room, of Longleat. The marble sphinx above was carved for the fireplace of another great house, Uppark. The objects below had more utilitarian uses. At left is an urn, which served as a wine cooler, on a pedestal, which served as a silver chest; the gilded creation beside it is a butter dish.

George Stubbs was the greatest painter of horses who ever lived, and by great good fortune he lived at a time when English gentlemen admired horses more than almost anything else in the world. These splendid animals belonged to the Prince of Wales, later George IV. Stubbs painted them with the royal coachman and the royal phaeton.

3. WEALTH FROM NATURAL RESOURCES

THE UNSINKABLE MOLLY BROWN

The legend of Molly Brown and Leadville Johnny is by now firmly established, beyond the reach of factual correction, in the folklore of the Western mining frontier. Molly was an Irish girl from Hannibal, Missouri, who arrived in Leadville, Colorado, at the height of the gold boom in 1884. James J. Brown was a mining man who married her and took her to live in his cabin. Gene Fowler, in *Timber Line*, tells what supposedly happened next:

In less than two months after his marriage to fifteen-year-old Molly, Leadville Johnny struck pay dirt. He was offered three hundred thousand dollars *cash* for his claim. He accepted, imposing but one condition.

"Pay me off in thousand-dollar bills," he said. "I want to take it home and toss it into the lap of the prettiest gal in this here camp."

He came bellowing into the cabin, did a bear dance with his young wife, then gave her the money, all of it. . . .

"I wanted you to see it; to hold it," he said. "That's why I didn't put it in a safe. But you got to hide it, even if it *is* all yours."

"Where?" asked Molly.

"You figure that out, honey. It's yours. I'm goin' down to celebrate at the Saddle Rock."

. . . He stayed at the saloon until early morning and was brought home by two of his intimates. He was sober enough to make two requests. One was that the "boys" would not disturb his pretty young wife; the other that they fetch some kindling and start a fire.

"I'm freezin' plumb to death," said Leadville Johnny.

The boys put him on a bunk, then made a fire. Molly, rousing from deep sleep, had an uneasy feeling. She sniffed as the new fire sent wisps of smoke through crevices of the stove. She felt the mounting heat. Then she screamed. She got up, while her husband's pals retreated hastily from the cabin. She scorched her fingers on the stove lids. . . . She almost set herself and the cabin on fire. She delved among the burning sticks, but it was too late. Of all places, she had hidden the money in the stove, and now her fortune had gone up the flue; three hundred thousand dollars floating in the Leadville morning sky. . . .

When Johnny sobered up next morning, he actually *laughed* about the loss. "It just goes to show how much I think of you," he said. "There's plenty more." . . .

Fantastic as it may seem, Leadville Johnny went out that very afternoon and located "The Little Johnny," one of the greatest producers of gold in Colorado history.

◄ PRECEDING PAGES: **A forest of old-fashioned oil derricks rises at the Signal Hill field in southern California.**
ANDREAS FEININGER AND TIME-LIFE PICTURE AGENCY

It was not precisely that way. Miners did not traffic in paper money. What Molly Brown hid in the stove was a few gold coins, and she fished them out of the ashes. But Molly loved a good story, and in later years, when she was moving among the rich folks of Newport and Paris, she made it better and better. Her husband was subject to the same fictional treatment in Molly's accounts. In real life Jim Brown was not a crazy old prospector but an able mine superintendent. And he was never known in Colorado as Leadville Johnny; that was the name attached to his boss, John F. Campion, who was the principal owner of the mine. But it was true that a vein of gold was discovered while Brown was superintendent and that Campion, in the openhanded way of frontiersmen, cut him in for one-eighth of the riches. That amounted eventually to about two million dollars, a pittance compared to the wealth of the real silver kings but enough to launch the Browns on a social career that amused two continents.

The indulgent Jim Brown bought his young wife a brownstone mansion in the best part of Denver; from there she mounted an all-out attack on the citadel of local society. Molly got herself up in furs and jewels, but when she went to call on the ladies of Denver, they were always out, and when she invited them to expensive parties, they did not come. Instead, they laughed at her errors of English and told jokes about her gaffes. Jim Brown retreated to the kitchen, where he took off his shoes, smoked his pipe, and drank whiskey with old friends from the mines.

Eventually Molly gave up on Denver and moved on to the richer social pastures of Newport, where people of wealth felt more sure of their position but were hard up for amusement. They found Molly a delight and her stories of the mines just the thing to liven up a dinner party. From then on Molly traveled with the international set of those days, and it was natural enough that, in April of 1912, she found herself among the glittering company that boarded the *Titanic* for its maiden voyage. In the bitter cold night when the ship was sinking, Molly, in her sable stole, boarded lifeboat No. 6, seized an oar, and got the frightened passengers singing. When one of the two men aboard wanted to give up, Molly told him to shut up and row; when the other questioned her orders, she threatened to throw him overboard. Thanks in large part to Molly, no one died in Boat No. 6. "I'm unsinkable," she informed the waiting reporters in New York, and ever after she was "The Unsinkable Mrs. Brown." Even Denver capitulated to an authentic heroine, though Molly returned only briefly to enjoy her social triumph.

Legends live on because they embody truth that transcends prosaic fact. The legend of Molly Brown and Leadville Johnny—how they struck it rich and what they did with the money—is a distillation of certain general truths about men who made their fortunes from the treasure buried in the earth and the wives or heirs who spent those fortunes. The very phrase, "struck it rich," tells what it is that sets these fortune makers apart from those who grew wealthy in trade or banking or manufacture. There is a great element of luck in finding gold or silver or copper or diamonds or oil. The men who made it big were not necessarily the ablest or the hardest working of all those who dug or drilled in the rock or sand. Often they were long on the spirit of adventure and the love of simple frontier pleasures but short on education or native business skill. Often they had no better idea of what to do with their money other than to drink it or gamble it away, though their wives might have grander notions.

This is not to say that all the mineral kings and oil barons were feckless dolts. The discovery and exploitation of natural resources has engaged some of the keenest minds in American business history. Herbert Hoover made his fortune as a mining engineer. John D. Rockefeller did not become the country's first billionaire without displaying a supreme talent for industrial organization. Everette Lee DeGolyer was not only the world's top petroleum geologist but a scholar and a distinguished patron of arts and letters. Nevertheless, many of the early oil and mineral barons—those who literally "struck it rich"—have possessed some or all of the characteristics embodied in the legend of James and Molly Brown.

THE SILVER KINGS

Let us look first at the four silver kings: John W. Mackay, James G. Fair, James C. Flood, and William S. O'Brien. We first meet Mackay and a companion in the spring of 1860, trudging eastward across the Sierra Nevada with packs on their backs and a joint remaining capital of fifty cents. As they reach the top of the divide and look down upon the

Molly Brown, the wife of a Leadville miner, wore her fanciest coat and carried her favorite cane for this photograph. Scorned by social Denver, she broke into the international set and in 1912 became a heroine of the *Titanic* sinking.

barren Washoe Valley, Mackay's companion takes the silver half dollar and tosses it grandly into the canyon. They walk into Virginia City penniless.

Mackay was a Dublin boy who had come to the United States with his family at the age of nine, joined the California gold rush at twenty, and spent eight years panning gold in the icy creeks of the Mother Lode. Now the stories of silver strikes had brought him, along with thousands of others, to Nevada and the Comstock Lode. He started work as a pick-and-shovel miner at four dollars a day, but after a few years he set up as a contractor and began to acquire shares in the mines he did jobs for. He was already a modest success in 1868 when he teamed up with James G. Fair.

Fair too was a Dublin boy who had emigrated and joined the gold rush; but, unlike Mackay, he had already established himself as a mine superintendent on the Mother Lode before crossing the Sierra to Virginia City. He and Mackay formed a plan to get control of the Hale & Norcross mine, which took its name from two of the early prospectors who had sold out for a pittance, but which was now controlled by William Sharon, the first Comstock king. It was a daring scheme, for it required buying shares in the mine on the volatile San Francisco Mining Exchange without arousing Sharon's suspicion. For such an operation they needed skillful brokers. They found them in James C. Flood and William S. O'Brien, who soon became their partners.

Flood and O'Brien too were young Irishmen who had followed the gold seekers to California but there set up as tradesmen, Flood in wagons and harness, O'Brien in marine supplies. Both fell victim to the boom-or-bust economy of the gold-rush city. Putting their heads together, they decided that the surest depression-proof business was a saloon; they established the Auction Lunch, so named because it served free lunch and was located near the trading center. O'Brien was the genial host who stood by the door, in broadcloth and a high silk hat, radiating Irish charm and drawing in the customers. Flood tended bar, not in the traditional white apron and shirt sleeves but in a fashionably tailored business suit. The saloon attracted brokers from the nearby Mining Exchange who often had tips on the mining shares. Flood and O'Brien made such successful use of this information that they had soon made enough money in speculation to sell the bar and assume the dignity of stockbrokers themselves. Such was their situation when Mackay and Fair came to them for help.

The scheme to buy up control of the Hale & Norcross mine worked like a charm. The four partners ended up with a property that returned several times its purchase price in a few years and established them as a new power on the Comstock. But much more was to come. Mackay and Fair had their eyes on two other mining properties—the Consolidated Virginia and the California—which lay between rich mines but had yielded only rock to previous drillers. They bought control and began tunneling deep in the mountain from the shaft of a nearby mine. Fair spent every working day at the face of the tunnel, in foul air and steaming heat—or so he liked to say in later years—until one day he spotted a knife-thin vein of silver quartz in the rock. The miners followed it, lost it, picked it up again, followed it on until it widened into an ore body twenty feet across. It was the Big Bonanza, the greatest single strike of any precious metal in history. It made the Comstock a name of magic throughout the world and transformed Virginia City from a shantytown

Gold Hill, seen at left in 1868, was the original mining camp that grew into Virginia City. The central structure in the city itself was the International Hotel, photographed above after it had been destroyed by fire and rebuilt in 1876. In its heyday Virginia City had 213 commercial establishments, including 100 saloons and a theater seating 1,600 people. Its most famous attraction for visitors, however, was the Big Bonanza mine. Carrying their lanterns in the center of the picture at top are President and Mrs. Ulysses S. Grant (fourth and fifth from right), with two of the Comstock kings, John S. Mackay (far left) and James G. Fair (far right).

With his profits from the Comstock Lode, James C. Flood built this Victorian gingerbread mansion, called Linden Towers, at Menlo Park, south of San Francisco. It was demolished in 1934, but Flood's other great house on Nob Hill is now the Pacific Union Club.

into the gaudiest center of luxury and high living between the Mississippi and the Pacific Ocean. Within four years of the time they gave up their saloon, Flood and O'Brien, like Mackay and Fair, were drawing an income of more than a quarter of a million dollars apiece every month.

O'Brien was the simplest as well as the most genial of the silver kings, and his life style was the least changed by his wealth. After returning to San Francisco, he bought a big house but spent most of his afternoons in the back room of McGovern's saloon, gambling with old cronies. A bachelor, he found his great enjoyment in lavishing wealth on his two sisters and their families. His partner from the barroom days, Flood, also went "down below" to San Francisco but found himself so besieged by claimants for his riches and so bedeviled by press attacks on the ill-gotten wealth of the bonanza kings that he

sealed himself off increasingly behind locked office doors. He built his monument in the form of two great houses—a mansion on Nob Hill, which is now the Pacific Union Club, and Linden Towers, a wedding cake of a country place at Menlo Park.

The Mackay and Fair families made splashes on a wider social sea. Soon after he had made his first modest winnings on the Comstock, Mackay married a pretty young widow named Marie Hungerford Bryant, who supported herself and her daughter by sewing for a dry-goods store. Because her first, alcoholic husband had been a member of the Bryant family (as in William Cullen Bryant) and her father, Captain Daniel Hungerford, had been a Mexican War hero (before he became the town barber in Downieville, California), Marie Mackay thought herself much too good for the dust and manual labor of a mining camp. She could not wait to drag her husband and family off on a grand tour of Europe. In 1873 she returned with Mackay to San Francisco, where he bought her a fine house, but she had left her heart in Europe, and there she presently returned, taking their two small sons with her. Mackay went back to Virginia City and took up bachelor quarters. In the next quarter century Marie Mackay returned only once to the United States, while Mackay lived in a succession of hotel rooms. With the Big Bonanza now pouring forth its torrent of riches, and an uncomplaining husband to support her, Mrs. Mackay bought a fine house in Paris and launched her social career with a splendid reception for ex-President Ulysses S. Grant, an occasion for which she had every piece of furniture reupholstered in red, white, and blue. Marie Mackay was no Molly Brown. In Paris and later in London she was judged to be a hostess of poise and charm as well as unlimited wealth, quite at home with lords and queens. Mackay visited her a few weeks every year, enduring her society friends but demanding a slug of bourbon in place of the wines at dinner. He always arranged in advance to be called back to America on business. If he resented his wife's desertion or the way she brought up their sons as young English gentlemen, he never complained about it in public. After selling his Comstock holdings, in the early eighties, he devoted his business talents to other enterprises, most notably the building of the Commercial Cable and Postal Telegraph companies. He was a generous friend to those in need, insisting always that his gifts and loans be kept secret. How little his fortune meant to him was revealed one day during a poker game. "I don't care whether I win or lose," he said. "And when you can't enjoy winning at poker, there's no fun left in anything."

Jim Fair, his original partner, never lost interest in money. He used some of it in 1879 to win election to the United States Senate, where during the next six years he seldom appeared and never made a speech. While he was in Washington his wife divorced him, charging "habitual adultery." She got a settlement of about five million dollars, the biggest granted by an American court up to that time. Thereafter the Fairs gave the world a textbook demonstration of the force of parental influence on growing children. Jim Fair, who had custody of the two sons, let them run wild while he lived at a San Francisco hotel and amassed blocks of city real estate. One of the boys, Jimmy, was soon dead, perhaps by his own hand or perhaps of acute alcoholism, and the other presently took to wife the proprietor of what was referred to by local newspapers as "a questionable resort." Mrs. Fair, meanwhile, had built a grand marble mansion on Nob Hill and launched the daughters, Tessie and Birdie, on social trajectories into the highest reaches of Eastern society, where Tessie married Herman Oelrichs and Birdie married William K. Vanderbilt.

Jim Fair was still alive to read about Tessie's wedding, pronounced by society editors the most magnificent ever staged west of the Mississippi. He had tripled his fortune by that time, far outdistancing his old partners on the Comstock, but friends would sometimes find him, across the Golden Gate in Marin County, sitting sodden drunk in a seedy hotel where rooms cost fifty cents a night. He was not invited to the wedding.

"I'VE STRUCK IT RICH"

It is no accident that most of the get-rich-quick stories in mining—and in oil as well—are American stories. In the countries of the European continent, mineral rights have traditionally belonged to the state, even though the land itself has belonged to private individuals. In England the sovereign's rights were restricted to precious metals, but in 1568 a court held that even the slightest trace of silver or gold in an ore body made it crown property. When Elizabeth and James I attempted to assert their right to copper and lead deposits, however, Parliament restricted the crown to silver and gold, leaving all other mineral rights with the owners of the land.

The wide-open American policy has often been condemned as a giveaway of public treasure; but its defenders argue that on balance more money has been lost in unsuccessful prospecting than has been made out of the few lucky strikes. In his memoirs Herbert Hoover wrote from personal experience: "If all costs are included—prospectors and subsequent equipment and operation of the more favorable properties—gold-mining is an unprofitable business in any country. Taking the world as a whole, the gold produced costs more than it sells for." Though Hoover was speaking only of gold mining, which he knew at firsthand, some claim that his words hold true for the baser metals and even for oil. Those who responded to the lure of big risks and big prizes have served an economic purpose in discovering and developing the resources of the continent. Some of them have also exhibited a gambler's engaging nonchalance toward the possession of great wealth.

The story of the Walsh fortune is the classic story of easy come, easy go. Tom Walsh had been roaming the Colorado mountains around Deadwood and Leadville for about twenty years, working at various jobs to support his family but always poking through abandoned mines and picking at rocks in search of gold or silver. Once he had passed up a chance to buy half interest in an old and apparently worn-out mine called the Homestake, which later enriched George Hearst to the tune of a hundred million dollars. His daughter Evalyn never forgot the day in 1896 when he made his great gold strike in another old silver mine, the Camp Bird at Leadville, and called her into his bedroom to say, "Daughter, I've struck it rich." Within two years he and his family had put the mining camps behind them and moved to Washington, where they presently built a mansion on Massachusetts Avenue, complete with a ballroom for three hundred guests. Nothing was too good for Evalyn and her younger brother Vinson. At the age of twelve she asked for and got her own victoria, with a span of sorrels and a liveried coachman to drive her to school. "I should be a liar," she later wrote, "if I tried to say I did not enjoy right down to the bottom of my soul the 'ohs' and 'ahs' that came from the other girls."

One of the boys she met at Washington parties was Edward Beale McLean, the heir to the family that owned the Cincinnati *Enquirer*; he asked her to marry him when she was fifteen. Ned McLean was, if possible, even more spoiled than Evalyn Walsh. It was partly to break up that juvenile romance that

Tom Walsh took his daughter to Europe, only to have her hotly pursued by what her brother termed "dago princes." Tom Walsh knew a fortune hunter when he saw one but, perhaps thinking of Ned McLean and ever solicitous of Evalyn's happiness, asked: "Are you sure you don't want this Prince?" Evalyn said no, she'd rather have a red Mercedes. She got the car, and a few years later she eloped with Ned McLean.

In later years her superstitious friends blamed Evalyn Walsh McLean's lifelong series of misfortunes on her possession of the Hope Diamond. But the bad luck began before she acquired that supposedly malign jewel. The first calamity occurred in 1905 when she and her much-loved brother Vinson turned over in an automobile accident at Newport. Vinson was killed, and Evalyn went through an operation that not only made her right leg an inch and a half shorter than her left but gave her, as a result of the drugs she had been given, an addiction to morphine. As soon as they were married, the McLeans took off on a European buying spree in which Evalyn acquired the Star of the East, a ninety-two-and-a-half-carat pear-shaped diamond, which she charged to her father. Having started out with a hundred thousand dollars apiece, they were seen cabling home for more. Writing ten years ago in *The Big Spenders*, Lucius Beebe noted that two hundred thousand dollars in 1909 bought about as much as a million dollars did in 1966, and commented, "It takes diligence and application to spend $1,000,000 in two months and have nothing more to show for it than three or four Mercedes roadsters and an outsize case of the shakes."

What with Ned's drink and Evalyn's drugs, the McLean marriage was off to a rocky start. But soon after they returned to Washington, it was blessed by the birth of Vinson Walsh McLean, known to the press during his short life as "the hundred-million-dollar baby." The infant was placed in a golden crib, the gift of King Leopold of the Belgians, who was an associate of Walsh in mining ventures. As Vinson grew up, the child was showered with presents from the McLeans and their friends, including a model of the U.S.S. *Olympia* in spun sugar, sent by Admiral Dewey. When the boy wanted to see the circus, his parents bought out an entire performance of Ring-

Tom Walsh discovered gold in Colorado in 1896. He took his family to Washington, D.C., where they built a mansion and began spending money at a rate that disposed of the fortune in two generations.

ling Brothers so that the clowns and acrobats might play for him alone. But one day, when he was eight, Vinson escaped from his nurses and guards, ran out into the street, and was fatally injured by a passing car. By that time his mother was the owner of the Hope Diamond, and her reputation for bad luck was firmly established.

The sale of the Hope Diamond to Evalyn Walsh McLean was the personal triumph of Pierre Cartier, the Paris jeweler. To make the sale he picked a moment when, according to her friend Lucius Beebe, Evalyn was most likely to feel the need of a jewel to revive her spirits: a morning in their Paris hotel when she and Ned were struggling to down their breakfast with the help of brandy milk punch. Cartier knew that on their honeymoon the McLeans had visited the sultan of Turkey and that Evalyn had seen, on the neck of the sultan's harem favorite, a great blue diamond that, she said, "made my fingers itch." Since then, Cartier reminded her, there had been a revolution in Turkey. The favorite, he heard, had been stabbed to death, and shortly thereafter a great blue stone had turned up in Paris. Of course no one could say for sure that this was the stone Evalyn had seen, but one thing was certain: this was the famous Hope Diamond that perhaps had brought misfortune to one more owner. The stone, it was said, had been plucked from the eye of an idol and had been brought to the French court by a dealer named Tavernier. The dealer, according to legend, was later eaten by wild dogs. The diamond became part of the French crown jewels and was supposedly worn by Marie Antoinette, with equally dire results. During the French Revolution it dropped out of sight. It was not seen again until 1830, when a stone of identical hue, recut and somewhat smaller, was bought in the London diamond market by Henry Philip Hope, a banker, as a present for his daughter, later the Duchess of Newcastle. It descended in the family to Lord Francis Pelham Clinton Hope, who gave it to his bride, the American musical comedy star May Yohe. When Lord Francis went bankrupt, it was sold to a Middle Eastern dealer named Selim Habib, who, it was said, presently drowned at sea.

Mrs. Tom Walsh pursued her social ambitions on two continents. Below, in the white dress, she is playing hostess to President and Mrs. William Howard Taft. In Europe the Walshes entertained King Leopold of the Belgians, who invested in Walsh's mine.

Pierre Cartier made this malign history sound so exciting that Evalyn McLean could not wait to possess the jewel. She wore it for the rest of her life, kept it under her pillow at night, and laughed at the friends who blamed it for her long succession of misfortunes: her divorce, the death of her husband in a mental institution, and the death of her only daughter from an overdose of sleeping pills. In her later years she found her true calling as Washington's greatest hostess and "Lady Bountiful." She entertained official Washington, from Presidents down to freshman congressmen, but she also held open house, at great cost in money and trouble, for busloads of disabled veterans. By the time she died in 1947 she had run through almost all of the fortunes that she and her husband had inherited. As for the Hope Diamond, it was bought from her estate by the New York jeweler Harry Winston, but he could not find a buyer for it and ended up giving it to the Smithsonian Institution, where it is now on view.

THE GUGGENHEIMS

Some of the mining kings, like John W. Mackay, were generous to a fault with friends and chance acquaintances in need. Some of their heirs, like Evalyn Walsh McLean, were impulsive benefactors of groups who aroused their personal sympathy. But of all the major American mining fortunes, the only one that served much social purpose in an organized way was that of the Guggenheims.

The founder of the family was Meyer Guggenheim, who came to the United States from a Swiss ghetto at the age of twenty and began his business career as a peddler in the Pennsylvania coal country. One of the items that he bought from a manufacturer and sold to housewives was stove polish. When customers complained that it burned and stained their hands, he took it to a chemist and found out what was causing the trouble. Next he set his family to work producing a polish that did not burn or stain, and that returned to the Guggenheim family the manufacturer's profit as well as the peddler's.

Meyer Guggenheim had only two interests in life: making money and raising sons. As his seven boys

SMITHSONIAN INSTITUTION

The Hope Diamond may not have brought bad luck to its last private owner, Mrs. McLean, but her misfortunes added to its evil reputation. Mounted in a setting with smaller diamonds, it is now on display at the Smithsonian Institution.

grew up, he put them to work in family enterprises ranging from lace to railroads. In time they concentrated on the processing of metals, and after a battle with Adolph Lewisohn and the Rockefeller interests, ended up in control of the giant American Smelting and Refining Company. It brought them a family fortune approaching two hundred million dollars—perhaps the greatest American mining fortune. Despite the founder's domineering rule, his family did not prove to have the lasting personal and financial solidarity of the Du Ponts or the Rockefellers. Partly this was because, by the chance of genetics, the sons did not themselves produce even the normal quota of sons. Partly it was because some of the heirs got themselves into a welter of marriages, liaisons, divorces, and scandals that drained both their energies and their purses. (According to the historian Karl Schriftgeisser, who must have done a lot of statistical research, they held the record among American families of wealth for the number of divorces per capita.) But probably the main reason for the financial decline of the Guggenheims was the fact that few of them took any interest in business.

What they did do, before the money was gone, was to set up a number of notably useful founda-

Mrs. Evalyn Walsh McLean (opposite) goes riding with her son Vinson, who was fatally injured soon afterward, at the age of eight, in an automobile accident. This straw cart, propelled by a peddler behind, was the only vehicle permitted at Palm Beach. Nothing dates it quite so shockingly as its name, the Afromobile.

85

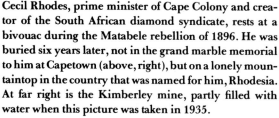

Cecil Rhodes, prime minister of Cape Colony and creator of the South African diamond syndicate, rests at a bivouac during the Matabele rebellion of 1896. He was buried six years later, not in the grand marble memorial to him at Capetown (above, right), but on a lonely mountaintop in the country that was named for him, Rhodesia. At far right is the Kimberley mine, partly filled with water when this picture was taken in 1935.

tions. One, the Fund for the Promotion of Aeronautics, supported many pioneers in that field, including Dr. Robert Goddard, the father of rocketry. Another provided free music every summer in New York's Central Park; still another free dental care for schoolchildren. The best known, the John Simon Guggenheim Memorial Foundation, awards greatly sought-after fellowships to talented writers and artists.

Almost alone among families of great wealth in the United States, the Guggenheims have patronized modern art and modern artists. Solomon, the last of the seven brothers to die, endowed the Guggenheim Museum of Contemporary Art, now housed in the spiral washtub of a building that Frank Lloyd Wright designed for it on Fifth Avenue. His niece Peggy was almost as influential in the world of modern art, although, as the daughter of one of the more spendthrift brothers, she had only a million or so to work with. Peggy was the friend of many of the significant artists of the first half of the twentieth century. After a flamboyant life in Paris and New York, she acquired a palazzo on the Grand Canal in Venice and filled it with the modern masterpieces she had collected. Visitors are faced at the entrance by a heroic sculpture of a man on horse-

back by Peggy's old friend Marini. As fashioned by the sculptor, the rider had an erect phallus, but Peggy had the phallus made detachable, so that it could be removed when dignitaries came to call.

THE DIAMOND SYNDICATE

While the great gold, silver, and copper fortunes of the nineteenth century were being gained and largely dissipated in the United States, the discovery of diamonds in South Africa launched a very different, much less free-and-easy kind of mining boom. Until the eighteenth century virtually all the diamonds had come from India, and especially the area around a fortress whose name—Golconda—became a legendary symbol of fabulous wealth. The rulers of Golconda allowed some of the diamonds to leave their state, but generally they wore them and displayed them or kept them in strongboxes inside their fortress. In the early eighteenth century diamonds were found in the sands along certain rivers in Brazil. By the middle of the nineteenth century India and Brazil accounted in about equal amounts for the world accumulation of diamonds. All this, however, was changed by a young boy named Erasmus Jacobs, who picked up a shiny stone on the banks of the Orange River in South Africa in 1867. Erasmus' mother gave the stone to a neighboring Dutch farmer, who sold it to an Irish ostrich hunter, who got it identified as a diamond and then sold it for two thousand five hundred dollars to the English governor of Cape Colony. Some say that Erasmus Jacobs got a quarter of that sum—six hundred twenty-five dollars; but he never got rich and neither did most of the diamond hunters who

BETTMANN ARCHIVE

BROWN BROTHERS

soon came flocking to South Africa with pick and shovel. The big prizes went to a few shrewd Englishmen who began buying up claims around the property of a farmer named De Beers, on a plateau where the town of Kimberley soon arose.

From among these many adventurers there emerged the figure of Cecil Rhodes, at that time an Oxford student of brilliant mind, magnetic personality, and messianic visions of British destiny. Rhodes formed De Beers Mining Company and soon had only one rival for control of the diamond fields, a Jewish Londoner of his own age named Barney Barnato. Not so much through financial power as through sheer personal charm, it would seem, Rhodes brought Barnato into a partnership, which became the diamond syndicate. "You can't resist him," said Barnato in wonderment as Rhodes took control.

Until the discovery of the fields near Kimberley, all the diamonds ever found had come from alluvial deposits on banks of rivers. But in the country around Kimberley they were found on a plateau, in an odd deposit of soft, crumbly yellow rock. Not until they had dug deep into this seemingly bottomless deposit did the miners realize that they had come upon the original source of diamonds—vertical "pipes" of volcanic material that had been forced up from deep in the earth's crust. Wide, yellow, and soft at the top, these pipes narrowed into a hard igneous rock, now called kimberlite, or "blue ground." Here was wealth beyond calculation—but also beyond the capacity of the world to absorb without destroying the market value of the stones. Rhodes and his partners, who then controlled ninety per cent of the world supply of diamonds, were quick to see the ne-

cessity to limit the production and set the price of the stones. For nearly a century the De Beers syndicate maintained a virtual monopoly. When new deposits of alluvial diamonds have been found, as in Angola, their owners have entered into a marketing arrangement with De Beers. No one has wanted to break the world market—not the owners of existing diamonds, not the dealers, not the discoverers of new fields, not the government of South Africa, not even the Soviet Union, which discovered a new field in Siberia in 1954 but has sold most of its production, using an intermediary, through the syndicate. Thus the diamond market flourishes, with De Beers deciding how many diamonds shall be taken from where, and how many parceled out to dealers, who are grateful to get them at whatever price the syndicate sets.

To Cecil Rhodes, the fortune that diamonds brought him was only a means to an end. While he was forming the De Beers syndicate he was also running for the Cape Parliament and building the base for a political party that made him prime minister of Cape Colony. He used both money and political power to further his dream of a British empire that would embrace the whole continent of Africa and establish Britain as the ruling power of the world. Rhodes was perhaps the greatest of all the European imperialists. It was his misfortune that he came upon the scene at a time when British faith in its imperial destiny was already waning, and what might have seemed like heroic conquest a century earlier appeared as mere power lust. In the aftermath of a crude attempt to seize the government of the Transvaal, Rhodes lost his political power and his dreams of empire. By the time he died in 1902 his fortune had been reduced through political spending and inattention to about five million dollars, which he left to establish the Rhodes Scholarships, that the elite sons of other nations might taste the greater glories of British civilization.

The man who ended up in control of the De Beers syndicate in the 1920's was Sir Ernest Oppenheimer, the son of a German-Jewish cigar maker, who had gone out to South Africa as a diamond buyer. Its present head is his son Harry Oppenheimer, who also controls the Anglo-American Corporation of South Africa, with vast interests in gold, platinum, copper, uranium, and silver. The diamond business has never been better. With brides now expecting diamond rings in Japan and Europe as well as the United States, prices have steadily risen. Sometimes it has been cheaper to meet the demand by retrieving stones from the sands on the southwest African coast, where rivers long ago washed them. But the original source is still there in the great hole at Kimberley—the pipes of "blue ground," still studded with diamonds, still reaching no man knows how far down into the earth's deep crust.

THE TIN KING

An aura of mystery and a whiff of danger have always hung over the business of mining diamonds, partly because of its attraction for romantic novelists, partly because of the tight security imposed by the mining companies to prevent theft. But the greatest mystery man of the mining world was Simon Patino, who made his fortune in tin.

"How does it feel to be so rich?" a reporter once asked Patino.

"How does it feel to be so poor?" snapped the tin king.

Patino knew quite well how it felt to be poor. He was a cholo—half Spanish, half Indian—born in the little town of Cochabamba, high in the Bolivian Andes. As a boy he went to work in a store that supplied prospectors who in 1905 were still looking for the gold and silver of the conquistadors. When one of them had run up a bill of several hundred dollars, he could offer nothing in payment but the deed to an old tin mine. The store owner, legend has it, fired Patino for letting the prospector run up such a bill and gave him the deed in lieu of back pay. Thereupon young Patino went up into the mountains with a burro, began picking away inside the mine, and eventually found himself the sole owner of

the greatest tin deposit on earth.

After World War I Patino was receiving a payment on two out of every three cans, cigarette packages, and gum wrappers sold in the U.S., along with everything else that used tin or tin foil. Though he had married a Spanish wife, the race-proud Bolivian aristocrats would have none of him. But since the taxes on his mines provided a large part of the revenues of the Bolivian government, he had no trouble in having himself appointed minister to Spain and later to France. Fortified with this dignity, the Patino family settled down in Paris and was soon rewarded with enough aristocratic attention to more than make up for any slights received from the provincial grandees of Bolivia. One daughter married a Spanish marquis, another a French count. In 1931, in a wedding that glittered all the more brightly in a year of deep depression, Patino's eldest son and successor in business, Antenor, was married to Maria Cristina de Bourbon, a cousin of King Alfonso XIII of Spain.

The tin king never went back to live in Bolivia, but he built three palaces there, just in case. Once when he was told that times were very hard in his native country, he thought to brighten the lot of the peasants by throwing open his palace at Cochabamba and inviting his countrymen to feast their eyes on the sumptuous rooms within. The visitors, never far from starvation, ran riot, covering the marble walls and velvet drapes with insulting words and drawings. In 1952 the tin mines were nationalized and the Patinos were left with the fortune they had already moved to friendlier places. Five years earlier the tin king himself had returned to his native land in death, to be buried in a great blue marble tomb, high in the mountains where he had been born.

HIRSHHORN: URANIUM AND ART

In the middle of the twentieth century, one new mineral was added to the list of those that have produced major fortunes. The mineral is uranium and the man who made his fortune out of it is Joseph Hirshhorn, a classically ambitious son of the Brooklyn slums. By the time he came on the scene the methods employed by the old silver and copper kings to build their fortunes had been brought under crippling regulation in the United States, but Hirshhorn found a virgin field in Canada. In the 1950's, when uranium was in sudden demand, he made a secret, lightning descent on the Blind River field, staking out claims in remote spots, disguising his agents with fishing poles and hunting rifles. He got in quickly, started up two great mines, and got out again, before the uranium boom subsided, with a fortune estimated as high as a hundred million dollars.

All the shrewdness Hirshhorn applied to his mining operations he applied in equal quantity to the collection of modern sculpture and painting. In 1966, when he had assembled one of the greatest collections of such art in the world, he offered it to the federal government—on condition that it not be merged with the collection of the National Gallery but kept by itself in a separate Hirshhorn Museum. This was a distinction that Andrew Mellon had refused and the other great donors of the National Gallery—Kress, Widener, and Dale—had not been offered. Not without some grumbling in Congress, Hirshhorn's offer was accepted and a circular concrete building erected on the Mall not far from the building that Mellon gave. Whether its collection deserves such special treatment is a question that will not be decided until time passes judgment on the artistic merit of the twentieth-century sculpture and painting that it contains.

THE ROCKEFELLERS

Though the mining kings have generally faded into the legend of the Golden West, some of their counterparts in oil are still with us. When *Fortune* compiled its list of the richest Americans in 1968, it found only one possessor of a mineral fortune among the sixty-six individuals whose wealth was estimated at one hundred fifty million dollars or more. But thirteen out of the sixty-six owed their fortunes to oil, and another five were Mellons, whose greatest single source of revenue was Gulf Oil. At the top of the list were two oilmen, J. Paul Getty and H. L. Hunt, together with Howard Hughes, whose fortune was founded on the manufacture of tools for the oil industry.

Five of the names on the same list were those of the Rockefeller brothers and their sister Abby Mauze— a reminder that the Rockefeller fortune is now in the hands of the third generation, and with brother Winthrop's death is beginning to pass into those of the fourth. Not only is it the oldest of the oil fortunes,

Simon Patino, the tin king, and his wife arrive in New York on a transatlantic liner not long before his death in 1947. According to the *New York Times*, he was reputed to have occupied half of a ship during one ocean crossing.

it is unique for the speed and ruthless efficiency with which it was accumulated, unique also for its influence on American life and the wide range of uses to which it has been put.

The great Rockefeller accumulation has been called a historical accident by its most distinguished chronicler, Allan Nevins. And so it was in the sense that it probably could not have been made at any other time or under other circumstances. But that is not to detract from the cold, moneymaking genius of its founder. As his sister Lucy succinctly put it, "When it's raining porridge, you'll find John's dish right side up."

John Davison Rockefeller grew up on a farm in upstate New York. His mother was an earnest, long-suffering woman who held the family together by hard work, sober living, and the fear of God. His father was a freewheeling commercial traveler with flashy clothes, a full beard, and an eye for the girls; he blew into town from time to time, scattered some money around, and then disappeared again. A century later his great-grandson Nelson Rockefeller, testifying before the senators who were passing on his nomination for Vice President, described his flamboyant forebear in these terms: "He was a gregarious, adventuresome and fearless man who worked hard and paid his debts promptly. Among other things, he got interested in botanic medicine, the selling of which occupied an increasing amount of his time. . . ." The description hardly does full justice to a man who, when he saw a sheriff coming, could never be quite sure whether the charge was bad debt or bigamy. The botanic medicine that he peddled was a phony cancer cure. Nevertheless, "Big Bill" Rockefeller was not without a sense of parental responsibility. "I cheat my boys every chance I get," he told friends. "I want to make 'em sharp. I trade with the boys and skin 'em and I just beat 'em every time I can. I want to make 'em sharp." With John D., the eldest, he had transcendant success, but it may be surmised that he exerted even greater influence as an example of how a man should not conduct himself in life or business.

John D. left home as soon as he prudently could, at fifteen, and went to work for a vegetable merchant in Cleveland. By the time he was eighteen he had a commission business of his own and by twenty was looking intently at the oil boom, which had begun with the discovery of oil in Titusville, Pennsylvania. His shrewd decision was to stay out of the chancy, chaotic producing end of the business, where hundreds of drillers, large and small, were in cut-throat competition. Instead he turned to the refining of petroleum. By 1863 he had acquired partners and made his Standard Oil Company one of the biggest refiners in the region. Associates of that time knew him, in the words of John D. Archbold, as a man who "always sees a little farther than the rest of us—and then he sees around the corner."

What Rockefeller saw for the future was an industry in which all the leading refiners were brought together in one great combine with himself in command. His means of achieving this end were breathtaking in their brazen simplicity. Under the name of the South Improvement Company, he went to the railroads that carried his oil and negotiated rebates, which brought his shipping costs well below those of competitors. This was fairly common practice in those days—a kind of quantity discount for big shippers—and was often expedited by some sort of largesse to accommodating railroad officers. But the innovation that ensured Rockefeller's success was an added provision that for every barrel his *competitors* shipped, the South Improvement Company should get a drawback equal to its own rebate. Thus not only did competing refiners pay more than Standard did for the same shipments, but their extra payments went straight into Standard's till. Not since a medieval baron threw a chain across the Rhine and levied a tax on every vessel that passed, had anyone found such a sure-fire scheme to collect money.

When the beauties of this plan were presented, in strictest secrecy, to the refiners he had chosen for his combine, a few of them ran to the press and the legislature, screaming of "monopoly" and "octopus"; but more of them threw in the towel and joined the combine. The South Improvement Company never really got off the ground because the courts soon declared drawbacks illegal, but by then the damage had been done. Rockefeller and his Standard Oil controlled most of the refining and shipping of oil in the area, and before long, by absorbing the biggest Eastern refiners, they controlled

The world's greatest collection of crown jewels is that of Iran. This is the crown of the Qajar dynasty, which was overthrown in 1925 by the father of the present shah. It is covered solidly with pearls and precious stones, including an eighty-carat emerald at center. The origin of most of the jewels is lost in history, but a red spinel at the top, partly hidden by sprays of diamonds and emeralds, was probably part of the loot captured from the Mogul emperors of India by a Persian shah in the eighteenth century.

ninety-five per cent of the business in the country.

Rockefeller never felt that his influence on the oil business was anything but beneficent. He had found chaos and created order. To a Sunday School class he explained it by this analogy: "The growth of a large business is merely the survival of the fittest. . . . The American Beauty rose can be produced in the splendor and fragrance which bring cheer to its beholder only by sacrificing the early buds which grow up around it."

Even if Rockefeller had been less abstemious in his personal tastes, he would never have had a fighting chance of spending the money that rolled in. He bought a fine house in New York, where he could eat his suppers of bread and milk, and a great estate at Pocantico Hills, where he could chip away at golf on his private course. He had already hired Frederick T. Gates, a former Presbyterian minister, to help him both in business affairs and philanthropy. Gates looked at the books and reported in dismay: "Your fortune is rolling up, rolling up like an avalanche! You must keep up with it! You must distribute it faster than it grows! If you do not, it will crush you and your children and your children's children."

Rockefeller's long life was hardly more than half over. He turned his back on business, leaving it to the able men he had recruited and trained. When he was called to testify before the congressional antitrust committee, he begrudged the time it took to defend himself. When a federal judge fined Standard Oil twenty-nine million dollars for accepting secret rebates in oil shipments, he paused in a golf game only long enough to hear the news and say to his companions, "Well, shall we go on, gentlemen?" When the Standard Oil trust in 1911 was broken into thirty-eight pieces by the Supreme Court, he showed no concern (nor need he have, since the parts turned out to be more profitable than the whole). From then on his interest was in giving away his money, a project he carried out with as great care and skill as he had devoted to making it. Of his millions, 256 went to the Rockefeller Foundation, 129 to the General Education Board, 45 to the University of Chicago, 59 to Rockefeller Institute for Medical Research (now Rockefeller University), and so on. The tradition of philanthropy he established was

carried on faithfully by his son and his five grandsons.

The extent of the donations has always been public knowledge. But not until the fall of 1974, at the Senate hearings on the confirmation of Nelson Rockefeller as Vice President, was the effect on the family fortune detailed in a revelation such as no other wealthy family in history has ever made. Out of something in the neighborhood of one billion dollars, John D., Sr. gave away more than half and left four hundred sixty-five million dollars to John D., Jr. After giving away another five hundred million dollars to charity, John D., Jr. left two hundred forty million dollars, divided in equal shares, to his five sons and one daughter. Despite gifts of two hundred thirty-five million dollars by the third generation, the fortune had grown again beyond the billion mark.

It was the purpose of the revelation to lay to rest the frequent charges that "the Rockefellers" control large segments of American industry. In this aim it succeeded, for the charts showed that the family holdings do not reach more than 2.06 per cent even in Standard Oil companies of New Jersey (now Exxon) and of California. Neither do the Rockefellers nor their representatives sit on the boards of directors of any of the oil companies in which their money is invested. If the Rockefellers exert great influence in American life, as they surely do in comparison with other families like the Mellons or the Du Ponts or single billionaires like J. Paul Getty, it is not because of their grip on corporations or their sheer financial weight. In some part it has been due to Nelson's public career, to which he and his family have contributed some twenty million dollars over the years. In some part it has been due to David's leadership in the banking community. But generally it has been due to the fact that three generations of Rockefellers have used the family fortune to support causes and undertakings that range from universities to museums to hospitals, from Lincoln Center to Jackson Hole, from conservation to population planning. All of these great enterprises, public and private, run in part on Rockefeller money. Many of those who run them, from Henry Kissinger on down, have risen to power as "Rockefeller men." This living network of productive relationships, not dead money, is the basis of the extraordinary Rockefeller influence.

J. Paul Getty peers glumly over the gold table service in Sutton Place, the English country house which he bought in 1959 and made the headquarters of his oil empire. He was generally regarded as the world's richest man.

FLAGLER'S FLORIDA

John D. Rockefeller's fortune was only one, though

John D. Rockefeller posed for this portrait in the 1880's when he was about forty-five. He had recently organized the Standard Oil Company, which controlled ninety-five per cent of the country's total refining capacity.

by far the greatest, of the fortunes produced by Standard Oil. Among his partners, in addition to his brother William, were Samuel Andrews, Stephen V. Harkness, Henry M. Flagler, Oliver Brewster Jennings, Charles Pratt, Henry Huddleston Rogers, Oliver H. Payne, John D. Archbold, and Jabez Bostwick. To this remarkable group of entrepreneurs, William H. Vanderbilt, who had met them on corporate battlefields, paid respectful tribute: "They are mighty smart men. I guess if you ever had to deal with them you'd find *that* out." All of them died multimillionaires, and some of them left significant memorials. Without Harkness gifts Harvard would not have its Houses nor Yale its Colleges. Without Pratt money there would be no Pratt Institute. Without Flagler there would have been no Florida East Coast Railway stretching to Key West. Without Bostwicks American polo would not have been the same.

Of all the partners, the one with the most original mind was probably Henry M. Flagler, who stood at Rockefeller's right hand in the battles over the South Improvement Company and is credited by some with inventing that diabolically clever scheme.

Christmas always gave John D. Rockefeller an opportunity to play his favorite role as giver of presents to the young.

Flagler was not cut out to be anybody's number two man, and once Standard monopoly was firmly established, he lost interest in the oil business and began looking for something to do with his money. This he found in Florida, where he first went on vacation in 1878. Florida at that time was already coming to be thought of as a winter resort, especially for wealthy people with chronic illnesses, but the railroad reached only to Jacksonville, with a narrow-gauge extension to St. Augustine, and the service was so bad that most northern visitors came by steamer. Flagler decided to change all that. In 1885 he began to build at St. Augustine the Ponce de Leon, a luxury hotel to rival the best in European resorts, and a new railroad to fetch guests from Jacksonville. Soon "Florida Specials" were making the trip from New York in thirty hours, which is just about what they do today. By 1894 Flagler had extended his railroad 285 miles south to Palm Beach, where he built an even grander hotel, the Royal Poinciana. Down the tracks from the north each winter, as faithfully as the whooping cranes and Canada geese above them, rolled the elegantly fitted railroad cars of the Whitneys, Wideners, Vanderbilts, Morgans, Goulds, McCormicks, Dodges, Fields, and Mellons. By looking down at the private "varnish" in the yards of the Royal Poinciana, guests of that hostelry could get a bird's-eye view of the Pullman-car aristocracy of the Gilded Age.

Flagler was counting on the citrus groves to provide freight for his railroad, and when he found that the frost line was somewhere south of Palm Beach, he extended his tracks to what was then a sleepy little settlement sixty miles farther down the coast. In 1896 Miami came alive at his touch. By now there was no stopping him. He would push his railroad to the southern tip of the peninsula and out over the ocean to the farthest of the keys. In 1912 the first train steamed out across the trestles that leaped from island to island until they reached Key West. Flagler lived just long enough to see his dream completed. It was not a sound economic venture, and after a hurricane washed out much of the roadbed in 1935, the island line was never rebuilt, though its trestles now carry the Key West Highway. But Flagler had not built it to make money. Altogether

Calouste Gulbenkian (left) posed in 1934 outside the temple of Horus in Egypt. The hawk god might have been a fitting deity for "Mr. Five Per Cent," who managed to get and hold for himself a twentieth share of the giant Iraq Petroleum Company.

he had sunk about fifty million dollars in his Florida projects, and he counted it well spent, though much of it never came back. He had opened up a state and, after all, had a hundred million dollars left.

MR. FIVE PER CENT

After John D. Rockefeller, Sr., the next oilman to present himself for membership in the billionaire's club was a wily Armenian named Calouste Gulbenkian. The son of a merchant in Constantinople, then the capital of the Ottoman Empire, Gulbenkian got his training in a land that derived its business practices from the Oriental bazaar and gave Western languages the word "Byzantine" to connote the utmost complexity in the management of human affairs. By training as well as by instinct Gulbenkian was fitted to move through the shadowy corridors of the international oil business in the early part of this century. Time and a passion for secrecy have long since covered his tracks. But somehow, before 1907, he must have played a part in bringing about the combination of Royal Dutch Oil and Shell Oil, for he emerged with a large block of stock in the greatest petroleum combine east of the Standard Oil Company. Sir Henri Deterding of Royal Dutch and Marcus Samuel, Viscount Bearsted, of Shell—both pretty imperial characters—were not ones to give away a piece of their merged company without having received something valuable in return.

Meanwhile, Gulbenkian had been making himself useful to Sultan Abdul Hamid II ("Abdul the Damned"), who massacred most Armenians he could get his hands on but seemed to like Gulbenkian. By 1911 Gulbenkian had put together a deal for the exploitation of the Mesopotamian oil fields by a consortium of British and German companies. This deal was blown sky-high by World War I, which removed the Germans from the international oil business, ended the Ottoman sultanate, and left the Mosul oil fields in the new country of Iraq. Patiently Gulbenkian worked out a new deal, which divided the pie among British, French, and American interests but left him five per cent of what became the Iraq Petroleum Company.

Just how rich this made Gulbenkian is impossible to say, since his wealth lay underground and could not be measured. The word "billionaire," which the press applied to him, was in his case more an accolade than a financial evaluation. What is certain is that before he died (and before the Iraqi government nationalized its oil fields), "Mr. Five Per

Nubar Gulbenkian, son of Calouste, lived and dressed as an Edwardian dandy until his death in 1972. He is seen here, with his customary lapel orchid and monocle, in the elegantly furnished car that was built for him on the model of a London taxi.

Cent" drew down some hundreds of millions in royalties.

In his private life Gulbenkian, though he had long since become a British citizen, did not desert the traditions of his Middle Eastern homeland. Since it was not legal to keep a harem in Paris or Lisbon, where he lived most of the time, he kept company with a string of beautiful young women. Seventeen was about the right age, he counseled his son Nubar —and change them every year.

Nubar went to Harrow and Cambridge, where he became known as a youth who could wear out "three stockbrokers, three horses, and three women" every day. Until he died in 1972 he cut an exotic figure on the London social scene, dressed in the formal morning clothes of an Edwardian gentleman, parting his bushy beard in the middle and wearing a tiny orchid from a florist who provided him a fresh one daily, whether he was in Cannes or in Katmandu. He drove about in a gold-and-black automobile that was built for him on the model of the London taxi; he liked it, he said, because it will "turn on a sixpence —whatever that is." Nubar's relations with his father were shaky at best. At one point, when he was working in his father's office, the old man discovered that Nubar had billed the company $4.50 for a lunch of chicken in tarragon jelly, which he had eaten at his desk. When Calouste refused to pay the charge, Nubar sued him for ten million dollars, claiming that the old man had promised him a share in the business. The case was settled out of court, but only after payment of eighty thousand dollars in legal fees.

During a long lifetime the elder Gulbenkian amassed one of the greatest art collections of the world, including paintings by European old masters as well as Turkish carpets, tapestries, manuscripts, furniture, and coins. When he died at eighty-six in 1955 he left most of his fortune to the Gulbenkian Foundation, which has built a museum in Lisbon to house the art collection. To Nubar and his sister he left only a few million apiece.

THE TEXAS OIL MILLIONAIRES

In the United States the first half of the twentieth century brought forth a new type of oilman—the Texas millionaire—by now as firmly established in the lore and legend of the West as the trailblazer or the cowboy. In public imagination he is a flamboyant figure in a Stetson hat and range boots who regards the rest of the world as a kind of Lilliput, buys His and Hers airplanes for Christmas, hands out hundred-dollar tips, and says, "Put me down for ten," when he means "ten million." There have been such oilmen, and the one that springs to most Texans' minds is the late James Marion West, Jr., known as "Silver Dollar" Jim for his propensity for scattering a roll of silver dollars and watching people scrabble for them.

West always said that he had to stay awake at night because that was when things went wrong with drills and derricks and he wanted to keep in touch with his crews. However that may be, he filled in the nighttime hours by cruising the streets of Houston, responding to police radio calls. His command post was a private midtown garage, where he maintained a fleet of thirty cars, including eleven Cadillacs, together with a force of mechanics and bodymen to keep them up. When West set out on one of his nightly forays, in company with members of the police force, he customarily wore his Texas Ranger's badge, mounted in a circlet of diamonds, and a gold belt buckle eight inches wide depicting cowboy scenes. To keep in touch with both business and crime he had four telephones under the dash—two connected to his private twenty-four-hour radio

network, one to the Houston police channel, and one to the county sheriff. To maintain law and order the car was equipped with one 28-gauge shotgun, one 30-30 rifle, one Tommy gun, and a canister of tear gas. Malicious gossips said that during one memorable shootout in a dark alley West missed the robber but shot his partner, Lieutenant A. C. Martindale, in the foot. His friends on the force indignantly denied this story and insisted that "Silver Dollar" Jim, with his 210-pound bulk and all his sparkling finery, was a sight to frighten any criminal.

There were more reliable witnesses to the episode one Halloween when a crowd of trick-or-treating youngsters ambushed "Silver Dollar" Jim in his traveling arsenal. Getting right into the spirit of things, West broke out the tear gas and gave them a trick to remember. Protective parents did not take the incident kindly. Among them and among civic leaders who were nourishing Houston's growing image of respectability, there was less than universal mourning when an early death in 1957 brought an end to Jim West's lifelong adventure in adolescence.

Except for Jim West, it is difficult to find any recent oilmen who live up to the image of the Texas millionaire. Certainly none has built a house that compares remotely with the mansions built by the very rich Easterners of the nineteenth and early twentieth century. It is revealing that when Warner Brothers was looking for a place to film *Giant* (a movie that reinforced the stock image of the flamboyant Texan), it could not find in all of Texas a house such as Edna Ferber described. The rich Texan is likely to live in a large but unremarkable house in some such suburb as River Oaks, to own a ranch in the cow country and perhaps a fishing camp, to keep a condominium at Vail and perhaps even apartments in New York and Paris. But all of these are for use, not for show, as is the private plane, which gets him where he wants to go but hardly rivals the old private Pullman for conspicuous luxury.

The most remarkable feature of Clint Murchi-

The men who struck it rich in the chancy business of oil drilling tended to be characters of independence and originality. Among his derricks on the opposite page is Hugh Roy Cullen, who gave more than one hundred million dollars to the University of Houston. At right is James Marion West, Jr., decked out in his gold belt buckle and diamond-circled Texas Ranger's star for an all-night patrol with the Houston police. His trousers were fitted with special pouches for the silver dollars he liked to scatter about.

son's house in Dallas was a large room with eight beds, "so a group of us boys can talk oil all night." Murchison and his close friend Sid Richardson, both centimillionaires at least, exemplified the "good-ol'-boy" life style of many Texas oilmen. Each morning they rose at four or five o'clock in their respective homes and spent half an hour or so on the phone together, swapping stories, passing on news, and discussing deals. Even when they branched out into fields of enterprise far removed from oil and Texas, they operated off the cuff. During one of their morning conversations Murchison asked Richardson to put up ten million dollars to help his friend Robert Young get control of the New York Central Railroad. Richardson said sure, passed on to other

matters, and had to call back later to ask, "What was the name of that railroad?"

Some of the oilmen have been generous to good causes. H. R. Cullen gave the Houston Symphony twenty thousand dollars a year, a gift for which the orchestra expressed its appreciation by playing Cullen's favorite tune, "Ol' Black Joe," whenever he attended a performance. Cullen also gave a hundred million dollars to the University of Houston, and then, when the football team won an unexpected victory over Baylor, added an extra two and a quarter million as a reward. The gesture was characteristically generous, even if it did not bespeak the careful purpose with which the Carnegie, Rockefeller, or Mellon wealth has been dispensed.

A few of the Texas oilmen have found some imaginative uses for their money. H. L. Hunt, an inveterate angel of right-wing propaganda outfits, went so far as to write a utopian novel called *Alpaca* to spread his ideas. In his ideal society those who pay the biggest income taxes have the most votes, and a citizen with only one vote can delegate his vote, if so minded, to someone better qualified. Hunt priced his novel reasonably and got his two stepdaughters to publicize it in a bookstore by singing, to the tune of "The Doggie in the Window:"

How much is that book in the window?
The one which my Popsy wrote.
How much is that book in the window?
You can buy it without signing a note.
Alpaca. FIFTY CENTS.

Hunt was a gambler, relying on a gambler's combination of luck and shrewdness. Men who had known him in the oil fields said that when he arrived in El Dorado, Arkansas, in 1921 he was a professional card player and that he won his first oil well in a game of five-card stud. Be that as it may, he multiplied his stake by trading in oil leases, the riskiest of investments, with almost consistent success. Even after he became a billionaire, he drove to work in an old car and carried his lunch in a brown paper bag. Never quite sure whether luck or skill had made him so rich, he said that sometimes he would like to "wake up stone broke" and see if he could make it all over again. He never found out, nor will his sons.

To a desert monarch in the Middle East, wealth may still be measured by the quality of his servants, his camels, and his hunting falcon. This is Sheik Isa of Bahrein, the offshore island state in the Persian Gulf that has been receiving oil revenues since the first great Arabian field was discovered in 1932.

Two of them, N. Bunker Hunt and Lamar Hunt, the owner of the Kansas City Chiefs in the American Football Conference, are already rated close to the half-billion mark.

GETTY THE BILLIONAIRE

About the only exception to the rather downhome complexion of life among the recent oilmen is afforded by another undisputed billionaire, J. Paul Getty. Unlike many of the others, Getty was born to wealth. His father, George F. Getty, was a Minneapolis lawyer who got into oil leases and left a drilling company worth about ten million dollars. The senior Getty gave his son an early training as a roustabout in the oil fields, and when Paul, who had spent two years at Oxford, thought of becoming a professor or a diplomat, steered him firmly into oil. But the boy made his own way. He went out wildcatting on his own, hit a gusher in the first well he drilled ("Pure luck," he candidly admits), and later, when George Getty put up money for partnership drilling, got only thirty per cent of the profits to his father's seventy. When Paul Getty had made a million dollars on his own before the age of twenty-four, he decided to retire and enjoy life, which he did for two years among the playboys and starlets of Hollywood. His father could never be quite convinced that Paul was not a playboy at heart, especially after he married three times within six years. When his father had a stroke, Paul went back into the business and ran it with signal success, but the senior Getty left control to his widow, Paul's mother, who shared the feeling that her son was not entirely to be trusted with money. Though he held both his parents in the admiring devotion of an only son, Getty found their limited support almost as much of a handicap as an asset during his struggle to expand the family enterprise. Getty began buying shares in the much larger Tide Water Associated Oil Company during the depths of the depression, when prices were at rock bottom. The acquisition took twenty years of wheeling and dealing, law suits, counter-suits, and bitter proxy battles, but when it was finally achieved, he had sole control of a major oil empire, with start-to-finish facilities not only for prospecting and drilling but for transporting, refining, and marketing oil. He was well on his way to his first hundred million.

A complex, articulate man, with interests ranging beyond the oil business to art, literature, conservation, and night life, Getty was capable of taking solid weeks at a time to learn foreign languages (fluent French, Spanish, and German, on top of academic Latin and Greek), to write a book on European culture in the eighteenth century, or to make himself an expert on French furniture or Oriental carpets. When he applied this concentration to business, he wore out his staff by letting his conferences run straight through mealtimes and far into the night. For such absorption he paid a high price in his family life. Many women found him a charming companion and a fascinating conversationalist, only to learn, when they were suddenly dropped, that nothing came before business. Later Getty looked back ruefully on his five marriages and divorces. "I hate to be a failure," he said, "I hate and regret the failure of my mariages. I would gladly give all my millions for just one, lasting marital success."

During most of his active years in business Getty lived abroad, at first in hotel rooms but after 1955 at Sutton Place, a seventy-three-room mansion outside London, which he later bought from the Duke of Sutherland. This was the center of the Getty empire, as he was its ultimate boss. When he died in 1976 he was planning to move to a house that he had kept at Malibu, California, during his years abroad. He got much of his pleasure from his art collection, which is strongest on eighteenth-century painting but includes also Persian carpets, tapestries, and antique sculpture. To house part of it he built a reproduction of a Roman villa, as authentic as scholars could make it, at Malibu. Predictably, the art critics sneered at the "phony villa," but the public lined up to see it.

Was he the last of the great independent oilmen? In his own view, emphatically not. "There are still plenty of places to wildcat," he said. "But you have to go where no one else is looking." And you don't get rich by working for some one else. "Going to work for a large company is like getting on a train," he says. "Are you going sixty miles an hour or is the train going sixty miles an hour and you're just sitting still? Operating men may manage a company's affairs very well—they manage the company's affairs better than their own fortunes. We couldn't do without them. But their choice wouldn't be mine. If I were starting again I'd do it the same way—exploring, wildcatting. If you hit it you get rich, if you don't you go broke."

MIDDLE EAST FORTUNES

If a young man in one of the oil countries of the Mid-

dle East felt inclined to follow Mr. Getty's advice, he would have a problem. The oil business in those lands is closed to private enterprise, since revenues flow directly to the rulers or ruling families or governments. In practice the new wealth of the Middle East is wielded by men like Sheik Ahmed Yamani, the oil minister of Saudi Arabia, who travel first class and doubtless relish their power but do not appear to be rich.

Nevertheless, some very great private fortunes are being made in the Middle East as a result of the enormous inflow of oil money. The possessors of these fortunes are little known in the Western world, except to a few bankers and businessmen. They do not deal in oil but in all the goods and services for which the oil boom creates a demand. Their style of business owes more to the tradition of the Levantine trader than it does to that of the Western oil driller.

One of these new multimillionaires is Abdul Azziz Sulieman, whose father was chief financial adviser to old King Ibn Saud, the founder of the Saudi state, and in 1933 signed on his behalf the original contract with the Arabian American Oil Company for exploitation of the Saudi Arabian reserves. The younger Sulieman is the head of a family enterprise that includes automobile assembly, cement, chemicals, hotels, and real estate. A reporter from *The Wall Street Journal*, who saw his new palace rising on the shore of the Red Sea at Jeddah in 1975, reported that it looked even grander than the next-door palace of the minister of defense, a Saudi prince.

Even so, it will not be easy for Mr. Sulieman to match in splendor the home of another new Middle Eastern merchant prince, Habib Sabet of Iran. His new home, on the outskirts of Teheran, is a replica of the Petit Trianon, complete with extras such as a swimming pool and an underground garage, which Marie Antoinette never enjoyed in the original. Mr. Sabet has specialized in joint ventures with companies like Pepsi-Cola, Revlon, Phelps-Dodge, and Johnson & Johnson. As an American banker told *Fortune*, "Sabet owns ten per cent of practically everything in Iran."

The flood tide of oil money on which these tycoons float has created a new wealthy class that includes royal princes and merchant princes alike. The signs of this affluence may be observed not only in the palaces and skycrapers they build at home but in the expensive hotels and stores and gambling casinos where they leave some of their money abroad. Theirs is the only extant wealthy class among whose members ostentation has not gone out of style.

A PORTFOLIO: WHAT A WAY TO GO!

THIS IS MRS. WILLIAM BACKHOUSE ASTOR, JR., THE REIGNING QUEEN OF NEWPORT SOCIETY, WITH HER COURTIER, HARRY LEHR, AT A GALA AUTOMOBILE RALLY IN 1899. AS THE PICTURES ON THE FOLLOWING PAGES SHOW, EACH NEW MODE OF TRAVEL HAS HAD ITS HEYDAY AS A MEASURE OF AFFLUENCE

For an afternoon's outing there was nothing like a coach-and-four. Below, bows are exchanged and hats tipped as one rig rolls past another. Footmen might handle the horses at the start of a festive jaunt, but it was a point of pride for the grandest swells to hold their own reins.

The ladies and gentlemen above, dressed in all the finery of the Gilded Age, are ready for a drive in their tallyho. This outsize four-in-hand was big enough to carry twenty or more people to the races or an elegant picnic. On the facing page, at top left, is Alfred Gwynne Vanderbilt I, a great horseman, who went down on the *Lusitania*. His grandfather, William H. Vanderbilt, hung original racing prints in his stable (top right). Outside the Newport Casino (opposite), Mr. and Mrs. Richard T. Wilson enter their surrey. Their three daughters married a Vanderbilt, a Goelet, and an Astor.

With flags flying, J. P. Morgan's *Corsair* leaves port for a cruise in 1894. To Morgan, who is preparing to disembark from his launch in the picture at right, his yacht was not only a thing of pleasure but a means of transportation and sometimes a place of business. At the end of a working week in the summer the *Corsair* would be waiting in the Hudson off Wall Street to take the owner and his guests upriver for the weekend. After spending Saturday night at his estate in Highland Falls, they would go aboard again on Sunday evening and get a good night's sleep before the *Corsair* started downriver very early next morning. Breakfast, with enough meats and fish to suit the financier's taste, was served on board in the shadow of the downtown skyscrapers.

The modern standard for luxury in motor yachts is set by the 380-foot *Atlantis* of Stavros Niarchos, the Greek shipping magnate. Built in 1974, it is here seen dwarfing the other craft in Monte Carlo harbor. The *Atlantis* has a dining room for twenty-eight, a movie theater for forty, a swimming pool, and twelve guest suites. For getting about in all elements, it carries two speedboats and two automobiles, and has a helicopter pad.

One of the most elegant of automobile interiors was turned out by Rolls Royce in 1927 for the wife of a French buyer. To recreate an eighteenth-century drawing room on wheels, the upholstery was woven by Aubusson and the ceiling painted with rococo cupids. A later standard of affluence is illustrated in the scene on the opposite page. Attended by his pilot and his chauffeur, Marcel Boussac, the French textile magnate, leaves his private plane for a short walk to his waiting Rolls.

4. WEALTH FROM TRADE

A MEDIEVAL PEDDLER

On the dusty roads of Lincolnshire, in the later years of the eleventh century, a young Englishman named Godric set out to make his living as a peddler. The son of a Saxon peasant, born in the hard decade that followed the Norman Conquest, Godric got his start by combing the sandy shores of the North Sea, picking up whatever the tide brought in from shipwrecked vessels. By selling such flotsam, he saved up enough money to buy a stock of the goods that commonly went into a peddler's pack—such items as pins and needles, scissors and knives, ribbons, religious charms, and whatever else might fill the needs of farmers' wives. Later he began visiting the cities and the annual fairs where he could buy fine cloths from abroad and metal objects to please richer customers. Now, with so much of value in his pack, Godric found it prudent to travel in a band with other merchants. Eventually he began going abroad to buy his own supplies and ship them back to England. Finally he joined with other merchants in outfitting their own vessels to trade along the coasts of England, Scotland, Norway, and Flanders.

At the age of forty Godric turned his back on worldly success, gave away all he owned to the poor, and retired to the forest of Finchale to become a hermit. In the decades that remained to him Godric won such renown as a holy man that a monk named Reginald wrote the story of his life, providing in the opening chapters a rare, authentic record of a medieval merchant's career.

◀ PRECEDING PAGES: **A caravan in Afghanistan travels the ancient highway of trade, the trans-Asian Silk Road.**
ROLAND MICHAUD, RAPHO-GUILLUMETTE

Up to the time he became a hermit Godric's story is essentially that of traders since civilization began. It is the story of the amber merchants who bore their precious loads down through the primeval forests of Europe from the Baltic coast to the Mediterranean markets before the time of Christ. It is the story of the caravan masters who followed the ancient Silk Road that ran across Central Asia from the borders of the Roman Empire to the Jade Gate of China. It is the story of the Polos of Venice. In its maritime phase it is the story of the Salem and Boston sea merchants who became the first wealthy men of the American colonies. Coming down to the last century, it is the story of Joseph Seligman, with a pack on his back trudging through the rural towns of Pennsylvania in the 1830's, or of Henry Lehman, driving his peddler's wagon around the back country of Alabama ten years later. One more step—the replacing of the peddler's pack with a small store—and it is the story of Marshall Field or the Hartford brothers or Frank Woolworth.

In ancient civilizations traders were the first men of business to make their mark on the historic record. Before the invention of money and banking, long before the start of manufactures, they were forming links between the separate civilizations of the Mediterranean world. In their packs and caravans and ships they brought not only goods but knowledge of foreign lands, the taste and smell of exotic products, and a rising standard of life. The cities they founded around the shores of the Mediterranean have come down to us in history and legend with an aura of wealth and luxury—Sardis, Sidon, Sybaris, Palmyra, Carthage, Corinth, Alexandria. To the warlike Romans these were places of corrup-

tion and decadence. But for all that Cato might censure or Caesar forbid, Rome was seduced by the traders with their tempting luxuries. The booty that Roman armies brought home furnished capital that flowed back to the East in payment for silks, jewels, spices, and delicate foods, enriching many a Roman merchant in the process. The most savage portrait ever painted of a trader is that of Trimalchio in Petronius' *Satyricon*, the gross merchant-shipper lolling in drunken revelry, boasting of vast estates he had never seen, having his wife's jewels weighed at the feast to prove their value.

Trimalchio is a burlesque figure; but many traders made great fortunes in Rome, and some of them surely found solace in luxury and revelry for the honor and office that aristocratic Rome denied them. The prosperity of the traders was made possible by the "great majestic peace" that Rome imposed on the known civilized world, and when at length that peace was destroyed, trade began a long, slow decline. In the darker centuries of the Middle Ages, when Islam blocked the Mediterranean sea routes and the Vikings made the northern seas too perilous for commerce, there was little opportunity for merchants. Few but fighting men and pilgrims traveled the roads of western Europe.

The appearance of peddlers like Godric of Finchale near the end of the eleventh century was a sign that at long last a measure of prosperity and safety was returning even to the distant marches of what had been the Roman Empire. By then the Vikings had given up raiding to settle down as merchants. In the south, after the First Crusade, most of the Mediterranean was again opened up to the trade of Venice, Pisa, Genoa, and French ports.

THE MERCHANT OF PRATO

Thanks to a chance find in modern times, we have the detailed records of one merchant who rose to affluence in Italy in the fourteenth century. His name was Francisco Datini, and he built a fine house in the city of Prato, twenty miles north of Florence. When some of its interior walls were taken down in the course of remodeling work in 1870, workmen found the complete records of his firm.

Born about 1335, the son of an innkeeper, Francisco Datini was thirteen years old when the Black Death took the lives of his father, his mother, and one of his two brothers. After working for a year as a shopkeeper's apprentice, the boy journeyed to Avignon, then the seat of the papacy. It was a good place for a store because money flowed into the papal court, creating a market for fine cloth, leather goods, jewelry, and religious articles. When the constable of France, Bertrand du Guesclin, laid siege to Avignon, Datini had no scruples about selling armor to the French attackers and the Provençal defenders alike.

Not until he was forty-six did Datini leave his business at Avignon with two partners in charge and return, with a twenty-two-year-old wife, a retinue of servants, and all his household goods, to make

The merchant-sailors who crossed the Mediterranean to trade with the infidel faced many challenges, as shown in these scenes from a thirteenth-century manuscript. At far left a storm has snapped the mast in two; while some remain on board others head for shore to buy and sell goods (center); only after a safe return voyage can they offer thanks at their own church (far right).

BIBLIOTECA DEL MONASTERIO DE EL ESCORIAL, MADRID

This wooden figure, from a church in Norfolk, England, represents the typical medieval peddler. The sculptor has given him a pack that seems far too small to hold all the wares he must have carried.

his headquarters in Prato. Soon his firm had branches in Pisa, Genoa, Spain, and Majorca.

Through his agents he bought wool in Spain, North Africa, and England, had it manufactured into cloth, and exported the cloth to markets all around the Mediterranean. His profits, the records show, ran pretty steadily at just under nine per cent a year. Much higher but less dependable profits were made in silk, velvet, and spices from the East. Unlike many merchants of his time, most notably the conscienceless Venetians, Datini drew the line at trading in slaves.

Perhaps most importantly the records of the house of Datini reveal the step-by-step transition from primitive accounting methods to the precise, double-entry bookkeeping that made it possible to keep track of large and various business transactions.

Iris Origo, who read the voluminous correspondence between Datini and his business associates, concluded:

He believed neither in the stability of any government nor in the honesty of any man. "You are young," he wrote to one of his factors in 1397, "but when you have lived as long as I and have traded with many folk, you will know that man is a dangerous thing, and that danger lies in dealing with him." It was these fears that caused him to distribute his fortune in as many places as possible, never sinking too much in any single company, never trusting too much to any partner, always prepared to cut his losses and begin again, to recover in one field what he had lost in another. And it was by this caution, this unceasing vigilance, that he made his fortune. But it was a weary life.

One of the first philanthropists among the merchant princes, he left his fortune to a foundation for the poor. A grateful city erected a statue of the merchant of Prato holding in his hand a sheaf of the bills of exchange with which he conducted his far-flung business.

TRADING EMPIRES

Maritime commerce was the basis of two remarkable seaborne empires, that of the Venetians and that of the Dutch. In each the state and all its machinery were controlled by men whose fortunes were based solidly on trade. Each of them rose at the edge of the sea and enlarged its realm with bits of land seized from the water and held fast against the attacks of tide and storm. But in their civilization and style of life they could hardly have been more different.

Venice, which "held the gorgeous east in fee," was half Oriental in its love of splendid costume, jewels, pomp, and state spectacles calculated to awe its people and advertise its power. It used captured seamen to row its galleys and sold European boys to be made into eunuchs for the court of Turkey. It was ruled by an oligarchy of merchant families, acting through a doge and the Council of Ten, which employed an official poisoner and used assassination as an instrument of policy. Its great men look out at us in splendid portraits by Titian and Giorgione and Veronese, swathed to their cheekbones in silk and cloth of gold, alive with intelligence and force, but silent, secret, hidden.

How different the Dutch! In their black woolen jackets and their starched white ruffs, the merchants of Holland face the world with expressions of shrewdness and confidence that need no finery to announce their power. Without the long hair and ruffs, the syndics of Cloth Hall, as they were painted by Rembrandt, could be the directors of United States Steel.

The astonishing Dutch mastery of seaborne commerce in the seventeenth century grew out of the long struggle by the Protestant Dutch to throw off the iron rule of Catholic Spain in the Netherlands. Driven out of Amsterdam in 1535, the Protestant grain dealers made common cause with the cutlass-wielding "Sea Beggars," who captured and sank the big ships of Spain. Amsterdam was retaken in 1578, and thereafter, with neither powerful nobles nor churchmen to dispute their sway, the merchants settled down to show how a sensible bourgeois state should be run. Having little land to farm and few resources to exploit, they became "the waggoners of the waves." At a time when all Europe had about twenty thousand vessels, sixteen thousand of them were Dutch. The fast, low frigates, built for trade and combat alike, opened up such a profitable trade with the Orient that for a period of one hundred ninety-eight years the Dutch East India Company paid an average annual dividend of eighteen per cent. One Amsterdam merchant named Beylant spoke for many when he said that if there was a profit to be made, he would "sail through Hell to get it, even if it scorched his sails." As if to prove their willingness to trade with the devil, they filled an order from the king of Spain for an entire fleet— which he promptly sent against Holland.

The possibilities for profit that exist in a state ruled by its businessmen were notably exploited by the members of the Bicker family. Andries Bicker,

Early traders carried their coins in pouches like the ones shown above. When they lacked merchandise that could be offered in exchange, they found gold was always an acceptable substitute. Other highly prized items of trade were spices. Cloves, nutmeg, cinnamon, pepper, gathered from the widely scattered shores of Asia, are displayed in the ornate box (below) as if they were precious jewels.

the burgomaster of Amsterdam, was a power in the East India Company. With his three brothers he divided up the trade of the world. While Andries established a monopoly of the Russian fur trade, Jacob took the rest of the Baltic for his sphere, Jan took the Mediterranean, and Cornelis took all the Americas; a son-in-law commanded the municipal garrison, and a cousin commanded the Baltic convoy patrol. When it came to nepotism, however, the Bickers had nothing on the family of Burgomaster Willem Munter, who ran the government of Amsterdam with two sons, a son-in-law, four brothers-in-law, two nephews, and a cousin.

Sir William Temple, who was British ambassador to The Hague in 1668, found among the Dutch a strange combination of wealth and frugality:

The merchants and tradesmen are of mighty industry. Never any country traded so much and consumed so little. They buy infinitely, but 'tis to sell again. They are the great masters of Indian spices and Persian silks, but wear plain woolen and feed upon their own fish and roots. They sell the finest of their own cloth to France and buy coarse out of England for their own wear. They send abroad the best of their own butter and buy the cheapest out of Ireland for their own use. They furnish infinite luxury which they never practice, and traffic in pleasures which they never taste.

Frugality and sobriety were not qualities with much appeal to an aristocratic visitor from the court of Restoration England. But from their own bourgeois point of view, which is much closer to our own, the Dutch created a life style of singular comfort, beauty, and homely pleasure. Not for them the pomp and panoply of the Venetian noble in his house of gold nor yet the grandeur of the English lord in his great, dark, drafty castle. The Dutch merchant built his house of brick and wood, with inside plumbing and large windows that flooded the rooms with sunlight. He adorned it with fine teak furniture brought from the other side of the world, with china and tile from his own Delft potteries, and especially with paintings.

Dutch painting of the seventeenth century—the high tide of the Dutch mercantile empire—is a sufficient answer to the charge that materialist civilizations do not encourage great art. Seldom has such a body of art sprung into being in so short a time or reached such peaks of genius in artists like Rembrandt and Vermeer. This flowering was nourished and supported by the patronage of the bourgeois merchant families. They did not pay high prices for the art; they bargained as closely as they did for wool or spices. But they bought steadily and in great quantity. It was not unusual, according to an historian of the time, for a Dutch burgher of relatively modest means to have on his walls a hundred or two hundred pictures, all painted by living artists of his country. The burgher might like a little flattery in the paintings of himself and his wife, but he wanted his surroundings—the rooms and furniture and streets and windmills and canals—to be painted with faithful realism. It is because of the buyers' taste as much as the artists' talent that we have a pictorial record of Dutch life in the seven-

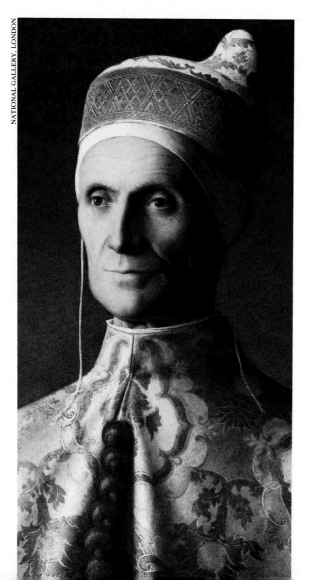

For more than six hundred years the republic of Venice was controlled by its businessmen—merchants, bankers, shipowners—whose names were written in the Golden Book of Venetian aristocracy. At their head stood the doge, elected for life. At left is a portrait of Doge Leonardo Loredano, by Giovanni Bellini, about 1501.

Auß dem Zornal ins Schuldbuch sein/
Darzu ins Capus trag ich ein/
Zur lincken hand den Debitor/
Zur rechten ghört der Crebitor.

Die Götter so mit grosser müe/
Wir auff die Meß zurichten hie/
Die wöll Gott glücklich bringen hin/
Daraus eruolg vil nuz vnd groin.

LIBERTAS.

This sixteenth-century Nuremberg merchant house must have been a noisy place as well-dressed clerks counted and bagged the large piles of coins. In the background workers pack goods for future shipment.

teenth century that is scarcely matched by that of any other place or time in history.

Holland's maritime ascendancy was the envy of the English, who got an early start at sea but did not catch up with the Dutch until late in the seventeenth century. Sometimes they too found their prey in the treasure galleons of the king of Spain. They called it privateering, but since they practiced it in peace as well as war, it was hardly distinguishable from piracy. When the Elizabethan sea dogs sailed forth to "singe the beard of the king of Spain," they went with the wild applause of the people, the solid financial backing of the courtiers, and the private blessing of the queen herself. Of the six hundred thousand pounds that Drake brought back in 1580 from his round-the-world voyage in the *Golden Hind*, it is believed that about three hundred was Gloriana's share. Its importance in the history of the British Empire has been underlined by John Maynard Keynes:

The booty brought back by Drake in the *Golden Hind* may fairly be considered the fountain and origin of British Foreign Investment. Elizabeth paid off out of the proceeds the whole of her foreign debt and invested a part of the balance (about £42,000) in the Levant Company; largely out of the proceeds of the Levant Company there was formed the East India Company, the profits of which during the seventeenth and eighteenth centuries were the main foundation of England's foreign connections; and so on.

Writing in 1930, Keynes went on to make the following calculation:

At the present time (in round figures) our foreign investments probably yield us about 6½ per cent net after allowing for losses, of which we reinvest abroad about half—say 3¼ per cent. If this is, on the average, a fair sample of what has been going on since 1580, the £42,000 invested by Elizabeth out of Drake's booty in 1580 would have accumulated by 1930 to approximately the actual aggregate of our present foreign investments, namely £4,200,000,000.

THE EXOTIC SASSOONS

Throughout the seventeenth and eighteenth centuries the profits of the East India trade flowed back into the hands of the aristocratic families, paying for their great stone country houses, their horses and carriages and servants, and the tiers of paintings that they hung on their walls. Of all these fortunes, perhaps the greatest, and certainly the most exotic, was that of the Sassoons. Unlike the Rothschilds, with whom they invite comparison, the Sassoons did not rise to affluence from a European ghetto. They had prospered for centuries in Baghdad, a crossroads of Near Eastern trade routes and the chief center for Jews in exile since the time of Nebuchadnezzar. The Sassoons claimed descent from King David and belonged to the Jewish commercial elite. Several of them had occupied the post of chief banker to the caliph, which entitled them to wear cloth of gold at court and to receive the bows of the populace.

By the early nineteenth century, however, Baghdad's long age of affluence had been ended by successive attacks of Mongols, Persians, and Turks.

David Sassoon (seated) was the founder of the family of Jewish merchants who profited from the exotic trade with the East. Sassoon David Sassoon (in Western dress) was the first of the family to leave Bombay and set up business in London.

STANLEY JACKSON, *THE SASSOONS*, HEINEMANN, LONDON, 1968

Casting about for revenue, the ruling pasha began seizing rich Jews for ransom. It was time for the Sassoons to move. In a chapter out of the *Arabian Nights*, David, the oldest son of Sheikh Sason Ben Saleh, made his escape by boat in the dead of night, muffled in turban and cloak, with a money belt around his waist and pearls sewn inside his clothes. The pasha sent agents to bring him back for ransom, but he reached Persia, and after a few years' stay he moved on to Bombay. He arrived there at a time when the monopoly of the British East India Company had at last been broken and the trade of the Orient was thrown open to Parsees, Moslems, Hindus, and Jews under the impartial protection of the British flag.

The house of Sassoon, which David founded at Bombay, flourished from the start. One source of revenue was the cotton trade, especially during the American Civil War, when the mills of Lancashire, cut off from their American supply, paid record prices for Indian cotton. But over the years the firm's greatest profits came from buying opium grown in India and shipping it for sale in China.

The importance of opium to the Eastern trade was simply this: there was almost nothing else that the Chinese wanted. Indeed, the history of trade with China, since long before the days of Marco Polo, had been a series of frustrating attempts to find goods that the Chinese would accept even as "tribute" from "the barbarians." The very rare items that pleased the Chinese rulers are enshrined in legend: the Golden Peaches sent from the Kingdom of Samarkand in the seventh century, and the Six Bayards, or "Heavenly Horses," that the Emperor T'ai Tsung received from "the Far West." On the other hand the Chinese always had one thing that the West craved, and that was silk, in which they enjoyed a monopoly for two thousand years. The Romans could never get enough of the precious silk until, in the sixth century, two Christian monks smuggled some silkworms out of China in a bamboo cane and brought them to the Emperor Justinian at Byzantium.

It was a cause for rejoicing among the foreign merchants when they discovered that Indian opium brought a high profit in China. The evil effects of opium smoking were perfectly well known at that time both to the British government and to the Chinese imperial court, which forbade importation of the "foreign mud." Yet for years the Chinese imperial factors at Canton winked at the illegal trade, and when in 1839 the emperor sent a special commissioner to enforce the embargo, the British fought the Opium War to open up the Chinese port in the name of free trade.

The Sassoons were not alone in reaping immense profits from the opium business. Among the other firms that shared in the bonanza was Jardine, Matheson & Co., which survives to this day as a vast complex of manufacturing and trading companies, with headquarters in Hong Kong. In a much smaller way opium swelled the profits of American merchant families, including the Forbeses, the Perkinses, and the Delanos (whence the maternal inheritance of Franklin Delano Roosevelt).

As the sons of David Sassoon came of age, he took them into the business, trained them, and sent them out to manage the firm's interests in Shanghai, Hong Kong, and London. Thus it was in 1858 that the third son, Sassoon David Sassoon ("S.D."), moved to England and became the first of his clan to wear Western dress. His experience there was so pleasant that over the next twenty years all but one of the brothers followed S.D. to London, the exception being Elias, who not only remained in the East but left the family firm to start his own immensely successful enterprise in Shanghai. In England the Sassoons bought great country houses, hired fine chefs, gave splendid parties, sent their sons to Eton and Harrow, and were soon welcomed into the racy, pleasure-loving circle of the Prince of Wales, later Edward VII. The clan was jolted when S.D.'s son Alfred married a Gentile, Theresa Thornycroft; but soon after that other Sassoons were marrying outside their faith.

By moving en masse to England, the Sassoons not only pulled up their social roots but ensured the eventual eclipse of their merchant house. None of the English sons in the third generation went into the family business, though several of them put their unquestioned gifts to use in other fields. Siegfried Sassoon, of the Thornycroft branch, won youthful renown as the poet of World War I. After that war his cousin Philip became parliamentary private secretary to Lloyd George. Philip's sister Sybil married the Marquess of Cholmondeley, the Lord Great Chamberlain of England, and became superintendent of the Women's Royal Naval Services in World War II.

The only Sassoon left in trade was Victor, grandson of Elias, who had founded the rival house in Shanghai. In the 1850's Elias had had the foresight to buy up, at prices in the range of two hundred dollars an acre, large tracts of the mud flats along the Yellow River in Shanghai. By Victor's time these flats had become the Bund, the greatest trading center in China. When he covered them with office buildings, hotels, and apartments, the land was worth about one million four hundred thousand dollars an acre and Victor Sassoon was considered the richest businessman in Asia. But the Japanese invasion and later the victory of Red China ended the last great Sassoon enterprise. Sir Victor's departure from China in 1948 put a period to a family mercantile venture that stretched back for many centuries and very likely to biblical times.

THE FIRST AMERICAN MILLIONAIRES

From the exotic splendors of the Sassoons, we may now turn to the spare beginnings of mercantile wealth in America. Because of the British ban on colonial manufactures, shipping offered virtually the

CONTINUED ON PAGE 130

Sir Victor Sassoon (below) leads his Derby winner, Pinza, at Epsom Downs in 1953. In the late twenties he spent a fortune building skyscrapers on land in Shanghai that the Sassoons had owned since it was a mud flat.

POPPERFOTO

The Europeans who traded with the East in the seventeenth and eighteenth centuries brought back spices, coffee, lacquered goods, indigo, porcelain, and tea. The English were the greatest importers of tea, shipped in boxes like the ones shown on the facing page. In the sixteenth century the Portuguese were the first to set foot in Japan; the Japanese paper screen above shows a large Portuguese ship flying the flags of both countries. The Chinese set about depicting those they called the "Ocean Devils." At left is a wood-and-ivory figure of a "barbarian" shown holding an umbrella. At right is a T'ang dynasty pottery figure of what looks to be a Near Eastern trader with his wineskin.

RUSSELL & C° FOO CHOW FOO.

ARGONAUT

L M

EXTRA CURIOUS

OOLOONG

Nº 10

A WAH

KATE HAYES

FB

EXTRA FINE

OOLONG

Nº 10

WYHING

CONTINUED FROM PAGE 127

only way by which an ambitious young man in the Northern colonies could rise above the level of a farmer or shopkeeper. In the quarter century before the Revolution, the ports of Massachusetts already had an elite of prosperous shipowners with names like Gray, Derby, Cabot, Crowninshield, and Hancock. But it was the Revolution that transformed their trading vessels into privateers—and the shipowners into America's first millionaires. During the Revolutionary years the Continental Congress issued six hundred twenty-six letters of marque, entitling the captains of armed trading vessels to prey upon British shipping, and the General Court of Massachusetts issued a thousand more.

After the Revolution, American maritime merchants built bigger ships and sent them to the Pacific to compete with the East India Company in its own waters. Boston's premier shipping king in the early years of the nineteenth century was Thomas Handasyd Perkins, whose firm provided some or all of the financial bedrock for many of Boston's first families, including Cabots, Lodges, Appletons, Shaws, Forbeses, and Russells. By Boston standards Colonel Perkins lived well, with a mansion on Beacon Hill and a resplendent coach. But he and others had before them the cautionary example of John Hancock, the proud and improvident shipping heir who had earned a lasting place in the history books but had spent his fortune in vainglorious display. Besides, there were deeper satisfactions. When Colonel Perkins attended church one Sunday, the minister pointed him out to the congregation from the pulpit, saying: "God bless you, sir! When you die angels will fight for the honor of carrying you to heaven on their shoulders." Until that day should arrive, Colonel Perkins never took a vacation in ninety years of life and work. When George Washington asked him to be the first Secretary of the Navy, he was able to answer quite honestly that since he owned more ships than the United States Navy, he thought he was more needed in his own business.

With the coming of steam on the ocean highways in the second third of the nineteenth century, New England's maritime primacy swiftly faded. By 1850 Nathaniel Hawthorne, who had filled the sinecure job of surveyor for the customhouse at Salem, could write of ancient seamen who "spent a good deal of time asleep in their accustomed corners, with their chairs tilted back against the wall; awaking, however, once or twice in the forenoon, to bore one another with the several thousandth repetition of old sea-stories, and mouldy jokes, that had grown to be

pass-words and counter-signs among them." Salem's port was too shallow for the new ocean-going packets. But even Boston missed out on the age of steam.

The whole nation was turning its back on the maritime world of its youth and facing the new challenge of developing the vast continent beyond the Alleghenies. The change is well illustrated in the lives of two brothers, Robert Bennett Forbes and John Murray Forbes. "Black Ben" Forbes went to sea as a cabin boy in a ship of his uncle, Colonel Perkins, commanded the brig *Nile* at twenty, and made a fortune at twenty-three. But he could read the figures on the ledgers, and in later years he turned his attention away from the grand but profitless clippers to begin experimenting with steamships and screw propellers. Meanwhile his brother, John Murray Forbes, who had also as a boy started out in the China trade, made a second fortune and was the chief organizer of the Chicago, Burlington and Quincy Railroad. From that time on, the fortunes of the New England merchant princes flowed increasingly into industrial enterprises outside New England.

The coming of steam on the seas brought a new kind of shipping magnate. On the premier North Atlantic run, no American operator succeeded in competing with the British line founded by Samuel Cunard of Halifax, Canada. But Captain Robert Dollar came out of the Northwest lumber camps to found the Dollar Line, which dominated the Pacific trade. And William R. Grace used his Grace Line to tie together his commercial and industrial empire in Latin America. In the twentieth century, however, all these carriers ran into heavy seas after the airplane took away their passenger traffic.

In the middle years of the twentieth century the greatest fortunes in the carrying trade were made by lone-wolf operators who built and chartered freighters and tankers. The spotlight of notoriety shone on two flamboyant Greeks, Stavros Niarchos and Aristotle Onassis, who not only built competing fleets but seemed bent on outdoing each other in the brilliance of their marriages, the size of their yachts, and the opulence of their private Aegean islands. Meanwhile their fortunes were equaled, if not surpassed, by an American so reclusive that his next-door neighbor in Darien, Connecticut, when interviewed, could not quite remember what he looked like. His name is Daniel K. Ludwig, but a stranger who telephoned him at the office of his company, National Bulk Carriers, was told by the operator

130

The antics of Greek shipowner Aristotle Onassis brought a seldom-seen smile to the face of American billionaire J. Paul Getty in 1963.

that no one of that name worked there.

Born in South Haven, Michigan, in 1897, Ludwig dropped out of high school to work at jobs on the waterfront at Port Arthur, Texas, where he learned to repair marine engines. He was nineteen when he made the crucial decision made by many fortune builders: that he had worked for his last boss. During the next twenty years in the chancy business of buying, building, and chartering boats, he stuck to that resolve, although he was often on the edge of bankruptcy. It was during those years that he mastered the business practices that brought later success in shipping. One was to register his ships in such flag-of-convenience countries as Panama and Liberia, where registration fees are low and safety regulations few. Another was to recruit his crews among such people as the Cayman islanders, who would put up with spartan accommodations on shipboard. Still another was to insist on speed and rigid economy throughout his business. (A senior ship's officer who sent in a report bearing a paper clip was admonished: "We don't pay to send ironmongery by air mail.") But the most important discovery he made was the way to build his ships with other people's money. Step number one was this: as soon as he owned one ship outright he chartered it for a long term of years to an oil company and assigned the charter to a bank as collateral for a loan to build another ship. Step number two, developed a few years later, was this: before he even built the ship, he arranged a long-term charter against which the bank advanced money for the full cost of building. By operating almost entirely with bank loans, Ludwig was able to hang on to the full ownership of his empire.

The boom that followed World War II, with its rising demand for oil and a shortage of tankers, sent shipping rates soaring. Ludwig was one of the first at sea with the new supertankers, which enriched him along with the Greeks and such other big fleet operators as Hilmar Reksten of Norway and Y. K. Pao of Hong Kong. But by the end of the 1950's he was already moving to diversify his operations, especially into real estate, which he identified early as the prime opportunity of the sixties. By the seventies,

when tanker fleets were struck by the Arab oil embargo, and the subsequent drop in gasoline consumption, Ludwig was better set than others to ride out the storm.

THE DEPARTMENT-STORE KEEPERS

These tycoons of the carrying trade are shipowners rather than traders on the model of the old New England merchant princes. Beginning about the middle of the nineteenth century the merchant princes of the future were to be found not on the decks of rolling ships but in peddler's wagons and country stores.

The man who originated the department store, according to most accounts, was Alexander Turney Stewart, a young Irishman who emigrated to New York in 1820 and presently opened a linen shop on lower Broadway, stocked with the products of his native land. He did so well that in 1846 he was able to build an ornate structure, which he called the Marble Dry Goods Palace and which Henry James

At the end of the nineteenth century Mrs. Potter Palmer (right) reigned as queen of Chicago society. Once, when Mrs. Jack Gardner of Boston came to call, she was proudly shown Mrs. Palmer's gold table service for fifty. "And what," asked the irrepressible "Mrs. Jack," "do you do when you have a large dinner party?"

condescendingly described as "vast, marmorean, plate-glassy." In a day when most retail business was done by small specialty shops, Stewart's store offered under one roof everything from mattresses to Oriental rugs to corsets. In addition to such novelties as fixed prices and free toilets, he hired handsome young men as clerks because he noticed that his lady customers seemed to prefer them. Toward the end of his life he opened a bigger store, the Cast Iron Palace, which after his death became Wanamaker's. By his merchandising flair, and by paying the lowest wages in the city and investing his profits in real estate, Stewart piled up a fortune of fifty million dollars, which put him in the financial league with Commodore Vanderbilt and John Jacob Astor.

Following in Stewart's steps, merchants in every major city found the department store a path to riches. Among them were Eben Jordan and Edward A. Filene in Boston; John Wanamaker in Philadelphia; Rowland Macy, Nathan Straus, and Bernard Gimbel in New York; Joseph L. Hudson in Detroit; Morris Rich in Atlanta. Most of them had been poor boys who started out by clerking in a small store or, in a few cases, by driving a peddler's wagon through the countryside. Some of their common characteristics may be seen in the men whose names were given in succession to the store that launched two of Chicago's greatest fortunes.

First it was Potter Palmer's store, founded by a young Quaker who arrived from upstate New York at a time when Chicago was still something of a frontier town and opened a dry-goods store on Lake Street. The store prospered, expanded to its own building, and branched out to include other lines of merchandise. Potter Palmer is remembered for his gracious way with lady customers, urging them to take their purchases home, try them out before their husbands, and bring them back if they did not satisfy. He is remembered also for the silver dollars with which he studded the floor of the barber shop in the Palmer House, which he built after selling his store. But he is remembered most of all for his wife, who was half his age and who outlived him by sixteen years.

Nothing was too good for Bertha Honoré Palmer, the daughter of a French family in Kentucky. Though Palmer found society something of a bore, he built for Bertha a huge turreted castle on Lake Shore Drive, where she reigned thenceforth as the queen of Chicago society.

When he was drawing up his will, which left everything to Bertha, his lawyer warned Palmer that if his wife should marry again, his entire fortune might end up in the hands of a stranger. "If she does," said Palmer, "he'll need the money." Mrs. Palmer did not marry again, and she proved herself a good business woman by managing the Palmer House herself and doubling the fortune her husband left her. If she knew how to spend money, she also knew how to get it back. Once at a dinner in Paris, where President McKinley sent her as a commissioner to the Paris Exposition of 1899, she lost a large teardrop emerald valued at forty thousand dollars. Her host, Tom Walsh, was eager to replace it, but she told him not to worry. Later, as Lucius Beebe tells it, she recouped the loss by marking up the prices on the Palmer House menu: "Ten cents on strawberries, a nickel on the coffee—little things that no one would notice."

While Potter Palmer was building up his Chicago store a boy named Marshall Field left his family farm in Pittsfield, Massachusetts, and got his first job in the local general store—a job from which he was presently fired with the well-meant advice that he seek some line of work for which he was better fitted. Instead, he went to Chicago and worked his way up to a partnership in the Cooley and Farwell store, a competitor of Potter Palmer's. When Palmer decided to retire, he sold shares in his store to Field and another young merchant, Levi Leiter. Under their direction the store prospered and moved into a handsome new building that became a showplace of Chicago. Though reserved and rather frosty by nature, Field, like Palmer, had the true merchant's touch for making his customers feel happy and cherished in the store. To a sales clerk who was arguing with a customer he once uttered an admonition that became thereafter the guiding principle of the store: "Give the lady what she wants."

A business relationship with Marshall Field was likely to be profitable but not warm. When he decided that Leiter had served his purpose, he calmly announced one day, "I feel that it is time that we part," and named a figure, giving Leiter the choice of buying Field's interest or selling his own. Taken by surprise and knowing that the figure was low, Leiter decided to buy. What he did not know, but soon found out, was that if Field left the store, most of the management team would go with him. The next day he gave in, saying: "Marshall, you win. I'll sell." Field had given Leiter no alternative but to sell his interest at the low figure they had agreed upon.

Both Leiter and Field subsequently multiplied

their fortunes by buying Chicago real estate. Leiter's wife became a hostess in London society, and their daughter Mary married Lord Curzon, eventually becoming Vicereine of India. Field kept on running the store and piling up a fortune, which at the time of his death in 1906 amounted to something over a hundred million dollars.

HARTFORDS AND WOOLWORTHS

After the department store, the greatest source of merchandising fortunes was the chain store, as pioneered by the Hartfords of the Great Atlantic & Pacific Tea Company. It all began with a little tea store that was opened in New York in 1859 by George Huntington Hartford and a partner. Hartford had a sound business idea—to cut the price of tea from a dollar a pound to thirty cents by buying direct from the producers in Japan and China, eliminating all middlemen. He was also a showman, and he painted his store bright red and gold, hung Japanese lanterns, put his cashiers in pagodas, and sent a red wagon through the streets to advertise prizes and premiums. Soon he added other goods and began opening other stores until by 1876 he was operating sixty-seven more or less conventional grocery stores that offered charge accounts and wagon delivery. It was his youngest son John who in 1912 got the idea of cutting prices still further by selling for cash only, without delivery, aiming at a large volume. With his father's grudging assent he opened such an economy store around the corner from a conventional A. & P., and quickly put it out of business. All the A. & P. stores were converted to the new formula, and new ones opened at the rate of one every three days. "We went so fast," John Hartford later reminisced, "that hobos hopping off freight trains got hired as managers." Under "Mr. John" and his older brother "Mr. George," the chain reached a total of 15,737 neighborhood stores in the period before the coming of the supermarket.

Frank Woolworth was another farm boy who had a hard time getting started in the business world. His first job, as a clerk in the dry-goods store of Augsbury & Moore at Watertown, New York, paid nothing for the first three months. In later life he gave B. C. Forbes, the financial writer, a classic account of a farm boy's first day on the job:

Mr. Augsbury was the first one I encountered. "Bub, don't they wear any collars in your neighborhood?" was

how he greeted me. I replied: "No." "No neckties either?" I again replied: "No." "Is this old flannel shirt the best you have to wear?" he next asked. "Yes, sir," I replied. "Well, you'd better go out and get a white shirt and a collar and a tie before you begin work."

I went and got properly rigged up, and shortly after I got back to the store Mr. Augsbury went to lunch. Nobody told me what to do. I hung around, feeling foolish, waiting for something to do. The clerks stared at me and sneered at me—I was a boob from the country accustomed to wearing nothing but old flannel shirts without collar or tie. At least, I imagined that was what they were thinking—and they afterward told me that that was exactly their sizing up of me. When most of the clerks had gone to dinner—lunch, as we call it nowadays—in came an old farmer and said to me: "Young man, I want a spool of thread." I didn't know where they kept the thread, so I went over to Mr. Moore, who was busy at his desk, and asked him. "Right in front of your nose, young man," he snapped without looking up from his writing. I pulled out a drawer directly in front of me and, sure enough, found it full of spools of thread. "I want number forty," said the farmer. I never knew till that moment that thread had a number. I fumbled all around the drawer looking for number 40, but could not find it. I appealed to Mr. Moore to know if we kept number 40. "Certainly; right in the drawer in front of you," he said quite sharply. I had to tell him: "I can't find any." "Just as I expected," he said testily as he got down from his desk and showed me the right kind of thread. He immediately returned to his desk.

"How much is it, young man?" asked the farmer. I had to turn once more to Mr. Moore. It was eight cents. The farmer pulled out a ten-cent shinplaster. "Mr. Moore, where do I get change?" I had to ask. "Come right up to the desk and make out a ticket," he ordered me. I picked up one of the blanks and studied it all over to see what I could do with it. But I was stumped. "Mr. Moore, I don't believe I know how to make this out," I had to confess. "Hand it to me; I will show you," he replied. Next I had to ask: "Where do I get my change?" "There's the cashier right there; can't you see him?" he said impatiently.

The young clerk survived his first day and was making $3.50 a week in three months' time. The idea that made him rich came from an experiment in the Watertown store with a five-cent counter for inexpensive items. What was needed, Woolworth decided, was a whole store full of nickel items, and with $315.41 worth of merchandise lent on credit by his employer, he opened The Great Five Cent Store in Utica, New York. It failed. Woolworth analyzed the difficulties: a poor location and not enough items of any quality at five cents. Four months later he opened the first five-and-ten cent store at Lancaster, Pennsylvania. It succeeded, and although the next two stores failed, he now had a formula that could be repeated in good locations all over the country.

The Woolworth formula brought riches not only to him but to rival chain owners like Kress and Kresge. The chains they built lived long after the rise in prices had made a mockery of the name "five-and-ten."

WHAT THE HEIRS DID WITH IT

The earlier retail fortunes have now passed into the hands of the second, third, fourth, and even fifth generations. Their possessors have run the gamut of possible responses to the inheritance of great wealth. In some cases, and particularly in the more tightly knit Jewish families, the heirs have maintained active management of the family business. The Lazarus family of Cincinnati not only kept control of the family stores in that city and Columbus but became the dominant influence in the Federated Stores chain, where Lazaruses swarm almost as thickly in the executive suite as shoppers in a bargain basement.

Marshall Field's son, Marshall II, died before his father, probably a suicide, and by the time Marshall III came of age the store had passed out of family hands. Not content with the life of the Long Island hunting set, he used his fortune to start a Chicago publishing empire, which includes the *Sun Times* and World Book Encyclopedia. It has been headed in succession by Marshall Field III, IV, and V.

Since Frank Woolworth had no sons, his fortune descended to two daughters, Helena Woolworth McCann and Jessie Woolworth Donahue, and a granddaughter, Barbara Hutton. During the 1930's the tabloid newspaper editors could never quite make up their minds whether Barbara Hutton or Doris Duke, the American Tobacco Company heiress, was "the Richest Girl in the World," but in the number of husbands, Miss Hutton won handily, seven to two. They were, in order: "Prince" Alexis Mdivani, a bogus Russian nobleman; Danish Count Kurt von Haugwitz-Reventlow; actor Cary Grant; Igor Troubetzkoy, an authentic czarist prince; Porfirio Rubirosa, a Dominican playboy who also married Doris Duke; Baron Gottfried von Cramm, a

On a spring evening in 1913 President Wilson pushed a button in Washington that turned on the 80,000 lights in the new Woolworth Building in lower Manhattan. The tallest building in the world had been paid for in full by the five-and-dime merchant Frank Woolworth.

German tennis champion; and Doan Vinh, a Vietnamese prince. Despite the inroads made by various husbands (notably excepting Cary Grant), Miss Hutton's fortune, which came to her in 1933 at a value of forty million dollars, is probably much larger now. Its future is not known since her only child, Lance Reventlow, who stood to inherit it, was killed in an airplane crash in 1972.

The Hartford brothers of A.&P., "Mr. George" and "Mr. John," had no children. Huntington Hartford, a familiar figure in New York café society in recent decades, is the son of a third brother, Edward, who never entered the family business but became an inventor and made a separate fortune of his own from the Hartford shock absorber. "Hunt" therefore received inheritances from both his grandfather and his father. After college he made a perfunctory stab at working in the family business but was presently fired by his crusty uncles for taking half a day off. For an heir to a great fortune Hunt showed, according to some of his associates, a rather dangerous combination of qualities: an urge to do something useful with his money but an unusually short attention span. He has devoted his earnest, if fleeting, efforts to a succession of what he calls "projects." These include a Gallery of Modern Art in New York, built to provide a showcase for realistic art, as opposed to the abstract art on view at the Rockefellers' Museum of Modern Art; a colony for writers and artists in California; a magazine of the entertainment world called *Show*; a resort in the Bahamas called Paradise Island; an agency for fashion models, which he started after his return from World War II; a handwriting academy to further his interest in graphology; and an open-air café which he proposed to build in Central Park at his own expense but which the city turned down. With very little to show for any of these "projects," Hartford had reduced his fortune, according to *The Wall Street Journal* in 1973, from one hundred million dollars to thirty million.

FRIED CHICKEN AND HAMBURGER

In recent decades two of the most spectacular merchandising successes have been made by fast-food chains. The businessman responsible for the growth of Kentucky Fried Chicken was not old Colonel Sanders but a young man from Kentucky who bought the rights to the colonel's image and the colonel's formula, John Y. Brown, Jr. It took Brown just seven years to expand Kentucky Fried into a national fast-food chain and sell out at a price that made him thirty-three times a millionaire.

Multiply the figures by fifteen and you have the story of Ray Kroc, the man behind the McDonald's hamburger chain. Kroc is perhaps the outstanding example in recent times of the truth that it is never too late to start on your first million. In 1954, at the age of fifty, he was selling something called a Prince Castle Multimixer, which shook six milk shakes at once. When he got an order for eight such mixers from a single restaurant in California called McDonald's, he began to think about the volume of business that the restaurant must be doing. After paying a visit to the owners, Richard and Maurice McDonald, he made a deal with them to franchise outlets in other states, and two years later he bought them out.

One of Kroc's secrets of success was to impose rigid standards of quality and service. From coast to coast each machine-cut sliver of ground beef

weighed 1.6 ounces and measured 3.875 inches across; its cooking was timed by winking lights; was served by employees whose costume, hairstyle, and manners were strictly regulated from headquarters. Franchise holders were told precisely how long the cooked hamburgers might be kept under infrared light before they were served (ten minutes), and how often to sweep the parking lot (every hour). So little was left to local discretion that the restaurants maintain the company standards with a turnover of help that averages one hundred per cent every six months. In 1973 McDonald's passed the U.S. Army as the leading supplier of food. So financially successful has the company been that Ray Kroc's secretary, who got ten per cent of the stock at the outset, is now retired with a fortune of fifty-four million dollars. Kroc himself, still in active charge at seventy-three, is estimated to be worth about three hundred million dollars.

MRS. JACK GARDNER OF BOSTON

With Huntington Hartford as a living example of how little can be accomplished with a huge fortune, we may now close with a backward look at a lady who accomplished an astonishing amount with a relatively modest fortune. This was the incomparable Mrs. Jack Gardner of Boston.

Born Belle Stewart in New York, she was the daughter of David Stewart, who began his career as an importer of fine linens and later became involved with iron and mining interests. Her husband, John Lowell Gardner, was a member of an old New England shipping family. Their combined fortune at its peak did not amount to more than six or seven million dollars, but Mrs. Jack knew how to·use every

dollar to good effect. Almost as soon as she arrived in Boston, she established herself as the hostess who gave the best parties and attracted the liveliest guests. Proper Bostonians' most polite word for her was "unconventional." Where they were generally content with one house on Beacon Hill, Mrs. Jack had two, back to back. Where their carriages had one footman on the box, Mrs. Jack had a matching pair. Her coachman drove faster than theirs. Her dresses were tighter than theirs. Her ropes of pearls were longer than theirs. They found it unsettling when she once rode about with two lion cubs on the seat beside her. Ladies professed shock when she invited them to tea in a drawing room where Sandow the Strong Man stood on exhibition behind a thin curtain, wearing only trunks—or, as some remembered, a fig leaf. Their sense of propriety was offended during Lent when Mrs. Jack made public display of her penitence by driving to the Church of the Advent with soap and a bucket of water, and washing down the steps.

At a time when Boston still liked to think of itself as the Athens of America, Mrs. Gardner held court for the brightest talents in the arts and letters.

Barbara Hutton, Woolworth's granddaughter, was dubbed "the poor little rich girl." Her seven husbands (in order, from left on the opposite page) have been: "Prince" Alexis Mdivani, a Russian, in 1933; Count Kurt von Haugwitz-Reventlow, a Dane, 1935; American actor Cary Grant, 1942; Prince Igor Troubetzkoy, another Russian, 1947; Dominican playboy Porfirio Rubirosa, 1953; Baron Gottfried von Cramm, a German tennis champion, 1955; and Doan Vinh, a Vietnamese prince, 1966. She once summed it up, "All the unhappiness in my life has been caused by men."

Among them were many young men to whom she gave encouragement, entree, and often financial support. But they included also the established lions of Boston and Cambridge: Henry James, Charles Eliot Norton, James Russell Lowell, Oliver Wendell Holmes, and Henry Adams.

The writers among them paid her tribute in words. "I think of you," wrote Henry James, "as a figure on a wondrous cinquecento tapestry—and of myself as one of the small quaint accessory domestic animals, a harmless worm, or the rabbit who is very proud and happy to be in the same general composition with you." Henry Adams addressed her as "Wonderful Woman!" Bernard Berenson said that to find her equal it would be necessary to go back to Isabella d'Este in the Renaissance court of Mantua.

The musicians were equally devoted. The Boston Symphony often came to play at her musical evenings, and Wilhelm Gericke, the director, would not start a public concert until Mrs. Gardner was in her seat. When Paderewski came to Boston, he played at her home for her alone, or so he thought—actually she had hidden a few favored guests behind a screen.

Puritan Boston jumped to the conclusion that many of the handsome young men in her entourage, and especially the artists among them, were her lovers. It is impossible to know because if Mrs.

Gardner bestowed favors she bestowed them on gentlemen who did not talk. The evidence is limited to such appealing scenes as one that Ellery Sedgwick witnessed in the gymnasium of Groton School at a time when Mrs. Gardner was forty-eight and John Singer Sargent was thirty-two. Sedgwick, later editor of the *Atlantic Monthly* but at that time a Groton undergraduate, was sitting behind some wrestling mats, reading *Ben Hur*, when

suddenly the gymnasium door was thrown wildly open and a woman's voice thrilled me with a little scream of mockery and triumph. Cautiously I peeked from my concealment and caught sight of a woman with a figure of a girl, her modish muslin skirt fluttering behind her as she danced through the doorway and flew across the floor, tossing over her shoulder some taunting paean of escape. But bare escape it seemed, for not a dozen feet behind her came her cavalier, white-flanneled, black-bearded, panting with laughter and pace. The pursuer was much younger than the pursued but that did not affect the ardor of the chase. The lady raced to the stairway leading to the running track above. Up she rushed, he after her. She reached the track and dashed round it, the ribbons of her belt standing straight out behind her. Her pursuer was visibly gaining. The gap narrowed. Nearer, nearer he drew, both hands outstretched to reach her waist. In *Ben Hur* the chariot race was in full blast, but it was eclipsed. "She's winning," I thought. "No, she's losing." And then at the apex of my excitement, "He has her!" But at that crucial moment there came over me the sickening sense that this show was not meant for spectators, that I was eavesdropping and, worse, that I would be caught at it. There was not one instant to lose. The window was open. Out I slipped and slithered to safety.

For me that race was forever lost and forever won. The figures go flying motionless as on the frieze of the Grecian urn.

What men or gods are these? What maidens loth?
What mad pursuit? What struggle to escape?

I knew not then whether it was lost or won. What I did know was that the Atalanta of that Sunday morning was Mrs. Jack Gardner and Melanion Mr. John S. Sargent.

Sargent and other artists who were inspired to immortalize Mrs. Jack in paint did not find it an easy task. In point of fact, she was a rather homely

Isabella Stewart Gardner (left) was painted in 1888 by young John Singer Sargent, who persuaded her to drape her pearls around her waist rather than her neck. The portrait now hangs in Fenway Court (opposite), the Venetian-style palazzo that Mrs. Jack built in 1903 to house her growing art collection and that remains to this day exactly as she left it.

woman. Luckily for the painters, she had some good points: sparkling eyes, fine arms and shoulders, and a magnificent presence. Sargent's best-known portrait of her, which hangs in the place of honor at Fenway Court, shows her standing regally in a plain black dress with a rope of pearls about her waist. The dress is tight and the neckline is cut a little lower than was the style of that day, but modern visitors to Fenway Court are usually at a loss to understand why the painting was regarded as so daring that her husband locked it up for his lifetime. The truth is that he had some provocation. John Lowell Gardner was a tolerant man who loved his wife, indulged her whims, and generally paid no attention to the gossip about her. But when the new Sargent painting was hung in an exhibition at one of his Boston clubs, some man made a remark that alluded, first, to the rumor of a previous affair with a writer named Crawford, and second, to a well-known geographical feature of the White Mountains. What the bounder said was, "Sargent has painted Mrs. Gardner all the way down to Crawford's Notch." It was when he heard of that remark that Gardner finally lost his temper and ordered the painting locked up.

For her education in art Mrs. Gardner had sought out Charles Eliot Norton, a professor in Harvard's Fine Arts department. Later she had made a protégé of a curly-headed undergraduate named Bernard Berenson, who was to become the world's leading authority on Italian Renaissance art. During her travels with her husband, she had come to know the museums and auction rooms of Europe, fallen in love with Venice, and begun to collect paintings on her own. Some of her purchases must go down as among the best bargains in modern art history. Berenson helped her get Titian's *Rape of Europa*, which Rubens had copied because he thought it was the greatest painting in the world. Vermeer's *The Concert* she bought for six thousand dollars. (Today it would be worth several million.) During her husband's lifetime they had talked of building a museum to house their treasures. When he died of a stroke in 1898 at the age of sixty-one, she knew exactly what she wanted to do with the time and money left to her. She bought a tract of reclaimed marshland in the Fenway and began to lay plans for a building that would be her home and monument.

Friends found her a changed woman. Where she had spent money lavishly, she began saving pennies. The big rooms of her Beacon Street house were closed off in winter to save fuel, and guests accustomed to her lavish lunches found themselves facing a single lamb chop. Mrs. Jack needed every dollar to create Fenway Court. It is a three-story building whose rooms turn their backs to the cold New England landscape and open onto a sunny Italian courtyard. The balconies that overhang it came from the Cà d'Oro in Venice. The entrance door and the lions that guard it are from Florence. The mosaic pavement of the courtyard came from the villa of the Empress Livia in ancient Rome. Though she employed an architect, Mrs. Jack was the true designer. She spent her days at the site, supervising every detail, eating her lunch with the workmen, summoning helpers with toots on a trumpet (one toot for a mason, two for steam fitters, and so forth). She did not hesitate to turn window casements inside out, to put the capitals of Roman columns under the columns they originally crowned, or to stick Victorian wooden tracery on a Renaissance wall. Thanks to her almost unerring taste, it all seemed to work.

Except for a few friends from overseas, like Ellen Terry and the Archbishop of Canterbury, no guests had been allowed in Fenway Court during its three years of building. Finally, on New Year's night in 1903, Mrs. Jack stood at the top of a horseshoe staircase in the Music Room and welcomed Boston society, friend and foe, to the grand opening. To heighten the suspense she treated them first to an hour-long concert by fifty members of the Boston Symphony. Then a mirrored door was rolled back to display the fairytale courtyard with its tropical flowers, its tinkling fountains, and its thousands of lighted candles. Beyond were the three floors of rooms, each planned to the last Turkish rug and Florentine sconce by the mistress herself.

After her night of triumph Mrs. Gardner lived on at Fenway Court until her death in 1924, a frail old lady at the last, wrapped all in white as Sargent painted her just before her death, and carried about in a gondola chair imported from Venice. In her will she left Fenway Court to the public, with an endowment to keep it up and strict instructions not to change a thing. Fresh violets are placed each morning, as Mrs. Jack placed them, before Giorgione's *Christ Bearing the Cross*. Even pictures that have been downgraded by changing taste or revised attribution hang where she hung them. As the embodiment of one brilliant woman's taste and dedication, it is a place without equal in the United States. In the history of artistic patronage, a few million dollars never bought more.

HOLLAND IN THE SEVENTEENTH CENTURY WAS RULED BY
ITS WEALTHY MERCHANTS, WHO CREATED A LIFE STYLE
OF BOURGEOIS LUXURY. IN HIS PAINTING OF AN *ARTIST IN*
HIS STUDIO, JAN VERMEER EXPRESSED THE DUTCH LOVE OF

century when Emmanuel de Witte painted the scene on the opposite page. In this busy courtyard merchants gathered daily to buy and sell the goods that poured into Holland from a worldwide trading empire. One such merchant was Pompejus Occo (below), who owned a fine library and corresponded with humanist scholars. Dirck Jacobsz painted him with symbols dear to artists of the time: a carnation (for constancy in love) and a skull (for the brevity of life). The Dutch passion for flowers finds expression in the detail at left below from Hugo van der Goes' *Adoration of the Shepherds*. The purple columbine in the glass vase symbolized the Sorrows of the Virgin.

Indoors and out, the prosperous people of Holland found their pleasures in every season. When the rivers froze, they turned out in their long dresses and pantaloons for a skating party such as Hendrick Avercamp painted (above). At home, music often filled a long winter evening. When Jan Molenaer painted the family at right, he not only arranged all the members with their instruments but posed them in front of the family portraits to include past generations as well.

Unlike the ruling classes of countries with an aristocratic tradition, the Dutch made little public display of their wealth. But at home they liked both physical comforts and cultural amenities. In his painting of *A Lady at Her Toilet* (above), Gerard Ter Borch shows the rather plain mistress of a Dutch household being dressed in her French finery with the help of a maid who laces her bodice and a page who holds a cruet. On the opposite page a young woman is playing the virginals, a sort of harpsichord, for her visitor. The artist, Jan Vermeer, has rendered the table cover, the chair upholstery, and even the objects reflected in the mirror with loving, meticulous detail. The water pitcher may be from the pottery at Delft, as is the plate at left.

5. WEALTH FROM FINANCE

RICHER THAN CROESUS

Crassus (left) was the richest man in ancient Rome. At immediate right is a relief showing Roman landlords of the second century A.D. collecting rent from peasants; next, a fourteenth-century miniature showing visitors to the office of a Genoese banker. The florin (far right), with the lily of Florence, became a standard in a time of highly fluctuating currencies.

Croesus, king of Lydia in the sixth century B.C., has been enshrined in legend as the symbol of inexhaustible wealth. But there must have been at least one time when he was short of cash, for Herodotus tells us that he applied to a local banker for a loan. The banker's name was Sadymatte, and he said no.

The origins of finance are lost in prehistory, but we may assume that something in the nature of banking sprang up in every culture as soon as one individual accumulated a surplus of wealth, by trade or plunder or any other means, and made the discovery that someone else would pay him a bonus for having the use of it for a period. More than a thousand years before Croesus' time the Code of Hammurabi set forth in some hundred and fifty paragraphs the laws governing loans, interest, pledges, guarantees, losses, theft, and so forth. In Babylon, as in Egypt of the same period, the chief storehouses of wealth were the temples, and priests functioned as bankers to agricultural economies. But as trade increased, merchants accumulated wealth of their own and set up as private bankers.

From the trading societies of Asia Minor the institutions of banking passed to Greece and later to Rome. But somewhere along the way both the trader and the banker lost some of the social status they had enjoyed in the Eastern world. Greece and Rome, having started out as societies of farmers and fighting men, accorded their honors to the ownership of land and the achievement of military glory. Even after Rome became a world trading empire aristocrats did not engage in trade, and when they lent money, they preferred to leave the handling of the actual transactions to hired servants or slaves. This did not prevent even the noblest of Romans from lending out money at high rates of interest. Cicero professed shock when he found that Brutus had been lending at forty-eight per cent to the residents of Salamis during his term as governor of

Greece, but Cicero himself did not think twelve per cent high.

The Roman banker was not a pure financial man but often combined the careers of military leader, plantation owner, politician, and what we would term racketeer. The most notable example of the breed, and the richest man in the Roman Republic of the first century B.C., was Marcus Licinius Crassus. People said, according to Plutarch, that Crassus got his wealth from Rome's greatest calamities, revolution and fire. The revolution that enriched him was that of Marius, which brought on civil war and Marius' defeat by the aristocrat Sulla. When Sulla proscribed the chief supporters of Marius, Crassus bought up their estates at distress prices and sometimes, it was alleged, added a few names of his own to Sulla's list to enlarge his holdings. Later he put some of this money to use buying slaves and training them in fire-fighting units. In those Republican days Rome, built largely of wood, was highly combustible but had no public fire department. When a fire broke out, Crassus' fire fighters would rush to the scene, then wait while their leader bargained with the owners of the burning house or adjoining properties over a price to put out the blaze.

Crassus said that no man should consider himself rich unless he could afford to put his own army in the field. That is about what he did in 54 B.C. when, through his wealth and the power it gave him, he got command of an expedition against the Parthians. He was an experienced general, having helped crush the slave rebellion led by Spartacus (it was he who crucified six thousand slaves along the Appian Way), but his army was overwhelmed by the Parthians at Carrhae in Asia Minor. His fame as the richest Roman had reached the Parthian camp. When they cut off his head, according to some accounts, they thought it only fitting to pour molten gold into the mouth.

A more sympathetic Roman banker was Gaius Maecenas, whose name has entered the languages of the Western world as a synonym for a generous patron of the arts. The lifelong colleague and adviser of

◄ PRECEDING PAGES: A detail from *The Money Changer and His Wife*, painted by Quentin Massys in 1514.
LOUVRE

the Emperor Augustus, Maecenas was described by a contemporary as a man "of sleepless vigilance in critical emergencies, far-seeing and knowing how to act, but in his relaxation from business more luxurious and effeminate than a woman." He was the patron of Horace and Virgil.

In the examples of Crassus and Maecenas we can discern some of the characteristics of bankers as a class. One is that while they often wield great political power, they do not generally wield it directly. They lack the crowd-pleasing gifts of the politician, the charisma of the front man. Even when they aspire to political power for its own sake and not just to protect their private interests, they generally work through other men, as Crassus did when, failing to achieve ultimate power himself, he threw his weight behind Julius Caesar. This is not to say that they simply "buy power." Often they have unusual gifts in judging and choosing men, and achieve their political ends by backing successful public figures.

Another characteristic of moneymen is their affinity for the arts. Maecenas' example as a patron was followed in later times by the Medici and some of the Rothschilds, and in this country by J. P. Morgan, the Mellons, the Lehmans, and others. The bankers' record cannot be explained simply by saying that they have been the ones who have had the money to act as patrons. In fact, they have often had less wealth than the landowners or, especially in the last century, the manufacturers. But whereas American industrialists have far outstripped the bankers in the field of philanthropy, the bankers have set the pace as patrons.

One might hazard the guess that the outstanding record of bankers in the political and cultural spheres reflects something of their natures. Bankers occupy central positions in the economic world, dealing with all types of men, making decisions that affect all aspects of the economy. The horizons of their business lives are necessarily broader than those of landowners or manufacturers. To succeed as bankers they must be judges of men, else they may lose their fortunes. It seems likely that the qualities that make a good banker include a breadth of vision which enables him to operate successfully in the political and cultural worlds.

They are not much loved, however. They do not arouse the same affection or admiration as the bluff landed squire, the romantically adventurous trader, the Horatio Alger type of industrialist. Quite frequently they have been considered to be grasping, hard-eyed, hardhearted men, if not downright rapacious and thieving. Their cautious reserve and lack of warmth may indeed be necessary traits for their profession; but their reputation probably springs from a very simple fact: men who are glad enough to borrow from bankers when they need money find very little pleasure in paying it back with interest. Thus the banker seems a greedy figure, forever squeezing money out of needier people.

The bankers' unlovely image was reinforced when the Christian Church set its face firmly against usury. To the Church Fathers the bankers of the Roman Empire appeared as rich men who were typically forcing poor people, mostly farmers, to pay back money they had borrowed to tide them over between crops or to pay the tax collectors, who as often as not were the same bankers—and to pay them, moreover, with interest that might run as high as twenty-five or fifty per cent. Why, they asked, should the banker, who had done no work, take such a cut of the earnings of the farmer, who had done all the work?

In their condemnation of usury the Church Fathers lumped all kinds of borrowing and all rates of interest together. The banker who financed a trader on a highly speculative venture, involving great risks of piracy, warfare, banditry, and natural calamity as well as all the vagaries of the marketplace, was as sure to forfeit salvation as the rich man who lent money to peasants. And a rate of six per cent was officially no less sinful than a rate of one hundred per cent.

The drastic effect of the Church's policy was to drive bankers out of business or underground throughout most of Christendom. Merchant bank-

ARCHIVES PHOTOGRAPHIQUES, PARIS

ers continued to flourish in Venice and a few other Mediterranean ports, but as often as not they were trading with the infidel, who deserved no protection from the Church. In western Europe much of the merchant banking that survived in the Middle Ages was carried on by the Jews, whose souls were not endangered by Christian edict. During the darkest centuries, when the Mediterranean was largely closed to European trade by the rise of Islamic power, the scarcity of bankers was less crippling than it might have been. For with most of Europe reduced to a subsistence economy, there was very little trade or manufacturing to finance.

Yet there was still need for bankers, not least on the part of princes. In England during the twelfth and thirteenth centuries Jews were forbidden to own land but enjoyed royal protection as moneylenders because the kings needed them to finance wars or crusades. When the royal needs were especially pressing, kings could squeeze the Jews for extra taxes or confiscate their property outright. The ill will fostered in the Christian population by the Jewish "usurers" was reflected, long after they had been expelled from England by Edward I, in Shakespeare's *Merchant of Venice*. As Miriam Beard pointed out in her *History of the Business Man*, both Shylock and Antonio are most unlikely characters. The idea that any moneylender, Jew or Gentile, would have forgone his interest in order to satisfy his desire for revenge would have struck the sophisticated merchant bankers of the Venetian Rialto as preposterous. As for Antonio, who lent money without interest and sent his ships out without insurance, he would have been written off as a fool.

As trade revived and wealth increased in western Europe during the late Middle Ages, the functions of

The merchant ship at left belonged to the fleet of Jacques Coeur, the fifteenth-century financier. Coeur raised the money that enabled Charles VII and Joan of Arc to drive the English out of France. But he was arrested (right) and deprived of his property by order of a thankless king.

bankers became indispensable. The Church itself required various items of merchandise that could not be found at home—incense for its altars, fine fabrics for its vestments. For these it had to rely on traders from the East, and the traders required a profit for carrying on a risk-laden business. To get around the canonical ban on usury various subterfuges were invented: extra "service" charges would be added to the merchant's bill or the banker would take shares in a trading enterprise to disguise his interest as "profit." By such polite fictions the door was slowly opened to Christian bankers. By the thirteenth century the Jews had lost their special advantages and most of the banking of western Europe had passed into the hands of the "Lombards," a term that derived from the barbarian people who had come down across the Alps in the sixth century but that came to denote the merchant bankers of the cities of northern Italy. The thirteenth century saw the rise of Italian international banking families: the Alberti, the Frescobaldi, the Barzi, the Peruzzi, and others.

JACQUES COEUR, KING'S BANKER

Early in the fifteenth century an ambitious young man named Jacques Coeur was beginning the spectacular career that made him probably the richest private man in Europe. He was the son of a fur dealer in Bourges, which was then the capital of the French dauphin Charles, who had been driven out of Paris by the English and was yet to be saved by Joan of Arc. Coeur's relationship with that inglorious monarch was both his making and his undoing. His first appearance in the historical record is in the year 1429, when, as assistant master of the royal mint, he was accused of striking coins of inferior alloy. This was a frequent recourse of hard-pressed rulers, and none was more hard pressed than the dauphin, whose troops were melting away for want of money to pay them. It may be surmised that Coeur was acting under orders; at any rate he was acquitted.

Having taken the rap for his royal master (if that is what he did), Coeur set out in 1432 to make his own fortune in the Eastern trade. From his experience in the fur trade he had a keen appreciation of the heady profits made by Venetian and Genoese merchants in luxury imports from Constantinople and Syria. Enlisting the help of the sultan of Egypt, Coeur set up his own routes from the Near East through Cairo to ports in southern France. To pay for the luxury imports from the East he wangled from Charles the

rights to old Roman silver mines in the Rhone Valley. Within a decade he was rich enough to be the financial power behind Charles' throne. When the English war broke out again in 1449, Charles' new army was financed in considerable part by a loan of two hundred thousand écus—nearly a ton of gold—from his moneyman. In place of the glittering, outmoded knights who had gone down to defeat at Crécy and Agincourt, France now had an efficient army, complete with artillery, which proceeded to drive the British back to the Channel.

Jacques Coeur had only a brief span of years in which to enjoy his wealth. He built at Bourges a house that bears in stone his family motto: "To valiant hearts (*coeurs*) nothing is impossible." He had also picked up estates, chiefly from nobles who had borrowed money from him and then could not pay it back. These men became his enemies, as did

153

others whom he had bested in trade and still others who resented his influence with the king. In 1451 they struck, charging Coeur with accepting bribes, with impressing citizens to row his galleys, with exporting silver to the Saracens, and—most important but most absurd—with poisoning the king's lovely mistress, Agnes Sorel. Charles could hardly have believed the poison charge—La Sorel had died in childbirth and her baby had survived; but this was the same prince who had made no effort to save Joan of Arc from the stake. Now he offered no help to the man who had financed his victories. Coeur was convicted, stripped of his properties, and thrown into jail. He escaped and made his way to Rome, where Pope Calixtus III thought highly enough of him to give him command of a naval expedition against the Ottoman Turks. On the island of Chios he fell ill and died in 1456.

THE MAGNIFICENT MEDICI

Coeur's rise to financial power coincided with that of Cosimo de' Medici in Florence. Coeur was ruined largely because of his inescapable dependence on a fickle monarch. The Medici went from triumph to triumph, partly because they had the good fortune to live in an independent city-state without a powerful ruler, partly because they had the good sense to seize political power themselves. The Medici had moved into a financial vacuum left by the collapse,

Cosimo de' Medici raised his family's banking house to the peak of its power in fifteenth-century Florence.

in the latter part of the fourteenth century, of the earlier Italian banking houses, which had suffered both from the usual trouble with princes and from the long economic depression brought about by the Black Death. The founder of the firm was Cosimo's father, Giovanni di Bicci de' Medici. Under his guidance the Medici moved in wherever they saw a profit: in the manufacture of wool; in the export of wool; in the import of silks and other luxury items from the East; in a monopoly of the trade in alum, the indispensable fixative for dyes; and, finally, in the lending of money at the best interest they could get. Their most lucrative client was the Holy See, which at times used the Medici branch in Rome as a bank of deposit and at times turned to the Medici for loans. At one time or another the Medici held as security not only papal revenues and papal estates but the papal miter, which was returned to the Vatican only under threat of excommunication. Cosimo was the real ruler of Florence, holding no public office but controlling those who did. The Medici policy was one that rich men through the ages have ignored at their peril: "Be as inconspicuous as possible."

Cosimo was a man of vision and culture, a friend and patron of philosophers, poets, and artists. He worried about the money he had made through charging interest on loans, and could not die in peace until he had spent long months debating the doctrine of usury with his friend Archbishop Antonio. To his great gratification the archbishop eventually came around to his view that if interest was truly the reward of risk-taking enterprise and not just the payment for safe use of money, it was no sin.

For all his humanist interests Cosimo was first and foremost a merchant banker. It was only with the accession of his grandson Lorenzo as head of the house that the Medici name came to stand first of all for magnificence of life and splendor of the arts. While Lorenzo pursued his destiny as the central pillar of the cultural Renaissance, the banking house slid slowly downhill. By the time Lorenzo died in 1492 it was outshone by its rivals.

JAKOB FUGGER THE RICH

In the next century the Austrian house of Fugger matched, if it did not exceed, the Medici in total wealth. Jakob Fugger was the grandson of a country weaver who had moved his family to Augsburg and started a business in the weaving of fustian. By Jakob's time the firm had expanded into mining, foreign trade, and banking, and had established connections with Austria's royal family.

The head of the house of Habsburg—and Holy Roman Emperor—was the young Maximilian I, described by a contemporary as a "king who would like to make war all the time but has no money." Such is the perfect client for any banker—a man with heavy financial needs and plenty of collateral but not enough ready money, who will therefore always be in debt to his banker. Fugger began lending Maximilian money to pay his army. When the emperor had trouble making payments on his loans, Fugger accepted liens on the royal tax revenues or mortgages on royal land. But as time went on, Fugger became increasingly choosy about the endless purposes for which Maximilian wanted money. At one point the emperor conceived the idea that he should crown his career by acquiring the papacy. "We have resolved never again to lie beside a naked woman," he wrote ingenuously, trusting that this would help assure him of "having the Papacy and becoming . . . after that a saint." Fugger took a dim view of his lord's whim and lent no money.

But another aim dear to the emperor's heart commanded Fugger's full support. That was to secure the succession as emperor of his young grandson Charles. The title of "emperor" had been held by Habsburgs for three generations, but in law they had no right to the succession. When an emperor died, his successor was chosen by seven imperial Electors, four of them princes and the other three archbishops. Young Charles, by dynastic chance, had already inherited the crown of Spain. If elected emperor he would rule not only Austria, much of Germany, and Spain but also the Spanish Netherlands and the Spanish possessions in the New World. This was a prospect disquieting to other rulers, most especially to the ambitious Francis I of France. It soon became apparent that this time there would be a fight for the imperial crown, and the seven Electors made it plain that the price would be high. With Fugger's backing, Maximilian promised the Elector of Brandenburg one hundred thousand guilders plus an annuity of eight thousand more and the hand of the Infanta Catharine of Spain, complete with dowry, in marriage to Brandenburg's son. The Elector Palatine settled for one

Lorenzo de' Medici, grandson of Cosimo, allowed the banking house to slide while he won the accolade *il Magnifico* for his patronage of the arts. Botticelli painted him in this proud stance as a figure in his *Adoration of the Magi*.

Jakob Fugger, the greatest moneyman of sixteenth-century Europe, was painted by Albrecht Dürer, who spoke of his sharp wrinkles and "shrewd, cold-blooded face." Fugger said: "Many are hostile to me. They say I am rich. I am rich, by God's grace, without injury to any man."

integrity of any one monarch. An account almost as lucrative as that of the Holy Roman Emperor was that of the papacy. The house of Fugger served as agent for the Holy See in collecting its revenues in Germany, Poland, Hungary, and Scandinavia. For this service the house charged five per cent plus whatever it could make on the exchange of the local currencies it collected for the guilders that it credited to the pope. The business brought Fugger profit but also obloquy after Pope Leo X discovered a new source of revenue in the sale of indulgences. When the notorious preacher John Tetzel barnstormed through Germany, selling slips of paper that promised the remission of sins, a representative of the house of Fugger was at his hand with a strongbox to receive the payments. The sight drove Martin Luther to bursts of vituperation against Fugger the Rich, who, he declared, got half the proceeds of the nefarious trade.

Jakob Fugger was a public-spirited man who enriched his native city with the Fuggerei, a colony of workers' cottages that still stands at Augsburg. His heirs in the second and third generations were famous collectors and patrons of art. But, like the Medici after Cosimo, they let their minds stray from business. Lacking his uncle's iron will, Anton Fugger went beyond the limits of prudence in lending money to Charles V, and when that monarch shrugged off his debts, the house of Fugger was brought close to collapse. Fortunately for the family, Jakob had hedged his bets by investing a sizable part of his wealth in landed estates. His descendants, now hyphenated counts (Fugger-Babenhausen, Fugger-Kirchberg-Weissenhorn, and the like), live in their castles in the hills about the upper Danube, relics of the decaying nobility that men like Jakob Fugger did so much to render obsolete.

FOUQUET'S FOLLY

The fading of the house of Fugger offers one more example of the peril that moneymen invited when they dealt with royal clients. The Bardi and Peruzzi were destroyed by the default of Edward III of England. Jacques Coeur was ruined by Charles VI of France. The greatest single blow to the Medici was the default of Charles the Bold of Burgundy. And the house of Fugger was brought down by Charles V.

Most of the bankers of the late Middle Ages and early Renaissance had got their start as traders. Those who stuck to trade as the cornerstone of their prosperity, in the way the Venetians did, might

hundred thousand guilders. And so it went. In 1519 in the midst of the bargaining Maximilian died, but Fugger kept his hand in the game by reminding Charles of what might happen if the house of Fugger went over to Francis. In the end the deal was made, at a total cost of more than half a million guilders—equal to three times the annual revenue of Florence.

Jakob Fugger's successful venture in emperor-making not only made him far and away the most powerful financial figure in Europe but gave him an independence such as no previous banker had dared display toward a royal client. Here is how he addressed the most powerful monarch in Christendom when a payment was slow in coming:

Your imperial majesty well knows how I and my cousins have been inclined to serve the House of Austria. . . . It is known and plain as daylight that your imperial majesty would never have obtained the crown of the empire without my aid. . . . For if I had wished to desert the House of Austria and favor France I should have gained much money and wealth, which were freely offered. But what disadvantages might have grown therefrom to your imperial majesty and the House of Austria, your majesty in your great wisdom might well ponder.

Fugger was too wise in the fickle ways of royalty to let the solvency of the house depend on the financial flourish for centuries. But those who lacked the security of the Venetian Republic and reached for the golden apple of royal finance almost without exception suffered for their ambition. As Fugger remarked, "These great princes do as they will."

As the rising monarchs of Europe established their dominance over their own nobles and found a new source of revenue in direct taxation of their subjects, the role of the moneyman in the public polity became even more precarious. The case of Nicolas Fouquet is instructive.

Fouquet was the superintendent of finance of France, a lover of the arts, a financial wizard, and by general belief the richest man in the kingdom. He was not, however, an infallible judge of human nature, at least of royal nature. In 1661 he invited the young king Louis xiv to a party at the magnificent chateau called Vaux-le-Vicomte which he had built in the country south of Paris. Fouquet had been a protégé of Cardinal Mazarin, the real ruler of France during Louis' years as a boy-king, and since the Cardinal's death three months before, Fouquet had seen himself as Mazarin's logical successor as

the king's first minister. What he did not know was that the young king was resolved to be his own first minister, and, furthermore, that Louis had been looking into the accounts of his finance minister to find out why Fouquet had so much money while the king, at least by Bourbon standards, had so little.

With all the rash pride of his ignorance Fouquet greeted the king at the gates of Vaux-le-Vicomte and led him proudly through the grounds of his new home. These were the work of André Le Nôtre, the greatest landscape architect of that or any other age. There were gardens, terraces, grottoes, lovers' nooks, long allées lined with statuary by Poussin, some fifty fountains and two hundred *jets-d'eau* sending their waters skyward to fall back in a grand cascade. A proud young king could not have failed to remark that there was nothing like this at his own

For three and a half centuries the descendants of Jakob Fugger have lived as landed aristocrats. Count Friedrich Karl Fugger, head of the main branch, was photographed with his handsome family at their seat, Schloss Babenhausen, near Augsburg, West Germany.

palace of Fontainebleau.

Next Fouquet showed off the chateau itself, the masterpiece of France's foremost architect, Louis Le Vau. Its splendid rooms with their soaring columns and endless murals had been decorated by the third of Fouquet's resident talents, Charles Le Brun. Everything seemed to bear out the motto that Fouquet had chosen for his armorial bearings: *Quo non ascendam?* ("How high can't I rise?")

No higher. Had it not been for his mother, who urged him not to spoil the party, Louis would have arrested his host on the spot. As it was, he stayed for the banquet. ("What fine plate," said Louis of the splendid dinner service. "Pardon, Sire, it is not plate, it is gold," replied Fouquet, plunging ever deeper into folly.) After a dinner created by Vatel, France's greatest chef, the guests were entertained by a play written for the occasion by Molière, France's greatest playwright, and staged in the garden theater—with the author in the leading role. Louis declined to spend the night in the royal suite laid out for him and drove back to Fontainebleau.

The king's marshals came three weeks later to take Fouquet into custody. He was tried, found guilty of embezzlement, sentenced to death, saved by royal favor to spend the rest of his life in prison. Louis took not only his lands and wealth but his whole team of stylistic geniuses, Le Nôtre, Le Vau, and Le Brun, and put them to work building a royal seat that would dwarf and shadow Vaux-le-Vicomte—the palace of Versailles. There, too, Vatel would provide the food and Molière, frequently, the entertainment.

JOHN LAW AND THE BUBBLE

Thanks to the austere Colbert, who succeeded Fouquet as finance minister, enough money was squeezed out of the French people to pay for the splendid seventy-three-year pageant of Louis' reign at Versailles. It was a marvelous show but a costly one. When the "Sun King" finally died in 1715, having outlived his own son and grandson, the kingdom was, for all practical purposes, bankrupt. The Duc

Nicolas Fouquet (below), the powerful finance minister of France in the seventeenth century, is an object lesson to all rich people who make too much show of their wealth. When he had built the splendid chateau of Vaux-le-Vicomte (left), he invited the young King Louis XIV to see it. Louis took it away from him, along with everything else he had.

d'Orléans, who now succeeded to power as regent for the old king's five-year-old great-grandson, Louis xv, was soon desperate for someone to relieve him of the tiresome problems of finance and allow him to concentrate on the all-night parties he loved.

The man to do it was at hand. His name was John Law, and he had been waiting for twenty years for just such an opportunity. The son of a Scottish goldsmith, Law had left England in haste after a duel in which he killed the rival lover of a lady he had known in London. In his travels about the Continent he had supported himself and his family in fine style by his winnings at gambling casinos. In the markets of Europe he had studied the workings of finance and in particular the system of "bank credit" evolved by the Bank of Amsterdam. By the time he presented his program to the regent, he was sure that he knew the secret of unlimited prosperity—for France and for John Law. The regent grabbed it as if it were a life preserver.

In studying Law's program, we soon become aware that we have entered a new financial era. It is rather as if we were looking at the modern structure of finance capitalism, seen in a distorting mirror. The basic problem, Law said, was a lack of money. So long as gold and silver were the only forms of money to finance the economy, there would never be enough. What was needed was a system of credit, so that a merchant with a hundred thousand livres could transact a million livres' worth of business. To show a skeptical ministry what he meant Law founded his own private bank, issuing paper money redeemable at any time for coin *of a fixed weight and amount*. Since the French coinage was subject to occasional devaluation, this meant that Law's paper money was, on the face of it, better than gold. Customers flocked to Law's bank. Commerce flourished. The regent was delighted.

The time had come for the Scotsman's next idea. Law proposed that all French industry be absorbed into one great state monopoly that would provide the government with unlimited, perpetual revenues. As a first step he got a royal charter for a company to develop and exploit the great province of Louisiana,

embracing the whole basin of the Mississippi River. Shares in the Mississippi Company were offered to investors. Colonists were invited. A royal government was sent out to found a city, which was named New Orleans for the regent. Rumors of a "giant emerald rock" led prospectors to the banks of the Arkansas River, where, in fact, they saw a lot of Indians and buffalo. Permanent settlers were hard to find until, by royal edict, tramps, vagabonds, and domestics out of work for more than four days were forcibly put on shipboard. Lest investors hang back, Law undertook to buy back for gold, in six months' time, at a price of five hundred livres, shares that were then selling for three hundred livres. Almost as an afterthought he announced that the company would redeem the entire national debt of France, paying all the government's creditors in bank notes, and would henceforth be the state's only creditor. John Law and the French treasury were now virtually one and the same.

What now began was the speculative frenzy known to history as the Mississippi Bubble. In the little rue Quincampoix, where the Mississippi shares were sold, noblemen came bringing their family treasure, shopkeepers their life savings. Fortunes were made between breakfast and lunch. Law's own chauffeur left him and hired a chauffeur of his own. The financier himself could not show his face without being mobbed. With some distaste "Madame," the regent's wife, observed the spectacle of a noble lady kissing the hand of the Scottish commoner. "If duchesses will kiss his hand in public," she remarked with her customary earthiness, "what part of him will they not kiss in private?"

By the time Mississippi shares, issued at five hundred livres, hit a price of ten thousand livres, prudent investors were showing signs of uneasiness. But, as in every speculative binge, there were gamblers who thought they could get in today and get out tomorrow with a profit before the bubble burst. If any one investor pricked the bubble it was an old enemy of Law's, the Prince de Conti, who sent three carts to the rue Quincampoix to collect the value of his shares in gold. Law found enough gold to redeem the prince's shares but then, in alarm, got the regent to outlaw the possession of more than five hundred livres of gold by any Frenchman. That only turned

John Law, a Scottish gambler, sold the regent of France on a scheme to refinance the national debt through a vast colonization project in the Mississippi Valley. French investors were swept up in an orgy of speculation before the Mississippi Bubble burst, ruining them and Law.

RUE
QUINQUEMPOIX
en l'année 1729

suspicion into panic. Within a month the price of shares had fallen to two thousand livres, redeemable only in bank notes at ten cents on the dollar. Threatened with hanging by investors who had lost their fortunes, Law fled across the border and kept on going until he reached Venice, where he spent his few remaining years in the gambling casino.

Some historians, disinclined to waste much sympathy on moneymen, have seen John Law as a classic charlatan. Yet he cared little for money as something to keep or spend. What he cared about was his System. It was all so new, even to its inventor, that once he got it going, he had no idea how to control it. But what he was trying to do was to use credit, the mainspring of the capitalist economy, on a grander scale than it had ever been used before. Modern money managers, who think the actual exchange of

At the height of the Mississippi Bubble, from mid-1719 to early 1720, the little rue Quincampoix in Paris was the center of frenzied trading. Fortunes were made overnight as shares in Law's Mississippi Company soared from 500 livres to 10,000.

metal money impossibly quaint and think nothing of raising a credit structure of trillions of dollars on no gold base at all, have no reason to scorn John Law.

THE HOUSE OF ROTHSCHILD

During the age of the great European princes, bankers were generally at the mercy of their royal masters. But a new age was coming, in which powerful bankers would build their own empires, capable of surviving the wars of nations and the rivalries of

In the Judengasse, the Frankfurt ghetto, the family of Mayer Rothschild had its home and began its rise to financial power.

kings. The family that showed how it could be done was the Rothschilds.

Mayer Amschel Rothschild, the founder, was born and brought up in the Judengasse in the city of Frankfurt. The narrow, crowded Jew Street was closed off with chains at night, and when a Jew went outside in the daytime, he would be taunted by German youths with the order, "Jew, do your duty," whereupon he had to step off the sidewalk into the gutter. Young Rothschild went to work in the family store, where, among other items of merchandise, he began a lively trade in coins. A neighboring prince, William of Hesse, was a coin collector, and one day, with a little wangling, Mayer Rothschild arranged an audience, at which he sold the prince some rare coins for less than they were worth. Prince William, who loved a bargain, kept the coin dealer coming back, and eventually Rothschild got to be friends with the prince's financial adviser, Karl Buderus. Rothschild now called himself a banker, and through Buderus he received a bit of business discounting some of the prince's foreign bills. Prince William had a lot of money coming in from England, a country to which Hesse had hired out its young men as mercenary soldiers (including those who had surrendered to George Washington at Trenton). Rothschild, meanwhile, was building up a business of importing cotton goods from Manchester. Soon Rothschild was handling the remittances in both directions, and before the old-line bankers of Frankfurt woke up to it, he was the prince's chief banker.

While Mayer Rothschild was establishing the banking business his wife Gutele was raising the five sons who would expand it into a vast international fortune. All five were thoroughly trained by their father, and when the middle son, Nathan, was twenty-three, he was sent off to England to handle the cotton business.

What enabled the Rothschilds to leap suddenly from modest success to great wealth was a disaster for the state of Hesse-Cassel—the appearance at its borders of the army of Napoleon Bonaparte. "It is my purpose," the emperor declared, "to put an end to the house of Hesse-Cassel" (which had supported the Prussians). Prince William took off in his carriage for the Danish border, but before he left, he entrusted his account books to Mayer Rothschild, who hid them in a secret cellar in his garden. During the Napoleonic occupation Rothschild and his sons had

Nathan Rothschild, head of the English branch, was caricatured in a familiar pose on the floor of the Exchange.

the assignment of driving around the German principalities, collecting monies due the prince and bringing them back in secret compartments of their coach. The best thing to do with the money, Rothschild kept saying, was to send it to London and invest it in British government bonds, the solid "consols." At length the prince agreed, and the first installment of the prince's fortune was put at the disposal of young Nathan Rothschild in London.

Neither father nor son had any intention of putting their first real stake into anything as safe and sane as government bonds. They figured that so long as the prince got the income he would have gotten in consols, whatever else they made was theirs. In later times bankers went to jail for this sort of thing, but during the Napoleonic Wars high finance was something new, and little understood by any but Rothschilds. Judging that Britain would soon be needing gold to finance the war, Nathan bought up all he could and presently sold it to the government at a

good profit. But then the government had the problem of getting the funds to Spain and Portugal, where the Duke of Wellington was fighting a Napoleonic army. Shipment by sea was risky. Nathan Rothschild undertook to make the deliveries— straight through the enemy's own country. The gold was shipped to Paris (with the full knowledge of the French financial authorities, who were gullible enough to believe that the Rothschilds were helping them by draining gold from England). There James Rothschild, the youngest of the five brothers, arranged to exchange it for drafts on Spanish, Sicilian, and Maltese banks; these were then smuggled across the border to Wellington. For this operation the house of Rothschild was well rewarded.

During the next few years the Rothschild fortune grew steadily greater. To provide the information that would give them a jump on rivals they built up the best messenger service in Europe, with riders standing by to carry messages, ships waiting at the

Here are four Rothschild brothers—Nathaniel, Lionel, Mayer, and Anthony—after they had all become English country gentlemen. They are the sons of Nathan, who appears on page 163. The brothers are riding to hounds in the Vale of Aylesbury.

Channel ports to sail at a moment's notice, even carrier pigeons when all else failed. On the London stock exchange Nathan Rothschild took his stand every morning at the same column—a short, tubby figure in top hat. Across the Channel the armies of Napoleon and Wellington were moving toward a showdown on the plains of Belgium. Everything was in readiness for the climactic scene in the rise of the house of Rothschild.

The battle of Waterloo was fought on June 18, 1815. On the morning of June 20, at about breakfast time, some forty hours before dispatches arrived from the duke, a courier brought the news of victory to Nathan Rothschild. He went first to inform the foreign minister, Lord Castlereagh, who was not inclined to believe the report, and then to the stock exchange. His first move, it was widely believed, was to ostentatiously start selling consols, thus leading other speculators to think that he had news of a British defeat. As prices tumbled, his agents bought the consols back at distress prices. There is no conclusive evidence that Nathan did or did not fleece the other speculators by that trick. What is known for certain is that he bought heavily. By the time the news of Wellington's victory was official, the Rothschilds were richer than ever and their golden touch had become legend.

Prince William of Hesse-Cassel got back his fortune, with interest, just as if it had been invested in bonds all along—and never suspected that it had generated a fortune many times greater than his own. By this time Nathan was, in effect, the official banker of the British government.

Meanwhile the other brothers were putting down the family roots in the money capitals of Europe. Amschel, the oldest, stayed in Frankfurt to take over from old Mayer. James, in Paris, rivaled Nathan in his success as a government banker and surpassed him in the elegance of his life style. Carl established the Italian house in Naples. Salomon founded the

Austrian house and built the Austrian state railway system, the model for Europe. It was Salomon who wangled from the Austrian government the hereditary title of baron, not only for himself but for his four brothers.

Before he died in 1812, old Mayer drew up a deed of settlement, designed to perpetuate the dynasty. It provided that the banking house should belong exclusively to his sons and their male heirs; no daughter or son-in-law should have any part of it. This plan of inheritance created a rather strong motivation for Rothschild daughters to marry their cousins, and in fact such matches were common in the first few generations. When Nathan's daughter Hannah strayed so far as to marry not merely outside the family but outside the Jewish religion, she was shunned by the rest of the family. But when his son Lionel married Carl's daughter Charlotte,

Waddesdon Manor, one of the great Rothschild houses in England, was built by Baron Ferdinand of the Austrian branch after he married an English cousin. Baron Guy de Rothschild (left), head of the French branch, appears at the Longchamp racetrack with his second wife Hélène and his son David, heir apparent to the French interests.

streams of splendid carriages bore Rothschilds, their guests, and retainers from the capitals of Europe to Frankfurt, where old Gutele, the mother of the clan, still lived on.

As their fortune grew—to a billion dollars, it was said, by the middle of the nineteenth century—the Rothschilds were not slow to match their life style to their means. Benjamin Disraeli, invited to a ball at James' house in Paris, marveled at "the unrivalled palace with a great retinue of servants, and liveries more gorgeous than the Tuileries, and pineapples plentiful as blackberries." The German poet Heinrich Heine, another friend of James', wrote: "I like best to visit the Baron in his office where, as a philosopher, I can observe how people bow and scrape before him. It is a contortion of the spine which the finest acrobat would find difficult to imitate. I saw men double up as if they had touched a Voltaic battery when they approached the Baron." On another

visit: "I saw a gold-laced lackey bringing the baronial chamber pot along the corridor. Some speculator from the Bourse, who was passing, reverently lifted his hat to the impressive vessel."

James had a sense of humor. When Delacroix boldly asked him to pose as a beggar because he had "exactly the right, hungry expression," James agreed and the next morning appeared, dressed in rags, at the artist's studio. A young friend of Delacroix's, who answered the door, handed him a franc. Later one of the baron's liveried servants brought the young man a letter: "Dear Sir, You will find enclosed the capital which you gave me at the door of M. Delacroix's studio, with the interest and compound interest on it—a sum of ten thousand francs. You can cash the check at any bank whenever you like. James de Rothschild."

In the second half of the nineteenth century the various Rothschilds strove to outdo each other in the

The elegance of the French Rothschilds has always owed as much to their taste as to their money. Baron Robert, who died in 1946, was photographed at left with some of his Limoges miniatures. Baron Philippe is shown below, standing in the cellar of his world-famous Mouton Rothschild vineyard. The wine label was designed for his bottles by the great French artist Georges Braque.

building of city palaces and country chateaux. In England Lionel's brother Mayer built Mentmore, a vast country house with towers, pinnacles, and a glass roof over the great hall. Upon seeing it Baron James summoned the architect and ordered another Mentmore, "only twice as big," which became the chateau of Ferrières outside Paris. The British Rothschilds became ardent hunters, famous hosts, and members of the inner circle of the Prince of Wales. As a banking house the English branch reached its zenith in 1875 when Lionel lent the British government the four million pounds with which it bought a large block of shares in the Suez Canal Company.

By the end of the nineteenth century the heyday of the Rothschilds, as of all private bankers, was coming to an end. In 1901 the original bank at Frankfurt closed its doors. The Italian house had disappeared long since, and the Austrian house would not outlast the two world wars. The English and French houses survive to this day, but they are as apt to be backing the Club Mediterranée or the ski resorts of Mégève and Chamonix as gold mining or steel companies. Meanwhile Rothschilds have added luster to the family name in other fields: Baron Henri and Baron Philippe for their Mouton Rothschild vineyards; Baron Edmond as chief backer of the Jewish settlements that became the state of Israel; Lord Rothschild as a distinguished biologist and the world's leading authority on human sperm; Baron Edouard and his son Baron Guy as the owners of famous racing stables.

In the realm of banking the name of Rothschild is still one to conjure with. One of the great ceremonies of the financial world occurs on each trading day in London when five men gather in the same room to set the opening price of gold on the world market. Of these five expert money managers, one is a representative of the house of Rothschild, and the room where they meet is in the Rothschild bank.

EARLY AMERICAN FINANCIERS

Turning now to the United States, we may notice that the earliest banking fortunes in this country, following a familiar pattern, had their origins in foreign trade. In the colonial period the greatest was that of Robert Morris, who got his start in the import and export business of Philadelphia's Willing family. By the time of the Revolution he had built up a prosperous shipping trade with banking connections in Europe and the West Indies. A big, genial, openhanded man, who set a fine table at his great house on the Schuylkill, he became the staunch friend and financial counselor of many of the revolutionary leaders. To them he was "the Financier," and when the new government found itself floundering ever deeper in debt, he was called to the rescue. His enemies said that Morris never did distinguish clearly between his own interests and those of the republic. Certainly he did not put his personal business into a blind trust, as modern Cabinet officers are expected to do. But he did better for the government than he did for himself because some years after the Revolution his own commercial empire fell apart, leaving him millions of dollars in debt. When George Washington came to pay his respects in 1798, he had to visit his old friend in the debtors' section of the Prune Street Jail.

Even those who questioned Morris' business ethics found him a good and likable man. Few thought that of Stephen Girard, who established another great Philadelphia fortune in the years after the Revolution. Like Morris, he made his original stake in shipping. After the first Bank of the United States was done in by its congressional enemies, he bought its building and assets and opened the Bank of Stephen Girard. Blind in one eye, burdened with a lunatic wife, childless, and virtually friendless, he seemed to most of his contemporaries a crusty, embittered man who prided himself on never giving a penny to charity. Yet when he died he left most of his fortune, upward of six million dollars, for the education of orphan boys.

An altogether sunnier and equally philanthropic financier was George Peabody of South Danvers (now Peabody), Massachusetts, who established a banking house in London. He used his fortune to build libraries, museums, lecture halls, and musical conservatories, and to establish the first true foundation, which rescued education in the Southern states after the Civil War. His chief business as a banker was handling the investment of English capital in American railroads, and his junior partner was Junius S. Morgan. Perhaps the most notable part his banking house played in U.S. financial history was that it served as the training ground and launching platform for his partner's son, J. Pierpont Morgan.

J. PIERPONT MORGAN

At the University of Göttingen, where he went to study after high school in Boston, J. P. Morgan's mathematics professor was so impressed by his

American student that he offered him a faculty appointment with the prospect of becoming the German scholar's own successor. All his life Morgan had the advantage of a quick mathematical mind that kept him one jump ahead of almost anyone he was negotiating with. At his breakfast table he amused himself by buying and selling foreign currencies to take advantage of small fluctuations in the money markets of the world. Arbitrage, which taxed some of the brightest minds in Wall Street as a full-time occupation, was for Morgan a breakfast game, like playing the horses or doing a crossword puzzle.

As the American correspondent for his father's London banking house, in the years after the Civil War, Morgan was plunged into the wildly competitive world of railroad finance. In that expansive era railroads were the victims of pirates like Jay Gould, Daniel Drew, and Jim Fisk, as well as empire builders like Commodore Vanderbilt and James J. Hill. Their securities were bandied from one buccaneer to another, driven up and down by speculators, often watered beyond hope of solvency. In 1885 the New York Central and the Pennsylvania, the two biggest Eastern roads, were on the verge of all-out war. The Pennsylvania had just acquired control of the West Shore Railroad, a rival line built across the Hudson from Vanderbilt's Central; in fact, it paralleled the Vanderbilt route all the way to Buffalo. It had been put together largely out of spite by George M. Pullman because the Vanderbilts scorned to use his parlor and sleeping cars. In Pennsylvania hands it would mean a bitter rate war, and so the Central had started building in its turn a railroad to parallel the enemy's. It was being graded and tunneled just south of the Pennsylvania main line, from Philadelphia to Pittsburgh. Observing the approaching conflict, Morgan knew it would be ruinous to stockholders, many of whom had bought Central stock through his firm. To avert all this folly, he invited the top executives of both companies aboard his yacht, the first *Corsair*, and practically kept them prisoner cruising back and forth in New York Harbor until they made peace. Each road acquired the other's competing line, and Morgan, for his work in setting it all up, cleared somewhere between one and three million dollars. So successful was the agreement, allowing both roads to stabilize their rates at a high

J. P. Morgan's cigar, wing collar, and gold watch chain went with him aboard his yacht, the *Corsair*. "I can do a year's work in nine months," he used to say to his business associates, "but not in twelve."

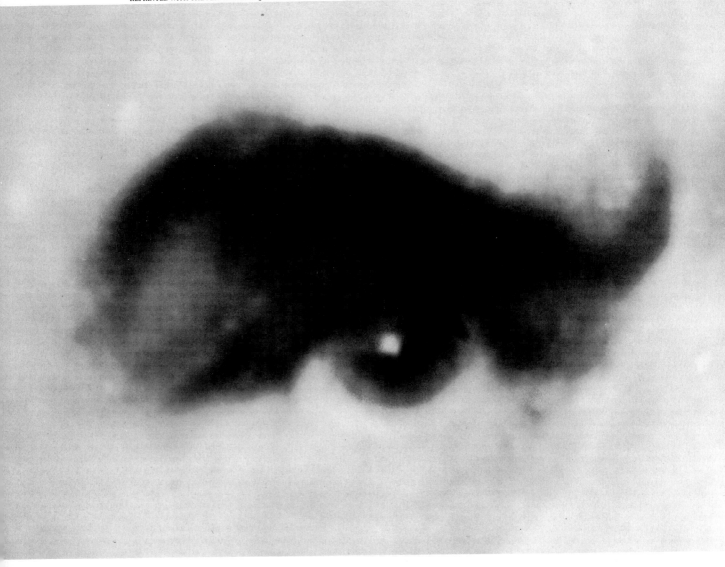

level, that other trunk lines began coming to Morgan to ask him to exercise his magic for them. After the decades of wild competition, the railroads began to enjoy the fruits of monopoly. Some of the customers complained about the high rates, but it all seemed good to Morgan, who believed that business should be run by gentlemen and that gentlemen did not poach on one another's territories.

Morgan's awesome power in the world of finance was demonstrated to the country in 1895. The U.S. Treasury had suffered an alarming drain of gold, which provided the only backing for the currency. Congress, filled with silver senators, was in no mood to worry about the gold supply. By late January it became evident that at the rate gold was flowing out, the Treasury would be empty in three weeks' time. On the night of February 5, in order to save the na-

tional credit, Cleveland called Morgan, who, having seen the crisis coming, was in Washington waiting for the call. In association with August Belmont, the American representative of the Rothschilds, Morgan put up sixty million dollars in gold—enough to stop the drain on the Treasury. Later, when Morgan was asked at a senatorial inquiry why, if the gold was available abroad, other bankers had not been asked to provide it, he replied simply, "They could not do it."

In 1901 Morgan brought off his greatest industrial coup by buying Andrew Carnegie's steel company for four hundred million dollars and combining it with eight others to make the nearly monopolistic United States Steel Corporation. He bestrode the financial world as no man has done before or since. When he happened to be quoted as

172

These are the eyes from the famous portrait of Morgan taken by the great photographer Edward Steichen. "Meeting his black eyes," said Steichen afterward, "was like confronting the headlights of an express train bearing down on you."

saying, "America is good enough for me," William Jennings Bryan's *Commoner* retorted: "Whenever he doesn't like it, he can give it back to us."

Morgan made no apologies for his power or his wealth. He liked to live well and he lived as well as any king, but he never built a house or bought a yacht for show or for keeping up with anyone else. As his biographer Frederick Lewis Allen remarked, "He preferred solid comfort, solid dinners, solid people." He also liked yachts and had a series of them, each bigger than the last and each fitted out with the things he liked—often the furnishings of the previous *Corsair*. He gave money to causes he cared about, never asking advice, always making the same swift decisions he made in business. When Harvard asked for help toward a new plant for its medical school, Morgan took only a moment to look at the plans, then pointed to three buildings and said, "I will build *that* and *that* and *that*. Good morning, gentlemen."

His interest in collecting was nearly lifelong. As a young man he had brought back from one European trip a crate of bits of stained glass he had picked up outside a cathedral. He was not a patron of living artists, most of whom he would not have found congenial, but his love of the art of the past was genuine. Over the years he bought such a volume of treasure —paintings, sculpture, carvings, tapestries, manuscripts, books—that it soon overflowed the storage rooms of his house and required a white marble library to be built next door.

Morgan enjoyed dealing with the owners and dealers who lay in wait for him at every step of his annual European tours. He never bargained. He ei-

173

ther paid the asking price—"Done"—or set his own price—"Yes or no." Few got the better of him. When Joseph Duveen was a young man, starting out as a dealer in his uncle's firm, he assembled a collection of Meissen miniatures for Morgan, artfully including mediocre ones with the real prizes. Morgan inspected the collection and asked, "How much for the lot?" Duveen quoted a price. With unerring eye Morgan picked out the six best pieces and paid young Duveen one-sixth of the total. "You're only a boy," Duveen's uncle consoled his nephew when the great collector had left. "It takes a man to deal with Morgan."

When Morgan died in 1913 he left, aside from his art collection, an estate of sixty-eight million dollars. In an age that was already getting used to billionaires, the figure was not very impressive. But in the power structure of the financial world he left an empty place that no private individual would ever fill again. In the gold crisis of 1895 and again in the Panic of 1907 he had functioned as the nation's lender of last resort. To fulfill this and other functions of a modern central bank it was necessary, within a few years of his death, to invent the Federal Reserve System.

JACOB SCHIFF

No one equaled Morgan as a financier, but Jacob Schiff came closer than anyone else. During the most adventurous period of investment banking, in the second half of the nineteenth century, there grew up in Wall Street a structure of Jewish banking houses that rivaled in size and influence the structure of Gentile banking. Without exception these Jewish banking houses were family affairs. Many of the founders were poor immigrants who had got their start as peddlers. (Whether on foot or on a wagon became in later years a social distinction among them.) The Seligmans were first in the field, followed by the Kuhns, Loebs, Lehmans, Baches, Goldmans, Sachses, *other* Loebs, Wertheims, and Warburgs. Sons were expected, virtually required, to go into the family firm. Sons-in-law were accepted as partners, but hardly ever anyone else. For forty-four years Kuhn, Loeb & Company never had a partner who had not been born into or had not married into the founding families. Jacob Schiff married Solomon Loeb's daughter Therese. Unlike the founders, he had not come up from the peddler's cart. He came from a family of German-Jewish bankers who at one time had shared the two-family

house in Frankfurt where Mayer Rothschild lived. Within a few years of his arrival in New York and his marriage to Therese Loeb, he had pushed his gentle father-in-law into the background and taken over the direction of the banking house. At a time when most of the capital for American industrial expansion came from Europe, Schiff used his contacts and knowledge of the European money market to good effect. Soon Kuhn, Loeb was deep into the great and risky business of railroad finance.

Schiff's name lives in Wall Street legend for his part in the greatest of stock-market epics, the battle for control of the Northern Pacific Railroad between E. H. Harriman (backed by Schiff) and James J. Hill (backed by Morgan). As the two sides struggled for control, the price of Northern Pacific shares soared in one week from under one hundred to over a thousand. On the record Hill won, some say because Harriman's last order to keep on buying arrived at Schiff's office on a Saturday, when Schiff was in the synagogue. Actually none of the principals got hurt much in the struggle, though some less-than-innocent bystanders paid for their folly in trying to mix in this battle of the giants. Hill kept control of the Northern Pacific, but Harriman still had his Union Pacific; Schiff, alone among investment bankers, was thereafter recognized by Morgan as his peer.

Schiff lived in the grand style, with a mansion on Fifth Avenue and a place on the Jersey shore for the early summer and another at Bar Harbor for the late summer. Except for August Belmont (né Schönberg), who was a bit of a bounder anyway, most of the rich Jewish families kept to their own social sphere (made famous by Stephen Birmingham in *Our Crowd*) and set their faces against intermarriage with Gentiles. By the end of Jacob Schiff's life this familial solidarity was breaking down, as was the orthodox faith of the founders. But for two or three generations theirs was a separate social milieu, which foreign visitors often found more cultivated and more aristocratic by European standards than the society of Mrs. Astor and her friends.

In the Panic of 1907, as in the gold crisis of 1895, both Wall Street and the federal government turned to Morgan. The crowd in the picture is gathered outside the Trust Company of America during a run on that institution. In addition to saving the trust companies, Morgan organized a syndicate to buy thirty million dollars' worth of New York City bonds on terms initialed by him in the superimposed memorandum. From the panic Morgan emerged richer and stronger than ever.

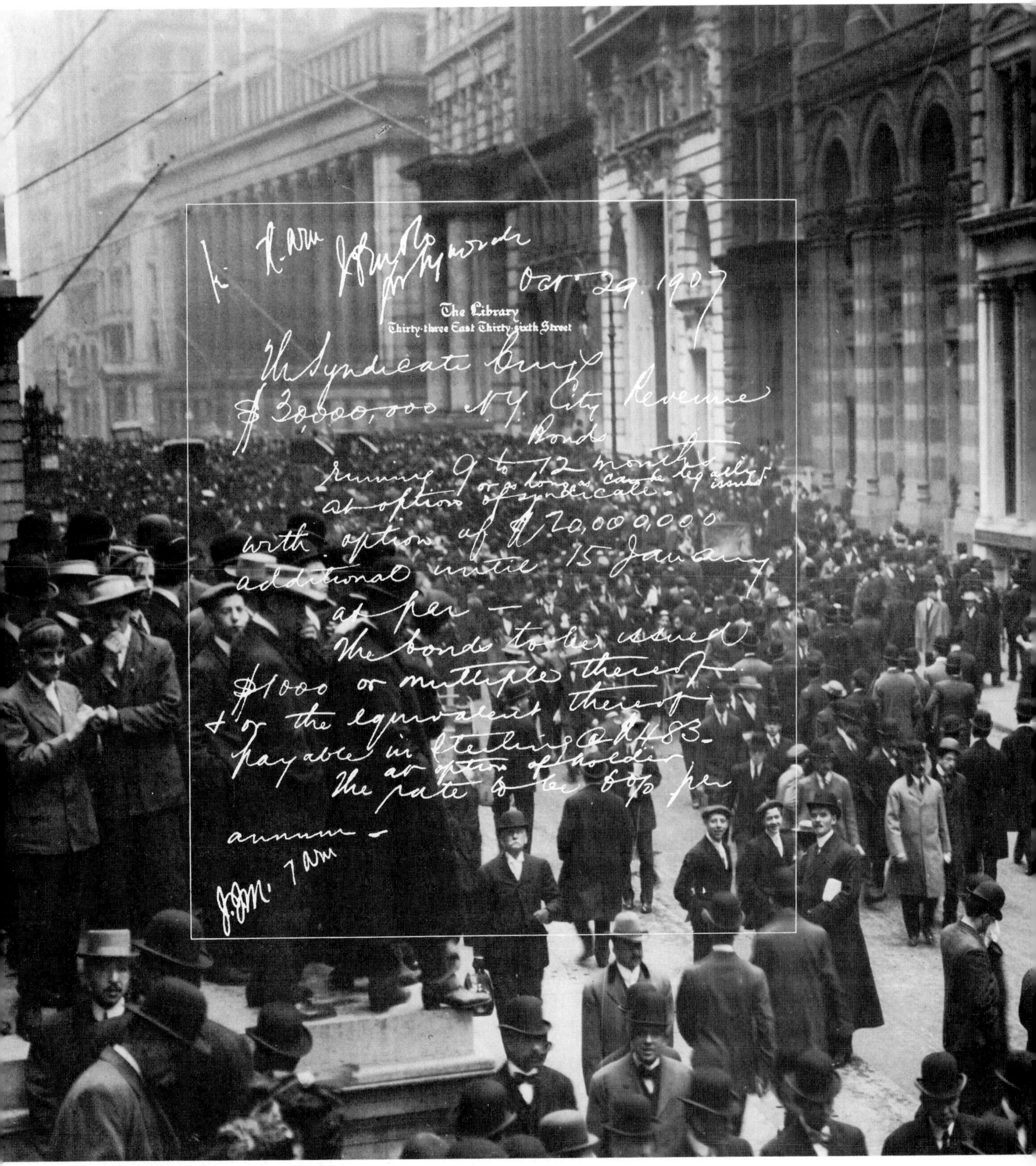

To R.—

Oct 29. 1907

The Library
Thirty-three East Thirty-sixth Street

The Syndicate buy
$30,000,000 NY City Revenue
Bonds
running 9 to 12 months
at option of syndicate as can be legally issued
with option of $20,000,000
additional until 15 January
at par —
the bonds to be issued
$1000 or multiple thereof
or the equivalent thereof
payable in sterling @ 4.83 —
at option of holder
the rate to be 6% per
annum —

J.P.M. 7 am

Jacob Schiff (far left) was J. P. Morgan's greatest rival in the banking world. Here he is marching in a Liberty Loan parade in 1918 with (left to right) bankers Walter Frew, George F. Baker, Jr., and Morgan the Younger.

No more than Morgan or Frick did they patronize contemporary artists. It remained for the Guggenheims, who were not bankers and were always a bit too unsteady to be fully accepted by "Our Crowd," to put big money behind modern art. But the Lehmans, Loebs, and Baches were notable collectors of old masters. Many were patrons of music—none more so than Otto Kahn, who was the best-known partner of Kuhn, Loeb after Schiff. A trim, dapper little man, impeccably dressed in a cutaway, cashmere trousers, spats, a tie with pearl stickpin, and a tiny orchid in his buttonhole, Otto Kahn became the organizational power and chief financial mainstay of the Metropolitan Opera.

HETTY GREEN, THE RICHEST WOMAN

It was an age when men of wealth thought it only right and natural to live with all the ease and show that their fortunes made possible. But not Hetty Green, the richest woman in the world and in some ways the strangest. One of the living landmarks of Wall Street in the age of Morgan and Schiff, she wore, year in and year out, the same voluminous dress, originally black but turning slightly brown and green with age. Sewn inside her petticoat were many pockets, each large enough to hold the contents of a safe-deposit box. She lived, most of the time, in furnished rooms, now in Manhattan, now in Brooklyn, now across the river in Hoboken. Each day she would travel by public bus or ferry to her Wall Street "office," which was the vault of the Chemical National Bank. Here she would sit on the floor, clipping coupons, reading the financial news, and receiving callers, among them some of Wall Street's most eminent figures. They came to pick her brains and sometimes, in moments of crisis, to ask for loans. Hetty, it seemed, was always solvent.

Hetty's forebears were shipowners in New Bedford, and she had got her first taste of finance as a girl of eight by reading stock-market news to her grandfather. She inherited a million dollars and married Edward H. Green, who had made about a million of his own in the China trade. His money was not hers, as she stipulated in a marriage contract, nor hers his. Eighteen years later, as if making good his wife's premonition, Green went broke, listing as his assets "seven dollars and a gold watch."

Hetty's secret of success, she always said, was to buy cheap and sell dear. The difference between her and others who pursued the same market strategy was that, by some reason or instinct, she seemed to know when was high and when was low. She made her first killing in Wall Street by buying depreciated U.S. government bonds right after the Civil War, when many investors feared they would never be redeemed at full value. After that she specialized in railroad bonds and stocks, often driving stocks up and down by heavy purchases or sales, sometimes bringing off a "corner" in which traders who had "sold short" were trapped until she sold them shares at her own price. Some sixth sense seemed to be working for her. One day in the spring of 1907 when she came home to her boarding house, her dress was bulging with securities. To a fellow boarder she explained that she had just taken all her holdings out of the Knickerbocker Trust Company. "If you have any money in that place," she advised, "get it out first thing tomorrow." The friend asked why. "The men in that bank are too good-looking," Hetty replied. "You mark my words." On October 21 a run began on the Knickerbocker Bank and by noon it closed its doors. That was the beginning of the Panic of 1907.

Hetty Green ate the cheapest foods in the cheapest restaurants she could find and left no tips. At a time when her money was earning something like five hundred dollars an hour she haggled over the price of a pair of shoes. When a druggist justified his charge of ten cents for a bottle of medicine by pointing out that the bottle cost five cents, Hetty went home to get a bottle of her own. Her son Ned was the saddest victim of her parsimony. When he hurt his knee Hetty would not call a doctor but treated it herself. Two years later, when it still had not healed, she dressed the boy in rags like her own and took him to a New York doctor, begging treatment as a charity patient. When the doctor learned who she was and demanded payment, Hetty took Ned away and never went back. Some years later the leg had to be amputated.

Hetty was not deliberately unkind. She went out of her way to help people—with favors, jobs, anything but money. Even though she had no use for her husband after he lost his money, she gave him enough to live, rather better than she did, at a genteel hotel and to pay his bills at the Union Club, where he spent his days. She trained her son carefully in business, and when he was twenty-four bought him a small railroad in Texas, which he ran well. She just could not bear to spend a penny when she did not have to. By her own lights she was magnificently successful. When she died in 1916 she left (to her son and daughter) a fortune of about a hundred million dollars. In hard cash that was about thirty million more than J. P. Morgan left.

THE QUIET MELLONS

The greatest banking fortune in the United States was not made on Wall Street but in Pittsburgh. It is that of the Mellons, and one might question giving it the label of "a banking fortune" since most of the money was made in industrial enterprises. But the Mellons began as bankers and have always operated more as bankers than as industrialists.

The founder of the family was Thomas, a farmer's son who lived, with singular appropriateness for the start of a rags-to-riches story, in the town of Poverty Point. He combined a career as a lawyer and county judge in western Pennsylvania with investing in real estate. When he was fifty-six and retired from the bench, he opened a bank, which he called T. Mellon & Sons, for the express purpose of launching his five sons in business. The other boys did well enough, but the two who took over the bank and made it the seedbed of a great fortune were Andrew W. and Richard B. As bankers the two brothers kept their

Hetty Green, the Wall Street miser, appears in the black dress she always wore. Under it, her petticoat was fitted with pockets to hold the bonds, stock certificates, and large sums of ready cash she carried about.

eyes open for attractive business opportunities, especially in the rising new industries of a high-energy, high-technology age. When they found one they liked, they would offer to put their own capital into it in return for part ownership.

One day in 1889 a young man named Arthur Vining Davis, just one year out of Amherst, came to Andrew Mellon, bringing with him a metallurgist, a chemical engineer, and a piece of light, shiny metal. It was a chunk of aluminum, produced by a new electrolytic process invented by Charles Martin Hall. Davis and his associates wanted to borrow four thousand dollars to pay off a loan that was being called by another bank. Andrew Mellon went to see Hall's little plant, thought a bit about the uses of this new light metal, and offered the men twenty-five thousand to set up a going business. Thus was born the Aluminum Company of America, the second greatest source of the Mellon fortune.

In this venture the Mellons applied one of their cardinal rules of management: set a company up right, provide it with enough money, find the right man to run it, and then, unless something goes wrong, leave him alone. This they did with Arthur Vining Davis, the young Amherst graduate, who ran Alcoa for nearly fifty years and made a fortune once estimated at over three hundred million dollars for himself, along with much more for the Mellons.

In much the same way the Mellons acquired control of the Koppers Company (coke), the Carborundum Company (abrasives), and a good many others. But their greatest single moneymaker was Gulf Oil. It had its beginnings at Spindletop in east Texas, where in 1901 a Yugoslav prospector named Anthony F. Luchich (soon Americanized to Andy Lucas) brought in the greatest of all gushers. In order to get enough money to finish his well Lucas had sold a controlling interest to a pair of operators named Guffey and Galey. Now they too had exhausted their money, and Colonel J. M. Guffey turned to the Mellons. While prospectors and speculators swarmed through Texas to get in on the great bonanza, the Mellons quietly bought out both Lucas and Guffey and brought most of the Spindletop dome under the control of a company that became Gulf Oil. In 1976 they still held nearly twenty per cent of the Gulf stock, worth just under a billion dollars.

For more than forty years Andrew W. and Richard B. Mellon worked together in a relationship of trust rarely found even in family businesses. Each had unlimited access to the other's funds. Each trusted the other to commit him in equal share to business ventures or charitable gifts. Because they worked behind the industrial scenes the men were little known to the general public, their wealth hardly guessed at. When A.W.'s name was proposed to Warren G. Harding as Secretary of the Treasury, the President-elect was said to have looked blank and asked, "Who is he?"

Andrew, especially, was a lonely, retiring man who did not marry until he was forty-five, and was divorced twelve years later. He lived in a big, dark, cavernous house in Pittsburgh, alone with his servants and in later years with his paintings. He walked softly and spoke softly when he spoke at all. During his years in Calvin Coolidge's Cabinet Washington wits liked to imagine a private conversation between the silent President and his Secretary of the Treasury, "consisting entirely of pauses."

Outside of business, Andrew Mellon's greatest interest in later years was his art collection. But he never collected art with the fierce joy of a Morgan or the whimsical prodigality of a Hearst. If he assembled the finest private collection in the United States it was because, in collecting as in banking, he looked for experts whose judgment he could trust. The principal expert he found—or rather the expert who found him—was Duveen, who by that time numbered Morgan, Hearst, Widener, and most of the other great American collectors among his clients. Duveen had trained his sights on the Mellon fortune early on, but though he was the most wily and aggressive of salesmen, it took him years even to meet Mellon. At last he accomplished it by taking a suite under Mellon's suite in Claridge's Hotel in London, where his valet arranged with Mellon's valet to get the old man in the same elevator. Before they reached the lobby Duveen had introduced himself and, as if on the spur of the moment, invited Mellon to visit the British National Gallery to "refresh their spirits" by looking at paintings. The resulting relationship altered the world balance of art. Under Duveen's expensive tutelage Mellon bought only the very best—as much as twenty million dollars' worth at a time. Before his death he gave it, along with a handsome marble building, to found the National Gallery in Washington.

On a street in Englewood, New Jersey, in 1927 a little girl is struck with delight at the sight of an honest-to-goodness, silk-hatted, chauffeur-driven multimillionaire. Andrew Mellon had just given money to build the National Gallery in Washington.

During Andrew Mellon's years in public life, as Secretary of the Treasury and later ambassador to Great Britain, his brother Richard Mellon managed the family interests. But the acquisitive period was over. In the third generation R.B.'s son, Richard King Mellon, took over the reins from his father but devoted as much time and energy to making over the city of Pittsburgh as he did to business. It was due in great part to his efforts that Pittsburgh was transformed from a harsh, grimy city beneath a pall of smoke from the blast furnaces and coke ovens into the bright and clean, if not exactly beautiful, city it is today. Meanwhile, Andrew's second interest, art, became the primary interest of his only son, Paul, who assembled the world's greatest private collection of English eighteenth-century paintings. Mellons of the fourth generation have applied their energies to such fields as education, city planning, and even banking, but they have yet to produce a financial captain in the mold of those who built the dynasty.

SOME RECENT MONEYMEN

In the twentieth century the world of finance has produced no fortune that remotely rivals the Mellons'. The stock-market boom of the twenties threw up some spectacular figures such as Jesse Livermore, who kept seven telephones on his desk so that one would always be cool to the touch during his hours of frenzied buying and selling. The device of the holding company enabled Samuel Insull to control a dizzy pyramid of electric utilities by a tiny capital holding at the top. But the 1929 crash took its toll of such highfliers. Jesse Livermore jumped out of a window, Samuel Insull fled the country, and the chairman of the New York Stock Exchange, Richard Whitney, who had speculated with clients' funds, went to jail. The most successful of the pure speculators was Bernard M. Baruch, who got out before the crash and left an enduring mark on American public life as adviser to presidents from Woodrow Wilson to Dwight D. Eisenhower.

Not until the 1960's did Wall Street produce another flight of venturesome moneymen, and for most of them the flight was short indeed. For a brief time a Texan by the name of H. Ross Perot was acclaimed as the latest addition to the select club of billionaires. He had begun as a star salesman for IBM, and then, with computers leased from IBM, he started Electronic Data Systems to provide services for industrial companies. Perot's real distinction

was that he managed to market a small portion of the stock in his company at the heady price of one hundred eighteen times earnings and then saw it rise to ten times the offering price. On that basis his own holdings were indeed worth over one and a half billion dollars on paper. But by the time the stock had fallen from $162 to $29 the billionaire's club had one less member.

More reminiscent of the great piratical days of Jay Gould and Jim Fiske was the lurid career of Bernie Cornfeld. While working as a salesman for a New York mutual fund, Cornfeld conceived the idea that by making his base outside the U.S. he could run his own fund without all the tiresome restrictions imposed by the U.S. government. "Do you sincerely want to be rich?" Cornfeld asked his salesmen and his customers alike. Enough of them answered yes to bring in a tide of money that flooded at just over twelve billion dollars. For a while he and his cronies lived like a Brooklyn boy's dream of the life of an Oriental sultan, complete with Swiss palace and jet-borne harem. Unfortunately Cornfeld was not as good at investing the money as he was at gathering it. When the market fell his empire was among the first to crash. Robert Vesco picked up the pieces and decamped to Costa Rica to escape the reach of the U.S. Department of Justice.

The crash of the go-go financiers left the financial world a rather staid place. In American cities, great and small, bankers tend to occupy central positions in business and public life. They are sure bets for company directorships, charitable contributions, patrons of whatever culture may be around, pillars of the Rotary, the United Fund and the country club. Their archetype, throughout the 1950's and 1960's, was David Rockefeller of the Chase Manhattan Bank. Early in the 1970's a reporter marveled: "He directs so many companies, supports so many worthy causes, knows so many people all over the world, that secretaries trail him with card files of all his interests and contacts." The financial clouds that gathered over many of the biggest banks in the last few years cast a shadow on his reputation as a financial titan but could hardly affect his personal life. He lives as well as it is possible to live in his New York townhouse and his homes at Seal Harbor and Pocantico Hills, but wholly without ostentation. For years he was the American Establishment personified. But it would have been as preposterous to think of him seeking more personal wealth as it would have been to think of Hugh Hefner wondering where the next girl was coming from.

A PORTFOLIO: THE WEALTHY PATRONS

PRIVATE WEALTH HAS BEEN THE CHIEF SUPPORT OF ART-
ISTS IN EVERY AGE. IN THE PORTRAIT ABOVE, COSIMO
DE' MEDICI IS ENTHRONED AMONG THE PAINTERS, SCULP-
TORS, ARCHITECTS, AND ENGINEERS WHO ENJOYED HIS
PATRONAGE. OTHER GREAT PATRONS, INCLUDING MANY
BANKERS, APPEAR IN THE FOLLOWING PORTFOLIO.

SCALA

oble English art collectors of the eight-
enth century headed for the Uffizi
allery in Florence to buy Renaissance
reasures from the Medici collections.
n this painting by Johann Zoffany, the
nglish envoy Sir Horace Mann (with
word and decoration), has joined a
roup inspecting Titian's *Reclining
Venus*. One of the Medici sculptures that
escaped them is Donatello's bronze
David (above), now on exhibit in the
National Museum at Florence.

This magnificent library reflects the taste of the man for whom it was built, J. P. Morgan. It was here that Morgan kept the leaders of Wall Street in all-night session during the Panic of 1907; here, too, that he received a stream of art dealers bringing him their greatest prizes from Europe. Today the Morgan Library is most famous for its collection of medieval manuscripts like the one on display in the right foreground. Among many treasures willed to the Metropolitan Museum of Art by the financier are: above, an eleventh-century Byzantine medallion of Saint Paul; below, a twelfth-century Limoges enamel reliquary; far right, a seventeenth-century silver ship's model from Nuremberg.

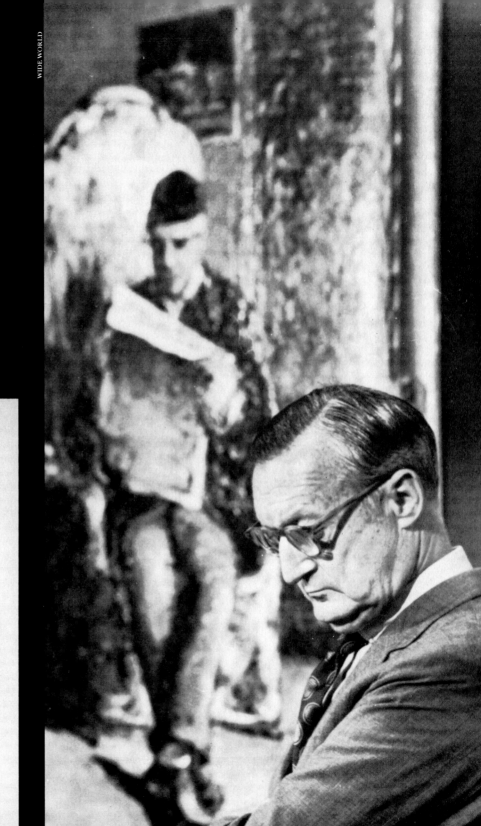

The special affinity of bankers for art collecting was demonstrated by Philip Lehman and his son Robert, senior partners in turn of the Lehman Brothers investment banking house. After Philip's death Robert Lehman turned his father's Manhattan townhouse into a private museum where the greatest treasures of the growing collection could be displayed in the period rooms of a rich man's house. When Robert himself died in 1969, he left the collection to the Metropolitan Museum, where it is now housed in a special wing. Around a central court, seven rooms from the Lehman townhouse have been installed, complete with paintings, furniture, wall paneling, and decorative objects. The picture above shows the entrance to the central court of the museum wing, with Robert Lehman's portrait. At right is the upstairs sitting room of the Lehman townhouse, with its early Italian Rennaissance and Flemish paintings.

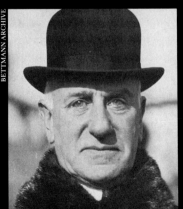

Among wealthy American patrons of the arts, the Guggenheims
have, as a family, been the most adventurous. Beginning about
1930, Solomon R. Guggenheim (left) set the pace by buying the
work of such European abstract painters as Kandinsky, Leger,
and Mondrian. Frank Lloyd Wright was commissioned to give
the collection a home on Fifth Avenue. Wright did not like the
kind of art that went into the museum ("crime without passion"),
and some painters do not much like the display that its spiraling
ramps afford. But the paintings and the building both testify to
Solomon Guggenheim's patronage of living artists.

His niece, Peggy Guggenheim, has also been a daring patron of
living artists. At her palazzo in Venice (opposite), Marini's *Horse
and Rider* greets visitors arriving by gondola on the Grand Canal.

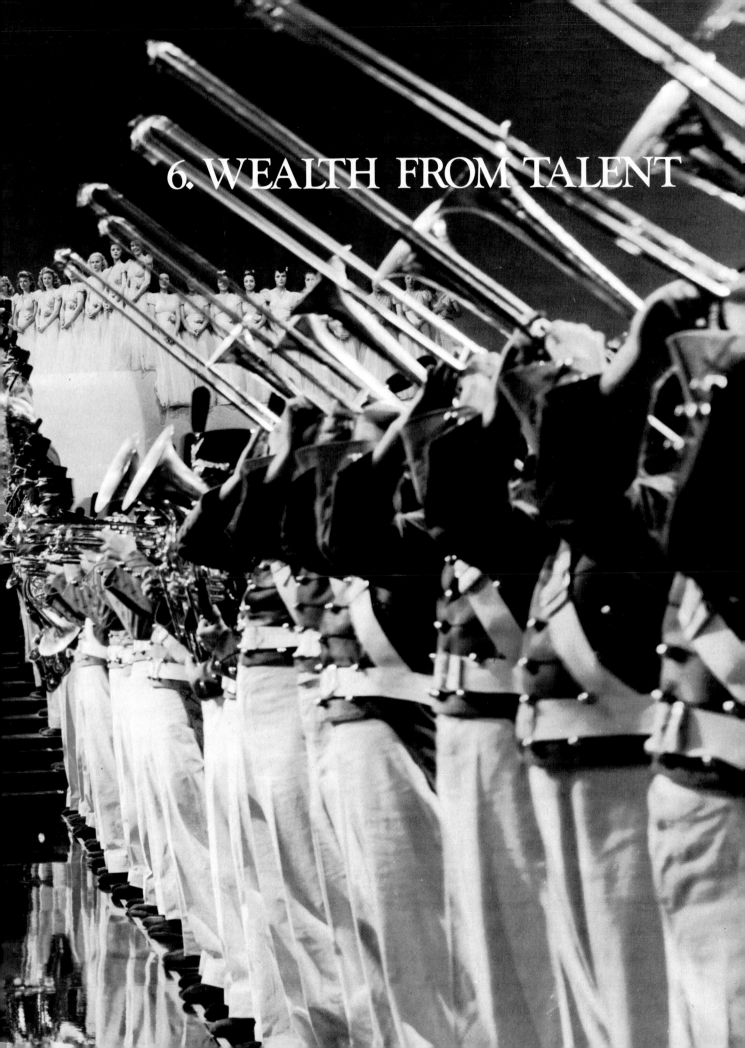

6. WEALTH FROM TALENT

If Voltaire resembles the cheery Dr. Pangloss in this engraving, it may be because economically he was living in the best of all possible worlds. The parsimonious Voltaire accumulated a considerable fortune and retired to a gracious villa, where he carefully regulated the use of candles to save cash. On the facing page, Charles Dickens, who wrote *A Christmas Carol* to defray the prodigious cost of his life style, reads his masterpiece to two of his children. Monte-Cristo (center) was the Paris home of Alexandre Dumas and the scene of the lavish entertainments that finally helped break him. At far right Dumas passes a reflective moment with one of his mistresses, the American actress Adah Isaacs Menken. Dumas boasted that he had fathered 500 children.

BROWN BROTHERS

THE AUTHORS

Although Dr. Johnson said that nobody but a blockhead ever wrote for any reason except money, it was not until the nineteenth century, when a large reading public evolved, that authors found a way to transform their creative writings into real wealth. When an author turned his pen over to the uses of the state, he could sometimes expect handsome payment, but when he listened to his own muse, he was apt to have a thin time of it. Milton was paid a thousand pounds for a properly dreary political treatise written to order for Cromwell's Parliament, but for *Paradise Lost* he received sixty-three pounds. Racine toiled as an early-day version of a publicity agent and was paid one hundred forty thousand francs for writing up Louis XIV's military exploits, but when he tried to raise the royalty for his plays to something more than forty francs a performance, he was accused of trying to ruin the French theater with his exorbitant demands.

An exception was Alexander Pope, the first author who succeeded in getting the public to really pay for its reading enjoyment. His translations of the *Iliad* and the *Odyssey* earned him a generous nine thousand pounds in royalties. He repaired to an estate in Twickenham in 1718, where, thanks to Homer, he "could thrive indebted to no prince or peer alive."

Few men were as assiduous as Voltaire in at-

tempting to amass a fortune, but his money came not from his writing but rather from speculations, lotteries, and profits from loans to impoverished noblemen at high rates of interest. A notoriously bad tipper, Voltaire was stingy in a dozen small ways; he especially disliked spending money on candles. He lived at other people's expense whenever he thought he could save a few francs. Needless to say, he died rich.

Other equally creative talents seem to have had a facility for losing fortunes rather than making them. Mark Twain had a good deal of fun at the expense of nineteenth-century American businessmen; but when he himself became wealthy, he built a Victorian mansion in Hartford that would have been the pride of any banker. Then Twain lost his money by investing in the hapless Paige typesetter. His business judgment, like that of many creative people, was clouded. When he had a chance to be an early investor in the telephone, he turned down the opportunity. He had already lost money on one impractical device and was not about to make the same mistake twice.

Charles Dickens wrote *A Christmas Carol* in 1843 to defray the cost of his lavish housekeeping. Even the sumptuous royalties from that classic were not enough, and Dickens had to move to Marseilles, where he lived for two years to save money. His literary successes eventually outstripped his own expensive tastes, however, and the master English novelist left an estate of ninety thousand pounds.

Alexandre Dumas, who often seemed to confuse himself with his legendary creation, the Count of Monte Cristo, ran through several fortunes during his lifetime. He left Paris for the last time with only a few gold napoleons to his name and moved to Dieppe to live out his days with his son.

Dumas ran an extensive fiction factory in Paris, exhausting some ninety collaborators during his career. Even so, he appears as a sputtering hack paralyzed by a virulent writer's block when his output is compared to the torrent of words written by the American detective-story writer Erle Stanley Gardner. Working on his thousand-acre ranch in Temecula, California, Gardner dictated into a battery of tape recorders and required seven full-time secretaries to transcribe his novels. In all, Gardner wrote one hundred forty books, including eighty about the portly defense counselor Perry Mason, his major creation. At the time of his death in 1970 Gardner's books had sold more than one hundred seventy million copies and had been translated into

◀PRECEDING PAGES: **Mickey Rooney and Judy Garland in the 1940 musical *Strike Up The Band* found that the Hollywood dream factory could produce pure gold.**
BETTMANN ARCHIVE

thirty languages. During his heyday in the 1960's Gardner's novels were selling at the rate of twenty thousand copies a day. His productivity was so astonishing that a newspaper reviewer once accused him of using ghostwriters. When this calumny was uttered, Gardner's publisher offered a prize of a hundred thousand dollars if the story could be proved. "It would be worth a hundred thousand dollars," he said, "just to find someone who can write like Erle Stanley Gardner." It would have been worth a great deal more. Gardner's total royalties have been estimated at something on the order of fifty million dollars.

Gardner was fortunate enough to come along at a time when royalties on hard-cover book sales were just a steppingstone to great literary wealth. Paperback sales and motion-picture and television rights now account for a huge portion of a successful author's income. The Perry Mason novels were made into a television series that earned Gardner another fifteen million dollars over a ten-year period, and what with reruns in lands as far away as Saudi Arabia, the end is not yet in sight.

Americans will pay dearly to laugh in troubled times, and no writer has made that circumstance pay as well as Neil Simon, the reigning king of comedy on the Broadway stage. In 1970 New York audiences had their choice of three Neil Simon hits: *Plaza Suite*, *The Last of the Red Hot Lovers*, and the musical *Promises, Promises*. That year Simon earned forty-five thousand dollars a week from his stage works alone. In addition to drawing a ten-per-cent royalty from the grosses of his plays in New York, throughout the country, and abroad, Simon was a major investor in Broadway shows. Not surprisingly, he invested heavily in Neil Simon shows, which gained him even more money. In a curious way, however, Simon owes much of his staggering income to the business judgments of others. He has a sense of foreboding about his plays when they are in rehearsal, and is convinced they will be flops.

"I always try to [convince producers to] close my shows down before they reach New York," he once said. "I tried to convince David Merrick to close *Promises, Promises* in Boston, and at one point I begged Saint Subber not to do *Barefoot in the Park*. The play seemed so dismal to me." Fortunately, no one payed much attention to Simon. *Promises, Promises* was the musical hit of the year, and *Barefoot in the Park* ran for 1,532 performances, making it the eighth-longest-running nonmusical show in Broadway history.

It is said that when a book is panned by the critics but is popular with the public, the author "cries all the way to the bank." If so, then Jacqueline Susann must have cried so hard she could scarcely have written out the deposit slips. Miss Susann's three soap-opera novels, *Valley of the Dolls*, *The Love Machine*, and *Once is Not Enough*, were all roundly panned when they first appeared; "sensationalist, sex-obsessed garbage," wrote one critic. All three books promptly made their way to the top of the *New York Times* best-seller list, an achievement that made Miss Susann the first author in history to type three consecutive number-one sellers. *Valley of the Dolls*, her *chef-d'oeuvre*, has sold more than seventeen million copies

The case of the very, very successful author was Erle Stanley Gardner, an attorney turned mystery writer. In his prime Gardner, working at his California estate, would write an entire Perry Mason novel in six weeks.

in hard cover and paperback, and has replaced the turgid *Peyton Place* as the best-selling novel of all time.

Miss Susann's novels earned the one-time minor actress eight million dollars in her lifetime, and no author worked harder for her success. She labored over her manuscripts through as many as five drafts on different colored paper, often crying in pain in the agony of creation. She was a tireless promoter of her books, and crisscrossed the country plugging them. "When you're number one," she said, "you have no place to go but down. And it's such a big drop from one to two." She died in 1975, but her popular mixture of sex and drugs and teasing insights into the lives of jet setters will continue to earn millions for her beyond the grave. She and her husband, television producer Irving Mansfield, were shrewd bargainers for the lucrative motion-picture rights. *Valley of the Dolls* was sold to the movies for a relatively paltry two hundred thousand dollars. *Once is Not Enough*, produced after her death, will yield Miss Susann's estate ten per cent of its gross revenues; the box-office figures are not complete, but if past performances are any indication, the total should be significant. *Valley of the Dolls* grossed twenty-eight million dollars.

The beau ideal of the successful author of our time is Harold Robbins, who lives like one of the extravagant characters in his own novels. A high-school

dropout at the age of fifteen, Robbins got a job in 1931 shoveling snow in Harlem and working for one of the local bookies. By the time he was twenty-one he had made and lost more than one million dollars in commodity speculation. Robbins settled down after that and went to work in the New York office of Universal Pictures as head of the statistical department. One of his duties was to wait for three hours every night for the receipts from the West Coast to be wired in, and the bored Robbins decided to pass the time writing. "The studio was buying a lot of crap and making movies out of it," Robbins recalls. "I thought I could do better." He may not have done better, but he did well enough. *Never Love A Stranger*, a novel reportedly modeled on the career of gangster Frank Costello, was a moderate success, and Harold Robbins, the popular novelist, was born. A flock of best sellers later, Robbins was one of the most successful authors in the country—so successful that Trident Press was set up specifically for the purpose of publishing Harold Robbins novels.

It takes a certain dash to write lines like "the room was filled with the smell of last night's love that hung in the air like old wine," and Robbins has plenty of dash. When he is not on the French Riviera he lives in Gloria Swanson's former house in Beverly Hills. He patrols the Mediterranean in his eighty-five-foot yacht and thinks little of losing a hundred fifty thousand dollars in a single night gambling at Monte Carlo. "My days are simple," he says innocently.

Robbins is one of the most reliable moneymaking "machines" of our day. He has become so successful that it is no longer necessary for him to actually write at all. Producers are willing to pay him huge advances for what he might someday write. Robbins sold the motion-picture rights for *The Adventurers* to Joseph E. Levine for one million dollars before the author knew what the book would be about. Gauging Robbins' total wealth is difficult; he is not like a publicly held corporation that must issue an annual report to its stockholders. Still, there are interesting indications of how large it must be. He was paid one million dollars for conceiving the idea for *The Survivors*, a television series that flopped. *The Inheritors* was good for one million two hundred thousand dollars in movie rights and two million five hundred thousand dollars in book rights. It all adds up. In an effort to be helpful, Robbins once told an interviewer in 1967 that he had already been paid about the same amount of money it cost to build the New York Public Library.

THE ARTISTS

The romantic tradition of the artist holds that a man of true aesthetic temperament scorns money and lives only for his art. Like the sixteenth-century ceramicist Bernard Palissy, who burned his house as fuel to keep his kiln fired, the artist is supposed to be consumed by his own creativity.

Nonetheless, more than one painter has been able to build up a considerable estate without damaging his stature as an artist. Certainly there is no reason to assume that the exuberant paintings of Peter Paul Rubens would have been improved if he had starved in some Flemish garret instead of being one of the most successful court painters of his day. In Rubens' life there was none of the Sturm und Drang that is so often the lot of the painter. After studying briefly for the law, he turned to art, and went to Italy in 1600 to study the paintings of Veronese and Titian. It seems that almost from the start he was a sought-after painter, who received a stream of high-priced commissions from the royal houses of Europe. Rubens and his students fashioned more than one thousand two hundred works during his lifetime, including such highly profitable commissions as portraits of King Charles I of England, King Philip IV of Spain, and Marie de' Medici, queen of France. His royal patrons paid him generously, not only with cash and jewels but with weighty honors of state. Rubens was knighted by both King Charles and King Philip.

Tended by five servants, Rubens lived almost as royally as his patrons. His home in Antwerp was the showplace of the city, and housed his private art collection, which included works by Brueghel, Titian, Raphael, Veronese, Tintoretto, Dürer, Holbein, and van Eyck and nearly one hundred of his own canvases. In 1635 Rubens felt the need of even grander quarters, and he purchased for ninety-three thousand florins a feudal castle at Steen, eighteen miles from Antwerp. He took the title Lord of Steen, and remained artistically active there until his death in 1640.

Like Rubens, the English portrait painter Sir Joshua Reynolds was not born to wealth but managed to accumulate a great deal of it by painting for wealthy patrons. Reynolds was not the appealing person the beloved Rubens was. He was particularly

Neil Simon relaxes during the rehearsal of *Gingerbread Lady*. A one-time gagman for television, Simon graduated to the theater, and in 1970 he had three shows running on Broadway, earning him about $45,000 a week.

tight-fisted when it came to paying his assistants. But few artists were better at the sometimes difficult business of extracting money from rich people. Reynolds was never the supplicant painter, wringing his hands in front of some prospective patron. His life style was calculated to remind his clients that he was as rich as they and that they should expect to pay accordingly. He owned a glorious rococo coach bedecked with paintings by Charles Catton showing allegories of the seasons. The wheels were ornamented with carved foliage and gilding, and the footmen who rode on top of this traveling display wore livery laced with real silver. For Reynolds, the coach was more than a personal ostentation. It was a form of advertising. He was usually too busy in his studio to go out during the day, so he had his sister ride about in the carriage as often as possible to draw admiring glances from Londoners and announce to everyone that Sir Joshua Reynolds was a man of prominence.

Reynolds had flat pay schedules for his work: twenty-five guineas for a head, fifty guineas for a half-length portrait, and a hundred guineas for a full-length portrait. He and his assistants ground out some three thousand of these works, earning Reynolds the equivalent of more than thirty thousand dollars a year. Although his customers were forced to pay handsomely, they got their money's worth. Reynolds ranked at the top of the English school, and his portraits invariably increased in value in a few years. He also did very well for himself. When he died in 1792 Reynolds had accumulated an estate equivalent to more than five hundred thousand dollars.

While few art historians would link Reynolds with Salvador Dali in terms of artistic style, the twentieth-century's mad genius of the art world is, if anything, Reynolds' master when it comes to shaking money from clients. Dali limits himself to one large canvas a year and sells it for as much as two hundred eighty thousand dollars.

The son of a Catalan notary, Dali loves money, and knows how to get it. He has become one of the foremost purveyors of art and related objects in the world today. Just as Michelangelo pocketed a fee for designing the uniforms of the Swiss Guards at the Vatican, and Flemish artists picked up extra money for designing furniture for their wealthy patrons, Dali is an artist for commercial hire. No job seems to be too small if there is enough money in it. He has designed coffee tables and coat hangers. A shop in Barcelona sells his shirts; Air India uses his ash trays; Schiaparelli sells his hats; and Guyana issues his postage stamps. Dali has turned his fine Spanish hand to the design of calendars, brandy bottles, ties, oyster knives, and bathing suits, receiving a cut from the manufacturer of each. He has spawned a number of cottage industries that are busy turning out his creations. French glass blowers in Nancy produce his crystal ware, and weavers at the Aubusson factory carry out his designs for tapestries. Bookbinders labor on his illustrated editions of everything from the Bible to *Alice in Wonderland* and the poems of Mao Tse-tung that sell for anywhere from thirty-five dollars to fifteen thousand dollars a copy. One company manufactures Dali playing cards at twenty-five dollars a deck. If artistic endeavor should fail, the master can always pick up extra money by just being Salvador Dali. He recently pocketed ten thousand dollars for doing a television commercial saying, "I am mad. I am completely mad . . . over Lanvin chocolates." He earned another ten thousand dollars for doing a commercial for Braniff Airways, although he spoiled the effect somewhat by announcing at the same time that he had never flown on any airplane and never would.

Dali's agent estimates that he has ten million dollars in the bank, or wherever it is that Dali puts his money. This would probably make him the richest artist of the twentieth century, if it were not for Pablo Picasso. When Picasso died in 1973 it was assumed that his estate might eventually be valued at some seven hundred fifty million dollars. But after a three-year examination by an insurance assessor, that estimate was raised to one billion one hundred million dollars. Approximately three-fifths of this comes from Picasso's personal art collection, including his own works and those of other modern artists. The remaining two-fifths is made up somewhat prosaically of real estate, houses, apartment buildings, and other investments.

Picasso was unquestionably the richest artist in history, and trying to make sense of his income is similar to reading the national budget. The numerals are written clearly enough, but they are so huge that they seem like abstractions instead of real figures. From January 5, 1969, to February 2, 1970, Picasso created one hundred sixty-seven oils and forty-five drawings, all of which were displayed at

Peter Paul Rubens, the prince of painters, repaired in appropriate splendor to the Chateau de Steen (right), where he lived out the end of a long and prosperous career as one of the foremost artists of the seventeenth century.

Salvador Dali, the mad genius of art, poses for his portrait in this famous photograph by Philippe Halsman.

Avignon the following summer. Art dealers estimated that if put on the market, Picasso's output for that period would fetch fifteen million dollars. As British art critic Michael Ayrton pointed out, "Currency is worth less in Picasso's hands than a sheet of blank paper."

A simple drawing by Picasso is worth upward of twenty-five thousand dollars. Oils from his last years bring anywhere from fifty thousand dollars to one hundred fifty thousand, and his masterworks are quickly becoming priceless. *The Nude Woman*, done in 1910, recently brought a reported one million one hundred thousand dollars from the National Gallery in Washington.

Picasso said he wanted to be rich enough to live like a peasant; except for a propensity for buying huge country estates—he once purchased two thousand five hundred acres on the north side of Mont Ste. Victoire, happily telling a friend, "I have just bought Cezanne's view"—he did so. During the later part of his life Picasso abandoned the furious womanizing of his youth and lived simply with his wife, Jacqueline Roque, in an electronically protected villa in Mougins in the south of France. He dined frugally in the kitchen of his country home, limiting himself to one glass of wine with his meal. His artistic energy was prodigious; he was capable of completing three canvases in a single day, earning himself somewhere between one hundred fifty thousand and four hundred fifty thousand dollars, if he still cared about such matters.

THE ACTORS

Society has frequently granted actors considerable wealth while denying them acceptance. Acting was deemed a respectable profession in ancient Greece, but in Rome it was stigmatized. Actresses were treated as prostitutes, which many in fact were. When the wife of a consul scandalized Roman society by appearing on stage singing and dancing, Sallust, the great pontificator of Roman morals, sniffed that she performed "more elegantly than is necessary for a respectable woman." Roman citizens who appeared in dramas were denied the right to own property and were disqualified from taking part in local governmental affairs. If actors were social pariahs, however, they could comfort themselves with sizable incomes. Performers received five hundred sesterces a performance, but, as always, stars could command higher fees for their work. Q. Roscius Gallus was, by all accounts, one of the handsomest men in Rome, although, because of a slight squint, he introduced to Rome the Greek practice of wearing masks on stage. An excellent comedian, Roscius earned five hundred thousand sesterces a year. He died in 62 B.C. a wealthy man. His contemporary, Aesopus, left an estate of twenty million sesterces.

The social lot of the actor had improved slightly by the eighteenth century. In England performers such as David Garrick and Mrs. Siddons were accepted as guests at the highest social levels, but it was not considered proper that they themselves should be hosts to the gentry at similar gatherings. Garrick accumulated a fortune of one hundred twenty thousand pounds as co-owner of the Drury Lane Theatre. In France an actor could make considerable amounts of money and be accepted by society while alive, but it was decreed that Christian burial grounds should not be befouled by an actor's corpse.

Sarah Bernhardt is the name most closely associated with the glamour of the early international theater. An extraordinarily gifted and versatile performer, the Divine Sarah was the most popular actress of her day. She acquired and lost several fortunes as easily as she did lovers, who included the fiery French Republican leader Léon Gambetta, an aging Victor Hugo, Prince Napoleon, the Prince of Wales (the future Edward VII), and numerous writers, artists, actors, and directors in Europe and America. Eternally strapped for cash because of her profligate spending, Sarah toured the world to rapturous reviews—"She recites as the nightingale sings, as the wind sighs, as water murmurs," wrote Lamartine—and a torrent of cash. But it was never enough to satisfy her creditors. She paid for her costumes with a "lunatic disregard of cost," said one biographer. She had her silks woven to order in Lyon. She imported her furs from Russia, and her velvets from Italy. There were always art dealers and decorators to pay, and a long line of tradesmen and couturiers waiting for their money. When she earned twenty thousand francs a year, she spent fifty thousand francs. To shore up her financial situation she toured America nine times, including four "farewell tours," and was hugely successful. She netted five hundred thousand dollars on her first tour alone. An indefatigable trouper, Bernhardt played large cities and small mining towns in America, crisscrossing the country in her special show train. She even managed to make some money playing poker, an American game she invariably won

because everyone had to play by her own Gallic rules. She would delightedly rake in everyone's counters, chirping brightly, "Cheeps, cheeps, cheeps."

Bernhardt should have been one of the wealthiest women in France. She earned almost six million dollars from her American tours alone. But before she died in 1923 at the age of seventy-nine, she acted in a silent movie despite an amputated leg because she needed the money.

Millionaire actors became almost commonplace during the 1920's when silent movies were in their glory days in Hollywood. "The public wanted us to live like kings and queens," said Gloria Swanson. "So we did—and why not? We were in love with life. We were making more money than we ever dreamed existed." Miss Swanson earned nine hundred thousand dollars a year from Paramount Studios and spent accordingly. In one year her perfume bill was six thousand dollars, and another one hundred nineteen thousand went for clothes.

The true royalty of Hollywood, however, were "America's Sweethearts," Douglas Fairbanks and Mary Pickford. As they emerged as major stars of the silent screen, both were ferocious negotiators. Sam Goldwyn said of Mary, "It took longer to make up her contract than it did her pictures."

Pablo Picasso stands in his cluttered studio, surrounded by creations made of paint, paper, iron, plaster, straw, and anything else that struck his fancy. His prodigious output of art ended only with his death in 1973 at the age of ninety-one. Assessors estimated the value of his estate at over one billion dollars.

Mary started in Hollywood in 1909 at the age of sixteen, working as a five-dollar-a-day extra. Ten years later she was earning one million dollars a year and was a co-owner of United Artists with Fairbanks, Charlie Chaplin, and D. W. Griffith. Fairbanks died in 1939—four years after a divorce from Miss Pickford—and in spite of a lifetime of wild spending, left an estate of three million dollars. Mary, who made her last film in 1933, continues to reign over their Hollywood estate, Pickfair, which, along with Harold Lloyd's forty-room estate, Greenacres, is still the premier Hollywood mansion. Because of ill health, Miss Pickford is rarely seen, but Pickfair is kept up as it was in the days when the king of Siam, Babe Ruth, Guglielmo Marconi, Charles Lindbergh, Albert Einstein, and Prince Hirohito came to dine on the solid gold service, with a footman poised behind each chair. A butler and five maids still live in a separate guest house on the property, and three gardeners arrive daily to look after the stately grounds. What with shrewd investments and land speculation during pre-inflation low-tax days, the delightful comedienne of *Daddy Long Legs* and *Little Lord Fauntleroy* is reportedly worth fifty million dollars.

Compared to Doug and Mary, our current on-again-off-again love team of Richard Burton and Elizabeth Taylor seems no more than affluent, for all her jewels and their clutch of villas in Mexico, Switzerland, and the French Riviera. Individually and as a team Liz and Dick have earned a great deal of money. At one time each could sign film contracts for one million dollars plus a percentage of the gross. Both careers have recently been becalmed, at least for the moment, and no one knows how much money they have left.

Two comics of modern Hollywood, Lucille Ball and Bob Hope, reign at the top of the economic scale. Lucille Ball's theatrical career started poorly. She was dismissed as a student of John Murray Anderson's dramatic school in New York, and was told by the instructor, "Try another profession. Any other." Lucy persevered through a long career of unimportant films, usually playing the wise-cracking girl friend of the star. She blossomed on television, however, and her *I Love Lucy* shows, twenty-one years of them, have been the most played, most profitable programs in the history of the medium. However, her comedic skills seem second to her business sense. With her husband Desi Arnaz—whom she later divorced—Miss Ball sold several seasons of her early *I Love Lucy* shows to Columbia Broadcasting Company for six million dollars. She took the money and bought three major television studios in Hollywood, later selling them and tripling her investment. The wealthiest woman in show business, Lucille Ball's fortune is estimated to be between fifty and seventy-five million dollars.

The undisputed king of the hill is Bob Hope, a poor kid from Cleveland who once tried to make a living as a club fighter in small-time bouts around the city. Estimates of Hope's total worth today range from one hundred fifty to seven hundred million. In addition to his vast revenues from his performances and a merchandising organization that bears his name, Hope is reputedly the largest single landowner in the state of California. He once bought a sixteen-thousand-acre tract in the San Fernando Valley for six hundred forty thousand dollars, and later sold off eight thousand five hundred acres for an estimated forty million dollars. He still holds title to the remainder, which is now valued at one hundred twelve million dollars.

When he wants to, Hope spends lavishly. He pays his gag writers seven hundred fifty thousand a year. Because he never likes to be too far from a golf game during his travels, he pays an estimated sixty thousand dollars in dues to some twenty clubs around the country. Hope's charity is legendary. His friend Bing Crosby estimated that Bob gives away twenty thousand dollars a week to various charitable institutions.

Remembering his early days on the vaudeville circuit, however, Hope can be tight-fisted. Although he arrived in Hollywood with a hundred-thousand-dollar annuity from his theater days and a lucrative motion-picture contract, his wife could not talk him into buying a house. Hope was willing to rent, but he did not want to be stuck with a mortgage. Today, however, he owns a home in Palm Springs that covers six city lots and is the largest single-family dwelling in a community known for spacious homes. Clearly he could retire, but the seventy-three-year-old comedian continues to work at a furious pace. As he often jokes, "I've got a government to support."

THE OPERA SINGERS

Of all the people in the arts, when it comes to sheer, unrelenting rapacity in the pursuit of cash, opera singers are probably without peer. Mary Pickford may have shaken her curls defiantly when wheedling money out of a reluctant producer, and Harold Robbins may have grandly demanded one million dollars for thinking about writing, but no group of creative artists invoke God on their side in salary negotiations with the regularity of opera stars. "One God and one Farinelli," was the spirited defense of the stratospheric fees demanded by the famous eighteenth-century castrato. An Italian soprano, Angelica Catalani, described herself with equal reverence: "When God has given to a mortal so extraordinary a talent as mine, everybody should honor and applaud it as a miracle. It is profane to deprecate the gifts of Heaven." It is difficult for even the flintiest impresario to bargain shrewdly with both a soprano and the Almighty.

When it comes to salary negotiations, the singers of today leave the details to their agents and managers. Few have the starch of Adelina Patti, who handled such matters herself. Patti was at the height of her career when she arrived at the Globe Theater in Boston for a performance of *La Traviata*. At two in the afternoon one of her employees went to see the

1

2

3

4

5

6

9

11

7

10

Hollywood was an El Dorado for young talent. Most never found it, but some were luckier: 1. James Cagney, 2. Edward G. Robinson, 3. Gloria Swanson, 4. Charlie Chaplin, 5. Shirley Temple, 6. Douglas Fairbanks and Mary Pickford, 7. Harold Lloyd, 8. Richard Burton and Elizabeth Taylor, 9. Lucille Ball, 10. Bing Crosby and Bob Hope, 11. Jackie Coogan. The tragedy of young Jackie Coogan is one of the enduring legends of Hollywood. He made millions as a child star, but his mother and father pocketed his income and kept it for themselves. Since then, child actors are protected by law from their own parents.

8

CONTINUED FROM PAGE 203

impresario, J. H. Mapleson, to fetch the five thousand dollars in cash that had been promised as her fee. Mapleson admitted he was one thousand dollars shy of the agreed amount. Dressed in her costume as Violetta, Patti waited in her dressing room without her shoes on. As soon as Mapleson came up with the remaining thousand dollars, she said, it would be her great pleasure to sing for the good people of Boston. The audience was streaming into the theater when the harried Mapleson arrived with eight hundred more. Splendid, said Patti, and put on one shoe. When the final two hundred arrived, she would put on the other, she told him. Seconds before the curtain was to go up, Mapleson scratched up the remainder. Patti slipped into her shoe and beaming radiantly went out to sing.

Patti was literally born to opera. According to legend, she was delivered backstage at the Madrid Opera House in 1843, two hours after her mother had finished singing the title role in *Norma*. An exquisite singer who ruled the international world of opera for forty-five years, Patti was also *diva assoluta* when it came to wringing money from theater producers. Patti sang at Covent Garden in London until 1881, when she began her incredibly profitable American tours. She had started at Covent Garden for a mere two hundred pounds a performance. When she arrived in America her price had risen to more than a thousand pounds. To go to far-off Argentina, Madame Patti required fifteen hundred pounds. Like other international stars, Patti found America much to her liking. She returned to do forty performances for an impressive one hundred seventy-five thousand dollars, and was persuaded to return once again for five hundred thousand dollars.

The most famous of the castrati, Farinelli, surely had the strangest career of any great singer in history. A Neapolitan born in 1705, Farinelli became a special favorite in the royal courts of Europe. He traveled across the Continent, pocketing huge fees, and arrived in London in 1734, where he was showered with gifts by the Prince of Wales. He traveled on to Spain, where he had planned to spend only a few months at the court of Philip v; he stayed for more than twenty years. The first Bourbon king of Spain suffered dreadfully from nervous depression, which

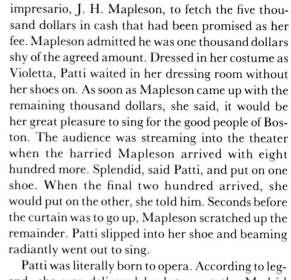

The usually flamboyant Enrico Caruso arrives at the Metropolitan Opera House in 1919 looking somber. He could not have been worrying about money. Caruso commanded $500,000 a year in appearance fees alone and was minting another fortune in royalties from records.

threatened his sanity. Philip found Farinelli's light voice soothing, and his melancholy lifted. The tenor was engaged as court singer *extraordinaire*. He was given an annual stipend of fifteen thousand dollars, plus a suitable coach and equipage. The king gave him a portrait set in diamonds valued at six thousand dollars, and the queen presented him with a gold snuffbox with two large diamonds set in the lid, good enough even for Caffarelli. For this Farinelli's sole duty was to sing to the king every evening. He sang the same six sentimental ballads each night, and never anything else. Philip lived for another ten years, and it is estimated that Farinelli sang the same six songs more than 3,600 times each. After Philip's death Farinelli stayed on under Ferdinand VI as court singer and confidential adviser, exerting great influence over the monarch and becoming, in effect, prime minister of Spain.

One reason why these operatic stars were so rapacious with theater managers was that there was no way for a singer to earn significant money except through personal appearances. There was no radio to prolong the career of an older singer; there were no Hollywood studios to magnify the inferior sound of a Mario Lanza and create an ersatz opera performer. Most of all, there was no record industry to extend a singer's income far beyond the opera stage. It is a tragedy of historical timing that no one got to watch Adelina Patti negotiate a record contract.

The first beneficiary of the new recording industry was Enrico Caruso. The ebullient Neapolitan tenor was a giant in the opera world, but thanks to recordings he became a world figure known by millions who never set foot inside an opera house. At the peak of Caruso's international career he earned five hundred thousand dollars in annual fees, and could command as high as fifteen thousand for a single performance. As a major recording star, he made nearly two hundred fifty records, which gave him immortality and his heirs an annuity. Caruso made more money than any successful recording star in history until he was passed more than thirty years later by Bing Crosby.

The tradition of the hard-bargaining singer is being carried on by conductors. Composer Igor Stravinsky had a simple rule when he appeared as a conductor. He wanted to know what others had been paid and then he asked for more. For a single appearance he received as much as seven thousand dollars—payable in cash, and in advance. A sizable sum but hardly in the league with Patti's fees of a century earlier.

Impresarios learned to fear the steely look of Adelina Patti. The soprano who ruled the international opera scene for a quarter century was known as a ferocious negotiator and had a splendid castle in Wales to prove it.

THE MUSICIANS

It has been possible for people engaged in the creation of classical music to live well. Rossini grew a businessman's paunch on the proceeds of his music, and Handel led a busy and prosperous life as London's favorite composer. But if a man of music wants to know true wealth, he must address himself to a larger audience. The music of Johann Sebastian Bach has enriched the world, but the proceeds from his entire life's work would not amount to more than a fraction of the royalties derived from "How Much Is That Doggie in the Window?"

Arthur Sullivan became a peer of the realm for writing serious works such as his lugubrious opera *Ivanhoe*, but *H.M.S. Pinafore* made him rich. By 1890 he and his partner, William Gilbert, had each earned a sumptuous ninety thousand pounds from their operettas, and they lived accordingly. Sullivan's quarters near Westminster Abbey were luxuriantly awash in Arabian clutter, with Persian hangings and antique screens. Gilbert, who for all his satires on the establishment of the day was really a stout Tory at heart, repaired to a Tudor mansion set on one hundred ten acres where forty servants tended to his cantankerous whims.

The rewards of writing successful popular music in the twentieth century can be almost without limit. Irving Berlin has probably written more hit songs than any other composer in history. Although he has written little in the last twenty-five years, his publishers list 899 Irving Berlin songs that are still bringing in royalties. And what royalties! His "God Bless America," introduced by singer Kate Smith in 1938, has earned some five hundred seventy-five thousand dollars—all of which Berlin has donated to the Boy Scouts and Girl Scouts. "White Christmas," written for a Bing Crosby movie in 1942, has sold more than one hundred five million records—a fair sale for a composer who could not read music and could play the piano by ear only by limiting himself to the key of F sharp.

Richard Rodgers has evolved into a major growth industry as a result of his Broadway musicals and related enterprises. In 1950 a friend tried to estimate Rodgers' annual income just as an exercise in mathematics. Rodgers' hit musical *South Pacific* was running on Broadway at the time, and he received $92,225 as the composer that year. He was also co-producer and received a generous but undisclosed share of the show's eleven thousand dollars weekly profit. Rodgers was also the producer of another successful Broadway show, *The Happy Time*, and there was a share of its twenty-eight thousand dollars weekly profit. Royalties from his earlier songs netted him additional thousands. Productions of Rodgers' and Hammerstein's previous hits, *Oklahoma!* and *Carousel*, were under way all over the world, and those royalties had to be calculated. Then the friend remembered that Rodgers was also the producer of Irving Berlin's enduring hit *Annie Get Your Gun*, and was due for a share of its enormous profits. He threw down his pencil in dismay. "It's impossible to figure out how much Dick makes," he said. "All I know is, it's a fantastic amount."

And all of this was before Rodgers got around to composing *The King and I* and *The Sound of Music*. A single successful theatrical property can become a major economic force, creating instant millionaires in its wake. Twenty months after the film version of *The Sound of Music* opened, Ernest Lehman, who wrote the screen adaptation, was still receiving a thousand dollars a day as his share of the profits. Robert Wise, the director, estimated that his own share would eventually come to eight million dollars. The movie single-handedly revived the flagging health of 20th Century Fox.

Leaders in popular music are financial ferrets. They are forever finding some unusual place to earn money. Paul Anka, for example, wrote the theme song for television's *Tonight* show in 1962, and has received a tidy thirty thousand dollars a year in royalties ever since. He got fifty thousand from Eastman Kodak to record their commercial jingle, "The Times of Your Life," and will receive additional royalties every time it is used. Anka has written more than four hundred songs, eighteen of which have been million-copy sellers. His royalties and performance fees have made the velvet-voiced baritone one of the richest entertainers in the world. He can command one hundred fifty thousand dollars for a single performance in Las Vegas, and estimates that he can earn up to ten million dollars a year if he wants to work that hard.

Money, it is said, makes a man cautious. And many of today's entertainment millionaires, when not engaged in the pursuit of their craft, appear to be highly respectable, even solemn, men of business. If it were not for his famous ski nose, Bob Hope could pass unnoticed in any corporate board room, and Richard Rodgers looks like the kind of person you go to for sound advice on insurance matters. But the kings of country and rock music will have none of that. They carry on the grand tradition which holds that there is no point in being rich if you cannot have fun tossing your money around.

Elton John, the exotic bird of paradise from England, has had a brief but astonishing career as a rock star. Hurling himself feet first on the piano, wearing costumes whose colors suggest an explosion in a pizza factory, Elton John earned seven million dollars in one year from screaming fans who attend his concerts in droves of seventy-five thousand and up, and buy his records by the millions. He has sold more than forty-two thousand albums; his *Captain Fantastic and the Dirt Brown Cowboy* sold 1,400,000 copies to retail outlets before it was even released in 1975. John's record-selling ability is so enormous that in 1974 he signed a deal with MCA Records for an unprecedented eight-million-dollar advance against royalties for any albums made in the next five years.

The son of an RAF squadron leader who was so strict he would not allow his son to purchase a

Irving Berlin only knows how to play the piano in one key, F-sharp major. Unable to read music, Berlin nonetheless became one of the country's most popular composers. As Jerome Kern once said, "Irving Berlin has no place in American music. He *is* American music."

mohair sweater favored by the young English toffs of the 1960's, John's passion now is buying things. Exotic eye glasses are one of his trademarks, and John does not stint. He has forty-thousand-dollars' worth. He owns pairs ringed with mink, encrusted with diamonds, and equipped with their own windshield wipers. One pair is fitted with miniature light bulbs, which spell out "ELTON" when turned on. His shopping sprees are legendary. He gave his manager an eighty-thousand-dollar yacht, and then threw in a ten-thousand-dollar Fabergé clock. His agent received a Rolls-Royce. Looking around for a birthday present for a friend, John sent him a nice etching: Rembrandt's *The Adoration of the Shepherds*.

Nashville, Tennessee, prides itself on being the "Athens of the South," and has a full-sized cement replica of the Parthenon to prove it. But, to the distress of the more elegant social set of old-line Nashvillians, the city is most famous today for being the center of the huge country-music industry. The most active recording center in the country, Nashville is so busy turning out country music that a hard-working studio musician can earn as much as a hundred thousand dollars a year playing in pick-up bands for recording sessions.

In 1937 Merle Haggard was born in a converted refrigerator-car in the Southern Pacific railroad yards in Bakersfield, California. By the time he was twenty-one Haggard had seen the inside of two reform schools, two county jails, and San Quentin for a series of crimes ranging from petty theft to armed robbery. Today Haggard earns one million dollars a year as a star of country music. He maintains all of the trappings of stardom; a seven-hundred-thousand-dollar mansion set on one hundred eighty acres with a one-hundred-thousand-dollar traveling bus in the garage, and a fifty-thousand-dollar set of model trains in the playroom.

Haggard is just one of the hundreds who have wandered into Nashville and walked out as millionaires. The countryside around the city is dotted with resplendent homes that start at five hundred thousand dollars and go up from there. Just as tourists come to New York to see the Empire State Building and the Statue of Liberty, country-music fans flock to Nashville to view Webb Pierce's swimming pool in the shape of a huge guitar and to gaze at the formidable walls outside the home of Johnny Cash. It is particularly easy to find the home of the famed comedienne Minnie Pearl. It is right next to the governor's mansion, and as country-music people say, "Minnie Pearl's is the nice one."

THE ATHLETES

The tradition of the sports celebrity is an old one. In the third century B.C. Roman fans could recall the glories of the gladiator Pacideianus, who had fought nearly a hundred years earlier, as easily as youngsters today can reel off Babe Ruth's home-run statistics. Pacideianus and the double-threat Hermes, who was equally adept at fighting on horseback or on foot with a net, could command fees as high as fifteen thousand sesterces per fight, and could look forward to a comfortable retirement on as much as two hundred forty thousand sesterces—assuming, of course, that they lived that long.

The highest rank in the Roman sports world was reserved for the chariot drivers, who raced for prizes at the Circus Maximus and lesser tracks throughout the Empire. The labor was hard. Drivers often averaged more than one hundred fifty races a year, but the rewards were prodigious enough for the successful ones to erect monuments to themselves, advertising their achievements. One driver chalked up 1,462 wins during a twenty-five-year career on the tracks, for prizes totaling just under four million sesterces. That tradition carries on today. Willie Shoemaker, the jockey, has won more than seven thousand horse races and has pocketed six million dollars for his efforts.

The millionaire sports figure is largely a twentieth-century American phenomenon. The first American to earn a million dollars in sports was boxer John L. Sullivan. He was also the first sports figure in America to spend a million dollars. When the great John L. found out on the night of September 7, 1892, that he could no longer "lick any son of a bitch in the place," he lost more than the world's heavyweight championship to James J. Corbett. He lost everything. There were no guarantees in the early days of boxing. The gross receipts for the Sullivan-Corbett fight were $101,577.80, out of which John L. received exactly nothing. Additionally, he lost a side bet of ten thousand dollars to "Gentleman Jim" Corbett and went deeply in debt. Fortunately, Sullivan remained just as popular with the American public as he had been when he was champion. For the next twenty-three years he toured the country in vaudeville and gave exhibition bouts, often dressed in his favorite costume of white tie and tails, thereby earning another $432,400.

The benefits of boxing have risen steadily since then. In 1927 Gene Tunney's share of the purse for the famous "long-count" bout with Jack Dempsey was over nine hundred ninety thousand dollars, the largest single prize that had ever been awarded to a boxer. Tunney, who was a surgically clean boxer, like to have things neat. He gave promoter Tex Rickard slightly more than nine thousand dollars in cash just so he could have the pleasure of seeing a check for one million dollars with his name on it. Tunney retired from the ring, married a Carnegie heiress, and entered the world of big business.

In 1974 heavyweight challenger George Foreman received five million dollars for getting beaten by the champion, Muhammad Ali, whose take from two fights that year was approximately eight million dollars—surely the best year's pay in the history of sports.

Traditionally, team players have to share. But in the case of Babe Ruth, the shares were anything but equally divided. Ruth towered over the rest of baseball. He was paid fifty-two thousand dollars for the

1922 season. That may not seem a high figure compared to today's pay scales, when a middling outfielder with a .285 batting average can command seventy-five thousand a year. In 1957 T. Coleman Andrews, the director of the Internal Revenue Service, calculated the ravages of inflation and the reduced buying-power of the dollar since 1922 and estimated that Ted Williams, the highest-paid baseball player at the time, would have had to receive one million dollars to equal the real value of Ruth's salary. In his heyday Ruth was paid more than the entire starting line-up of lesser teams. In 1927 he earned seventy thousand dollars. The next highest-paid player on the Yankees was Herb Pennock, who received seventeen thousand five hundred dollars. Lou Gehrig was paid eight thousand dollars. (Ten years later, after Ruth's retirement, Gehrig became the highest-paid player in all of baseball; he got thirty thousand dollars.) Ruth received one more raise. In 1930 he signed a contract for eighty thousand dollars, which was five thousand more than the salary of the President of the United States. One of the enduring legends of baseball holds that when Ruth was asked to justify earning more than President Hoover, he replied reasonably, "Why not? I had a better year than he did."

The story is almost certainly apocryphal, but the sentiment is true enough. The year 1930 was much better for Babe Ruth than it was for Herbert Hoover, Ruth set the style for wealthy sports figures, and no one carries on in his exuberant tradition better than today's basketball stars. The undisputed prince of the court is Wilt Chamberlain. In 1973 he was the highest-paid team athlete in America, earning four hundred fifty thousand dollars a year. He quit, accepting a hundred-fifty-thousand-dollar raise to become the highest-paid team coach in history. A confirmed sybarite, Chamberlain built himself a bachelor pad on a two-acre hilltop lot in West Los Angeles. He had originally planned to spend four hundred thousand dollars on his home, but as the nobility of Europe often found when building their palaces, housing costs have a way of getting out of hand. He now estimates that his hilltop snuggery is worth close to four million dollars. The appointments of Ursa Major, as he calls his home, are sumptuous by any standards. Never one for understated elegance, Chamberlain kicked off a storm of protest when he let it be known that the spread in the sunken conversation pit in his bedroom was fashioned from the muzzles of seventeen thousand Arctic wolves. Chamberlain, who bought up an entire year's sup-

KEN REGAN, CAMERA FIVE

Sports stars have become the new nabobs of America. Walt Frazier (left), the hard-running guard of the New York Knickerbockers who is paid $450,000 a year for his services, shows off his luxurious bachelor pad, featuring a massive circular bed covered in white mink. Joe Namath (above), the quarterback of the New York Jets, may be near the end of his playing days, but a perfumer is willing to pay him as much as five million dollars.

TED ROZUMALSKI, BLACK STAR

Babe Ruth (left) paved the way for giant salaries when he was paid more than the President because he had a better year (1930). Arnold Palmer (above) is a business conglomerate all by himself.

211

ply to be used as design accents in his home, defended himself by saying that the killing of the wolves was necessary to maintain Alaska's ecological balance.

The wealth for a sports figure comes not so much from his high salary as from the sale of equipment bearing his name and the endorsement of products often only dimly related to sports. When a tennis star goes out on the court at Forest Hills, he is a walking billboard. His sneakers, his racket, even the cup he drinks from are all paid advertisements for whatever products the athlete is pushing that day. The golfing professionals on the tour have their slacks, golf hats, and even their gloves carefully selected for them by the sponsoring manufacturer. The bigger the star, the more his income from such endorsements is likely to be until his actual winnings become an almost secondary consideration. In 1975 Joe Namath, the weak-kneed but strong-armed quarterback of the New York Jets, appeared to be nearing the end of a spectacular career. To help smooth the way he signed an eight-year contract with the Fabergé cosmetic company. Under the terms of the contract Namath will receive two hundred fifty thousand dollars a year for splashing Brut cologne over his resplendent face and extolling Fabergé's line of men's products. The contract has two six-year options, and Namath could eventually realize five million dollars on the deal.

The highest plateau of sports wealth, however, is the domain of the professional golfer. No other group in sports has been able to cash in on the ancillary moneymaking activities in the way golfers have. Johnny Miller is regarded as the finest middle-iron player in the sport today, but it is a wonder that he finds the time to play. Miller averaged two thousand five hundred in tournament winnings for every day he spent on the golf course in 1975; every day he spent working on endorsements in America, however, earned him twenty-eight thousand, while his overseas endorsements yielded him forty-two thousand a day. As one observer put it, players like Miller only play in tournaments "to keep the franchise warm."

Even so, Miller is merely a prince among kings. Far and away the richest figure in sporting history is Arnold Palmer, with Jack Nicklaus coming in second. Palmer, who now owns the country club where he was once denied the use of the pool facilities because his father was an employee, is many times a millionaire. Although he has not won a major tournament in several years, his income from various enterprises yields him an annual personal income of more than a million dollars, even after a savage tax bite. Palmer is himself an international corporation, grossing somewhere close to sixty million dollars a year. As befits his high station, the name of Arnold Palmer is associated with the products of some of the country's largest concerns, including Alcoa aluminum cookware, Coca-Cola, Marx toys, RCA, Lincoln-Mercury, and United Air Lines. It must be pleasant for the son of the country-club golf professional from Latrobe, Pennsylvania, to realize that he earns more than the president of any of those giant corporations.

THE SHOWMEN

The rise of the industrial age changed the shape of popular entertainment in America. Just as cottage industries gave way to sprawling factory complexes, the small entertainment of a century earlier turned into "show business." Troubadours, dressed up in striped pants, appeared in black face at traveling minstrel shows. Strolling players boarded railroad trains and crisscrossed the country in touring productions, taking culture to the hinterlands and bringing back gold for themselves.

A different breed of theatrical personality was born, the showman who found new sources of wealth in amusing an affluent young nation. One of the first and most famous was Phineas T. Barnum, who put mass entertainment on a scale that had hardly been seen since the circuses of Rome.

P. T. Barnum almost certainly never said, although it has been widely attributed to him, "There's a sucker born every minute." Even if he believed in the sentiment, the syntax was too crude for a man who took pride in his own refinement, as Barnum did. However, he did say, "The American people like to be humbugged," and amassed a considerable fortune proving his point.

In 1835 the twenty-five-year-old Barnum gave up his New York City grocery store to put on his first attraction in Niblo's Garden. Credulous New Yorkers paid out one thousand five hundred dollars to view a supposedly one-hundred-sixty-one-year-old black woman named Joice Heth, who was billed as George Washington's nurse. The next year Miss Heth died, and an autopsy revealed her to be a relative stripling in her eighties. But soon P. T. Barnum was working on a much grander project. In 1842 he opened the doors to his famous American Museum, which featured such humbug items as a "Feejee" mermaid and a woolly horse. When the crush of the crowds became too intense, Barnum put up a sign directing the people to that rarest of avises, the "Egress," and customers looking for it found themselves out on the street.

Barnum was a master of publicity. He transformed Charles S. Stratton, a twenty-five-inch midget from Bridgeport, Connecticut, into General Tom Thumb, one of the most famous attractions in American entertainment history. Some twenty million people in America and abroad paid to see the diminutive marvel whose career lasted nearly forty years and who earned, according to one biographer, "several million dollars." Tom became a solid if small citizen. He was a thirty-second-degree Mason and a Knight Templar, with a fine taste for expensive cigars and pedigreed horses. When Tom died of apoplexy in 1883, more than ten thousand mourners came to his funeral. Tom always drew a good crowd.

Barnum's greatest publicity accomplishment, however, was Jenny Lind, "the Swedish Nightingale." In 1849 Barnum was thirsting to be known as something more than a "mere showman," and opted for culture. Barnum contracted to pay Miss Lind a thousand dollars per concert if she would come to America. When she agreed, the mighty Barnum set about making the name of Jenny Lind, until then known in America only to a very few serious musicians, into a household word. He bombarded newspapers with publicity releases recounting the glory of her voice and the purity of her soul. The effectiveness of the eight-month build-up may be gauged by the fact that when Jenny Lind stepped off the S.S. *Atlantic* in New York City on September 1, 1850, some thirty thousand people, who had never heard her sing a note, were waiting at the pier.

Barnum built himself a pleasure dome that must have startled his neighbors in Bridgeport. Erected at a cost of one hundred fifty thousand dollars, Iranistan was a replica of King George IV's Brighton Pavilion which Barnum had once admired. A jumble of Turkish, Moorish, and Byzantine architecture, dotted with a series of minarets and towers, Iranistan was dominated by a gigantic dome reaching ninety feet above the ground. The structure, which contained its own astronomical observatory, was set in a fenced-off park where tame elk grazed. The life of a showman is never an easy one, and three times Barnum was pushed to the edge of bankruptcy; by the time of his death in 1891, however, he had amassed a fortune of some four million dollars.

Another legendary showman who found that the

P. T. Barnum poses with two of his most famous attractions, Lavinia Warren and General Tom Thumb. Commodore Nutt, another midget who posed with them, has been cut out of the picture. The Commodore loved little Lavinia, but she married Tom instead.

213

road to wealth could be somewhat precarious was Florenz Ziegfeld. He opened his first Follies in 1907, and for the next twenty years his name was synonymous with lavish spectacles and beautiful girls. Throughout his long career Ziegfeld served up a series of images to the American people that became part of the popular heritage: Sandow the Strong Man with his prodigious feats of strength; Gilda Gray dancing the shimmy; Anna Held, whose marvelously silky complexion was supposed to be the result of milk baths; and a moonbeam of a girl named Marilyn Miller. While enriching the American scene, Ziegfeld did not do badly himself. By 1922 he had a mansion on the Hudson and an estimated two million dollars in cash.

Ziegfeld was a moody, mercurial man who ruled his shows with autocratic perversity. He would

spend fifty thousand dollars to put on a single skit and then try to avoid paying composers their royalties. One afternoon in 1926 he hid in his office in the company of an amorous chorus girl while Victor Herbert raged outside about money owed him. Herbert turned purple and stormed out; shortly afterward he was felled by a stroke and died.

Ziegfeld lavished money and care on the long-legged ladies of the Follies, but he was notoriously stingy with the comedians, whom he considered a necessary evil in a musical comedy. He found W. C. Fields particularly unfunny and deducted the cost of the lost tennis balls Fields used in juggling from the comedian's salary.

Ziegfeld was persuaded to take his large cash holdings and buy stocks on margin in the boom market of 1927. When the market collapsed on Oc-

tober 29, 1929, his brokers frantically tried to reach him, but Ziegfeld was busy in court, locked in a suit over his refusal to pay the cost of a one-thousand-six-hundred-dollar electric sign for one of his shows. When he left court that afternoon, Florenz Ziegfeld had lost everything. He died three years later, more than a million dollars in debt.

During his career Ziegfeld had made a try at motion pictures, but he did not find Hollywood to his liking. The film capital bred its own great entertainment moguls—executives like Louis B. Mayer patrolled their studios with the hauteur of the true monarch. In fact many kings in recent history might have envied the power and money of a Hollywood studio chief. One of the most imperious was Darryl F. Zanuck, who had been a hard-driving one-hundred-and-twenty-five-dollar-a-week writer of

Rin Tin Tin movies at Warner Brothers until one day he was named executive producer and given a $4,875-a-week raise. He later became the ruler of 20th Century Fox. He was so autocratic that he once had to remonstrate with one of his associates as follows: "For God's sake, don't say 'yes' until I finish talking." One underling trying to outdo his fellows in fealty to the chief proclaimed, "When I die I want to be cremated and have my ashes sprinkled on Mr. Zanuck's driveway so his car won't skid."

Zanuck's remuneration was princely by any standards. In 1950 he received two hundred sixty thousand dollars in straight salary and had a portfolio of 20th Century Fox stock valued at $2,616,250. In 1950 his total income from salary and dividends came to $465,000. However, with his penchant for polo ponies and high living, he found it was not quite enough to make ends meet. "I manage," he said, "only by going a few thousand dollars into my savings each year. I won't change my way of life to save a few lousy bucks."

Zanuck was eventually forced into a reluctant retirement, taking with him the proceeds of his last great success, *The Longest Day*. An all-star recreation of the Normandy landing in World War II, the movie was a prodigious moneymaker that earned Zanuck six million dollars.

There is a nice symmetry to the story of Samuel Goldwyn. He arrived in America in 1896, an impoverished immigrant with twenty dollars in his pocket, and he died seventy-eight years later, leaving behind an estate of twenty million dollars. Goldwyn was a lone wolf. He was instrumental in the creation of Paramount and Metro-Goldwyn-Mayer, but left them both when he could not have absolute authority. He became an independent producer in 1922, annoucing, "It's dog eat dog in this business, and nobody's going to eat me."

The producer was famous for his somewhat antic use of the English language, and Hollywood columnists were always anxious to publish the latest "Goldwynism." Unfortunately, most of the more engaging ones, such as the legend that he once shrugged off a bad review of one of his pictures saying, "It rolls off my back like a duck," have been traced to other sources. One authentic Goldwynism, however, was a perfect reflection of the man: one day

Even in the worst of times the circus brought cheer to its audiences and cash to its promoters. The grand entry of the Ringling Bros. and Barnum & Bailey circus plays to a packed house under the canvas in Brooklyn in 1934.

a director warned him against filming a new play, saying "It's too caustic." "To hell with the cost," Goldwyn replied, "if it's a good picture we'll make it."

Goldwyn never did mind the cost when it meant quality. In 1947 he was unhappy with the progress of a movie called *The Bishop's Wife*. He ordered nearly one-million-dollars' worth of expenses written off, and started the film over again so that it came out the way he wanted. He was ruthless in securing the high style of film making that became known in the industry as "the Goldwyn touch." Author Ben Hecht said he dealt with writers like an "irritated man shaking a slot machine."

Goldwyn usually managed to shake successes out

of his staff, and he lived like a nabob on his seven-acre estate in Beverly Hills. His pride and joy was a lush croquet field where he royally entertained the greats of Hollywood, cheating them unmercifully whenever he could get away with it. Life included Sam Goldwyn out in 1974, and the last of the great Hollywood moguls passed from the scene.

THE LORDS OF THE PRESS

The rise of the large-circulation popular press in the nineteenth century created a new kind of millionaire, the press lord. The first great baron of the penny press in this country was the dour Scot James Gordon Bennett, who founded the New York *Herald*

Louis B. Mayer, the highest salaried man in America in 1943, sits flanked by the stable of stars at Metro-Goldwyn-Mayer. The studio boasted, with what for Hollywood was only moderate exaggeration, that it had under contract "more stars than there are in heaven." Every studio had its own galaxy of performers, but none could compete with MGM for depth of talent. The star system was expensive and could not survive the ravages of post-World War II economics, but while it lasted, it gave a lovely light. From left to right, first row: James Stewart, Margaret Sullavan, Lucille Ball, Hedy Lamarr, Katharine Hepburn, Mayer, Greer Garson, Irene Dunne, Susan Peters, Ginny Sims, Lionel Barrymore. Second row: Harry James, Brian Donlevy, Red Skelton, Mickey Rooney, William Powell, Wallace Beery, Spencer Tracy, Walter Pidgeon, Robert Taylor, Jean-Pierre Aumont, Lewis Stone, Gene Kelly, Butch Jenkins. Third row: Tommy Dorsey, George Murphy, Jean Rogers, James Craig, Donna Reed, Van Johnson, Fay Bainter, Marsha Hunt, Ruth Hussey, Marjorie Main, Robert Benchley. Fourth row: Dame May Whitty, Reginald Owen, Keenan Wynn, Diana Lewis, Marilyn Maxwell, Esther Williams, Ann Richards, Martha Linden, Lee Bowman, Richard Carlson, Mary Astor. Fifth row: Blanche Ring, Sara Haden, Fay Holden, Bert Lahr, Frances Gifford, June Allyson, Richard Whorf, Frances Rafferty, Spring Byington, Connie Gilchrist, Gladys Cooper. Sixth row: Ben Blue, Chill Wills, Keye Luke, Barry Nelson, Desi Arnaz, Henry O'Neill, Bob Crosby, Rags Ragland.

in 1835. The *Herald* put some zip into contemporary journalism, and under Bennett led the way in aggressive reporting. His packet boats raced out into the Atlantic to intercept the incoming sailing ships for news. If necessary, he would go even farther for a story. It was the *Herald* that sent Stanley to darkest Africa to find Livingstone.

In 1868 the *Herald* passed into the hands of James Gordon Bennett, Jr., whose chief interests did not lie in journalism. Although nominally in command of the paper, James, Jr., took his million-dollar-a-year income and devoted himself to being the absolute playboy of the Western world. He earned himself, if nothing else, a minor footnote in the history of social scandal when he participated in the last known duel in New York City. The ludicrous affair grew out of a minor scandal that rocked the elevated reaches of the city's social elite. It seems that Mr. Bennett arrived at a New Year's Day reception at the home of his fiancée, Caroline May, in a vigorous partying mood. After consuming prodigious quantities of wine, Bennett proceeded to relieve himself in the astonished lady's fireplace. Mr. Bennett, his overcoat, and his top hat were all flung out into the street, and the next day Caroline's brother Frederick waylaid Bennett outside the Union Club and attacked the publisher with a horse-

whip. Bennett challenged young May to a duel, and the two men repaired a few days later to Slaughter Gap, Maryland. Both were excellent shots and fortunately settled the matter by firing in the air.

Bennett was always the master of the grand gesture. On a bet, he once coaxed a cavalry officer to ride his horse into the library of the august Reading Room, Newport's most distinguished men's club. When the club's board of directors chastised Bennett, the publishing scion was annoyed by what he considered their stuffy attitude. He purchased a huge plot of ground nearby and airily summoned architect Stanford White to conjure up the magnificent Newport Casino, which took its place as the most extravagantly elegant club in Newport, or just about anywhere else for that matter.

Bennett had a passion for mutton chops, and particularly savored those served by a small restaurant in Monte Carlo. He arrived for lunch one day and found every table taken. He marched over to the manager and bought the place on the spot for forty thousand dollars. As the new owner, he had a table cleared, and sat down to his lunch. After the meal Bennett was feeling mellow. As he departed he tipped the waiter most generously. He handed the astonished servitor the deed to the restaurant, with the proviso that there must always be a table

Publisher William Randolph Hearst owned seven castles around the world, but his restless spirit was always happiest at San Simeon. More than an estate, San Simeon was a kingdom where Hearst could reign supreme amidst the jumble of art treasures he loved to collect. Hearst struggled to bring back the past and create another Versailles. The opulence of the swimming pool (left) might have startled the "Sun King" himself. Italian artisans labored over the marble and gold mosaic pleasure spa for more than three years. The pool cost more than one million dollars.

Despite the grand appointments, luncheon was informal. On the opposite page Hearst and his faithful mistress, the actress Marion Davies, entertain their weekend guests. As seen in an aerial view (below), San Simeon seems a remote fairy-tale principality. But the isolation was not complete. Hearst kept in constant contact with his newspaper empire, and at any hour a message might be dispatched beginning, "The Chief says . . ."

reserved for him and that mutton chops would forever be on the menu.

William Randolph Hearst took Bennett's idea for a penny newspaper and parlayed it into a vast publishing empire over which he ruled as a supreme autocrat. At the time of his death his publishing holdings alone were valued at one hundred sixty million dollars and included eighteen newspapers, nine magazines, and a clutch of related news-gathering enterprises. In 1922 Hearst newspapers showed a net profit of twelve million dollars. Even so, it was not quite enough to keep pace with the press lord's spending. It was estimated that with Hearst spending a million dollars a year on art and antiques alone, his annual personal expenditures totaled something close to fifteen million dollars. In spite of his profitable newspapers, magazines, mining, and real-estate interests, and a huge inheritance, Hearst, according to his biographer W. A. Swanberg, "actually lived from hand to mouth." He regularly pilfered his own till for ready cash and left standing instructions for the New York *Journal* to send him twenty-five thousand dollars in spending money every week.

In the 1930's his profligate spending caused a serious cash crunch within the Hearst empire, and he lost a degree of control over his own properties. He remained the despair of his business department all of his gaudy life. Although he owned seven castles around the world, he was always happiest at San Simeon, the most incredible private residence ever constructed in America. Hearst spent thirty million dollars on San Simeon, which may be compared with such royal keeps as Louis XIV's Versailles and Frederick the Great's Sans Souci. As Swanberg has pointed out, San Simeon represented the publisher's personal revolt against history. It was "a kingdom that was hermetically sealed against the republic that surrounded it." Hearst's domain began with a fifty-mile strip of oceanfront property midway between Los Angeles and San Francisco, and stretched into the mountains, encompassing a total of two hundred forty thousand acres. The construction of the gardens alone cost a reported one million

LONDON DAILY EXPRESS—PICTORIAL PARADE

WIDE WORLD PHOTOS

Three press lords go about the day. Hearst (left) scans daily reports in his retreat at San Simeon. Canadian-born mogul Lord Roy Thomson (right, above), who only likes to spend money buying more newspapers, saves a few shillings taking the subway to work. Malcolm Forbes (below) gazes down from the basket of a balloon that serves both his pleasure and his business.

dollars. And like the rest of the estate, these were never finished. Squads of full-time landscape architects and gardeners were kept at work, altering and improving the floral displays. While on a trip Hearst was enchanted by the smell of daphne. He wired his chief gardener, Nigel Keep, to plant a row of the aromatic shrub all around the main castle. Keep had to buy up every single available daphne in the state of California at a cost of twelve thousand dollars to fulfill the chief's wish. Once, Keep and his crew worked under floodlights through the night so that Hearst's guests could awaken on Easter morning to see the castle surrounded by thousands of blooming Easter lilies.

Hearst's weekend parties were legendary. Guests usually arrived on Friday night by private train, and could see the lights illuminating the twin towers of the main house from miles away. The weekends were active. Those who wanted to play tennis were likely to find themselves on a court with Bill Tilden or Alice Marble. The more adventurous were dispatched on horseback picnics, champagne and caviar having been trucked ahead. If the weather was not fine, guests could poke about the main house and view Hearst's collection of antiques. (One dealer alone provided the avid collector with eight million dollars' worth of artifacts.) San Simeon was an interior designer's nightmare, an eclectic jumble of pieces culled from the great houses of Europe.

Dinner at San Simeon was a raffish gathering of actors, newspaper people, and international celebrities who had wangled an invitation to the great house. There was one major restriction: guests were permitted only a single cocktail before dinner and were forbidden to drink in their own rooms. These prudish rules required his more hard-drinking guests to resort to evasive tactics. Actress Carole Lombard recalled that she and Hearst's mistress, Marion Davies, used to repair to the ladies' room for a convivial cup. "That's one place Hearst couldn't get at us," she said.

Lord Roy Thomson, a Toronto barber's son, shares Hearst's acquisitive instinct for buying up newspaper properties. Of the four hundred seventy companies Lord Thomson owns, one hundred eighty are newspapers. While the world-famous *London Times* is in his stable, Thomson's specialty is buying up small-town papers in such unlikely communities as Punta Gorda, Florida, and Kamloops, Canada. Lord Thomson finds that small newspapers can be perfect targets for a corporate take-over. Generally poorly managed, they can often be made more cost-efficient and turned into money spinners. "Anybody who can lose money with a small-town newspaper is a near genius," Thomson says. "It's a matter of how much you're going to make."

Although Lord Thomson is reportedly worth about three hundred million dollars, he is notoriously parsimonious in his personal spending. He flies only tourist class and carefully weighs his own baggage before each flight to make sure he does not spend a penny for overweight. Once on the road, he favors drip-dry shirts, which he washes out in his hotel room himself.

Malcolm Forbes may own a drip-dry shirt, but he certainly does not do his own laundry. Forbes is not cut in the mold of the man who makes millions and watches the pennies. The editor and publisher of the successful business magazine that bears his family's name, Forbes actively enjoys his considerable wealth. He became interested in Fabergé *objets d'art*, and now owns perhaps the largest private collection outside Russia—some one hundred twenty items valued at close to five million dollars. He likes historic old houses and snaps them up as if they were pieces in a Monopoly game. When he flies from place to place around the world in his company-owned DC 9, named, naturally enough, "Capitalist Tool," he can lay his head in any number of historic structures. He owns the Palais Mendoub in Tangier, the venerable Chateau de Balleroy in Normandy, and the Old Battersea House, in London, built by Sir Christopher Wren in 1699. For relaxation he can nip off to Zane Grey's former fishing camp in Tahiti.

Forbes is adept at mixing business with pleasure. He enjoys motorcycling and has turned that into a business: he is co-owner of the largest motorcycle dealership in America. He is also fond of hot-air ballooning. When he rises up into the sky aboard a balloon, the name of FORBES appears on the bag, which therefore becomes a business expense.

Playwright Neil Simon found himself strangely disenchanted with his newly found wealth. "I never suddenly screamed, 'now we can do the things and buy the things we've always wanted,' " he said. "Money brings some happiness. But, after a certain point, it just brings more money." Perhaps because Forbes is an old hand at wealth—he says with more modesty than accuracy that he owes his success to "sheer ability, spelled i-n-h-e-r-i-t-a-n-c-e"—he has a different view. For him money brings the chance to "do what is exciting to do if you could do what you would like to do."

ONE OF THE ADVANTAGES OF BEING RICH IS THAT YOU CAN INDULGE ALMOST ANY WHIM. THESE CARS WERE HALF BURIED IN A WHEAT FIELD BY STANLEY MARSH, A SUCCESSFUL, IF ECCENTRIC, BUSINESSMAN IN AMARILLO, TEXAS. HE JUST LIKES TO SEE HOW PEOPLE LOOK AND HEAR WHAT THEY SAY WHEN THEY SEE HIS "CADILLAC RANCH."

In the design of beds and baths some of the rich find scope for their most extravagant fancies. The picture above shows the children's bathroom in the London home of Richard Gangel, an associate of Bernie Cornfeld during the halcyon days of Investors Overseas Services. Designed to look like the interior of a Turkish tent, it has twin toilets with velvet covers and arms, beneath a gilded coronet.

At upper right on the opposite page is a solid silver bed designed for an Indian rajah. When he lay on the bed, his weight caused the nude ladies to wave their fans and whisks, thus cooling him and keeping the flies away.

At bottom right on the opposite page, Sarah Bernhardt reclines in the Turkish nook of her Paris apartment. The furs of bear, beaver, tiger, moose, and jaguar all gave sensuous delight to the Divine Sarah.

Directly to the right on the opposite page is a bed that belonged to La Paiva, a famous French courtesan of the Second Empire. It was carved out of solid mahogany and weighed one and a half tons.

KOLLAR—CHRISTOFLE, PARIS

COLLECTION OCHSE, PARIS

One of the ways in which the rich are different is that they have a wider choice of pets. On the opposite page: Irénée Du Pont, retired president of E.I. Du Pont de Nemours & Co., was photographed with an iguana in 1957 on his estate in Cuba. He trained his iguanas to come on call and stand at attention. Below: On his estate outside of St. Louis, August A. Busch, Jr., president of the Anheuser-Busch brewing company, kept a zoo that included not only this elephant but camels, mules, and buffalo.

Rich people's pets enjoy their own special advantages. Mrs. Marjorie Merriweather Post's schnauzer (right) slept on a bed that once belonged to Belgium's royal family. The rich dog's life at a resort is, of course, more informal. At Lyford Cay in the Caribbean, where thatched houses are in style, a miniature hut (below, right) is reserved for Lady Anne Orr-Lewis' terrier, Mr. Boffin.

Mᴿ BOFFIN
LYFORD CAY

Miss Alice Brayton, a spinster member of Newport society, inherited from her father an estate at nearby Portsmouth and a passion for topiary sculpture. Her garden included a menagerie of animals cunningly clipped out of privet. The giraffe at left has been in place for sixty years and, like the whimsical bear below it, requires a skilled gardener to prune it without losing either the shape or the expression. The estate, called Green Animals, is now open to the public.

The building of odd structures is a favorite preoccupation of
the rich. The seven-story stone edifice on the opposite page,
known as Horton's Tower, was built by a Mr. Sturt in Dor-
set, the heart of the English "folly" country, in the eighteenth century. He thought he might use it as an observatory
but never did.

Right: The Chinese Dowager Empress Tz'u Hsi built
his marble "boat" in a lake on the grounds of her summer palace near Peking. It served her as a pleasant place to
drink tea on warm afternoons, and now serves the Communists as an object lesson in the wicked waste of the old
regime.

Above: This brick maze was built in 1957 for Armand G.
Erpf, a Wall Street financier, on his estate in the Catskills. It
was inspired by the Greek myth of the labyrinth at Knossos
in Crete, where the Minotaur devoured Greek youths and
maidens until he was slain by the hero Theseus. In the central chambers of the maze stand sculptures of Daedalus, the
craftsman who built the original labyrinth, and of the
Minotaur.

Right: At Niles, Illinois, a suburb of Chicago, an industrialist named Robert A. Ilg built this half-size replica of
the Leaning Tower of Pisa in 1932. After living in it during
the summers for seventeen years, he was so far off balance
that he moved to a level place in California.

Labels on statues: RICHARD BARILE · MARIO BALESTRO · MELINDA BOIARDO · RUGGERO BOIARDO III RO · MAURICE GRASENZI · · BOIARDO ·

It is easy enough for the rich to adorn their gardens with conventional sculpture, but it takes some imagination to produce the arrays of statuary shown on these pages. The group in the picture above stands by the driveway leading to the estate of Ruggiero Boiardo, a middle-rank Cosa Nostra leader, in Livingston, New Jersey. Boiardo himself sits astride a horse in the best tradition of the Sicilian don. Ranged about him are busts of members of his extended family, carved of wood or molded of plaster.

"Lord" Timothy Dexter, a merchant, looked farther afield for the subjects of the statues that he placed about his mansion at Newburyport, Massachusetts, in the early years of the nineteenth century. On the central arch stand Washington, Adams, and Jefferson. Other figures were listed by Dexter as follows: "Doctor Franklin, John hen Cock, and Mr. hamelton and Rouffous king and John Jea—2 grenadars on the top of the hous, 4 Lions below; 1 Eagel *is* on the Coupulow, one Lamb to lay down with one of the Lions—one younecorne, one Dogg, Addam and Eave in the Garden—one horse."

When a wealthy Italian conceives some really wild idea, he is likely to give it expression in his garden. The sphinx at upper left and the face on the opposite page are both among the fountains of the Villa d'Este at Tivoli. Cardinal Ippolito II d'Este, the sixteenth-century prince of the church for whom they were built, delighted in the splash of waters on hot summer afternoons, as have many visitors since his time.

At about the same period the fantastic sculptures in the two pictures at right were carved out of natural outcroppings of rock in the garden of the Villa Orsini at Bomarzo. The mysterious aristocrat for whom they were created, Vicino Orsini, seems to have had in mind a Sacred Wood, inhabited by giants and monsters. In the picture at top a dragon does battle with mastiffs; at right is a mythological giantess balancing an urn of flowers.

7. WEALTH FROM THE INDUSTRIAL REVOLUTION

THE LUNAR SOCIETY

Dr. Erasmus Darwin, the grandfather of Charles, did not believe in traveling light. When he set out from his home at Lichfield in Staffordshire to make the rounds of his patients, he expected to spend much of the day in his carriage, and he equipped it accordingly. In front of him, a table served for eating and writing alike. At his left was a hamper of food and drink. To his right were shelves of books. As he drove from call to call Dr. Darwin put every moment to use. He was not only a physician but a botanist and zoologist, a poet, an inventor, and something of a philosopher. He set forth his ideas in long didactic poems that were greatly admired in the later decades of the eighteenth century, when he wrote them. In one of these, a treatise on the vegetable kingdom entitled *The Botanic Garden*, he speculated on the love life and conscious behavior of plants. In another, called *Zoonomia, or the Laws of Organic Life*, he advanced many of the ideas about evolution that, when stated in sober prose and scholarly form, made his grandson a great figure in the history of science.

Darwin the poet was not restrained by the rigidities of systematic science. In 1789 when he was writing *The Botanic Garden* he asked his friend James Watt for material about his steam engine, designed for pumping water out of mines. Watt obliged but remarked, "I know not how steam-engines come among the plants. . . ." This is how Darwin described the engine (shown in the sketch opposite):

Bade with cold streams the quick expansion stop,
And sunk the immense of vapour to a drop.—

◀ PRECEDING PAGES: **The glow of the blast furnaces at Coalbrookdale heralds the Industrial Revolution. This scene was painted by Philippe de Loutherbourg.**
SCIENCE MUSEUM, COURTESY OF HAMLYN PUBLISHERS , LONDON

Press'd by the ponderous air the Piston falls
Resistless, sliding through it's iron walls;
Quick moves the balanced beam, of giant-birth,
Wields his large limbs, and nodding shakes the earth.

Once every month Dr. Darwin drove fifteen miles to Birmingham for a meeting of the Lunar Society, so named because it met on the Monday nearest the full moon. As Dr. Darwin was its guiding spirit, so Watt was to be, in the eyes of history, its most famous member. But among the others, who never numbered more than twelve, were some of the most remarkable minds of eighteenth-century England: Josiah Wedgwood, the potter; Matthew Boulton, the manufacturer and Watt's partner in the development of the steam engine; Joseph Priestley, the discoverer of oxygen; James Keir, the Scottish chemist; Richard Lovell Edgeworth, the educational theorist; and Thomas Day, one of the great English eccentrics. It is not recorded that the members of the Lunar Society had any special interest in the moon except as a source of light for the drive back to their homes at night. But they were interested in everything else that came over the intellectual horizon of their day. Dr. Darwin, for one, expounded ideas on air travel, animal camouflage, artesian wells, auroras, birds, canals, prisons, gill slits in human embryos, the Portland vase, steam turbines, water closets, and dozens of other topics. Wedgwood, the queen's potter, was also a builder of canals and an experimenter with agricultural fertilizers. The members of the Lunar Society even lent their sober attention to a project of their fellow member Thomas Day who, failing to find the perfect wife, adopted two foundling girls and set about raising them to embody his ideals of womanhood. (When it came time to choose a wife, Day found them both deficient and married someone else.)

WEDGWOOD

WEDGWOOD

WEDGWOOD

DARWIN

WATT

BOULTON

The Lunar Society invites comparison with the other, more famous intellectual circle of that time, which revolved around Dr. Samuel Johnson in London. Darwin and Johnson were alike in many ways: big, shambling men with clumsy bodies and pock-marked faces, brilliant in their conversation, caustic in their comments. Accounts of the few occasions when they met leave a reader with the impression of two huge animals circling each other warily. The fact is that the interests of their two groups were far apart: the Johnson coterie in letters and art; the Lunar Society in science and technology. Therein lies the reason why the Lunar Society, which had no Boswell and kept no records, was nevertheless far more influential on the course of history. It was a seedbed of that great overturn in human life that is called, with some oversimplification, the Industrial Revolution.

As with every great flowering of human genius, it is appropriate to ask, Why then? and Why there? The men who met in Birmingham were the heirs to the surge of scientific discovery which had begun with Copernicus and reached a culmination in Newton, but which had yet to be applied to the material welfare of humanity. They were caught up in the libertarian political ideas of Rousseau, and in economics the doctrines of laissez faire developed by the French physiocrats and expounded by Adam Smith. On a practical level, the flood tide of prosperity in oceanic trade had brought to the English upper and upper-middle classes a prosperity that enabled men like Edgeworth to devote their lives to unremunerative studies and made it possible for others like Boulton to find investors for their manufacturing enterprises. At the same time the expulsion of yeoman farmers from the estates of the great landowners provided a ready source of labor for the new factories.

These conditions may help to explain, Why then. But, Why there? Why in England, and not, say, in France, where the world of ideas was in even greater ferment? The French were ahead of the English in harnessing water for power; at one time France had the greatest waterworks in the world, but they were

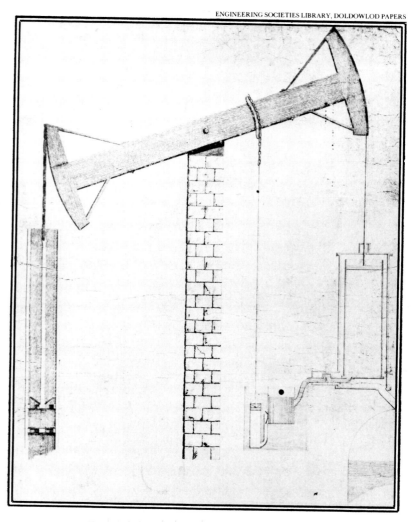

These two inventions launched the Industrial Revolution. At top is James Watt's own sketch of the steam engine, which he designed about 1765 to pump water out of coal mines. At bottom is a model of a water-powered spinning machine, which was used in Richard Arkwright's factories. Of the four members of the Lunar Society who appear on the opposite page, the two at left are seen in medallions made at Wedgwood's potteries.

JAMES REYNOLDS, *DIAGRAMS OF THE STEAM ENGINE*, LONDON, 1848

used to run the fountains in the gardens of the royal palace of Versailles. Instead of being applied to the invention of looms and pumps, French technology was squandered on the works of elaborate automatons, which were nothing but toys to delight the ladies of the court. Something was lacking in the political climate.

Why, then, in the Midlands, and not in London, where all the wealth and power and intellect of England had long had its center? There were several good, practical reasons. When the combined inventions of Hargreaves, Arkwright, Crompton, and Cartwright produced power looms for the weaving of cotton, water power was needed to run them. That meant building factories near convenient streams, such as those in the Midlands. Later, when Watt's steam engine was adapted for the textile mills, the power source needed was coal, and that, too, was to be found in the Midlands. But there were less material reasons. In London the hand of government and ancient tradition lay heavily on new enterprise of any kind. Parliament ruled for the benefit of the landowners and, to a smaller extent, of the monied interest and the nabobs, who had come home rich from the Indian Empire. Business enterprise loves freedom from political regulation, and this was what the new entrepreneurs found in the Midlands. Because the Midland towns had no royal charters or ancient privileges, businessmen had free

In the early nineteenth century steam was used to power the railroad locomotive. This cutaway drawing of 1848 shows how hot gasses from the firebox ran through pipes in a boiler. The surrounding water, heated to steam, drove the pistons, which turned the driving wheels.

rein to build where they wanted, hire whom they wanted, and generally do as they pleased. Labor and capital were, of course, needed, and neither was plentiful in this backward country. But the laborers who were being evicted from their ancestral farms could be brought to the factories. And the London capital market could be tapped, if need be, as Wedgwood did for his pottery and Boulton for his engineworks. But, it now appears, most of the capital that financed the Industrial Revolution was generated directly out of the new industries.

A revealing case history of how it was done was uncovered by T. S. Ashton, author of *The Industrial Revolution*, in the diaries of ironmaster Samuel Walker of Rotherham. Here are some entries:

1741. In or about October or November of the same year, Saml. and Aaron Walker built an Air Furnace in the old nailer's smithy, on the backside of Saml. Walker's cottage at Grenoside, making some small additions thereto, and another little hutt or two, slating with sods etc., with a small Garth [yard] walled in: and after rebuilding the chimney or stacks once, and the furnace once or more, began to proceed a little, Saml. Walker teaching the school at Grenoside, and Aaron Walker making nails and mowing and shearing, etc., part of his time.

1743. Aaron Walker now began to be pretty much imploy'd, and had 4 shillings a week to live upon. . . .

1745. This year Saml. Walker, finding business increase, was obliged to give up his school, and built himself a house at the end of the old cottage, then thought he was fixed for life; then we allowed ourselves ten shillings a week each for wages to maintain our families.

After accumulating a capital of four hundred pounds in the nail business, and borrowing one hundred fifty pounds from others, the Walker brothers built a casting house and, in 1748, a steel furnace. By 1774 their capital had increased to £62,500 and, after windfall profits from the manufacture of guns during the American Revolution, to £128,000.

On a larger scale this was the story of the Darbys of Coalbrookdale. In 1709, on a little stream that ran through coal beds in Shropshire, Abraham Darby had built a furnace for the smelting of iron with coke, and by the time of the Lunar Society, the Darby furnaces were filling the sky with a glow that looked to some visitors like the fires of the nether world. On a window pane of one factory in Scotland, Robert Burns scratched these lines:

We cam na here to view your warkes,
In hopes to be mair wise,
But only, lest we gang to Hell,
It may be nae surprise.

It was to pump water from flooded coal mines that James Watt perfected the steam engine; only later was it made to turn the wheels of the textile industry.

Thus it was that the Industrial Revolution occurred in the half century between 1760 and 1810, in the backward province of an offshore island of the Eurasian continent. Around Birmingham and Manchester the factories sprang up along rivers and amid coal fields. Workers poured in from all over England, and then from Scotland and Ireland, to tend the flying shuttles of the new looms and to live in the makeshift cottages that were thrown up in the shadows of the mills. In the dark cellars of these instant slums, as the Industrial Revolution unfolded, the death rate soared, and from them children six and eight years old went forth to work at the machines. The green hills of the Midlands were stripped bare to yield their coal, and the vegetation that remained turned black and dry from the soot of belching smokestacks.

But this did not happen at once. To the benevolent manufacturers who belonged to the Lunar Society the future into which they were leading mankind looked something like utopia. In contrast to the dirty, smoky kilns at which potters had worked before, Josiah Wedgwood's plant was light and clean, and kept in strictest order. He got his workers under one roof, not because any machines required it, as they did in the case of textile mills, but because the work could be broken up and organized more efficiently. Division of labor, he demonstrated, was no less important than machine production in bringing about the Industrial Revolution. He called his works Etruria, after the "Etruscan" designs which had come into fashion since the excavation of Pompeii and which Wedgwood adapted for his finest china. He might be seen stomping along the rows of workmen on his wooden leg, inspecting pots and plates; once when he found a flawed plate, he wrote on the workman's bench with chalk, "This won't do for Jos. Wedgwood."

Like Wedgwood in his pottery, Boulton in his engineworks at Soho, near Birmingham, required skilled craftsmen to make metal parts to tolerances not known before. Watt's engine had failed on its early trials because, until Boulton joined him, no one seemed able to make a piston that came within a quarter of an inch of fitting its cylinder. Boulton knew the importance of what he was doing in his engineworks. One of his visitors, James Boswell, never forgot what the manufacturer told him: "I sell here, sir, what all the world desires to have— Power." But Boulton clung to the belief that the machine could be put to use within a paternalistic economic order symbolized by Soho, where on family holidays the workmen paraded behind a band, to dine on whole roasted oxen.

The cotton mills proved him wrong. No skill was needed to tend the spinning bobbins; a woman could do it as well as a man, and a child as well as a woman. Success rewarded the owner who hired the cheapest labor, built the least expensive housing for his workers, and kept his looms running day and night.

Would a wise and humane society, if it had been able to foresee the price of "progress," have tried to halt the Industrial Revolution? Evidently not, for in the two centuries since that time other parts of the world have had the same choice, with the English example before them, and all have chosen to take the course that England took. Each country paid the price, during the time of transition, in disruption and disease, in the shackling of human rhythms to the rhythm of the machine, in the loss of rural peace and the ravage of fair lands. None held back, because all knew that beyond the dark valley of industrial transition lay wealth no man had dreamed of. Now, for the first time, man could use nature as a stockpile of raw materials to fashion what seemed then like an unlimited supply of the goods he wanted.

But that was in the future. The first profits of the new factories went to the men who had the wit and the enterprise to build them and run them and find markets for their products. The new monarch of the economic world was the manufacturer. In the century that followed, he and his ilk, in England and Europe, and most of all in the United States, would pile up fortunes to surpass any before them.

RICHARD ARKWRIGHT

The prototype of this new fortune-builder was Richard Arkwright. The youngest of thirteen children, Arkwright had gone to work as a barber's apprentice

at the town of Bolton in Lancashire, where the spinning and weaving of cotton was a cottage industry. In many of the cottages the yarn was being spun on a jenny, which James Hargreaves had invented in about 1764 and named for his wife Jane. The trouble with the jenny was that it spun a loose yarn, which could be used by the weaver for half of his work—the horizontal weft—but not for the interlacing threads of the warp. In 1769 Arkwright applied for and was granted a patent for a frame that used rollers to make a coarser but tighter yarn that could be used in the whole process of weaving. Because the frame required more power than human muscles could supply, the cottage industry was doomed. Thenceforth cotton would be spun and woven in mills powered at first by water and later by steam.

Whether Arkwright himself invented the frame or got it from John Kay, a clockmaker whom he had hired and then fired, was the subject of a lawsuit that lasted for four years. In the end Arkwright lost his patent, but it made little difference to him because by that time he was the biggest and richest

Richard Arkwright, first of the great millowners, had his portrait painted with a model of the spinning jenny that made him rich. To house the workers who thronged into the manufacturing centers, instant slums were created. Time and the photographer's art have lent a certain beauty to these rows of houses at Newcastle-upon-Tyne.

millowner in England. In 1785 the former barber was made a baronet and eagerly assumed the trappings that went with the title. Two years later the Manchester *Mercury* was able to report: "On Sunday last Sir Richard Arkwright, knight, High Sheriff of the County, arrived at Derby, accompanied by his javelin men . . . dressed in the richest liveries ever seen here. . . . The trumpeters were mounted on grey horses, and elegantly dressed in scarlet and gold."

Beneath such finery, Richard Arkwright looked like what he was: a shrewd, ruthless, hard-driving manufacturer. During the next century the world would come to know many like him. With his sharp eyes, his heavy jowls, and his swollen belly, he might have been the model for the later American caricature of the robber baron.

THE FIRST AMERICAN MILLOWNERS

The opportunities opened up by the Industrial Revolution in England did not go unnoticed by men of enterprise in the American colonies. But before they could bring the factory system across the Atlantic, they had to get around the obstacles placed in its path by the British government. Until the American Revolution, Britain forbade the manufacture of many articles in the colonies in order to preserve the market for British exports. After that Revolution, British law forbade the export of machines or designs for machines, and even refused to permit the emigration of skilled labor.

The first significant breach in this protectionist wall was made by a young Englishman named Samuel Slater. As a boy, Slater had been apprenticed to Jedediah Strutt, a partner and financial backer of Arkwright, and had risen to a position in which he had superintended the building of the latest Arkwright mill. In 1789 he assumed the guise of a farmer and boarded a ship for New York, carrying in his head a complete set of plans for a textile factory on the Arkwright model.

Slater quickly found a backer in Moses Brown of Providence, the possessor of a family fortune made

in ocean trade. The Browns had been one of the early New England families to get into shipping and one of the first to get out. Even before the Revolution, Moses and his brothers had begun shifting their interests ashore, establishing a cannon forge that supplied the Continental Army. By 1789 Moses Brown had given up active business and was making atonement for the profits his family had made in the slave trade by leading the Abolitionist movement in Rhode Island. At the same time, he had put some money into a spinning mill, with small success, and when Slater sought him out, he was glad to offer him a partnership. The mill that Slater built was so successful that within a year it was turning out more yarn than local weavers could use. Brown was warning Slater: "Thee must shut down thy gates or thee will spin all my farms into cotton yarn." However, wider markets were found, and the enterprise was soon swelling the fortune that went to endow Brown University.

FRANCIS CABOT LOWELL

Though built on the Arkwright model, the Brown mill was not established on the Arkwright scale. Neither were any of the other small spinning mills that began to dot the New England landscape in following years. It remained for Francis Cabot Lowell of Boston to establish the fully developed factory system in the United States. Lowell had begun a career in shipping, but because of the maritime depression brought on by Jefferson's embargo, he was looking for another field of opportunity. In 1812 he visited England and spent a good deal of time in the textile mills, studying their latest machines and methods. It is likely that he also visited the mills operated by Robert Owen at New Lanark in Scotland. Owen was not only a successful businessman but a social reformer who had proved that he could make a profit while providing good houses and good schools for his working families.

When Francis Cabot Lowell returned to Boston, he had in his mind both an understanding of the latest methods used by the English manufacturers and a conviction that a textile factory did not have to be a dark, satanic mill. With capital raised mostly from Boston shipping families, Lowell and his brother-in-law, Patrick Tracy Jackson, formed the Boston Manufacturing Company and acquired a site on the Charles River in Waltham, Massachusetts.

Lowell was not a reformer like Owen, but he had found a solution for the problem of labor, which had kept most New England mills small and left them at the mercy of part-time workers, who came and went as the crops and their fancies dictated. There was no supply of displaced agricultural workers in New England, and Massachusetts farmers were not about to send their wives or children to work in factories where they might be exposed to injury, illness, or the devil's temptations. Lowell's plan was to build rows of dormitories, put a woman of good character in charge of each, and invite the farmers to inspect the premises. If the farmers would let their daughters work, Lowell would provide them with a clean, bright place to live, good food, Christian supervision, and the opportunity to earn a dowry before they married.

Boston Manufacturing was a quick success, both in its textile operation and perhaps even more in its machine shop, which was soon supplying other mills with equipment. In 1823 a bigger plant was built on the Merrimack River, along with the new town of Lowell. By that time Francis Cabot Lowell was dead, at the age of forty-two, but his visions were realized in the town that took his name. The new factory was filled with industrious young women who found the mill work an agreeable way to earn some money of their own between the time they finished school and the time they married. The hours were long—as much as six days a week and twelve hours a day—but the work was not hard and the pay was good ($3.50 a week, of which only $1.25 went for board and room). One of the "young ladies of Lowell," Lucy Larcom, who later became a writer and editor of some renown, reported that some of the girls had time to cultivate window boxes and read books while they kept one eye on the dancing bobbins. They were a far cry from the ignorant, woebegone children who grew up in the mills of Manchester and Birmingham; after work some of them earnestly attended lectures by such visiting luminaries as Emerson and Whittier.

Even that dyspeptic tourist Charles Dickens, who

Francis Cabot Lowell, pioneer of the factory system in the United States, and his wife Hannah Jackson had their silhouettes cut during the heyday of that art. He made the family fortune, but she contributed the chin.

disliked the United States with almost as much fervor as he abhorred the bleak house of English industrialism, could find no fault when he visited Lowell in 1841. He wrote: "I cannot recall or separate one young face that gave me a painful impression; not one young girl whom, assuming it to be a matter of necessity that she should gain her daily bread by the labour of her hands, I would have removed from those works if I had had the power."

But the idyll was not to last much beyond the middle of the century. In the aftermath of the Irish potato famine in the 1840's, the first great wave of immigrants began to roll into the port of Boston. Here was a source of labor that did not have to be tempted by pretty cottages or protected by housemothers.

Tenements, thought the next generation of mill-owners, were good enough for the Irish girls, and the priests would see to their morals. By 1860 the mills along the Merrimack were beginning to look and sound like their counterparts in the black country of England. That was the year when one of them, shoddily built and overloaded with machinery, collapsed at Lawrence, the nearby town that was named for another Boston Brahmin (and Lowell in-law), Abbott Lawrence. There were ninety dead—Yankee girls and Irish girls alike—and relations between capital and labor were never the same in the Merrimack Valley.

In their days as merchant shippers, the rich men of Boston had kept their offices on the docks where their ships came in and had sent their sons to sea.

These three illustrious Lowells belonged to the tenth generation of the family in this country: President Abbott Lawrence Lowell of Harvard (above); his brother, the astronomer Percival Lowell; and their sister, the poet Amy Lowell. The 1957 family gathering of the eleventh, twelfth, and thirteenth generations was held at the home of Ralph Lowell, a banker and trustee.

But the owners of the textile mills did not live in Lowell or Lawrence. They lived on Beacon Hill, and few of their heirs went into the business. Thanks in part to their own Puritan tradition and in part to the Massachusetts trust law, which has made it relatively easy to safeguard family fortunes from spendthrifts, the Brahmin aristocracy of Boston has probably been the most durable in the country. As they retreated from business, they did not lapse into the pleasures of idleness but devoted themselves to achievement in other fields and to good works. Their charities bear such wondrous names as the New England Society for the Protection of Little Wanderers, the Animal Rescue League, and for the suppression of vice, the Watch and Ward Society.

No wealthy family in the United States can look back on a record of greater distinction than the Lowells. In the generation after Francis Cabot Lowell, its most eminent member was James Russell Lowell, the poet and ambassador to the Court of St. James's. In the third generation it produced President Abbott Lawrence Lowell of Harvard, the astronomer Percival Lowell, and their sister, the poet Amy Lowell. President Lowell remembered how their father had impressed on them the family's point of view on wealth: "Somehow he made us feel that every self-respecting man must work at something that is worth while, and do it very hard. In our case it need not be remunerative, for he had enough to provide for that; but it must be of real significance." In later life, admittedly, President Lowell had some qualms about such lofty indifference to material affairs. Ac-

cording to Boston's social historian Cleveland Amory, he confided to a Cabot, "I'm getting rather worried about the Lowell Family, George. There's nobody in it making money any more."

THE VANDERBILTS

Much greater fortunes than any made in the textile industry were to be generated by the steam engine in its other capacity as the driving power of the railroad locomotive. As early as 1804 Watt's engine had been adapted by Richard Trevithick to run the first true locomotive at an ironworks in Wales. In the next two decades the locomotive was developed, largely by George and Robert Stephenson, father and son, for the new railways that were beginning to spread over the countryside. Presently England had the world's first railroad king in the mountainous person of George Hudson.

American technology followed a few years behind British. In the quarter century before the Civil War, there was a burst of railroad building as many independent lines crisscrossed the Eastern states. It was not until the end of that period that Cornelius Vanderbilt appeared on the railroad scene.

The Commodore was no stranger to steam propulsion, but his experience had been wholly on the seas and rivers. From the age of sixteen, when he talked his mother out of a hundred dollars to buy his own boat, he had always been ready for a race or a fight. He had run ferries in New York Harbor and paddle-wheelers up the Hudson, and during the gold rush, he had operated a service to carry passengers from New York to San Francisco by way of Nicaragua, where they crossed the isthmus by lake steamer and stagecoach. That service alone, he said, made him a million dollars a year. At the same time he built two oceangoing steamers and mounted a challenge on the North Atlantic run, which was then being fiercely contested by the American Collins Line and the British Cunard Line. In the aftermath of two disastrous sinkings, the Collins Line collapsed, leaving the field to Vanderbilt. But he was still at a disadvantage. The Cunarders had strong subsidy support from the British government, which was determined to regain in the age of steam the

Cornelius Vanderbilt stood over six feet tall and was looking every inch a captain of industry when a photographer (perhaps Brady) took this picture of him. The informal title of "Commodore" stuck to him from the years when he operated merchant ships.

primacy England had lost to American ships in the final decades of the age of sail. Congress, on the other hand, had turned to the development of the continent and was reluctant to support American shipping with subsidy. Sizing up the situation, Commodore Vanderbilt turned his attention to land transportation. He was then sixty-six years old.

Vanderbilt began by buying control of two railroads that ran north from New York to Albany, roughly parallel to the Hudson River. There they connected with the New York Central, which had just been put together from a string of local railroads that reached from Albany to Buffalo. Business for Vanderbilt's Hudson Line was good in the winter when Central passengers and freight were transferred to it for the run between Albany and New York. It was not so good in the summer when the Central ran its own steamers down the Hudson. In the winter of 1867 the wily Commodore found a solution for the deplorable state of affairs. He simply stopped running his trains into Albany, leaving the Central passengers stranded about two miles away on the opposite shore of the river. When the owners of the Central screamed in protest, the Commodore expressed his great regret for the inconvenience but called their attention to a law, which had long lain forgotten, that did indeed forbid the Hudson Railroad to cross the river. To be sure, the Commodore was not one to be held up very long by laws that stood in his way. ("What do I care about the law," he once roared. "Hain't I got the power?") But this particular law suited his purpose, and he was most scrupulous about observing it. In this impasse the bosses of the railroad world took a sober look at the lion who had entered their midst. They decided not to fight him. At the earnest behest of the Central's stockholders, who included such powerful men as John Jacob Astor, Vanderbilt took over the Central, and it was his thereafter.

In the course of running and expanding the Central, Commodore Vanderbilt lined his own pockets with a fortune that amounted to over a hundred million dollars before his death nine years later. Legislatures were bribed and judges bought. The stock was devalued by the issuance of new shares worth twenty million dollars to the new boss. But during the following years Vanderbilt put money into building the line and improving service. He ran a good railroad.

What makes the Commodore seem like a true empire builder and almost an attractive figure is the crew of scoundrels who fought him in his next great battle. For sheer rascality, there has never been in the history of American business a trio to match Daniel Drew, Jim Fisk, and Jay Gould. "Uncle Dan'l" Drew was a man of the Commodore's own age, a sanctimonious old fellow who wore the same seedy clothes year after year, along with a cattleman's hat in memory of the time when he made his living by driving cattle to market. During that period it was Drew's practice, not unfamiliar in the West, to give his cattle a good feeding of salt and then let them drink their fill of water to increase their weight at market. When he came to Wall Street, he brought with him the same standards of ethics and the same sly tricks. Even the phrase, "watered stock," followed him to Wall Street, where it perfectly fitted his practice of issuing securities representing assets whose value was greatly diluted. Drew was about the only man on the Street who had the audacity to challenge Vanderbilt at the game of manipulating stocks to make a killing. On several notable occasions Drew lost and had to come whining to his "old friend" for mercy, but by 1867 he gained control of the Erie Railroad, which was the Central's chief rival for the western route. Vanderbilt wanted the Erie in order to shut out the competition, and began buying its stock. But as fast as the Commodore bought shares, Drew found ways of issuing new shares, at length turning them out on a printing press as if they were counterfeit money.

In addition to his bag of financial tricks, Drew had the benefit of two younger partners, Fisk and Gould. Fisk was a gaudy, expansive salesman who later operated the Fall River Line of "floating palaces" (partly, it would seem, so that he could appear in glittering naval uniforms of his own design) and conducted his business as if it were the P. T. Barnum circus. Gould was a dark, slight, morose man, afflicted with tuberculosis but gifted with as sharp a mind as existed in the age of the robber barons.

The struggle for the Erie lasted four years and reached a high point of farce after Vanderbilt got one of his tame judges to issue a warrant for Drew's arrest in order to make him quit issuing fraudulent stock. A force of deputies was dispatched to seize him, but Drew, Fisk, and Gould, gathering up the money in a satchel, beat the deputies to the dock and crossed by ferry to the Jersey shore, where they were outside the jurisdiction of New York courts. In Jersey City they fortified themselves in the Taylor Hotel, which was promptly dubbed "Fort Taylor" and was surrounded by their own plug-ugly "detectives."

By the time the war was over, the Erie had been

CONTINUED ON PAGE 252

249

UPI

BILL CUNNINGHAM

Since the Commodore's time, Vanderbilts have never been out of the public eye. Herewith a sampling:

On the opposite page, upper left: Reginald was a sportsman who bred and drove carriage horses.

Opposite, upper right: Consuelo Vanderbilt goes bicycling in Paris in 1893 with her mother Alva Smith Vanderbilt (Mrs. William K.) The strong-willed Alva had already decided on a husband for her daughter (the Duke of Marlborough) and a new husband for herself (Oliver H.P. Belmont).

Opposite, lower left: Alva's two sons, Willie K., Jr. and Harold, clown on the beach, with Harry Lehr (right), who was a sort of court jester to Newport society. In later life Harold became famous as the skipper of America's Cup yachts and the inventor of contract bridge.

Opposite, lower right: Mrs. Alfred Gwynne Vanderbilt holds her son William Henry III about 1905. The boy became governor of Rhode Island from 1938 to 1940.

On this page, above: Alfred Gwynne Vanderbilt II, owner of a fine racing stable, dances in 1937 with Joan Crawford.

At right: Gloria Vanderbilt, who was married for a time to the conductor Leopold Stokowski, is now Mrs. Wyatt Cooper. She paints pictures and designs fabrics such as the one used for the dress she is wearing.

CONTINUED FROM PAGE 249

brought to such a state of near collapse that it was hardly worth fighting for. Vanderbilt turned his back on that railroad, confident that it would not give the Central any serious competition. Drew had already been cast aside by his own partners, and ended his days on the charity of relatives. Fisk would soon be shot dead by a rival lover of his mistress, the actress Josie Mansfield. Gould, that "man of disaster," turned west to visit his evil talents on the Union Pacific.

In a sort of sabbatical between the period when he made his first eleven million in shipping and the period when he made his next ninety million or so in railroads, Commodore Vanderbilt took his family on a cruise to European waters aboard a yacht, the *North Star*, which he had built for the purpose. It was a mixed triumph. The Vanderbilts were banqueted by the Lord Mayor of London but snubbed by the English nobility. At least one London newpaper, the *Daily News*, was so carried away by the yacht ("said to surpass in splendor the Queen's yacht") that it

Society's last citadel was the Vanderbilt house on Fifth Avenue at 50th Street, and its last grande dame was Mrs. Cornelius Vanderbilt III. Mrs. Vanderbilt spent hours choosing her guests and planning the seating for a dinner party like this, but, as always in such matters, her best efforts could not guarantee that the table would sparkle with conversation. Beginning at the bottom left corner of the picture, and proceeding along the near side of the table, we may notice first that Mrs. Grafton H. Pyne seems to be having difficulty in getting the attention of Mr. J. Norman de R. Whitehouse away from his plate. Next, Miss Julia Berwind is not doing much better with Dr. Hamilton Rice. Next, Mrs. Truxtun Beale, herself a famous hostess in Washington, D.C., has given up completely on the Hon. Alfred Anson, who has turned his back and retreated into thought. Not until we come to Mrs. J. Borden Harriman, one-time U.S. ambassador to Norway, and Mr. Frank Lyon Polk do we find a pair of guests who seem to be enjoying a lively conversation.

On the far side of the table, at center, is Mrs. Vanderbilt herself, wearing as usual a jeweled bandeau on her forehead. On her right she has seated James W. Gerard, one-time ambassador to Germany, and on her left Mr. Godfrey Haggard, British consul general in New York. But at the moment Mrs. Vanderbilt has turned to deliver a few words to a gentleman for whom a chair has been pulled up beside her. He is identified as Mr. Elmendorf L. Carr, who had been asked to lecture after dinner on South American affairs.

Mrs. Vanderbilt, who had a sense of her place in social history, allowed this picture to be taken for *Vogue* shortly before she closed the house forever in 1945.

scolded social London as follows: "The Montmorencis, the Howards, the Percys, made the past world—and they had their reward. Let them give place to better men.... It is time that *parvenu* should be looked upon as a word of honor." And things went better at the next port of call, St. Petersburg, where the Grand Duke Constantine came aboard.

If nothing else, the cruise of the *North Star* put the Old World on notice that a new American plutocracy had made its appearance.

Considering the fact that he was the richest man in America, the Commodore was not a very great spender. He liked fast boats and fast horses, and he built a substantial house near Washington Square, to which he dragged his protesting wife, who wanted only to stay on Staten Island. But he did not care enough about society to cut out his cussing or to learn to spell or to improve his manners. He liked to play whist and to chase after the housemaids in his new mansion, but mostly he liked to think up schemes to trap old Daniel Drew. It remained for his descendants to show the world what it meant to live like a Vanderbilt.

The Commodore had eleven children, of whom eight were girls. The sons were cruel disappointments. George, the youngest and most promising, died at age twenty-five, after graduating from West Point. Cornelius Jeremiah was an epileptic and a wastrel. That left William Henry, who seemed to his father such a weakling that he sent him back to Staten Island to run a farm and a tiny railroad. In the end William Henry made a go of both and slowly won the old man's grudging respect. In his will the Commodore put Cornelius Jeremiah on a small allowance, cut off the daughters with modest bequests, and left everything else—upward of ninety million dollars—to William Henry and his line.

William Henry lives in legend for one single remark, "The public be damned." When he made it, he was being badgered by reporters who could not understand why he wanted to abandon passenger traffic on one line where it was losing money. If the public did not want the service enough to use it, Vanderbilt snapped, they could not expect it to be continued. It was a sensible point, echoed by every railroad man who ever sought to give up an unprofitable run, but never expressed with quite such memorable ill temper.

William Henry was a heavy, plodding, unadventurous man, but cautious and astute—just right for consolidating the empire his father had built. He

Jay Gould dressed like a gentleman, lived like a king, was a model husband and father. But even the other robber barons thought his business ethics beyond the pale, and he was never accepted by society.

doubled the family fortune, and when he died, divided it among his children. William Henry had built a brownstone mansion, all stuffed with bronzes, marbles, and tapestries, but it was his children who established the Vanderbilts as the greatest house-building family in American history. Willie K. and his brother Cornelius II built neighboring "cottages" at Newport, called respectively Marble House and The Breakers and costing in the neighborhood of ten million dollars apiece in old money. A third brother, George Washington Vanderbilt II, something of a loner, went down to North Carolina to build the greatest of all American mansions, Biltmore, set in a domain of one hundred thirty thousand acres, where he developed some of the principles of scientific forestry that were later adopted by the National Park Service.

It was Mrs. Willie K. who brought Vanderbilt magnificence to its zenith in the Gilded Age. It was she who got Richard Morris Hunt to design her New York mansion on the model of the Chateau de Blois and to borrow from the Temple of the Sun at Baalbek for her Newport cottage. It was she who forced her tearful daughter into a loveless marriage with the Duke of Marlborough. And it was she who created the greatest society scandal of the time by divorcing her husband and marrying Oliver Hazard Perry Belmont.

After that generation the Vanderbilt wealth was spread more widely. The last grande dame to live like a Vanderbilt was Mrs. Cornelius III, who held court at the last Vanderbilt townhouse in Manhattan before she moved out in 1945. During her travels abroad, there sometimes arose the question of where to seat her among the titled aristocrats. On one such occasion she helpfully explained: "In America I take a rank something like that of your Princess of Wales."

THE SPENDING GOULDS

While the Vanderbilts were establishing themselves as the prime case history of what Thorstein Veblen called "conspicuous consumption," the Goulds were not far behind. Jay Gould had provided that each of his six children should inherit nearly equal shares in an estate of about seventy-five million dollars. But the estate, with its vast railroad holdings, was to be kept intact, with George Jay Gould, the eldest son, acting as trustee for the other children.

In the Gould spending derby George was first off the mark with his marriage in 1884 to Edith Kingdon, an actress with an inordinate fondness for ropes of pearls. To show them off properly she required large houses and lavish parties. Even on their private railroad car, formal dress was *de rigueur* at dinner. It is told that on one journey, through some mix-up, the Gould car was placed in the center of a train instead of at the rear. This meant that travelers who wanted to get from one end of the train to the other had to pass through the Goulds' car. The situation was saved, to a degree, by the Goulds' English butler, who stood at the door and announced each stranger before he passed through.

But George was soon outdistanced in the spending race by his youngest sister Anna, who married

Edith Kingdon was an actress noted for her hour-glass figure when she married Jay's oldest son, George Jay Gould. It was said that when she lost her waist line, she lost her husband. She found consolation in her pearls.

Count Boni de Castellane. Boni was everything that red-blooded American men imagined when they thought of a foppish, decadent, profligate European nobleman. In order to win acceptance by French society, Boni informed his bride, it was not enough for a plain American girl to marry a fixture of *tout Paris* like himself, she must also make a splash by really fantastic spending. Boni would show her how it was done.

Boni and Anna began by building a replica of the Petit Trianon, buying jewels and clothes and furnishings without asking the price, and entertaining three thousand guests, by special permission of the French parks administration, in the Bois de Boulogne. What Boni did not quite grasp was the

fact that his wife was only getting the *income* of her fortune, and that was a mere six hundred thousand dollars a year. Soon the builders of the house were laying down their tools for lack of pay, the yacht was attached by creditors, and the jewels were on their way back to the jewelers. Boni had also been spending a good deal of his wife's money on mistresses, and in 1906 Anna divorced her expensive consort. Two years later she married his nobler and richer cousin, the Duc de Talleyrand-Périgord, who did not need to live wholly on her income.

Anna and her youngest brotherFrank continued to chafe under the restrictions of their father's will and to blame brother George for their paltry allowances. In 1916 they brought suit to remove him as trustee, on the grounds that he was mismanaging their property. Unhappily this proved to be true. George had worked harder at running railroads than his father ever had, but he lacked the old man's cunning. The legal battle that Frank and Anna started went on for years, and by the time lawyers and tax collectors had taken their portions, the estate had shrunk to less than half its original value. There was enough left for Helen Gould to keep up her father's ugly old mansion, Lyndhurst, at Tarrytown, New York, and for Frank to build a sumptuous gambling casino called the Palais Méditerranée at Nice, and for Jay Gould II, son of George, to become the perennial United States champion of court tennis. But the inheritance received by Jay Gould's grandson and namesake could be counted in six figures.

George Jay Gould (at left on the opposite page) takes a ride at Palm Beach with Henry Clay Frick. Frick was the coke king of Pittsburgh when Andrew Carnegie made him his partner and chairman of the Carnegie Steel Company.

The Big Four who built the Central Pacific Railroad were, left to right: Collis P. Huntington, Charles Crocker, Leland Stanford, and Mark Hopkins. They worked as a team, but Huntington (who wore the skullcap to keep his bald head warm) ended up as the dominant partner.

THE BIG FOUR

While marble cottages and steam yachts proclaimed the wealth of the Vanderbilts and Goulds in the East, the mansions rising on Nob Hill in San Francisco signaled the arrival of a group of railroad kings in the West. These were the Big Four—Stanford, Huntington, Hopkins, and Crocker—who built the Central Pacific and ran it east to its historic meeting with the Union Pacific at Promontory Point. It had not been their idea. All four had been storekeepers in Sacramento in 1861 when a singleminded engineer named Theodore Dehone Judah came to ask their backing. What inspired Judah was the dream of a railroad spanning the Western states to the Pacific coast. But what the merchants saw was the prospect of great personal wealth flowing in large part from subsidies that Congress would provide. They were a well-matched team: Charles Crocker, the hard-driving construction boss who got the tracks laid; Leland Stanford, the shrewd politician who was soon to be elected governor of California and who knew how to get favors from the state legislature; Mark Hopkins, who handled the money; and Collis P. Huntington, who arranged the federal subsidy by whatever means of persuasion or bribery the situation required. In this company Judah did not last long. He was too insistent on building a track that would hold up and too honest to get the subsidy raised by swearing that mountains existed on stretches that were flat plain. He sold out his minor interest to the Big Four and went back East, where

257

Three of the Big Four built mansions on Nob Hill in San Francisco. Above, left to right, are the houses of Crocker, Stanford, and Hopkins. All three houses were destroyed in the earthquake of 1906.

he died before the Golden Spike was driven.

The Big Four went on to form the Southern Pacific Company, which dominated California political life for decades. In time the partnership began to loosen and Huntington was left in active control of the company. But each of the four partners retained a quarter interest, and each ended up with a great fortune. Of the four, only Crocker founded a family that has played an important role in California financial and social life. Among the other three there was a shortage of direct heirs, a circumstance that led to the founding of two great institutions. After Stanford's only child died young, he and his wife devoted some thirty million dollars to building, in memory of Leland, Jr., the greatest private university in the West. Huntington's estate of seventy-five million dollars was divided between his second wife, Arabella, and his nephew, Henry E. Huntington. But Henry and Arabella, who were of about the same age, put it back together again by marrying. Henry had made a considerable fortune of his own as the sole owner of the Los Angeles city transportation system, and had begun collecting rare books and manuscripts at his marble mansion in San Marino. After his marriage to Arabella, they took an even more expensive fancy to eighteenth-century English portrait painting. Their purchase in 1921 of Gainsborough's *Blue Boy*, stage-managed by Sir Joseph Duveen, was the best publicized American art acquisition of the early twentieth century. *The Blue Boy* cost six hundred twenty thousand dollars and was followed to California by many other notable paintings of the same period, along with manu-

scripts and letters of even greater scholarly, if not monetary, value. The estate at San Marino, filled with all these treasures, is now the Henry E. Huntington Library and Art Gallery.

CYRUS HALL McCORMICK

Along with the growth of industry in the first half of the nineteenth century, there was an outburst of invention. In most cases it was not the inventor who got rich from his invention; more often it was a businessman who knew how to raise money and run factories and find markets for a new product. But if the inventor had some of these talents, too, the patent laws gave him a head start in the race. One who succeeded was Cyrus Hall McCormick.

Farmers long before McCormick's time had wished for some mechanical device to help with the harvest. The ancient Romans had experimented with such devices, and so had the English in the eighteenth century. But the need for a reaper was felt most acutely in the United States, where the increasing size of farms and the chronic shortage of manpower created a crisis at every harvest. No matter how much grain a farmer might plant, he could only reap as much as could be cut with a sickle or scythe in the brief time of its ripening.

Among those who were trying to invent a machine to do the harvesting was Robert McCormick, a prosperous wheat farmer in Virginia. He and his eldest son Cyrus kept tinkering in their shop until they had a horse-drawn machine that could cut the wheat and lay it flat without too much loss of grain. The basic design was Robert's, but the improvements that made it successful were largely Cyrus'. In the early 1830's they demonstrated it in wheat fields, where it cut as much wheat in an hour as a man could cut in a day.

Whether the McCormick reaper was a better machine than the reapers invented by Obed Hussey and others is a matter of argument. But there is no doubt that Cyrus McCormick's talents as a business promoter were greatly superior. He set a firm price of one hundred twenty dollars and, knowing that few farmers had much cash, asked for only thirty dollars down. If crops happened to be poor that year, he did not press the farmers for money, as most manufacturers did, but gave them more time to pay. He built his main factory in Chicago but spotted assembly plants around the wheat belt, so that a farmer could get quick delivery on his reaper and quick help if it broke down. As a farmer himself, he knew that crops do not wait.

McCormick was the kind of boss that workmen liked. One of them told his biographer, Ernest Poole:

He knew how to get spirit into his men. At Blue Island we worked from seven A.M. to five-thirty, with half an hour for lunch; and when there was a rush of orders, it would often be midnight for us. I don't mean we had to stay unless we wanted, but most of us did—not only because we got overtime pay but because he could make us feel like that—because he was one of us, understand? No white-collar boss but right out on the job, workin' hard with his sleeves rolled up on some new gadget that had gone wrong. He knew machines like his own mother. While he was livin' we had one boss—and if anything went wrong, you could go right to him and get it fixed up. In these new days of big companies, you have a dozen bosses—and where are you? With Old Cy we knew. When he died there were mourners in our crowd, for now we had lost him, and we knew we'd never have a boss like him again.

THE SINGERS AND CLARKS

The American product that first and most successfully captured the world market was not, however, the harvester. It was the sewing machine. And the man whose name is linked forever with this saga of Yankee enterprise was Isaac Merrit Singer.

Singer cannot be called the inventor of the sewing machine. The idea had been around at least since 1790, when a patent for a leather-stitching device was granted in England. Nothing came of that, but by the 1830's two other fairly successful machines had been developed. The prize of fame and fortune that eventually went to Singer might well have gone to Barthélemy Thimonnier of France, who had set

Vizcaya was built at Miami by James Deering, son of William Deering, whose farm-equipment company was merged with that of Cyrus McCormick and others to form the International Harvester Company. Finished in 1916, the house is an approximation of an Italian Renaissance palazzo. To furnish it Deering raided villas, cloisters, and palaces from England to Sicily, at a cost above ten million dollars. It is now a museum.

up a factory to turn out his machine. But the factory was wrecked by a mob of angry tailors who feared that it would put them out of work. The prize might then have gone to Walter Hunt, an American, had he not showed his machine to his fifteen-year-old daughter. Sharing the concern of the French tailors, she appealed to her father's Quaker conscience not to market something that would put seamstresses out of work. Reluctantly, Hunt put his invention aside, thus allowing his place in history to rest on such other inventions as the safety pin and the paper collar. The next man up was Elias Howe, Jr. Howe's machine actually reached the market in the 1840's, but like the others patented at about the same time, it had enough "bugs" left in it to give its users frequent trouble.

It was into this situation that chance directed Isaac Singer. The son of a poor German millwright, Singer had run away from home and from a stepmother at the age of twelve. In 1850 he was thirty-nine years old and had spent the intervening twenty-seven years pursuing one professional career, for which he was unfitted, while resisting another, for which he had a genius. The career that claimed his heart was that of actor and impresario. It might seem at first sight that nature had indeed destined him for theatrical life. He was a giant of a man, with a voice fit for Shakespeare and an animal vitality that could capture any audience.

Unfortunately, even in that heyday of melodrama, the critics' unanimous verdict was that Isaac Singer was a hopeless ham. In consequence, he drifted between the theater and manual labor, where his true talent of inventor kept bubbling forth. While he was digging ditches he invented a rock drill, and while working for a printer he developed a type-carving machine. One day in 1850, as he was working on this latter invention in a Boston machine shop, he noticed a sewing machine that had been brought in for repair. After a casual inspection Singer pointed out to the shop owner, one Phelps, that the machine would work better if the shuttle moved in a straight line instead of a circle and if the needle moved up and down instead of horizontally.

Singer was, as usual, stone broke. But a three-way partnership was worked out between Singer, Phelps, and a businessman named Zieber, who could put up forty dollars. In the next eleven days Isaac Singer per-

fected the two crucial inventions, which, when added to all the others, produced a reliable sewing machine.

The enterprise was just getting off the ground when it was struck by a suit brought by Elias Howe for violation of patents, demanding twenty-five thousand dollars. By that time Phelps had dropped out in despair over trying to deal with the obstreperous Singer; Zieber would soon follow. In fear that the Howe suit would destroy the fledgling company, Singer turned to a lawyer named Edward Clark. Here at last was the combination of talents that would make Singer a household name in about every country of the civilized world.

If any man in the business world was likely to be put off by the vulgar, swaggering Singer, it was Edward Clark, a prim, careful young man, a graduate of Williams College and a Sunday School teacher. When Clark learned something of Singer's personal life, he could barely conceal his distaste. Somewhere in New York City, Singer had left behind the wife of his early years and their two children. He was now living with a mistress named Mary Ann Sponsler, who had borne him eight more children. And along the way he had fathered two more children by other liasons. When all this intelligence became known to Edward Clark's wife, her advice was clear: "Sell out and leave the nasty brute." But Clark decided no, and it was he, of all those who had crossed Singer's path, who went on to share the resulting fortune.

The patent suit was settled by a pooling of patents. Howe got a royalty that eventually earned him some two million dollars. Meanwhile, the only thing that saved the Singer-Clark partnership was probably the fact that, as soon as the money began to roll in, Singer found he had better things to do than sit at a desk. He made small improvements on the machine from time to time, and he was a hit on the Chautauqua circuit, where his theatrical talents enabled him to get laughs with such jokes as this: "Why is a Singer Sewing Machine like a kiss? Because it *seams* so good."

Clark was left in the office to develop the business techniques, which, even with no advantage in patents, enabled Singer to dominate the world market. Since husbands of that day tended to doubt that their simple wives could run such a complicated machine, Clark set up young women in store windows to demonstrate how easy it was (and thus to gather crowds on any sidewalk). Buyers who had been so foolish as to buy a different make were offered fifty dollars turn-in against the "superior product." Salesmen were imbued with such crusading spirit that one representative from the West went so far as to shoot the salesman of a rival company, whereupon he was lynched by the dead man's friends.

But Isaac Singer was a stranger to most of this business expansion. The time had come to enjoy the delights of affluence that had passed him by in his youth. In 1859 he moved his consort and brood to a house on Fifth Avenue, and shortly thereafter he acquired the most remarkable conveyance seen on the streets of New York. It was a mammoth carriage weighing two tons and painted canary yellow, with room for thirty-one passengers. It was fitted out with a nursery at one end for the proliferating Singer progeny, and seats for a small orchestra on the outside. Nine horses were needed to pull this princely equipage.

For twenty-four years Singer had been promising to get a divorce from his first wife and make an honest woman of Mary Ann Sponsler. But by the time he finally got around to getting a divorce in 1860, he had found a new love in Mary McGonigal, the mother of five of his other children. It was too much for Mary Ann Sponsler, who at last blew the whistle on the old rascal, suing him for support and telling all to the papers. Singer hastily took off for Europe in the company of Mary McGonigal's younger sister Kate. There, against all probability, Singer began to settle down, though not with either of the McGonigal sisters. His last love was a young woman named Isabella Boyer, with whom he passed a sunny old age, fathering six more children and building a grand house near Torquay on the Channel coast of England.

When Isaac Singer died in 1875 the count of his children stood at twenty-four, of whom eight were legitimate. The estate was divided among the children, with the youngest ones getting the most. In succeeding generations the Clarks and the Singers both ran true to form. Few in number and quiet in nature, the Clarks have used some of their wealth to restore Cooperstown in New York and to endow the Clark Art Institute at Williamstown, Massachusetts, with its fine collection of French impressionists. The numerous Singers, on the other hand,

After a long and lecherous life, Isaac Singer had finally settled down with his second wife, Isabella, when this picture was taken about 1870. Winaretta, one of their six children, is seated by her mother. The boys, seated by two unidentified ladies, may be Washington and Paris.

scattered many of their smaller inheritances to the winds. Isaac's true spiritual heir was the next-to-the-youngest son, Paris Singer, so named for the city of his birth. A blond giant like his father, he had a tempestuous romance with the famous dancer Isadora Duncan, who called him her Lohengrin. In Florida during the 1920's he was the owner of the exclusive Everglades Club and thereby the arbiter of Palm Beach Society.

THE DU PONT DYNASTY

Among American families who have risen to wealth through manufacture, the Du Ponts are a case apart. It is perhaps best to think of them not as individuals in the American tradition, but as an aristocratic European family transplanted to the colonial world.

The founder of the family, Pierre Samuel Du Pont, was the son of a Paris clockmaker, lame from a childhood illness and hard pressed to earn a living. Growing up in the 1760's, he displayed such brilliance as a student of economics and a pamphleteer that he won acceptance by Dr. François Quesnay, the leader of the physiocrats, and later by Anne Robert Jacques Turgot, the royal finance minister. In the intellectual sunburst that preceded the French Revolution, he was a champion of laissez-faire economics, a reformer but not a radical. On the one hand he was loyal to the king, who made him a *seigneur*, and he added "de Nemours," the place name of his family, to signify his own subtle translation to the aristocracy. On the other hand, he wrote pamphlets about the rights of man and dreamed of utopias. To Thomas Jefferson he was "the most brilliant man in France."

When the French Revolution got out of hand and passed into the control of the radicals, led by Robespierre, Pierre Du Pont was jailed for a two-month period. Some time later he decided that the course of prudence was to leave the country. With his family retainers and worldly goods, he set sail on an American vessel in 1799.

It was a long and difficult voyage, during which the ship lost its way, wandered about the Atlantic, and ran out of food. The behavior of the Du Ponts was in the French aristocratic tradition. Distrusting the American crew, they stood armed guard night and day over the cases and trunks of goods that they had brought with them. When they landed, tired and hungry, at Newport, they stopped at the first substantial house they came upon. As it happened, the family was at church, but through the windows they could see a table set for New Year's Day dinner and a hearty meal ready to be served. Upon Pierre Samuel's order, they broke into the house and consumed the meal, then left a gold coin in payment and departed. It is not recorded what the owners of the house thought of this assertion of aristocratic prerogative.

Pierre Du Pont's idea was to establish a colony in Virginia, to be called Pontiania, that would serve as a home away from home for chosen exiles of good

CONTINUED ON PAGE 268

Eleuthère Irénée Du Pont (on the opposite page in a painting by Rembrandt Peale) founded a company to make gunpowder in 1802. He had been encouraged by his father's friend President Thomas Jefferson at a meeting depicted in a later painting below. Those present were (left to right) Du Pont, Paul Revere, Secretary of War Henry Dearborn, and Jefferson. The company's product was kept in canisters like those at left.

The album of the Du Ponts goes back to the beginning of the Republic. Pierre Samuel (medallion at top) transplanted the family from France to America. His son E. I. Du Pont built the powder plant, including the drying house (top). Alfred Victor (left) succeeded E. I. as senior partner in 1834. At left above is Winterthur, filled with the greatest private collection of American antiques. Directly above are two sportsmen of the 1930's: Henry Belin Du Pont, a glider pilot and later chairman of TWA, and J. Simpson Dean, who married Polly Du Pont and became a Du Pont executive.

Du Ponts have made news in unexpected ways. At right is Mrs. Margaret Osborne Du Pont, who won the Women's National tennis title at Forest Hills three years running (1948–50). Farther right is Ethel Du Pont, who married Franklin D. Roosevelt, Jr. in 1937, at a time when their fathers were bitter political opponents. Zara Du Pont (below), a determined supporter of labor and liberal causes in the 1930's, often appeared on Boston picket lines, where she was known to union organizers as "Aunt Zadie." Irénée Du Pont, president of the company, liked to swim at Xanadu, his stately pleasure dome in pre-Castro Cuba.

In 1957 three Du Pont company presidents and the family members of the board of directors sat for this portrait for *Life*. Beginning at left are successive chief executives: Irénée Du Pont (1919–26), Walter Carpenter, Jr. (1940–48), and Crawford Greenewalt (1948–62). The others, in order, are Henry B. Du Pont, Lammot Du Pont Copeland, Sr., Pierre Du Pont III, Hugh R. Sharp, Jr., Henry F. Du Pont, Eugene E. Du Pont, Emile F. Du Pont, and William Du Pont, Jr. At the same time family members were active at other levels of the company. At right, F. George Du Pont operates a laboratory firing range at the Du Pont-controlled Remington Arms Company. At far right, Irénée Du Pont, Jr. holds flasks of Teflon.

CONTINUED FROM PAGE 262

birth and high intellect; but this idea fell through because land east of the mountains was too expensive. Instead the family settled first in New Jersey and later on the banks of the Brandywine in Delaware. It was Pierre's younger son, Eleuthère Irénée, who came up with the winning scheme. Irénée had been appalled at the poor quality of gunpowder produced in America. This was something he knew about, for he had served an apprenticeship in the laboratory of the great French scientist Antoine Lavoisier. With money provided by the French and other investors, he built a gunpowder mill on the banks of the Brandywine and found a ready customer in the United States government, then headed by his father's admirer, Thomas Jefferson. During Irénée's lifetime the mill and its profits grew slowly but steadily, enabling him to shake out almost all the investors and make it into a family enterprise. Thereafter, for a hundred years, the Du Pont company stuck to explosives, making a surge forward during every American war. Between wars the new capacity was taken up by the need for explosives to prepare roadbeds for railroads, to clear forest land of stumps, and to blast coal from mines, as well as to provide ammunition against birds and beasts.

During the coming four generations the family established certain policies and traditions that find no duplicate in any other American family of wealth. For many years the family wealth was held in common and no salaries were paid to family members who worked for the company; instead, they had drawing accounts to meet their expenses. Pierre Samuel had explicitly encouraged his descendants to marry their first cousins, the better to maintain family solidarity and concentrate family wealth. This policy was remarkably well followed through most of the nineteenth century with no apparent ill effects. Even after Colonel Henry A. Du Pont, the head of the family in the early twentieth century, began to worry about the genetic perils of inbreeding and issued a decree against first-cousin marriages, they did not entirely cease. But as Du Pont daughters began to marry outside the clan, the sons-in-law were virtually adopted into the family and taken into the company. As in any hereditary enterprise, the problem of succession was crucial. Perhaps the greatest achievement of the Du Ponts in their steady rise to affluence was their success in finding, among the family members or in-laws, men capable of running the enterprise at every period in its history. This was not accomplished, however, without rows and palace revolutions, which sometimes burst into angry public scandals.

Following the death of Eugene, who had run the company for thirteen years, there was a moment in 1902 when his heirs were about to sell it to a rival powder company. But three young cousins, Alfred, Coleman, and Pierre, took control. Alfred emerged as the dominant force until, in 1906, he committed an unpardonable offense against family rules by divorcing his wife and then remarrying. Alfred was ostracized, both socially and in business, while Pierre took command of the company. Even at New Year's, when the Du Ponts set out in their carriages to drop off presents at the many houses of their cousins, it was noticed that few carriages crossed the Brandywine to the vast estate of Nemours, which Alfred built on the west bank.

It was Pierre and his younger brothers Irénée and Lammot who turned Du Pont from a powder maker into a chemical conglomerate, making everything from rayon and nylon to paint, synthetic rubber, and plastics. For decades it also held a controlling interest in General Motors, but in 1955 the Supreme Court compelled it to cut that company loose.

As the generations passed, the Du Pont estates in the valley of the Brandywine grew both in numbers and in size. Alfred's Nemours was rivaled by Henry F.'s Winterthur and by Pierre's Longwood. The central control of the fortune ceased long ago, but the individual shares add up to many billions of dollars. Du Ponts contributed to charities, and cancer research in particular, but mostly in Delaware. They ran for national office but only to represent Delaware in Congress. They owned Wilmington newspapers, exercised influence over the Delaware legislature, and in general made Delaware something of a Du Pont family fief. But since World War II, Du Ponts have increasingly tended to break away from the family tradition, scatter to other parts of the country, and lose interest in the company. Perhaps the symbolic end of the family dominance of the company may be said to have occurred in 1970 when Lammot Du Pont Copeland, Jr., son of the chairman of the board, went bankrupt as a result of bad private investments, reporting assets of twenty-six million dollars and liabilities of nearly sixty-three million dollars. In consequence, his father resigned the chairmanship, which is now held not by a Du Pont cousin or even a Du Pont son-in-law but by Irving Shapiro, an unrelated career executive. At last, it would appear, the Du Pont company has ceased to be a family fiefdom and has become in all respects a modern corporation.

AMERICAN WEALTH REACHED ITS FLOOD TIDE OF OSTENTATION IN THE QUARTER CENTURY THAT ENDED WITH THE FIRST WORLD WAR. IT WAS A TIME WHEN LADIES PRIDED THEMSELVES ON THEIR ELEGANT COSTUMES AND GRACEFUL CARRIAGE. THE YOUNG WOMAN ABOVE, ON HER WAY TO THE RACES, IS MISS NATICA RIVES,

Newport was society's summer capital, and the high point of the season was the annual New York Yacht Club race. Some spectators drove out to Castle Hill in carriages to watch the race from land, while others got a closer look from small boats offshore.

The social center of Newport life, and the capital of the new sport of tennis, was the Casino. In the picture below, Colonel John Jacob Astor IV, in white pants, stands outside the Casino with a bevy of belles in uniform white dresses.

The two ladies in the circular picture on the opposite page are Miss Lota Robinson and Mrs. Stuyvesant Fish, advancing in full regalia. "Mamie" Fish made it her career to liven up the party scene. Once she required her guests to speak only in baby talk through dinner.

Newport's marble "cottages" were for use in the two-month summer season. At left is Marble House, which William K. Vanderbilt built for his wife Alva in the early 1890's at a cost of two million dollars for the building and nine million for the furnishings. He lost it to Alva when she divorced him a few years later. Its cost and splendor were matched by that of his brother Cornelius' place, the Breakers (at top on this page). Chetwode (center) was built for W. Storrs Wells but later sold to John Jacob Astor. The Elms (bottom) was the home of E. J. Berwind, a Pennsylvania coal baron, and later of his sister Miss Julia Berwind, one of the last of Newport's grande dames. All these houses are now open to the public.

In the days of automobile racing, its greatest patron was William K. Vanderbilt. He is seen in the picture at top of the opposite page (second from left) with fellow car buffs. The Vanderbilt Cup Races were held on a private motor parkway on Long Island.

Car races were too noisy and dusty for most society people. The elegant young ladies in the picture below are leaning on the rail at the horse-racing track at Tuxedo Park, New York.

Saratoga was the premier racing resort, and attracted the greatest swells. The one with the magnificent paunch (in the picture at left below on the facing page) is Diamond Jim Brady, who liked to begin a meal with six dozen oysters. For Brady, who sold railroad equipment, the Saratoga track was an ideal place to meet wealthy buyers. One of these grandees (in top hat and greatcoat in the next picture) was William C. Whitney, the New York traction king and owner of Saratoga's finest stable.

BROWN BROTHERS

OVERLEAF (pages 276–77): On Easter Sunday in 1898 New York society paraded on Fifth Avenue. Across the street in this picture is the Croton Reservoir, which supplied the city with water; the site is now occupied by the New York Public Library.

It was a time of sumptuous dinners and lavish parties. In the picture on the opposite page, the turn of the century is being celebrated by the friends of Harrison Grey Fiske, the theatrical producer and husband of the actress Minnie Maddern Fiske. The guests, possibly fancying themselves to be noble Romans, wear laurel wreaths.

Mrs. William K. Vanderbilt's costume ball, given in 1883 to open her new Fifth Avenue house, challenged the creative imaginations of her guests. On this page are some of those who attended. In the top row left to right: Miss Constance Rives as a Bumble Bee and Mrs. Cornelius Vanderbilt, the hostess' sister-in-law, as Electricity. In the bottom row: Miss Kate Strong as Puss and Alva Vanderbilt herself, with stuffed

Albums of the rich reveal some of the simpler pleasures enjoyed by younger family members. At left are three young ladies with the pets they have entered in a society dog show. The two little girls with balloons (above) are granddaughters of Jay Gould, with their mother (in black) and a friend. The children on the pony, photographed in 1923, belong to a younger generation. They are Ruth and John Medill McCormick, great-grandchildren of Cyrus Mc-Cormick, the harvester king, and Joseph Medill, the founder of the Chicago *Daily Tribune*.

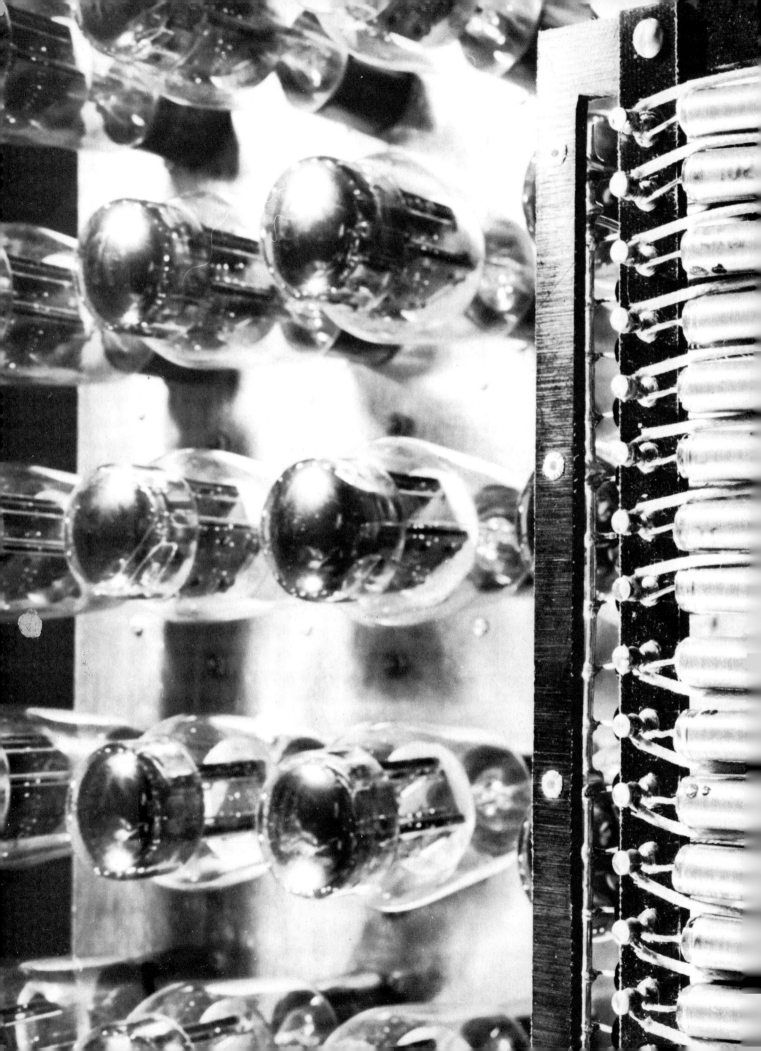

8. WEALTH FROM MODERN INDUSTRY

HENRY FORD

In Aldous Huxley's novel *Brave New World* the divinity of his society of the distant future was venerated as "Our Ford"; worshipers made the mystic sign of the T in commemoration of their dim folk-memory of the legendary Model T, and the great clock that sounded over the city was called Big Henry. Huxley was writing with tongue in cheek, but it was not surprising that he should pick Henry Ford as the man to be transmuted into the deity of a technological society. Henry Ford, more than any other man of this century, typified mass production; no one else has so changed his society, and even the appearance of the land, by what he has done.

Henry Ford was born in Dearborn, Michigan, in 1863 and died there not quite eighty-four years later. During those years, without wandering far from Dearborn, he contrived to make himself not only the wealthiest man of his time but one of the wealthiest Americans of all time.

Ford was one of those men who seemed born to tinker with machinery. After a miscellany of jobs that gave practical experience—apprentice in a

◀PRECEDING PAGES: **These are some of the components that go into the construction of an IBM computer.**

machine shop, watch repairman, traction-engine operator, engineer for an electric lighting company —he began experimenting with internal combustion engines in his own workshop. His first creation was a "quadricycle" in 1896—a real horseless carriage, the kind that looked exactly like a buggy without a horse in front.

Henry Ford had decided that there was a future in the new machines that were beginning to appear on American roads and streets. For a time he designed and built racing cars and sometimes drove them, and his Arrow set a speed record on the ice of Lake St. Clair in 1904. It all drew attention.

Bolstered by his added experience and publicity, Ford returned to making commercial motor vehicles at the Ford Motor Company, which he had formed in 1903. He was entering a very chancy and competitive market. As early as 1900, when pioneer automobile makers were just beginning to venture into the field, twelve companies turned out a total of 4,192 machines. Ten years later the competition had become so cutthroat and chaotic that more than two hundred makers among them made only 181,000 automobiles, not only internal combustion types but a fair sprinkling of electrics and a steamer or two.

During the first few years of this century the motorcar was a sporting vehicle, an expensive plaything of the affluent, and one better suited to ostentation and

competitive events such as hill-climbing, considering the miserable condition of the roads, than to transportation. This was the situation in which the Ford Motor Company operated modestly for five years. But Henry Ford had other ideas about the proper role of the automobile in American society, and in 1908 he brought out the first of his Model T's, the homely little motorcar that would be a true peoples' wagon—and that would set off a revolution in American life. That first 1908 Model T sold for about eight hundred fifty dollars; it was possible to buy another make for a comparable price, but to get one as ruggedly built would have cost about a thousand five hundred.

This was only the beginning. Ford's special talents did not end in the shop but extended to production. He worked out the moving assembly line, where a worker with a minimum of training could learn to perform a simple task and repeat it endlessly as the Fords came inexorably down the line. It was a wonderful system for speeding up work, but it was dehumanizing in its deadening drudgery. In 1914 Ford began paying his employees the then-unheard-of wage of five dollars for an eight-hour day. In part this was to compensate his workers for the gray routine of their jobs; mainly it was because Ford, unlike most capitalists of the period, recognized the contradiction between paying low wages and at the same

time expecting to sell in an affluent market.

There are men and women today already grandparents who were born after the last Model T rolled off the assembly line in 1927, and so it is necessary, as it never would have been before, to describe this vehicle, which put America on wheels and made Henry Ford very rich. It was a simple, sturdy, angular, and far-from-elegant machine, eleven feet long and with a twenty-horsepower, four-cylinder engine. Until the later years of production the basic model was an open touring car with a folding top like that on a buggy; there were side curtains that could be laboriously attached with little turnbuttons for winter driving or in case of rain, but the closure was poor, and this, combined with the lack of a heater, made winter driving an Arctic adventure, while the difficulty of putting on the curtains often meant that in sudden rain storms driver and passengers were soaked before they could get themselves shut in. As far as color was concerned, Ford reportedly once said that a customer could have any color—so long as it was black.

The acres of Model T chassis, so neatly ranked below, were a single day's output by the Ford Motor Company in 1913. By then Henry Ford's mass-production assembly-line techniques had reduced the price of a Model T to $550; it would be even lower in subsequent years.

The power plant was of the utmost simplicity: the engine block was simple and unencumbered; a magneto, integral with the flywheel, generated low-tension current, which, passing through spark coils, was transformed to high-tension current, and then distributed to the four spark plugs. A very elementary carburetor completed the engine, except for the simple cooling system. The Model T ran hot, and removing the radiator filler cap on a hot day not only required precautions against scalding but resulted in a spectacular geyser of steam and boiling water shooting a dozen feet into the air. Most mechanical ailments of the Model T could be taken care of with nothing more than an adjustable wrench, a screwdriver, and a pair of pliers.

This graceless but uncomplicated machine was designed by Ford for the great mass of Americans, and it served them so well that it has become a national legend. It was the flivver, the tin lizzie, the affectionate butt of countless jokes and cartoons. It was no beauty, but it did its job. Being high and light, it could crawl and wallow through rutted quagmires where most other cars hopelessly bogged down, a priceless advantage in an era when the bottom dropped out of even main highways during spring thaws and when rural roads were none too good even in the best of weather. It was farmers to whom the flivver especially endeared itself. Besides being able to travel over rough or sodden country roads, it could be pressed into service to pull a mower or grain binder, or haul a load of hay or a calf

to market. With a pulley bolted to a rear wheel and the wheel jacked up, the Model T could be used to supply power through a belt for anything from sawing wood or shelling corn to pumping water or washing clothes.

And while Americans in increasing numbers saved their dollars to buy a Model T, Henry Ford was making it easier and easier for them to own one. The initial price of eight hundred fifty dollars had been reduced to below five hundred dollars by 1914; in 1925 a runabout model was selling for only two hundred sixty dollars. At the same time production was climbing rapidly; from fewer than eighteen thousand in 1909 it reached thirty thousand in 1914 (two-fifths of the automobiles manufactured that year were Model T's). The next year sales reached over half a million, and nearly two million in 1923.

During all these years the flivver did change—but not very much. Ford had said in 1909 that the Model T would always remain, with "no new models, no new motors, no new bodies, and no new colors." It was a rather arrogant, public-be-damned statement, suggesting that customers could accept whatever Ford chose to produce, and it was this attitude that eventually cost Ford his undisputed leadership in the automobile field. For the fact was that there were many things on the Model T that could have been improved—some at little or no cost—and Ford stubbornly refused to make the changes.

Take the matter of the flivver's gas tank. It was located under the seat, and to fill it or even find out

Henry Ford had a number of cronies, famous in their own right, with whom he enjoyed forgetting about business for a time. He is pictured above, posing with several of them at an old grist mill in the West Virginia mountains during a camping trip in 1918. They are, from left to right: Thomas A. Edison, the inventor; Harvey S. Firestone, Jr.; John Burroughs, noted naturalist and author; Ford; and Harvey S. Firestone, founder and head of the Firestone Tire and Rubber Company. The seated man is R. J. H. de Loach. At far left, Henry Ford, then eighty, relaxes in the sunshine on the steps of his plantation in Georgia. At near left, in 1902, he stands beside Barney Oldfield with Ford's 999, which Oldfield drove in races.

Henry Ford takes the steering rod of his 1896 "quadricycle," his first gasoline vehicle. With him are his wife and grandson, Henry Ford II.

how much gasoline remained, the driver and anyone else in the front seat had to get out, the seat cover had to be removed, and the tank cap unscrewed. The gasoline gauge was a wooden stick that had to be poked down into the filler hole; the height to which the stick was wetted indicated how much gasoline was in the tank. Endless letters begged for a filler neck on the side of the car, but Ford stubbornly refused to make any change until 1926, when he moved the fuel tank forward into the cowl. Then there was the strange case of the missing door on the driver's side on the touring car model—which included most Model T's produced. If anyone needed to get in and out of the car it was the driver, and yet no door was cut through on his side. The other three were there, but the driver had to climb over the side, or if the top was up and the side curtains fastened, he had to enter from the opposite side, climbing over anyone sitting there to get to his seat. There seems to have been no explanation for this strange design quirk, and again Ford did nothing to correct it. But even with its shortcomings, the Model T was what millions wanted and needed in an automobile at the time: low price, ruggedness, versatility.

In the beginning Ford had raised twenty-eight thousand dollars in cash from other investors, including John and Horace Dodge, to get the company started. But as time went on he found them a nuisance—"parasites" was how he described them to the press—while the investors grew alarmed by Ford's constant talk of cutting prices and building new plants. In 1916, when he announced that no more dividends would be paid and all profits would

be plowed back into the business, the Dodge brothers brought suit. In the end Ford bought out all the investors for one hundred five million dollars and, as one of his associates recalled, "danced a jig all around the room." He was now the sole owner.

Sales and profits continued phenomenal, and Henry Ford not only became very rich, he became very famous. His name was known to peasants in Russia and to Asian villagers who did not recognize the names of such famous Americans as Coolidge, Wilson, or Edison. While another man of enormous wealth, John D. Rockefeller, had come to be hated and reviled, Ford continued high in the esteem of his fellow Americans. For Rockefeller was accused of becoming rich at the expense of the public; Ford, just as assiduously accumulating his hundreds of millions, managed to maintain his image before a grateful public as the modest, homespun provider of the Model T.

By the middle of the twenties the Model T was losing some of its charm. Roads were improving, and it was no longer as necessary to have a mud wagon to get around. Much of the public was beginning to yearn after automobiles with more class than the boxy, unlovely black flivver. Model T sales dropped; those of Ford's competitors climbed. Ford at last gave way to the inevitable, and on May 26, 1927, the last of 15,007,003 Model T's came off the assembly line and Ford shut down his huge River Rouge plant for eighteen months while he retooled for a completely new automobile, the Model A. The coming of the new Ford was a nationally anticipated event: newspapers speculated, comics made jokes, thousands of buyers paid for the car in advance, without the slightest idea of what it was going to look like. The secrecy, carefully protected by the Ford people, resulted in one of the greatest publicity build-ups in industrial history and did wonders for the sale of the Model A, but other automobile makers had gained an advantage during the time Ford was off the market that Ford never was able to overcome.

With the great competitive advantage of the Model T gone, the Ford Motor Company headed into rougher and rougher waters. Ford followed a stubborn anti-union policy, which was effectively and brutally carried out by Harry Bennett, Ford's long-time lieutenant. Bennett's policy led to bloody violence; labor at Ford plants became bitter and productivity sagged. Moreover, accounting methods at Ford were still those of the Model-T days: there was no modern record-keeping and data-reporting system. Nor was there any clear-cut organizational structure, with the result that the executive suite was divided into feuding factions.

The Ford V-8 saved the company during the 1930's, and the involvement of Ford in war production kept it busy through the mid-1940's, but the future after that did not look promising. Henry Ford II, grandson of the founder, became president of the company in 1945, and one of his first acts was to fire Bennett. He made peace with the United Auto Workers, and in time brought the Ford Motor Company back to a healthy and competitive position. That, though, is another story.

Henry Ford, the founder, died in 1947, quite comfortably provided with wordly goods—his personal fortune amounted to well over a billion dollars. In becoming wealthy Ford had quite literally changed the face of America. As automobiles proliferated, the demand for more and better roads grew, and with the spreading network of roads and highways, the nation's pattern of hamlets, small towns, and cities changed. The country store and the crossroads village withered, urban centers grew, suburbia and the shopping center rose, and the inner city decayed. Even without Ford the motorcar would have been inevitable, but it would not have conquered so fast or in the same way.

Aside from his automobile, the thing nearest to Ford's heart was his Greenfield Village in Dearborn, where he amassed all kinds of early Americana; not just old bootjacks and coffee grinders and circus posters, but entire buildings—schoolhouses and blacksmith shops and inns—which he had moved bodily and reassembled, with all equipment and furnishings, to form a nineteenth-century village. There was something paradoxical in Ford's nostalgic endeavor to preserve an embalmed semblance of a vanished small-town way of life, for no one had done more than he to destroy that easy-paced era in American history.

Henry Ford and the Model T may stand as symbols of the second phase of the Industrial Revolution, which began around the turn of the century. An outpouring of consumer goods, from old industries and new, brought a rapid rise in the gross national product and the standard of living. In all this activity many new businesses were founded and many new fortunes made. Those who got rich are far too numerous even to be mentioned in this book. We can single out only a representative few.

In the automobile world alone, there were many other giants, many of whom left their mark on the industry and some of whom left their names on its products: Ransom E. Olds, David Buick, John and Horace Dodge, William C. Durant, Louis Chevrolet, Clement Studebaker, Charles W. Nash, James Packard, Walter Chrysler. Perhaps the most important, though no car bore his name, was Alfred P. Sloan, Jr., who was put in control of General Motors by the Du Ponts after Durant, its founder, almost wrecked the company. With the help of such innovations as annual model changes and choice of colors and all manner of extras, Sloan raised General Motors' share of the market from twelve per cent when he took over in 1920 as vice president in charge of operations to sixty-five per cent when he retired as chairman of the board in 1956. Even more important was Sloan's contribution to the science of business management. Probably more than anyone else, he developed the system of organization, with centralized control at the top and decentralized operations, that was widely copied or adapted by other big corporations.

The automobile age also brought many peripheral industries supplying parts and equipment— and men who profited very well from them. Harvey S. Firestone was one shining example. After trying bookkeeping, and then selling patent medicine, Firestone went to work for the Columbus Buggy Company. One day while driving a buggy with hard rubber tires (still a novelty on streets noisy with steel-rimmed wheels), it suddenly occurred to him, as he put it later, "my future was right on the wheels of my buggy." In 1899 he organized the Firestone Tire and Rubber Company. Solid tires gave way to pneumatics, buggies to automobiles. His original factory had employed ten persons and produced twelve tires a day; at the time of his death in 1938 Firestone Tire and Rubber had, besides its Akron plants, twelve factories in the United States and eight abroad, and was supplying about one-fourth of all the tires used in this country.

THE CEREAL KINGS

The shelves of our supermarkets are filled with packages bearing the names of men who got rich in the food industry. Two of the most famous came from the single modest city of Battle Creek, Michigan, and both built their empires mainly on breakfast foods.

In 1866 Mrs. Ellen White opened a health institute in a farmhouse just outside Battle Creek. The place catered to Seventh Day Adventists, people whose Sabbath is Saturday and who do not eat

Ready When You Stop

A food immediately ready for use. Add a little cream (or milk) and a sprinkle of sugar.

It is put up in double sealed packages—impossible of contamination from dust or moisture.

Post Toasties

the deliciously toasted bits of wafer-like corn are the food for picnics, auto tours and any kind of trips—and for the home.

Its convenience does away with a lot of bother to whoever prepares the meals.

The delightful flavor of Post Toasties makes new friends

GENERAL FOODS CORPORATION

To school well fed on
Grape-Nuts
"There's a Reason"

meat. However, to be very effective the place needed a doctor, and Mrs. White and her husband picked out young John Harvey Kellogg and encouraged him to go to Bellevue Hospital Medical College in New York, from which he returned in 1876 a doctor and surgeon.

Dr. Kellogg took over the post of superintendent of the institute in 1876. He was a dynamo of energy and ideas. One of his first acts was to rename the place the Medical and Surgical Sanitarium, arguing that a new word was needed since the accepted word, "sanatorium," meant a hospital for invalid soldiers. The sanitarium became popular; Kellogg's regimen of fresh air, rest, exercise, and diet did wonders for tired businessmen and flabby middle-aged women. The place grew and grew.

In 1880 Will K. Kellogg, brother of the Doctor and his junior by eight years, went to work at the sanitarium. The Doctor dominated his brother, as he had when they were growing up; Will referred to himself as a "bookkeeper, cashier, packing and shipping clerk, errand boy, and general utility man." He answered the mail, took care of complaints, worked fifteen hours a day, even on Christmas and July Fourth, and waited seven years for his first two-week holiday. It was the Doctor's custom to exercise in the evening by riding about the grounds on a bicycle; Will had to trot alongside while they discussed the day's business.

Dr. Kellogg had been making and marketing by mail on a small scale, through his Sanitas Food Company, various kinds of health foods he concocted. In 1894 the brothers found a way to roll wheat grains into thin flakes; these were added to the Doctor's line under the name Granose and were immediately popular. But the secret of flaked wheat was too good to keep. It leaked out, and Battle Creek became a boom town. Forty-four firms, most operating on a shoestring, were producing wheat flakes, plain or laced with apple juice, maple syrup, or some other flavor, and bearing such titillating names as Hullo-Boena, Hello-Billo, Fruit-Cerro, Flake-Ho, and Abita. The boom quickly collapsed, and with it the sales of Granose.

In 1891 an emaciated businessman in a wheelchair arrived at the Battle Creek Sanitarium. He was

Two pioneers in the breakfast-food industry built their companies into the giants in the field: W. K. Kellogg, whose fortune was founded on corn flakes, and C. W. Post, who started with Postum and Grape-Nuts. At left, early advertisements.

in his late thirties, and his career was at a low point, for he had failed in several enterprises. Several months under Dr. Kellogg's regimen put forty or fifty pounds back on his frame, and the man, Charles W. Post, went forth improved in health and bearing memories of a cereal coffee substitute served at the sanitarium. Outside, he concocted his own cereal coffee, which he called Monk's Brew and which he first marketed in 1894. After two years with no success, he changed the name to Postum and established the Postum Cereal Company.

Post then hired an advertising agency, and the lean Monk's Brew years were quickly left behind. Post found all sorts of wonders in a cup of Postum. "MAKES RED BLOOD!" Postum packages claimed. Charles Post himself invented a disease called "coffee neuralgia" and warned the public against it. He found a tragic case in Aurora, Illinois, and publicized it nationwide: "Lost Eyesight through Coffee Drinking." At the beginning of 1898 he added another product he called Grape-Nuts (which, Dr. Kellogg noted, somewhat resembled his own Granola of toasted grains). By 1900 sales had soared so

that Post was said to be netting three million dollars a year. A corn flakes product named Post Toasties was added to the line. There were eventually others, but those three were the foundation of the Post fortune.

Post's company was later merged with the Jell-O firm and others to become the huge General Foods Company. His fortune went to his daughter Marjorie, whom he had trained in the business while she was in her teens and who became one of the richest women in the country.

The Kelloggs, meanwhile, were not doing as well as their former patient. With their market for wheat flakes much reduced, they had turned to selling corn flakes, again through the Sanitas Food Company. Will Kellogg now had some control over the policies of the company, and he received a quarter of the profits, but he was finally getting fed up with his brother's arrogant and dictatorial ways. He also wanted to advertise aggressively and sell corn flakes in stores, but the Doctor remained conservative and insisted on selling the flakes as a health food through discreet ads in his health journal. The break be-

CONTINUED ON PAGE 295

ALFRED EISENSTAEDT, TIME-LIFE PICTURE AGENCY©TIME INC.

GENERAL FOODS CORPORATION

Mrs. Marjorie Merriweather Post, daughter of the cereal king, greatly increased the value of the business he left her. She also created for herself a life style that could hardly be matched for its combination of magnificence and taste. The picture above was taken in 1944 when she was married to Joseph E. Davies, one-time U.S. ambassador to the Soviet Union. At left is her estate, Mar-A-Lago, at Palm Beach. The pictures on the following pages were taken there and at her other homes in Washington, D.C., and in the Adirondack Mountains.

For the hot summer months Mrs. Post had an Adirondack hideaway she called Camp Topridge. No road led to the isolated spot; the last stage of the trip in could be made only by boat. At left is the canopied cable car that carried guests uphill from the boathouse to the main house. It was only one of the amenities of the mountain retreat, where guests had individual cabins.

Hillwood, her Washington estate, was home to Mrs. Post. There (opposite page) she makes a final inspection of the dinner table before a party that will include the French ambassador. Mrs. Post, meticulous about details, spent all day before a party making sure everything was correct. At right, a footman polishes the silver-gilt service, a task that occupied almost his full time. Above, butlers carry food for a garden party.

CONTINUED FROM PAGE 291

tween the brothers finally came over the building of a fifty-thousand-dollar factory to house machinery for making wheat flakes. After it was finished. the Doctor announced that he had not authorized it, and so his brother would have to pay for it. Will Kellogg was able to obtain the money to pay this sudden debt, but he told his brother that after more th.n twenty-two years he had had much more than enough of him and was quitting as his flunky at the sanitarium.

Will Kellogg was still manager of the Sanitas Company, but there he was an agent of the corporation and not an employee of his brother. Nevertheless, the Doctor had a leading voice in setting Sanitas policies, and Will was impatient with his brother's cautious methods. Finally, after a great deal of haggling, he was able to purchase an option on the Doctor's rights to make and sell corn flakes, and in 1906 he incorporated the Battle Creek Toasted Corn Flake Company.

Will Kellogg's first factory burned down in July, 1907, a year and a half after his company went into business; but within five months it was operating again, with a capacity of four thousand two hundred cases of corn flakes a day. That was only a small beginning. In time corn flakes were being shipped out by the freight carload. One Kellogg advertisement showed a locomotive pulling a string of twenty-one cars consigned to a single broker; it carried the caption, "THE LARGEST SHIPMENT of Breakfast Food Ever Sent to One Person."

Skillful promotion was the key to Will Kellogg's success. Early on he started putting his facsimile signature on packages, and the line, "The original has this signature—W. K. Kellogg," became a dominant theme in advertising. He used such gimmicks as proclaiming a Wink Day. ("Give the Grocer a Wink! And see what you'll get.") The shopper got a sample box of corn flakes, and although at that time the idea of a woman winking was considered a bit daring, the campaign was a success. Kellogg advertised heavily in the leading magazines and in 1912 had what was then the largest sign in the world at Times Square in New York.

It took some time and several lawsuits before Will Kellogg finally disentangled himself completely from the legal ties that had bound him and his brother together. From that point on, his story was one of almost continuous growth and success. There were new Kellogg's breakfast foods—Shredded Wheat, Krumbles, All-Bran—but Toasted Corn Flakes remained the mainstay of the growing Kellogg fortune. When Will Kellogg died in 1951, that fortune—from a business he had started in his late forties—amounted to approximately fifty million dollars.

EASTMAN AND KODAK

Post and Kellogg made their fortunes by giving people something they needed in new forms and packages. George Eastman made his by giving the people something most of them had no idea they wanted. His contribution was a simple camera that anyone could use and the film to go with it, and in doing so he turned photography from a profession into a hobby.

Eastman was born in 1854; his father died when he was eight, and his schooling ended in the seventh grade when he went out into the world to earn his own living and help his widowed mother. He began as an office boy earning three dollars a week in an insurance company. He was intelligent and a hard worker, and by the time he was in his early twenties, he was a junior officer in a bank with a salary of fourteen hundred dollars a year, a respectable sum in that day of uninflated money.

So far nothing in his career suggested a man who might risk his money and position on a venture into strange territory. He seemed destined most likely to be a moderately successful banker. Then, by chance, photography came into his life in 1877, when he was twenty-three. He had planned to make a vacation trip to Santo Domingo, and a friend suggested that a photographic record of his trip would be valuable. The art had advanced little since the days of Mathew Brady; the photographer still required a heavy camera and tripod, a small laboratory of chemicals, scales, graduates, and other equipment, glass plates and boxes for storing them, a darkroom tent, and miscellany. Eastman gamely bought everything he would need, and took lessons in how to use all his chemicals and equipment.

The trip to Santo Domingo fell through, but photography had put its hooks into Eastman. At that time photographs were made by the wet-plate method: the photographer dipped a clear glass plate into light-sensitive chemicals, put it in the camera,

The Japanese garden on the opposite page is only one corner of the grounds of Hillwood, where Mrs. Post lived until her death in 1973. The plantings are immaculately tended, and a large staff is kept busy caring for the huge greenhouse and for the acres of gardens.

took his picture, and developed the plate in his darkroom before the chemicals dried. It was time-consuming, messy, and had no room for spontaneity. George Eastman began to believe that there was a better way, and set out to make a dry plate that could be prepared well ahead of time, used when needed, and then developed at leisure. Other amateurs were engaged in the same quest, but Eastman kept at it with dogged singleness of purpose, going to work in his kitchen laboratory every evening after dinner and often working most of the night till it was time to eat breakfast and return to his job at the bank. By 1880 he had created a dry plate with the sensitized surface protected by a coating of gelatin.

His assets were the dry plate and three thousand dollars in savings. He quit the bank and took as his partner Henry Strong, a genial maker of buggy whips; the two men went into business as the Eastman Dry Plate Company on one rented floor of a factory building in Rochester on the first day of 1881. The new business was almost immediately successful, thanks to Eastman's hard work in managing every phase of the operation, from finding customers and publicizing the firm to keeping an eye on production and improving the plates. Before the end of the year the company moved into a four-story building and opened offices in England.

"The idea gradually dawned on me that what we were doing . . . was not merely making dry plates," Eastman remarked of his first year of business, "but that we were starting out to make photography an everyday affair." But even the dry plates were fragile, heavy to carry, and bulky to store. In 1884 Eastman and his co-workers discovered that collodion, spread on a paper backing, gave a tough, flexible film that could be rolled. The firm devised a roll holder so that any camera could use the new film. But to create a mass market for the film a camera was needed that even a child could operate. The Eastman plant brought forth that marvel of simplicity in 1888. Eastman named it the Kodak.

Eastman once explained how he coined the name. "The letter 'K' had been a favorite with me—it seems a strong, incisive sort of letter. Therefore, the word I wanted had to start with 'K' . . . The word Kodak is the result. Instead of merely making cameras and camera supplies, we made Kodaks and Kodak supplies. It became the distinctive word for our products. Hence the slogan: 'If it isn't an Eastman, it isn't a Kodak.'"

The first Kodak was a model of simplicity, requiring no juggling with focusing or exposure time. It was a rectangular box about six by three by not quite four inches. The user simply aimed the camera and clicked the shutter, then advanced the film with a key and cocked the shutter for the next picture by pulling a cord. The buyer paid twenty-five dollars for this first real family camera, but it came loaded with enough film for one hundred pictures, and when they were used up, he sent the camera to the Eastman plant, where technicians removed and developed the film and made prints. The camera, reloaded and ready for another hundred snapshots, was returned to the owner for ten dollars. The pictures were round and only two and a half inches across, but it was the first time the absolute novice had been able to take any kind of photographs. The Eastman company capitalized on this heady experience in its advertisements with the slogan, "You Press the Button, We Do the Rest."

Even before the first Kodak appeared, Eastman was working toward a film that would not need paper or other backing. In this search he was urged on by his friend Thomas Edison, then working on his motion-picture machine and needing a film able to stand the strain of being drawn through a series of sprocket wheels. In 1889 Henry Reichenbach, a chemist working for Eastman, discovered a celluloidlike material that was everything they needed. Amateur photographers would no longer need to send their cameras back to the factory but could take the exposed rolls to local developing centers—or even develop them themselves.

Eastman made the most of his products, soon building his firm up into a multimillion-dollar empire. The corporation was heavily attacked as a monopoly, to which Eastman blandly replied that at least eight other film-makers, four camera manufacturers, and a fair number of suppliers of other photographic goods were all competing with Eastman Kodak. He was not being completely candid, for the great Eastman complex had tied up more than eighty per cent of the market; the competitors he spoke of had to divide the remaining crumbs among them. Eventually, to avoid federal action, the company did allow retailers to sell competitive goods, and in 1921 divested itself of a number of small subsidiaries to end an anti-trust action brought during the Wilson administration. It made little difference; when Eastman died, his company still controlled between seventy-five and eighty per cent of the American photographic market.

The manufacture of photographic products produced a large quantity of by-products, and thus

George Eastman, en route to Europe in 1890, was photographed holding one of his first Kodaks, which had recently come on the market. The photographer used the same kind of camera, which took a round picture.

gave rise to an industry in such nonphotographic products as wood alcohol, cellulose, and synthetic fabrics. Eastman found himself rather adrift among the chemists and their formulas; although he remained in charge and made the final decisions, he could no longer contribute much by tinkering in the workshops. With time to spare, he turned to good works. He was very generous to the city of Rochester —an orchestra, a theater, municipal buildings, and buildings and endowments for the University of Rochester. His benefactions extended to schools beyond Rochester; in all he gave away almost seventy-five million dollars.

In 1931, when he was seventy-seven, Eastman began to suffer from a spinal ailment that threatened to cripple him. A lifelong bachelor and now alone, he considered his situation, made up his mind, and in March of 1932 went into a bedroom and shot himself. He left a brief note on a bedside table: "To my Friends: My work is done. Why wait?"

LAND AND POLAROID

Edwin H. Land is another American who made himself wealthy—enormously so—through photography, but there is little other resemblance between him and George Eastman. Eastman was essentially a tinkerer, a pragmatic experimenter; Land, the inventor of the 60-second camera, was a brilliant scientist, a man with the theoretic background to solve his basic problems before ever going near a laboratory or workshop.

Land was in New York City in 1926 on a holiday fling during his first year at Harvard when a seemingly trivial incident occurred. He was walking along Broadway, he recalls, when it occurred to him

that filters that could polarize light would cut out the glare of headlights and make night driving easier. He was only seventeen at the time, but the moment and the idea marked the beginning of a life career.

Land got a leave of absence from Harvard and plunged into research that within two years produced his first sheets of polarizing materials, which he named Polaroid. In 1929 he returned to Harvard, which provided a laboratory where he could continue his experiments, but after three years Land was so impatient to start marketing his now-improved Polaroid that he left college again, though

Girls at the Kodak plant in Harrow, England, during the 1890's (above) processed film from Great Britain and Europe. (At that time the entire camera had to be sent to the factory to have the exposed film removed and new film loaded.) On opposite page, George Eastman tries out one of his company's new cameras in his garden on his seventy-fifth birthday.

he was within a few courses of his degree. He never did get his diploma.

For a time Land and a physics professor ran a research laboratory and made polarizers; then in

1937 he organized the present Polaroid Corporation. His reputation was already such that he was able to get backing from a silk-hat group of financiers not known for supporting shaky enterprises. He was introduced to several Wall Street moneymen, among them W. Averell Harriman, Lewis Strauss, and James P. Warburg, and so impressed them that they not only put up an initial three hundred seventy-five thousand dollars in capital but let him keep a majority of the stock in the new company.

Polaroid sales climbed steadily, from one hundred forty-two thousand dollars to a million dollars a year between 1937 and the outbreak of the war at the end of 1941. Polaroid sunglasses were increasingly popular; the company marketed a glare-free study lamp; a variety of Polaroid filters went to scientific laboratories and photographers. The war brought a change in tempo as the company turned to military optics and Land concentrated on infrared searchlights and gun sights, but it was only a temporary interruption for Polaroid.

His work with polarized light has made Land the world's leading authority on the subject, and he holds hundreds of patents for inventions and discoveries in this and related fields. But the idea that would make him one of the wealthiest men in the world came while he was taking snapshots of his daughter one day during World War II. When she asked somewhat petulantly why she had to wait to see the finished pictures, it suddenly occurred to Land that photography still had a long way to go. A person who buys another commodity—an automobile, a pair of gloves—can use it immediately. But when he takes a picture he has to wait days, or at least hours, to see the result.

Beginning in 1944, Land spent his spare time considering how to produce a finished photograph in the camera. It was an awesome challenge. After more than a century of research, photographers still developed, fixed, washed, and dried their negatives; then from them printed, developed, fixed, washed, and dried the prints—this in a dark room. Land was attempting to accomplish the equivalent of all this in a camera, and in only a minute or so. His scientific friends told him it could not be done, yet within only six months he had solved the basic problem, and by 1947 all the details of camera and chemistry had been worked out.

The first 60-second Land camera went on sale with limited advertising in a single outlet—the Jordan Marsh department store in Boston—on

November 26, 1948. The crush to buy was so frantic that harried salesmen sold some display models from which parts were missing. After a breathing spell to build up its inventory, Polaroid put on a big promotion in Miami, reasoning that most of the buyers would be prosperous vacationers who would carry the camera and its praises to all parts of the country. That first year, 1949, Polaroid sales zoomed to $6,680,000, more than five million of it from the new camera and film.

Land is a social visionary who believes that industry should provide every worker with "a worthwhile, highly rewarding, highly creative, inspiring daily job." As a scientist he likes to lock himself away in the laboratory for days and nights while working on an idea. Thanks to the continuing stream of innovations and improvements that came out of that laboratory, Polaroid became one of the most renowned growth stocks on Wall Street. An investor who put one hundred dollars in Polaroid in the 1930's would have had two hundred thousand at the peak of the market in the 1960's. As for Land himself, with assets in the hundreds of millions, he may well be the richest inventor in history.

PATTERSON AND WATSON

John H. Patterson is remembered not so much for the size of his fortune as for inventing high-powered salesmanship; to put his cash registers in as many places of business across the country as possible he became the first of the supersalesmen—and showed countless other businessmen how to get a reluctant public to buy their products.

Patterson was born in 1844 near Dayton, Ohio, and unlike most businessmen of his era, he was a college graduate. It was a distinction he ever after denigrated as a waste of time. After college he variously helped on the family farm, collected tolls on one of the Ohio canals, ran a coal yard with his two brothers, developed Ohio coal and iron mines, and then for several years was general manager for a mining company in an Ohio town.

Patterson discovered that the company store was losing six thousand dollars a year instead of making twelve thousand as the books said it should, and the cause was easy to find: dishonest clerks were dipping often and heavily into the store's cashboxes. Patterson learned that a Dayton saloonkeeper, James S. Ritty, had solved a similar problem by devising a sort of mechanical cashbox. A clerk registered the amount of the sale by pushing keys that opened the cash drawer, publicly exhibited the amount of the sale, and gave out a resounding *bong*. He then deposited the money from the customer, made change, and closed the drawer, aware that the sonorous bell note had called attention (especially that of the manager) to what he was doing. The device was, of course, the first cash register, and it enforced honesty.

Patterson bought two of the machines, known as "Ritty's Incorruptible Cashier," and pilferage at the store ended. He and his brothers at once bought Ritty's stock, and two years later, in 1884, gained complete control and changed the name to National Cash Register Company.

Patterson had his product; now he set out to sell it. He improved the cash register first of all, but mechanical imperfections were not his main problem. Most of his prospects had never heard of a cash register and so could see no reason why they should put out a lot of money to have an unnecessary gadget in their stores.

To build a dedicated work force that would go out and break down this opposition, Patterson started from the ground up. In a day when industrial doctrine called for paying employees as little as possible and not worrying about their working conditions, he went completely against tradition by building a factory whose walls were eighty per cent glass and whose spacious grounds were landscaped with flowers. The inside was even more revolutionary: swimming pools, showers, hot lunches, medical care, inspirational lectures. And National Cash Register wages were high. Whenever he was asked why all this folderol that could only ruin good workers, Patterson's answer was to the point. "It pays," he would say. Outside his office door he hung a sign, "Be Brief—Omit All Compliments About Welfare Work."

As the spearhead of his entire organization, Patterson created what he called "the American Selling Force." By cajolery, pleading, exhortation, praise, and sarcasm, he imbued his salesman with an evangelical belief in what they were doing, until they saw this machine with its nickel plate and bonging bells as a Great Cash Register in the Sky. From a group of average men Patterson built one of the most aggressive bodies of salesmen that has ever existed.

Patterson was the inventor of the standardized sales talk. It was a period when salesmen depended on charm and personality; sell yourself first and then sell your line. Not Patterson's men. It was all down in the *N.C.R. Primer*. At first the methods in the Primer were only recommended but later were made compulsory when it proved that they sold more registers and earned more commissions than the personality approach.

Patterson's salesmen were not allowed to carry a screwdriver lest they get sidetracked into service work. They were to concentrate entirely on selling, and after finishing Patterson's training program, they were ready for the most reluctant customer. Demonstrations were usually staged in a sample room in a first-class hotel, often with such trappings as backdrop curtains painted to represent the interior of a store. Clocks were never in evidence; they might remind the prospect that he had an appointment elsewhere.

The salesmen were prepared to handle deftly such simple objections as these: "I don't have the money." "I don't need one." "My present system works fine." And once the prospect was softened, the closing was done with finesse—no blunt, "Let's sign the order and wrap this up." Instead, the salesman might ask, "What color do you want?" or "When do you want delivery?"

Patterson had blackboards and sketch pads everywhere in his offices so that he and others could follow his precept, "Visualize! Analyze! Dramatize!," by sketching out problems or ideas. He held frequent conventions and conferences, which combined the most frenetic aspects of a carnival and a revival; there were flags, songs, and competitions with prizes, and his salesmen went home tired but fired with determination to fill the land with National Cash Registers.

Patterson was a great believer in slogans and maxims, which he strewed liberally about the premises. Among his idiosyncrasies was a belief that regular fresh starts were important, so he would go through his executives' desks from time to time, emptying the drawers and burning the entire contents, even personal photographs. He was also likely to fire any executive who had been around long enough to begin to seem indispensible—there were few old-timers at National Cash Register. He also went in for a succession of health fads: horseback-riding one time, no salt, pepper, eggs, or butter at the executive table during another period, no tea or coffee yet again. And his men went gamely along with all of them.

CONTINUED ON PAGE 304

John H. Patterson (with mustache), the cash-register man, looked like a conservative, Victorian businessman, but he was, in fact, the inventor of many of the most aggressive modern selling techniques.

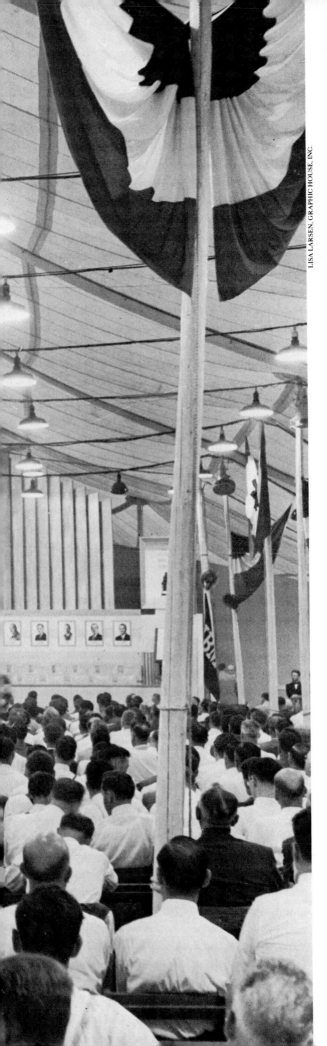

Thomas J. Watson exhorts a 1947 revival-style meeting of International Business Machines top salesmen (left) to go forth and do even better in 1948. Below, son Thomas Watson, Jr. poses before some of the products IBM was promoting in that postwar year. At bottom, two IBM salesmen pause before an honor roll of supersalesmen and draw inspiration from one of the ubiquitous slogans of their leader, Thomas Watson.

THERE IS NO SUCH THING AS STANDING STILL

CONTINUED FROM PAGE 301

Patterson's eccentricities did not interfere with NCR sales. By about 1910 the company controlled ninety per cent of cash-register sales in the United States and was coveting the remaining ten per cent. In 1922, the year Patterson died, annual gross sales were twenty-nine million dollars. The crotchety old man left a healthy organization; its annual sales have exceeded the two-billion-dollar mark, though not on cash registers alone any more, for it now also makes various accounting machines and data-processing machines.

One of John Patterson's supersalesmen was a young man named Thomas J. Watson, who would later go out and become a great success on his own. Watson's methods would never quite lose the stamp of his former chief and mentor; in fact, the slogan "Think," which would become so closely associated with him, was one that had bemused him in the halls of National Cash Register.

Thomas Watson went to work for the National Cash Register Company in 1898 at the age of twenty-four, after a few years of selling pianos, sewing machines, organs, and cash registers for another company. At NCR Patterson had his usual galvanizing effect, deeply impressing Watson with the philosophy of the "company spirit." Watson related how, in his early days, when he was discouraged, he was "fortified with certain tried and true homilies." This incident is credited with Watson's copious use of maxims and slogans to stimulate employes: "Sell and Serve." "Aim High." And the omnipresent "Think."

After leaving National Cash Register at the age of thirty-nine, Watson became president of the Computing-Tabulating-Recording Company, which later changed its name to the somewhat less cumbersome International Business Machines Corporation. Watson financed growth with loans, with the result that gross sales increased from two million to more than thirty-three million dollars between 1914 and 1949, and company personnel in the same period went from two hundred thirty-five to twelve thousand. When he handed over the reins as chief executive officer to his son in 1956, just a month before his death, IBM had one hundred eighty-eight U.S. offices and six plants, and another two hundred twenty-seven offices and seventeen smaller plants were spread through eighty nations. In 1975 IBM was the second biggest money-maker (after Exxon) among all U.S. corporations.

Thomas Watson's long leadership of IBM was pointed to as a classic example of one-man rule in business. His relationship with his employees was paternalistic, and at times domineering. But he paid well, provided welfare benefits including sick insurance, paying full salary up to six months when such ideas were not popular among businessmen, and even set up country clubs for his workers. In return for all these good things, he constantly exhorted his people to THINK THINK THINK. That, and to be loyal and to work hard. His paternalism was often criticized, but there is no quarreling with his results.

The revolution in electronics has created considerable quick wealth. Consider briefly David Packard and William R. Hewlett of the Hewlett-Packard Company who started their business in 1939 when they came out of Stanford University with fresh electrical engineering degrees. Their capital investment at the outset was five hundred thirty-eight dollars, their shop Packard's home garage, their stock in trade a new type of audio oscillator, which Hewlett had developed while in school. They made an early big step forward when they sold eight of the devices to Disney studios, which used them to produce sound effects for *Fantasia*.

Twenty years later Hewlett-Packard had become a leading manufacturer of electronic measuring instruments. Its sales in 1967 were almost a quarter of a billion dollars and rising, and both founders were tremendously rich, with about a quarter of a billion dollars worth of stock each. Since that time the amazing development of pocket calculators has come about and Hewlett-Packard has been one of the principal names in the manufacture of the miniature calculating machines.

COSMETIC KINGS AND QUEENS

It does not always take a Model T, the manufacture of electronics, or the invention of a magic camera to produce great wealth. There was, for instance, King Gillette. Gillette for years had been obsessed with the idea of inventing something—if possible, something that would be discarded after using. In his search for an idea he even made lists, going through the alphabet, but the light came one day while he was shaving and found his straight-edge razor dull. What the world of men needed, he decided, was disposable razor blades, made of thin metal and clamped in a holder.

It was eleven years, however, before Gillette made anything from his idea. There was a long, long time of experimentation with clock springs and other thin metal strips and hones and whatnot while friends and others joked and told him to drop the whole thing. But eventually he found twenty backers willing to put up two hundred fifty dollars each, and with the money, he purchased equipment and hired an expert mechanic. The first Gillette safety razor became a reality in 1903 and fifty were sold that year. Two years later the number had increased to more than a quarter of a million. Unfortunately for King Gillette, he did not retain much of the huge earnings from his idea. He sank much of his money into real estate, overextended himself in planting huge date orchards, and spent money publishing books advocating a corporation-run world. When he died he had only about a million dollars left.

Gerard Lambert found his way to a considerable amount of money by playing on people's insecurities, by making them afraid that they might be offending others. Lambert was general manager of a moderately successful firm founded by his father, the Lambert Pharmacal Company, which made Listerine, a mouthwash for which various valuable therapeutic properties were claimed. The story goes that an employee was reading aloud a clipping from a medical journal when he came to the word "halitosis." "What's halitosis?" Lambert asked, and the employee replied, "bad breath."

It was all Lambert needed. Shortly thereafter he was writing the first of a great number of tragic little stories, of women who faded away into spinsterhood never knowing why romance had cooled, of men whose dream of a home and slippers and fireplace and loving wife had faded when their fiancées' kisses turned cold. And all because even their best friends wouldn't tell them. The nation learned from Listerine advertisements the tragic consequences of halitosis.

By the time the great halitosis campaign finally ran its fantastically successful course, Gerard Lambert also had a Listerine toothpaste on the market and was promoting Listerine as a specific for sore throat and dandruff, and even as an after-shave lotion. His agile mind had increased the company's earnings and his own income many times; any limit on his mounting wealth seemed far away when he became bored with making millions. He sold all his

Helena Rubinstein learned, while still in her teens, that beauty could be packaged in jars and tubes and vended like any other commodity; she capitalized on the discovery so well that she became a multimillionaire. Here she is photographed in her laboratory, whence came many of the beauty aids that made her rich.

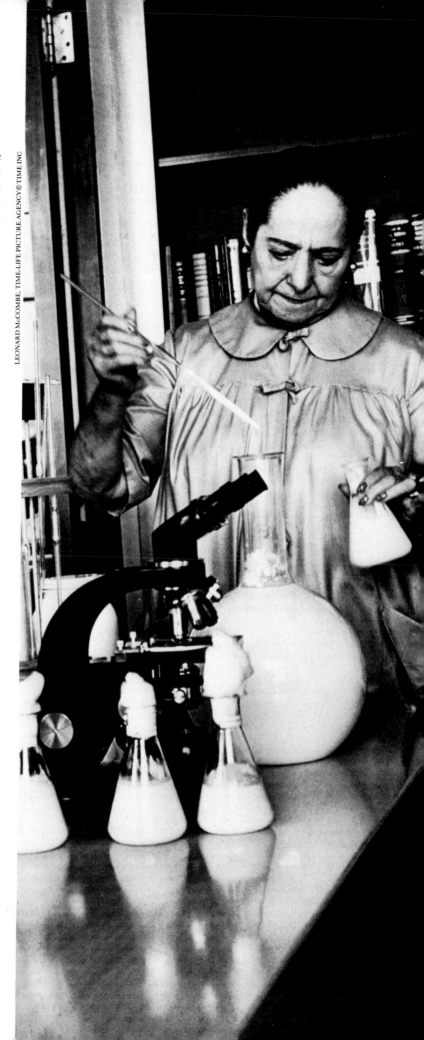

own holdings, and, as he said, "from that day to this I have never tried to make another dollar."

One of the greatest markets is the demand for beauty. Women without it want to make themselves beautiful; those who are attractive, work to remain that way; those who are fading, fight to keep or regain what they had. It is a billion-dollar business: cosmetics, beauty parlors, body salons, all the rest. Beauty is a commodity like any other, and one of its chief purveyors was Helena Rubinstein.

Miss Rubinstein, a Polish girl, was visiting relatives in Australia when her career began. Australian women, their skin dried and roughened by the arid climate, admired her complexion and asked to use some of her creams. Miss Rubinstein smelled a business opportunity, and sent home for a supply of cosmetics and opened a shop. A year and a half later, at the ripe age of nineteen, she left Australia with a hundred thousand dollars and went into business in London's fashionable Mayfair section.

During World War I, Helena (by then Madame) Rubinstein decided to make New York her base, and moved there in 1915. She began to open beauty salons across the United States, which not only sold her various beauty preparations but also offered clients skin analyses with their jars of cream. She had been one of the first dealers in cosmetics to realize that dry skins and oily skins should not be treated with the same product—and, being an excellent businesswoman, she capitalized on the fact.

The Rubinstein line of cosmetics ran into the hundreds of items. At one point a count showed 629 items: 62 creams, 78 powders, 46 perfumes and colognes, 69 lotions, and 115 lipsticks, along with a number of soaps, rouges, eye shadows, and the like. Rubinstein girls told customers that such a large number was necessary so that exactly the right product would be available for every woman's particular beauty needs, but the real reason for such an abundance was that Madame Rubinstein was competing with her archrival Elizabeth Arden.

Madame Rubinstein also operated a very plush body shop on New York's Fifth Avenue, where women could come for a morning of stretching, vibrating, massage, heat rays, sweating in hot blankets, exercise, and a bath in milk; then, after a lunch of raw vegetables, they were kept occupied during the afternoon with foot massage, face mask treatment, shampoo, and hair setting. The cost was considerable.

Madame Rubinstein died in 1965 at the age of ninety-four. The personal fortune she left showed

A portrait of King Gillette, founder of the Safety Razor Company, looms behind a later president, Joseph Sprang. Gillette had a unique idea, spent years developing and marketing it, and then lost his company and most of his fortune through unwise investments.

how much money can be found in a jar of cream; she was worth more than a hundred million dollars.

JAMES LING, CONGLOMERATOR

During the booming postwar economy—and especially during the great Wall Street bull market of the 1960's—a new phenomenon appeared in American business. This was the conglomerate corporation, a kind of enterprise that, as its name indicates, was a collection of widely diverse enterprises under one management roof.

The pioneer and wonder boy in conglomerates was a young man named James Ling, who returned home to Dallas in 1946 after two years in the U.S. Navy, sold his house to raise money, and with an initial capital of three thousand dollars started an electrical contracting business. The times were in his favor; the postwar building boom provided a wide-open market, and by the early 1950's his business, which he called Ling Electric, had gross annual sales of more than a million dollars.

Ling incorporated to escape some of the taxes that were taking most of his profits, but when he proposed selling stock, Texas bankers were amused at the idea of such a small company going public. Ling was not fazed. He got authorization to issue eight hundred thousand shares of stock, kept half, and put the rest on sale—at $2.25 a share. He and a small group of friends sold the stock door-to-door and by telephone—even from a booth at the Texas State Fair—and disposed of the entire offering.

Now, with new working capital, Ling bought out another electrical contracting firm, paying cash. Ling's corporation was now twice as big as before; he issued more stock, and on his next two moves, when he gathered in electronics firms, he was able to do so by a stock-trade deal, using little cash. Each acquisition increased the value of Ling stock.

Ling's operating method was to issue new stock each time he added a new company to his holdings, and to use that stock as the wherewithal to acquire still more companies. In 1960 he made his largest acquisition to date, a Dallas-based firm called Temco Electronics, and Ling changed his letterhead to Ling-Temco Electronics. Next came Chance Vought, a large maker of aircraft and missiles. Ling bought up a controlling interest in the company's stock and took over against the wishes of Chance Vought management. Now Ling headed Ling-Temco-Vought—or LTV as it became known in business circles.

Next Ling went after Wilson and Company, in a maneuver that a news magazine called something like Jonah swallowing the whale. Wilson was already a conglomerate of meat packing, sporting goods, and pharmaceutical businesses, with annual sales of about a billion—twice those of LTV. But Ling quietly bought up Wilson's stock, and the first intimation that Wilson's president had of what was happening came when he got a personal visit from one of Ling's men.

For a time there was no stopping Ling. He took in almost anything not tied down, including Jones and Laughlin Steel, and Greatamerica Corporation, which was also a small conglomerate in itself, owning Braniff Airways, National Car Rental, and various insurance companies. By 1968 LTV was number 38 on *Fortune*'s list of the five hundred leading corporations; its annual sales were $1.8 billion. Ling spoke expansively of his plans for 1970: "I'll say here and now that if we're not closer to five

When James Ling (above) competed in a two-mile run for executives in 1972, his reputation as the wonder boy of conglomerates had all but vanished; his Ling-Temco-Vought stock was worth less than a tenth of what it had been three years earlier, and its prospects were dim.

billion dollars than four, then my name won't be associated with this company."

But the career of the wonder boy had depended mainly on the bull market and easy credit. In 1969 and 1970 the bears took over. LTV stock sagged to nine dollars by 1971; it had soared to one hundred thirty-five dollars in 1968. Ling is not quite a poor man today; but compared to the days when he was riding high, his fortune is all but gone.

HOWARD HUGHES

Howard Hughes, too, depended on a diversity of enterprises to eventually amass the one and a half billion dollars, more or less, that he had when he died. Unlike such men as Henry Ford, George Eastman, and Will Kellogg, he did not stick to one business. Unlike such financial wizards as Jimmy Ling, he used real money, not the paper profits of a boom, and most of it was his own. Though his personal life was secretive to the point of obsession, there was nothing secret about his major business affairs.

Hughes got his start at the age of eighteen when his father died, leaving him a three-quarters interest in a business called the Hughes Tool Company. It was a small company, but it manufactured a product in considerable demand: a bit for drilling oil wells invented by the elder Hughes and superior to all other types on the market for cutting through rock. For years the Hughes Tool Company would finance other Howard Hughes ventures.

As a minor, Howard Hughes had to get court permission to vote his own stock, but then he took over completely, first buying out the remaining quarter share in the company, which his father had bequeathed to a number of relatives. He hired capable men and put them in key positions, and when he was satisfied that the firm was working smoothly, turned its operation over to them and moved to southern California. Though he refused ever to dilute his absolute ownership of Hughes Tool, he hardly ever set foot inside it again during the rest of his life.

In California he was talked into backing a motion picture. The result was a disaster called *Swell Hogan*, never released. But in watching it being made, Hughes was bitten by the movie bug and proceeded to produce a number of pictures, with mixed success. In 1927 he became director as well as producer of an opus called *Hell's Angels*, a World War I aviation story. Hughes spent lavishly, among other things buying and rebuilding dozens of old airplanes. Then, during production, sound came to the motion-picture screen, and Hughes decided to turn *Hell's Angels* into a sound picture. It meant scrapping much of his existing footage, especially since his leading lady, Greta Nissen, had an almost impenetrable Norwegian accent. In her place he

In becoming a billionaire Howard Hughes punctuated his life with dramatic—and often enigmatic—episodes. Above, he is given a ticker-tape parade in New York after his 1938 around-the-world flight. At far left, he sits with Jean Harlow, an unknown until he made her a star with *Hell's Angels*. At left center, Hughes testifies at a 1947 Senate hearing, where he lashed back at those who were attempting to impugn his handling of wartime airplane contracts. At near left, in 1972, Hughes leaves his London hotel in a limousine whose windows are blocked with newspapers.

hired an unknown named Jean Harlow, who was paid one hundred twenty-five dollars a week. The picture was released after three years in production; it had cost three and a half million dollars, an enormous amount for that time, and had taken the lives of four stunt fliers.

Hughes continued making motion pictures until 1932. Critics found them empty and in poor taste, but Hughes had a feeling for the common denominator—for corn—and laced his pictures heavily with sex, violence, and sentimentality. In 1939, after a hiatus of seven years, he returned to motion pictures to make a Western of thin plot called *The Outlaw*. In it he starred Jane Russell, a nineteen-year-old dentist's receptionist, whose abundant talents he emphasized even more by designing a special brassiere. *The Outlaw* cost three million four hundred thousand dollars, and was notable for the long battle (much of it for publicity purposes) that Hughes fought with the censors over scenes that were too extravagant with Miss Russell's cleavage.

When Hughes gave up motion pictures in 1932, it was for another consuming passion, this time flying. He had been flying for a long time, ever since he first took lessons at the age of nineteen. During the filming of *Hell's Angels*, he crashed while trying to prove his stunt fliers wrong in saying that a certain aerial maneuver was impossible; he crushed the bones of one side of his face badly, but the accident did not dampen his enthusiasm. Now in 1934 he became obsessed with speed, and with an aeronautics engineer and a pilot-mechanic to help him, set out to design a faster plane. He had a knack for aircraft design, and he and his assistants created a plane designated the H-1, flush-riveted and with retractible landing gear —both new ideas—to reduce drag. When Hughes took it on its speed test flight in September, 1935, the H-1 amazed the nation with a clocked speed of 352.39 miles an hour, almost forty more than the previous record. A few months later he set a coast-to-coast record of nine hours and twenty-seven minutes in a Northrup Gamma he had modified, and a year later in his H-1 he raced across the country in seven hours and twenty-eight minutes.

Looking for another record to break, Hughes modified a Lockheed Lodestar, filled it with extra gas tanks, named it "New York World's Fair, 1939" (there was a promotional tie-in), and with a hand-picked crew of four left New York on July 10, 1938, to fly around the world. The flight, with stops at Paris, Moscow, Omsk, Fairbanks, Minneapolis, and finally New York again, took three days and

nineteen hours, half the time required by Wiley Post for a similar flight. Hughes was lionized; his honors included one of New York's ticker-tape parades.

In 1937 Hughes went into the airlines business, buying a controlling interest in a struggling carrier called Transcontinental and Western Airways. He renamed it Trans World Airways and bought more of its outstanding stock until he owned a commanding seventy-eight per cent; thereafter he refused to permit any public offering of stock that would dilute his overwhelming control, just as he so jealously guarded his absolute ownership of Hughes Tool Company.

With the approach of war, Hughes turned to producing military hardware. The Hughes Tool Company successfully carried through a contract for the centrifugal casting of aircraft cannons, while Hughes undertook to design aircraft for the armed forces in a hangar at Burbank, California. From these aviation-related activities a new enterprise was formed, the Hughes Aircraft Company.

A bizarre Hughes creation of this period was an eight-engine plywood flying boat designed to ferry seven hundred soldiers overseas safely above enemy submarines. Nicknamed the "Spruce Goose," it was flown just once by Hughes, for one mile at a height of seventy feet and then was retired for further work. From that time on it sat in a huge shed on the Long Beach waterfront under close guard, while the coming of jet aircraft made obsolete any potentialities it may have had. It cost Hughes some fifty million dollars, and to the day of his death he refused to junk it.

Business slumped drastically for Hughes Aircraft at the end of the war, but the firm soon made its contacts with the burgeoning young electronics industry. Under vigorous leadership, headed by Charles B. Thornton, a clever administrator, and Drs. Simon Ramo and Dean Wooldridge, brilliant young scientists, the company grew rapidly, filling government needs for radar, weapons guidance systems, and various space hardware.

In 1948 Hughes got into the motion-picture business again by buying almost nine-million-dollars' worth of stock in RKO, and six years later he made the studio completely his with a further twenty-four-million-dollar purchase of stock. But motion

Kokichi Mikimoto (opposite), the cultured-pearl king, had his picture taken in 1946 in a black cape and a derby hat that he had brought home from London. At that time he was reporting the highest income in Japan.

pictures had never been one of Hughes' strong points, whether he was producing or directing, and he did little better as an owner. In 1955 he sold out, making a million-dollar profit, a poor showing for seven years' investment and involvement.

By the mid-fifties the Hughes empire was beginning to show signs of strain because of Hughes' erratic management. Time meant nothing to him: he would call his executives as readily at 3 A.M. as at 3 P.M. He often could not be reached on matters requiring his personal decision; all that could be done was to leave a message—and Hughes might call back in the next few hours, or two weeks later. And as Hughes became more and more of a recluse, and as his phobia about germs increased, it became exceedingly difficult to arrange personal meetings with him.

Hughes Aircraft was the first to suffer from this deterioration; in July of 1953 Ramo and Wooldridge left to found their own very successful business, and Thornton soon joined the exodus. Hughes was left with a demoralized company unable to fulfill large and critical government contracts, and was faced with a choice of either loosening his jealous personal control or losing control altogether. He chose the former course, putting Hughes Aircraft under the administration of a newly created Hughes Medical Foundation, although he remained president.

There had been rumbling in TWA for a long time over Hughes' methods, until in 1966, after long litigation, Hughes was deprived of his voting rights on the grounds of mismanagement. The airline had been very close to Hughes' heart; deprived of control over it, he decided to give it up completely. He received a check for $546,549,771 for his seventy-eight per cent share of the stock, probably the largest single check ever issued to an individual.

With all this loose change in his pocket, Hughes changed his base of operations completely, going to Las Vegas, where he immediately secluded himself in a hotel and began buying up gambling casinos, hotels, and great tracts of land in and around the city. Hughes saw little or nothing of what he was buying, for he had by now become an almost total recluse, seldom venturing outside his hotel suite, where he was served by a small group of trusted retainers (most of them Mormons, whom he believed to be more honest).

Howard Hughes fled Las Vegas in 1970 just as suddenly and unexpectedly as he had arrived. During the next six years he lived variously in the Bahamas, London, Managua, and finally Acapulco,

although so secretive were his moves that seldom at any given time was the public certain of his whereabouts.

In the seventies the Summa Corporation, a holding company, became the keystone of the Hughes empire, replacing the Hughes Tool Company, which for so many years had produced large and steady profits and provided the foundation for Hughes' growth. In 1972 the tool company itself was sold to a group of major employees for one hundred forty million dollars.

Hughes' methods and personality quirks seem designed more to destroy a business empire than to build one up. Yet when Howard Hughes died in April, 1976, he left a fortune estimated at around one and a half billion dollars. He had begun with a factory worth about a million dollars.

Howard Hughes was such a rare bird that we can hardly expect to see his like again. But it is not impossible to imagine future Eastmans and Pattersons, Rubinsteins and Kelloggs. Where they will come from is, as always, a matter for speculation. Will men twenty years from now be making fortunes from new sources of energy? A windmill king perhaps. Or from some machine to harvest the produce of the seas? A Cyrus McCormick of the deep, it might be. If these ideas seem fanciful, consider the case of a Japanese who did indeed make a great fortune—surely the most improbable fortune of the twentieth century—from one particular product of the oceans. He was Kokichi Mikimoto, the pearl king.

Mikimoto was a peddler of dried seafoods when he got the idea of putting oysters to work for him. Pearls are produced, in nature's way, when an oyster accidentally gets a grain of sand inside its shell and, to ease the irritation, begins covering it with layer on layer of a substance it secretes called nacre. Since this happens infrequently, divers had to bring up and shuck an enormous number of oysters to find one pearl. Mikimoto set out to perfect a method known to the Chinese since the thirteenth century. By a long process of trial and error, he learned to insert a granule of mother-of-pearl into the oyster's flesh at a precise spot between the stomach and kidney where it would bother the oyster most. The resulting pearls were indistinguishable from natural pearls, except by x-ray, and could be marketed for a quarter of the price, with plenty of profit for Mikimoto. By 1946, nine years before his death at ninety-six, he paid the highest income tax in Japan.

So long as a man can make a fortune by outwitting oysters, the economic frontier is not closed.

A PORTFOLIO: THE AFFLUENT LIFE

THE LAST OF THE GREAT DANDIES, LUCIUS BEEBE,
WAS PHOTOGRAPHED ABOVE BY SLIM AARONS
IN THE GARDEN COURT OF THE PALACE HOTEL IN
SAN FRANCISCO. SUCH ELEGANCE OF PLACE AND
DRESS IS NOW OUT OF STYLE. BUT THE MODERN
RICH, AS SEEN ON THE FOLLOWING PAGES, FIND
MANY OTHER REWARDS FOR THEIR WEALTH.

SLIM AARONS, PHOTO RESEARCHERS

In the twentieth century the homes of the rich acquired a new feature: the luxurious swimming pool. This one, with its Greek temple and black sphinxes, was built for Mrs. Frederick Guest, the daughter of Andrew Carnegie's partner Henry Phipps, on her oceanfront estate, Villa Artemis, at Palm Beach. The young lady by the pool is her daughter-in-law, Cee Zee Guest.

The bathing pavilion shown at right is also in Palm Beach and belongs to Mrs. Albin Holder, whose first husband was Howell Tyson Lykes, a New Orleans shipping magnate. The bathing beauty on the steps is Mrs. Arthur Lee Kinsolving, Jr.

OVERLEAF (pages 316–17): Thomas Felix Bolack and his family share their home at Farmington, New Mexico, with some of Mr. Bolack's trophies. Bolack got rich by finding oil in an area where geologists told him not to look. Now he spends his spare time hunting beasts around the world. The polar bear was shot on the ice of the Churki Sea, off Siberia.

JOHN LANNOIS, BLACK STAR

Few of the present-day rich seem to have either the homes or the flair to give the fancy parties their predecessors did. It took Truman Capote, a writer of moderate means, to give a masked ball that, judged by its guest list, was the most glittering of recent times. In the picture on the opposite page, a properly masked couple arrives for the party at New York's Plaza Hotel.

More in vogue than masked balls are small parties like the one shown in the picture at left at the home of Mr. and Mrs. H. Bradley Jones in Pasadena, California. And for dining out, there is always Maxim's in Paris (above).

OVERLEAF: It would be hard to find a more spectacular site for a swimming pool than this one. It belongs to the former president of the Research Institute of America, Carl Hovgard, whose house overlooks the desert at Carefree, Arizona.

Elegance has not completely vanished from modern life, as these pictures show. At left on the opposite page are two ladies from Brooklyn Heights, Miss Mary Appleton and Mrs. Helen Appleton Reed, at the opening of an art show. Miss Mary, a friend of Gertrude Vanderbilt Whitney, worked at the Whitney Museum of American Art for forty years. She and her sister, though never rich, always came to openings in antique jewelry, satins, and Venetian lace.

At right on the opposite page are two great beauties of their respective generations, Mrs. Winston (Cee Zee) Guest and Mme. Jacques Balsan, who was once the Duchess of Marlborough, and before that Consuelo Vanderbilt.

Grey toppers and picture hats, as seen in the picture at left above, are proper garb on the opening day of the Ascot racing season, even as they were in the time of *My Fair Lady*.

The lawn tennis courts of the Newport Casino look very much as they did when the game was introduced there in 1880. This was the scene of the national championships until 1914, when they were moved to Forest Hills. More recently the Casino's president, James H. Van Alen, an heir to the Astor fortune, originated the "sudden death" system for tennis that is now used to decide games in championship matches.

International polo also made its first appearance in Newport. In 1875 James Gordon Bennett, Jr., had brought back some balls and mallets from England and ordered a carload of cow ponies from Texas. In 1886, in the first international match, a British team beat the Americans, two games to one.

One sport that makes no compromise with the casual modern world, in either its dress or its horsemanship, is fox hunting. This is Mr. Henry Robertson Fenwick, Master of Foxhounds of the Green Spring Valley Hunt in Maryland, with his whippers-in

9. WEALTH & SOCIETY

THE GOSPEL OF WEALTH

Just before New Year's Day, 1868, Andrew Carnegie sat down to assess his business and his life. This, in part and with its own quixotic spelling, is what he wrote:

> Thirty three and an income of 50,000$ per annum.
>
> By this time two years I can so arrange all my business as to secure at least 50,000 per annum. Beyond this never earn—make no effort to increase fortune, but spend the surplus each year for benevolent purposes. Cast aside business forever except for others. . . .
>
> Man must have an idol—The amassing of wealth is one of the worst species of idolitary. No idol more debasing than the worship of money. Whatever I engage in I must push inordinately therefor should I be careful to choose that life which will be the most elevating in its character.

The young Carnegie did not fulfill this contract with himself on the schedule he set. During the next thirty years he went on to build the world's greatest steel company and to make a fortune that by the end of the century was probably second only to that of John D. Rockefeller. Yet through all those years the memorandum lay in his desk drawer and lay, it may be presumed, on his conscience. Then, when he was sixty-seven, he sold his business for four hundred eighty million dollars and devoted the rest of his long life to giving almost all of that fortune away.

More faithfully than anyone else, Andrew Carnegie represents, in his life and his ideas, the American dilemma of wealth. He never doubted that in the business world, at least, men worked for money, and he firmly believed that the best work should bring the greatest rewards. Money was the incentive that during his lifetime spurred the ablest Americans to the greatest leap forward in material wealth in the history of the human race.

Still, the making of money was not in itself a worthy goal for a man. "The man who dies rich dies disgraced," he wrote at a later time. And here he parted company with most of the other captains of industry. He sounded more like the radicals and reformers of his own time, or the students and professors of recent times.

It is worth inquiring where Carnegie came by these very distinct, and some would say antithetical, sets of ideas. He grew up, to the age of twelve, in the Scottish highland town of Dunfermline. His father had made a decent living as a weaver in the time when weaving was done on hand-powered looms in cottages all over Scotland. But his father's living was wiped out by the coming of the factories, which employed women and children at power looms. The boy never forgot the day when his father came home in despair and said, "Andra, I canna get nae mair work."

In that emergency it was Andrew's mother who borrowed enough money from her friends to pay for the family's passage to New York in steerage and thence to Pittsburgh, where they had relatives. It took the combined efforts of the father as a weaver, the mother as a leather stitcher at home, and young Andy, who got his first job as a bobbin boy in a cotton mill, to make ends meet. Andy was the kind of boy who was always being offered better jobs, the kind of boy who, when asked when he would like to start, answered, "Right now, sir, if you please." By the time he was eighteen, he was private secretary to Thomas A. Scott, the superintendent of the Western Division of the Pennsylvania Railroad, with the munificent salary of thirty-five dollars a month. "I couldn't imagine," he recalled later, "what I could ever do with so much money." To his hard-working father he promised: "It won't be long before you and Mother shall ride in your own carriage."

When Scott became vice president of the railroad in 1859, Carnegie was promoted to Scott's old job as superintendent of the Western Division, and when Scott was called to Washington at the outbreak of the Civil War, Carnegie went with him to help run the Union Army's rail service. By that time Carnegie was already putting his savings into companies that were growing with the railroad boom. One of these was a company that built steel bridges, and thus he was led into the business of making steel.

As a businessman Carnegie was a tough, hard-driving boss, quite in the mold of others who came to be labeled robber barons. He was always pushing his executives and his workers to turn out more steel at a lower cost. When the market was soft, he had no qualms about cutting wages. The men Carnegie took into partnership, especially Henry Phipps and Henry Clay Frick, were even tougher than he was. If it was Frick who actually broke the union in the bloody Homestead strike of 1892, Carnegie had only the lame excuse that he had been in Scotland at the time.

The struggle of his youth, followed by brilliant success as a young man, goes far to explain Car-

---

Nothing refreshed Andrew Carnegie more, after a hard year's work, than to go back to Scotland and lie down on his native heath.

negie's faith in hard work and high rewards. It was the classic life pattern of men who ended up as right-wing defenders of the unregulated capitalist system. But such men often found Carnegie's other ideas puzzling, if not dangerous.

These ideas too went back to his youth. Though his father had come upon hard times, the members of Andrew Carnegie's family on both sides were tradesmen who had enough money to get an education and enough education to read books. They were leaders in the agitation for political reform that led to the Chartist movement in the 1830's. The sight of one uncle thrown in jail for helping to organize the local Chartists made a lasting impression on Andrew. "As a child," he wrote many years later, "I could have slain king, duke, or lord, and considered their death a service to the state." And he never failed to compare the narrow, greedy businessmen whom he met in later life with the visionary working-class reformers he had admired in his youth.

What made the Carnegies and others like them such enthusiastic Americans was the idea of a society in which every man had an equal voice and every man had an even start. While it was admirable to make money, it was not right to inherit it. As Carnegie himself put it: "I would as soon leave to my son a curse as the almighty dollar." (Whether he might have modified his view if he had had a son is impossible to say, since his only child was a daughter.)

Carnegie's philosophy of giving was set forth in a two-part essay, which he wrote for the *North American Review* in 1889 and which became known as the "Gospel of Wealth." His central thesis was that great accumulators should regard their surplus wealth as a public trust and should distribute it for the public good, preferably in their own lifetime.

He went on to list the good works that deserved primary consideration: 1) universities, 2) free

This cottage in Dunfermline, Scotland, was Andrew Carnegie's birthplace on November 25, 1835. The Carnegies shared the second floor with another family; on the ground floor Andrew's father made his living as a weaver until the coming of the power loom destroyed his trade.

libraries, 3) hospitals "and other institutions connected with the alleviation of human suffering," 4) parks, 5) halls suitable for meetings, concerts, etc., 6) "swimming baths," 7) churches—but only the building of them.

Not everyone was pleased with that list. As noted by his biographer Joseph Frazier Wall, religious leaders were especially nettled to find churches "seventh on the list—just after swimming baths." Nevertheless, coming from one of the country's richest industrialists, the "Gospel of Wealth" created a sensation.

In the thirty years that remained to him, Carnegie was as good as his word. As a largely self-educated man, he set great store by books and colleges. He treasured his friendships with men of letters like Mark Twain and Matthew Arnold more than those with men of industry. It was natural, therefore, that the first and most widespread use to which he put his money was the building of libraries. His policy was to build a library and turn it over to a town to keep up and stock with books. By the end of his life he had built 2,509 libraries, in the United States, Canada, and Britain.

THE CHALLENGE TO WEALTH

The dilemma that inspired Carnegie to propound his "Gospel of Wealth" was created by the burst of industrial expansion and fortune building that followed the Civil War. In most developed societies since the dawn of civilization there had been rich men and poor men. But in most places wealth was based on political power and sanctified by long existence. Even the Christian Church, which for many centuries turned an unfriendly eye on the acquisitors of new fortunes, condoned the possession of long-established aristocratic wealth. The political system offered no easy way of changing the balance between rich and poor.

In the United States in the second half of the nineteenth century matters stood differently. Men were making fortunes of unprecedented size, with unprecedented speed, in unprecedented numbers. Yet they did so at the sufferance of a democratic society, which could have stopped them by law had it wanted strongly enough to do so. In fact, the people and their representatives appeared to accept the view of Adam Smith that if men of enterprise were left alone to pursue their own interests, they would advance the material welfare of all. The first part of Carnegie's "Gospel" was in fact the prevailing view of the majority, as repeatedly expressed at the polls, from Horace Greeley's day to William Jennings Bryan's.

Part I of Carnegie's "Gospel of Wealth" found an eloquent champion in the Reverend Russell Conwell, a Baptist minister of Philadelphia. In a lecture entitled "Acres of Diamonds," which he is said to have delivered six thousand times, he proclaimed: "Money is power. Every good man and woman ought to strive for power, to do good with it when obtained. Tens of thousands of men and women get rich honestly. But they are often accused by an envious, lazy crowd of unsuccessful persons of being dishonest and oppressive. I say, Get rich, get rich! But get money honestly, or it will be a withering curse."

William Lawrence, the Episcopal bishop of Massachusetts, went on from there. "In the long run," he wrote, "it is only to the man of morality that wealth comes. . . . Material prosperity is helping to make the national character sweeter, more joyous, more unselfish, more Christlike. . . . Godliness is in league with riches."

Despite this ecclesiastical chorus, Part I of the "Gospel of Wealth" did not command universal support. There was, first, the matter of the size of the

Carnegie realized the poor boy's dream of returning to his homeland and buying the great house on the hill. Every summer he filled Skibo Castle with guests from the worlds of education, literature, and politics, whose company he preferred to that of his fellow industrialists.

new fortunes. In the earlier decades of the Industrial Revolution it had been easy to see that a man who built up a cotton mill or an iron foundry deserved the fruits of his enterprise. Society was the richer, and the man would not have worked so hard or taken such risks without the hope of making a lot of money. But it was not so easy to see why John D. Rockefeller required a billion dollars to bring out his best efforts.

There was also the question of how much social good these titans of wealth had done. Andrew Carnegie had been largely responsible for building up an American steel industry, which furnished an essential base for the great surge of economic growth and which turned out more steel than all the other countries of the world combined. It could be argued that his reward was not excessive. But what of Rockefeller, who owed his fortune not so much to any special ability in refining and distributing oil as to his skill in arranging secret rebates that drove his competitors to the wall?

The railroad industry offered a gamut of empire builders, ranging from highest to lowest on the scale of social utility. No one had a good word to say for Jay Gould, who boasted that he never built railroads, only bought them—and, he might have added, sometimes wrecked them. The Big Four of the Central Pacific—Huntington, Stanford, Crocker, and Hopkins—made fortunes that they owed in part to heavy government subsidies and the corruption of legislators, but they did build the railroad. Perhaps, considering all the risks, it required the incentive of huge rewards to get the job done. But there was also the example of James J. Hill, who built the Great Northern—an equally important and difficult job—without either subsidy or corruption.

The protest against the inequities of wealth was never more graphically expressed than by Edward Bellamy, who published *Looking Backward* in the year before Carnegie published his "Gospel of Wealth." In that utopian novel the narrator pretends to be looking backward from the year 2000 to the economic system of the 1880's. He wrote:

Perhaps I cannot do better than to compare society as it then was to a prodigious coach which the masses of humanity were harnessed to and dragged toilsomely along a

very hilly and sandy road. The driver was hunger, and permitted no lagging, though the pace was necessarily very slow. Despite the difficulty of drawing the coach at all along so hard a road, the top was covered with passengers who never got down, even at the steepest ascents. These seats on top were very breezy and comfortable. Well up out of the dust, their occupants could enjoy the scenery at their leisure, or critically discuss the merits of the straining team. Naturally such places were in great demand and the competition for them was keen, every one seeking as the first end in life to secure a seat on the coach for himself and to leave it to his child after him. By the rule of the coach a man could leave his seat to whom he wished, but on the other hand there were so many accidents by which it might at any time be wholly lost. For all that they were so easy, the seats were very insecure, and at every sudden jolt of the coach persons were slipping out of them and falling to the ground, where they were instantly compelled to take hold of the rope and help to drag the coach on which they had before ridden so pleasantly. It was naturally regarded as a terrible misfortune to lose one's seat, and the apprehension that this might happen to them or their friends was a constant cloud upon the happiness of those who rode.

But did they think only of themselves? you ask. Was not their very luxury rendered intolerable to them by comparison with the lot of their brothers and sisters in the harness, and the knowledge that their own weight added to their toil? Had they no compassion for fellow beings from whom fortune only distinguished them? Oh, yes, commiseration was frequently expressed by those who rode for those who had to pull the coach, especially when the vehicle came to a bad place in the road, as it was constantly doing, or to a particularly steep hill. At such times,

It does not take a great deal of money to win enduring fame as a philanthropist. Cecil Rhodes provided in his will for the Rhodes scholars (one of whom, basketball star Bill Bradley, appears in the Oxford archway at top left). Below, in descending order, are three other instances of men whose names have become household words through relatively modest donations. Alfred Nobel, a Swedish munitions maker and the inventor of dynamite, established the Nobel prizes. (In the picture, the peace prize is awarded in 1964 to the Reverend Martin Luther King, Jr.). James Smithson, the illegitimate son of the Duke of Northumberland, never set foot in America but left his estate to found the Smithsonian Institution "for the increase and diffusion of knowledge among men." John Harvard (bottom), teaching elder of a church in Charlestown, Massachusetts, left his private library and half of his estate to a fledgling college in Cambridge, which was thereupon named for him.

the desperate straining of the team, their agonized leaping and plunging under the pitiless lashing of hunger, the many who fainted at the rope and were trampled in the mire, made a very distressing spectacle, which often called forth highly creditable displays of feeling on the top of the coach. At such times the passengers would call down encouragingly to the toilers of the rope, exhorting them to patience, and holding out hopes of possible compensation in another world for the hardness of their lot, while others contributed to buy salves and liniments for the crippled and injured. It was agreed that it was a great pity that the coach should be so hard to pull, and there was a sense of general relief when the specially bad piece of road was gotten over. This relief was not, indeed, wholly on account of the team, for there was always some danger at these bad places of a general overturn in which all would lose their seats.

Now that we ourselves can look back on three-quarters of the twentieth century, we may observe that the great coach did not overturn, despite a very bumpy stretch of road in the 1930's. Conditions of work have been vastly improved for most of those who must drag the coach. The seats on top are not quite as soft as they were in the Gilded Age, but they are at least as stable, and many more persons have scrambled up to occupy them.

Throughout the twentieth century, waves of legislation, ranging from anti-trust laws to the income tax to the securities laws, have restricted the freedom of private enterprise and widened the sphere of government. And with each new wave, there have been those who predicted, either in hope or in despair, the end of the capitalist system and the eclipse of private wealth. In 1937 John D. Rockefeller, Jr. stated his belief that in thirty years there would be no great fortunes left. Yet in 1974, after giving away about three-quarters of a billion dollars on top of the half billion given by John D., Sr., the Rockefeller family still had assets of over a billion. Meanwhile, several other men have risen to billionaire status in the years since John D., Jr. made his prediction.

The income tax had, to be sure, ended the period when a man could draw a high salary and keep all of it. But fortunes are not built out of savings from high salaries. They are the fruits of new enterprise, not taxed until they are realized as capital gains, and then only at about half the rate of salaries, dividends, or interest. In the fourth quarter of the twentieth century that route to wealth was still open.

The case for allowing the accumulation of great fortunes rests in part on the importance of providing high incentives for men who devote their efforts and risk their capital in enterprises that add to the wealth of nations. This logic was widely accepted in the nineteenth century when business was young and the need for development was clear. It is questioned now when many of the basic industries have passed into what economists like to call a "mature" phase, with supposedly less need for invention and innovation.

Even large, established corporations need to offer financial incentives for hard work and ability, as the British are finding out. But they do not generally provide ambitious young men with avenues to great wealth. It has already been noted that recent industrial fortunes have been made in what seem like peripheral fields of the economy, such as pet foods or retreaded tires, or in small firms that supply big firms. These areas are, in fact, the present industrial frontier, as railroads and farm machines once were. Who is to say that the transistor is less important, or less deserving of reward, than the telephone? Or that the inventor of the instant camera in the twentieth century contributes less to human happiness than the builder of a steel mill in the nineteenth?

The belief in high rewards is certainly not dead in the land. In 1972, when George McGovern was campaigning for President, he was surprised to find, in working-class districts, so little response to his proposal for raising the capital gains tax. "What do they think?" he asked. "That they are all going to win the state lottery?" Perhaps—or else that they were going to sell their house for twice what they paid for it, or start a small-town restaurant and run it into a Howard Johnson chain.

THE INHERITANCE OF WEALTH

Whatever may be thought of the social utility of high rewards for new enterprise, it is much harder to justify the inheritance of great wealth. Even some of those who were on the receiving end have found it a doubtful advantage. Here is William K. Vanderbilt, grandson of the Commodore:

My life was never destined to be quite happy. It was laid out along lines which I could foresee almost from my earliest childhood. It has left me with nothing to hope for, with nothing definite to seek or strive for. Inherited wealth is a real handicap to happiness. It is as certain as death to ambition, as cocaine is to morality. If a man makes money, no matter how much, he finds a certain happiness in its possession, for in the desire to increase his business he has constant use for it. The first satisfaction and the greatest, that of building the foundation of a fortune, is denied him. He must labor, if he does labor, simply to add to an over-sufficiency.

In the dynamics of the economic system, inherited wealth plays some useful part. In the form of "venture capital" it often provides backing for enterprises started by "new men" who have not had the luck to inherit money themselves. Thus at second hand it may stimulate economic creativity. But it does not generally have the direct effect of stimulating its own possessors to extraordinary efforts or innovations.

Some special consideration may be given to those who have not been content to enjoy their inherited riches but have followed their fathers into family businesses or used their money to start new enterprises of their own. In such cases inherited wealth has provided a head start for individual heirs and, if they were men of ability, may have contributed to the smooth running of an enterprise, with some benefit to the public as well. Many a captain of industry has dreamed of founding a dynasty that would carry on the family business he built. There was Meyer Guggenheim, calling his seven sons together, holding up to them a fistful of twigs, and saying: "Separate, you are easily broken. Together, none can break you. My sons be as one." As it turned out, the Guggenheim sons did not stick together, and the Guggenheim enterprise faded away. But there are still some families that retain control of great businesses, among them the Du Ponts, the Fords, the Uihleins of Schlitz Brewing, the O'Neills of General Tire and Rubber, the McGraws of McGraw-Hill, the Houghtons of Corning

Glass, and the Stevenses of the J. P. Stevens textile company. Recently Henry Ford II, while speculating from a hospital bed on the future of his company, ventured the thought that people want a Ford somewhere near the top of the company. He did not reveal the source from which this intelligence had come to him. Generally, the tide has been running strong against family dynasties, partly because of inheritance taxes but partly also because of a feeling that merit should govern the choice of executives in great businesses.

Up to a certain level, there is general support for the inheritance of wealth. Even among the advocates of near-confiscatory death taxes, few would deprive the widow and young children of enough to maintain their standard of living. And there is thought to be merit in allowing sons to keep control of small family enterprises. As recently as the spring of 1976 President Gerald Ford was pushing legislation that would make it easier for farmers to pass their family homesteads on to children and thus keep them out of the clutches of giant ''agribusinesses'' (which at the same time his Secretary of Agriculture, Earl Butz, was busily encouraging). There has always seemed to be some special virtue in the Jeffersonian figure of the independent farmer on the family homestead. But there would seem to be no less merit in the owner of an independent corner filling station or an independent local newspaper.

In the case of large fortunes, even their possessors have not recently advanced many arguments for inheritance, beyond the assumption that a man's property is his to do with as he wants. In England, where the socialist ethic has gained more ground than it has in the United States, the attempt to justify inherited wealth has just about collapsed. In 1975 the London *Sunday Times* sent a reporter to interview some of the remaining holders of inherited wealth, and reported the results in a feature entitled: ''The Rich: Backs Against The Wall.'' A typical response was that of the Duke of Devonshire, who viewed himself as really no more than the caretaker of his stately home and its agricultural land. He pointed out that if the government wanted to preserve the stately homes, the cheapest way to do it was to let the owners live there. His somewhat apologetic attitude may be contrasted with that of his ancestor who, when advised that the rising cost of living might make it prudent for him to dispense with his second pastry chef, protested: ''Can't a fellow even have a biscuit?''

American heirs to great fortunes have not been so sadly reduced as their counterparts in England. Inheritance taxes, reaching to the ninety-per-cent bracket, have indeed made it difficult to pass on the bulk of a huge fortune or to retain family control of a big company. But with early and careful planning it is not impossible, as John D. Rockefeller was one of the first to demonstrate. While giving a large part of his fortune to a foundation, he was able to pass on another large part to his son. And by making the transfer many years before his death, he paid only a gift tax, which is substantially lower than an inheritance tax, and also ensured that the natural increase in the fortune during the rest of his lifetime would go directly to the son. This kind of estate planning keeps many lawyers busy and accounts for the fact that many of the richest men die relatively poor. It has also brought about a great proliferation of charitable institutions into which the wealthy channel part of their fortunes in order to safeguard the rest.

THE UTILITY OF FOUNDATIONS

It would be unfair, however, to ascribe the growth of charitable institutions entirely, or even primarily, to motives of tax avoidance. The United States enjoys a tradition of philanthropy that antedates the inheritance tax laws and is quite unmatched by any other country in the world. The case for allowing very rich men to dispose of their wealth as they see fit, rather than surrender it to the tax collector, rests to a large extent on the worth of their philanthropies. In particular it rests on an assessment of the social utility of that uniquely American institution, the foundation.

The prototype of the American philanthropist was Peter Cooper. He is best remembered perhaps as the inventive fellow who built the locomotive Tom Thumb in 1830 and raced it against a horse. (The horse won, but the locomotive was also a success.) Cooper made a fortune from a glue factory, a locomotive works, and New York real estate. But during the heyday of the robber barons he was saying, ''There is fast forming in this country an aristocracy of wealth, the worst form of aristocracy that can curse the prosperity of any country.'' To satisfy his conscience and to set an example for his peers, he gave most of his fortune to found Cooper Union, a New York institution that for more than a hundred years has offered free instruction in art, science, and technology. At his funeral the minister could say of Peter Cooper: ''Here lies a man who never owned a dollar he could not take up to the Great White Throne.''

The motives that have led men to practice philanthropy have been as various as the men themselves. Andrew Carnegie was a man in Cooper's mold. The fact that he hugely enjoyed his philanthropy, and basked in the applause he got whenever he attended the dedication of a new library, does not detract from the purity of his motives. John D. Rockefeller was precipitated into philanthropy to some extent by the wave of public animosity against himself and the Standard Oil trust; but once he had turned from moneymaking to money giving, he pursued his new purpose with the same intensity that he had pursued the old. Henry Ford showed little interest in wholesale philanthropy, as opposed to pet hobbies, until the Ford family faced the prospect of losing control of the company upon his death. Only by giving ninety per cent of the fortune to the Ford Foundation, in nonvoting stock, was the family able to maintain control of the company at least through his grandsons' generation.

One man who would surely have been horrified by what happened to his fortune was Russell Sage. Among the robber barons of the nineteenth century, Sage was a shadowy figure who stayed out of the

CONTINUED ON PAGE 340

Russell Sage kept his eyes on the ticker tape, pinched every penny, and gave little thought to charity during his forty-three years as a Wall Street financier. To his second wife Olivia, a lady of gentle manner but firm purpose, he left a fortune of seventy million dollars. Feeding the squirrels in the park (above) was the least of her good works. In the twelve years before her own death, she gave away almost all of the fortune to colleges, hospitals, museums, and other charities. The Russell Sage Foundation stands as a memorial to the strangely assorted pair.

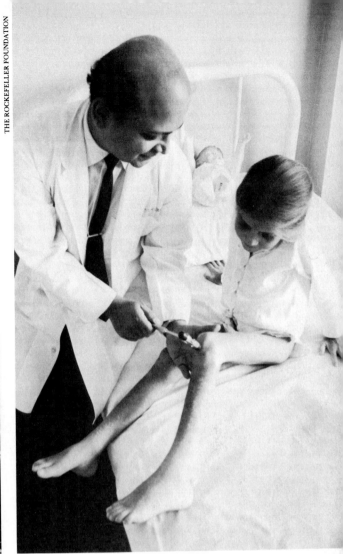

Foundations large and small—some 26,000 of them at latest count—support a wide variety of good works. The largest of all is the Ford Foundation, whose staff members work, somewhat like goldfish, in glass-walled offices looking out on the garden court of the headquarters building in New York. Two of the hundreds of projects to which they dispense money appear at left: a program for training young conductors at the Peabody Conservatory of Music in Baltimore, and the Sesame Street television program, featuring Big Bird. Above are two projects of the Rockefeller Foundation: at right, a community health-care program in Cali, Colombia; at left, a program to develop high-yielding, disease-resistant wheat in Mexico.

Rockefellers of four generations appear in this photograph taken at Pocantico Hills, the family estate, in the early 1930's. They are: John D., Jr., John D., Nelson and his son Rodman.

CONTINUED FROM PAGE 337

public eye as much as he could, manipulated the market in railroad stocks, and piled up a fortune of a hundred million dollars. A miser on the model of Hetty Green, he wore the cheapest clothes he could find, and walked to save streetcar fare. After his first wife died, he married a schoolmistress whose father he had ruined, and proceeded to make her life miserable by such petty tyrannies as denying her a dog, which she wanted, and filling the house with cats, which she hated. As soon as Sage was dead, his widow came into her own. She gave most of the fortune to universities, churches, and in particular to the Russell Sage Foundation, whose philanthropic

work would have been the furthest thing from the mind of the man whose name it bears.

The important question, however, is not what led the donors to set up foundations, but what purposes the foundations have served. In the case of the largest of them, it takes a pretty captious critic to say that on balance they have not done a great deal of good. The Rockefeller Foundation, specializing in medical and scientific research, has to its credit such achievements as the cure for yellow fever and the hybridization of grains that brought about the "Green Revolution." The Carnegie Foundation, in addition to building libraries, was a powerful influence in raising college standards and professors' salaries. The Ford Foundation has drawn some fire because it has operated in more controversial fields, including the arts and contemporary social problems. It could hardly expect the same degree of approval for its backing of drives to register black voters in the South or its grants to militant Chicano politicians in the Southwest as other foundations get for medical research and higher education. In any case, such projects have used up only a small proportion of its vast income, which is almost triple that of any other foundation.

The purposes served by some of the small foundations range from the routine and worthy to the highly imaginative. Some are trivial but engaging, such as the Dr. Coles Trust Fund for Ice Cream for the Pupils of South Plains and Fanwood (New Jersey). Others have impulsive moments, as shown by the David and Minnie Berk Foundation, which normally presents an award for "a major achievement in prolonging or improving the quality of human life," but also on one occasion bought a new horse for a Brooklyn fruit vender named Angelo Angioletti when his old one dropped dead. If the work of small foundations seems unimportant, consider the Dorr Foundation. Dr. John Dorr, its donor, thought up the idea of painting white lines along the edges of highways to make driving safer at night. It is impossible to guess how many lives have been saved by the foundation's backing of this simple procedure.

The argument is made that while some of the great foundations served an important purpose in their earlier days, their functions have been superseded by government. Certainly it is true that the kind of medical research that the Rockefeller Foundation pioneered is now supported in far greater volume by the federal government. But the federal agencies that support this work, the National Science Foundation and the National Institutes of

340

Health, were modeled on the Rockefeller Foundation, and might not have been so effective so soon without that model. Moreover, the fact that so many Nobel Prizes in science and medicine have been won by Rockefeller scientists testifies to the continuing importance of the work they are doing.

The strongest arguments made for the foundations are that they are less bureaucratic in their operations than government agencies and that they sponsor innovative work that the government is slow to recognize or fearful to pursue. It was not hard to get appropriations for heart research through a Congress made up in large part of potential heart cases. It was much harder, if not impossible, to find federal money for programs aimed at population control at a time when that was a politically sensitive subject.

THE FUTURE OF PRIVATE WEALTH

In arriving at any judgment on the social utility of private wealth it is necessary to consider both what the fortune builders contributed to economic progress in the making of their money and what they contributed to social welfare in its use. If all of them had been pirates like Jay Gould it would not be hard to conclude that the country would have been better off without them. If they had all developed products of recognized utility, like Cyrus McCormick and George Eastman, it could be said that they contributed far more to the general welfare than they got in the way of reward.

Another judgment must be made on the social utility of these fortunes after they pass out of the hands of their builders. If all the heirs had spent their riches on conspicuous consumption, as some of the Vanderbilts did, it would be easy to say that such fortunes might better have been forfeit to the tax collector. But if they had all been devoted to the public good, like those of Carnegie and Ford, it would not be hard to conclude that they have served a better purpose than they would have served if thrown into the general revenue of the federal government.

But the final assessment is not likely to be made by any such careful calculation of social utility. Voters may be moved by feelings of envy toward those who strike it rich or—to put it more sympathetically—by feelings that gross inequalities in wealth are offensive to public morality. On the other hand, they may be moved by the hope that they too may find the gold at the end of the rainbow or—again to put it more sympathetically—that the hope of high re-

Laurance Rockefeller, Jr. (below) spent three years living in an East Harlem slum while he worked as a volunteer for VISTA. His sister Marion worked in hospitals for the retarded and terminally ill.

wards still spurs men on to works that benefit society at large.

There is another question too that may be crucial to the outcome. That is whether young people—and especially the ablest young people—in our society have the same driving desire to get rich that their fathers and grandfathers did. Lord Beaverbrook spoke for his generation when he said: "The money brain is in the modern world the supreme brain. Why? Because that which the greatest number of men strive for will produce the fiercest competition of intellect."

Lord Beaverbrook was remembering the time

341

when he had been plain Max Aitken, a poor Canadian boy making his way to wealth in the lumber business. Aside from the fact that he ended up with an English title, his story was that of the American captains of industry.

More than half a century has passed since that time. And during these years the goal of moneymaking has been under consistent attack, especially on the college campuses. Young people cannot but question whether the pursuit of wealth is worth the effort, and equally important, whether it is worthy of their talents. It was not until about the middle of the last century that moneymaking became the most important goal for American youth. In other times and places ambitious young men have striven equally hard to become Roman senators or medieval abbots or knights in armor. In our society, fortune makers have been steadily losing prestige. In the period that began with the election of John F. Kennedy and ended, for the time at least, with the resignation of Richard Nixon, some of the brightest of them found politics a more compelling life interest. It is not easy to see where they will turn next, or whether the lights they follow will be more worthy than those followed by Andrew Carnegie or Henry Ford. It would hardly be a great step forward if they created a society that glorified golf pros and rock singers over captains of industry.

For some clue to the shape of things to come, we may perhaps return to the family which, more than any other, has been representative of the history of great wealth in this country, namely the Rockefellers. It was John D. who piled up the first of the billion-dollar fortunes and occasioned the greatest uproar over "ill-gotten gains." It was he and his son and his grandsons who created the model for the philanthropic use of great fortunes. But a new generation of Rockefellers has come of age, the children of the five brothers and hence known as the Cousins. In a book published in 1976 Peter Collier and David Horowitz gave a fascinating report on the attitude of the Cousins toward the family wealth. There is among them little inclination to devote their lives either to conserving their money or to governing its use for philanthropic purposes. Rather, it would seem, they wish they did not have it. To many of them the name Rockefeller has itself been a burden, a cause for cringing when they are introduced to strangers, and an obstacle to establishing their own identities. John D. III's daughter Sandra dropped the family name, becoming Sandra Ferry, and others seem to have rushed into marriage to replace it.

Some of the Cousins, to be sure, have followed traditional paths, such as Nelson's son Rodman, who runs IBEC, the Latin American investment firm founded by his father, and John D. IV ("Jay"), who is president of West Virginia Wesleyan College. But several of the Cousins have been active in left-wing movements, and several have spent long periods of "penance" working in ghetto projects, insane asylums, and the like. Laurance's daughter Marian is married to a Ph.D. candidate at the University of California and spends her summers in a converted railroad caboose in the hills of northern California. They get by on seven hundred dollars a month for a family of four and hope, by growing their own food and making their own clothes, to get down to three hundred dollars or less.

Among the twenty-two Cousins, not one has become a playboy or a spendthrift or a loafer. All appear to wrestle with the same Rockefeller conscience that burdened their fathers, but on their own very different terms. Having tried so hard to distance themselves from their overhanging trust funds, they were dismayed when Nelson, in order to win confirmation as Vice President, spread the family finances over the front pages of the nation's press. His son Steven, an assistant professor at Middlebury College in Vermont, and the most articulate of the Cousins, says of the family as an institution, "Isn't it just an anachronism, a dinosaur that is trying to keep me from going out and getting involved in American life just like everyone else? . . . The dynasty stuff—that's all finished." Says his cousin Laura: "There is no way to justify the money."

It would be rash to conclude, on the evidence of one very special family, that private wealth has lost its appeal to the young. In the first half century many prophets, including the second Rockefeller, have predicted that the age of great fortunes was ending, and so far they have been wrong. But ideas and attitudes that begin in the upper levels of a society have a way of working themselves down through the whole pyramid. If the young Rockefellers do indeed reflect a feeling that is widespread among members of their generation, it may be that Carnegie's "Gospel of Wealth" will soon have run its course. When that day comes the multimillionaire will follow into the gallery of history the Roman senator, the medieval abbot, and the armed knight.

A grand Newport mansion of the Gilded Age, fallen into decay, awaits the wrecker's ball. They do not build them like this any more.

STAFF FOR THIS BOOK

Editor   Joseph J. Thorndike, Jr.
Managing Editor   Sandra J. Wilmot
Art Director   Elena M. Bloomfield
Picture Editor   Mary Z. Jenkins
Associate Editor   Kaari Ward

SPECIAL CONTRIBUTIONS

We wish to thank the following for their contributions to this book:

Oliver Jensen for editorial counsel

Peter Andrews for writing Chapter 6 on "Wealth from Talent"

Ralph K. Andrist for writing Chapter 8 on "Wealth from Modern Industry"

William Wolman for consultation on economic history

Laura Lane Masters, our librarian, and her assistant Pamela Lehrer

Douglas Tunstell for pictorial consultation

Carol Caldwell, Susan Green, Toby Kahn, and Linda Keller for research

ACKNOWLEDGMENTS

We wish to thank the following institutions and individuals for their special help in obtaining illustrations:

___

Slim Aarons
Ansel Adams and his assistant, Mrs. Andrea Turnage
Caroline Bancroft
Brown Brothers—Mr. & Mrs. Harry Collins
Culver Pictures—Bob Jackson
Bill Cunningham
The Eastman House—Susan Stromer
The English Speaking Union— Mrs. Helen Hettinger
Andreas Feininger, New York
Florida State Archives—Mrs. Joan Morris
The Ford Foundation—Jocelyn Saitta

General Foods Corporation—John Whiteman
Raymundo de Larrain, New York
The Morgan Library
The Museum of the City of New York—Esther Brumberg
Otto Nelson, New York
The New York Times—Shirley Baig
Palm Beach News—Susan Hixon
Rockefeller Family & Associates— George Taylor, Audrey Guthrie
Rockefeller Foundation—Jane Klang
Nancy Sirkis, New York
Sygma—Mrs. Monique Lafonte
Time-Life Picture Agency—Phyllis Grygalin, Marthe Michelle Hallett
Town & Country—Missy Becker
UPI—Stan Friedman, Nat Andriani
Weidenfeld & Nicolson Publishing Company, London

Grateful acknowledgment is made to the authors and publishers of the following works for the use of quotations.

___

Fowler, Gene, *Timber Line,* 1974, Comstock Editions, Inc., Sausalito, Calif.; Origo, Iris, *The Merchant of Prato,* 1957, Alfred A. Knopf, Inc., New York, N.Y.; Keynes, John Maynard, *Treatise on Money, The Pure Theory of Money,* Vol. 5, 1972, St. Martin's Press, New York, N.Y.; Sedgwick, Ellery, *The Happy Profession,* 1946, Little, Brown, and Company, Boston, Mass.; Ashton, T.S., *The Industrial Revolution,* 1948, Oxford U. Press, New York, N.Y.; Poole, Ernest, *Giants Gone,* 1943, McGraw-Hill, Inc., New York, N.Y.

INDEX *Numbers in bold face refer to illustrations.*

Aarons, Slim, photograph by, 313
Abdul Azziz Sulieman, 102
accounting methods, 122, 288
"Acres of Diamonds" (Conwell), 332
actors, 201–3, 205
Adams, Henry, 138
Adoration of the Magi (Botticelli), **155**
Adoration of the Shepherds (Goes), **143**
Adventurers, The (Robbins), 196
Aesopus, 201
Aga Kahn, 6, **7**
Ahmed Yamani, Sheik, 102
airplanes, 18–19, 310
Aitken, Max. *See* Beaverbrook, Lord
Alba, Duchess of, **8**, 9
Alberti (family), 153
Alcoa. *See* Aluminum Company of America
Aldrich, Winthrop W., 22
Alexis, Grand Duke of Russia, 108, **109**
Alger, Horatio, 16
Allen, Frederick Lewis, 173
Almanach de Gotha, 11
Aluminum Company of America, 179
American Indians. *See* Indians, American
American Museum, 212
Amin, General Idi, 19
Amory, Cleveland, 14, 248
Amsterdam Exchange, **142**, 143
Andrews, Samuel, 94
Andrews, T. Coleman, 210
Anka, Paul, 208
Annenberg, Walter, 22
Annie Get Your Gun, 208
Anson, Hon. Alfred, **252–53**
anti-trust suits, 93
A. & P. *See* Great Atlantic & Pacific Tea Company
Appleton (family), 130
    Francis, **279**
    Helen. *See* Reed, Mrs. Helen Appleton
    Mary, **322**, 323
    William, 14
Archbold, John D., 90, 94
Arden, Elizabeth, 306
Arkwright, Richard, 239–40, 242–44, **242**
Armstrong, Anne, 22
Armstrong, Rebecca (Mrs. William Backhouse Astor I), 52
Arnaz, Desi, 203, **216–17**
Arp, Jean, sculpture by, **187**
Arrow car, 284
art
    artists, 197–201
    patrons of, 86, 89, 98, 102, 124, 136–40, 150–51, 154, 156, 173, 176, 178–80, **181–91**, 221–22, 258
Artist in His Studio, An (Vermeer), **141**
Ascot races, **323**
Ashanti tribe (Ghana), 19, 26
Ashton, T. S., 240
Astor (family), 11–12, 21, 107, 324
    Caroline, **50–51**
    Carrie, 52
    Charlotte Augusta, **50–51**
    John Jacob I, 9, 47–56, **48**, 249, 273
    John Jacob II, **52**, 53

John Jacob III, 24, **52**, 53
John Jacob IV, **50–51**, 51, 53, 55, **271**
    Mrs. Ava Willing, 50, **51**
    Mrs. Madeleine Force, 50
John Jacob V, 53
John Jacob VI, **53**, 56
John Jacob VII, **50**, 53
Vincent, **50**, 56
Waldorf (2nd viscount), **51**, 53
    Lady (Nancy Langhorne), **51**, 53
William Backhouse I, 48–52, **52**, 53
    Mrs. (Sarah Todd), 52
William Backhouse, Jr., 50, 52
    the Mrs. (Caroline Webster Schermerhorn), 48, **49**, 50, **51**, 52–53, 55, **103**, 174
William Waldorf (1st viscount), 53, **53**, 55
Astoria (Irving), 47
athletes, 209–12
authors, 194–96
automobiles, 18, **108–9**, 284–89
Avercamp, Hendrick, painting by, **144**
Ayrton, Michael, 201

Bach, Johann Sebastian, 207
Bache (family), 174–76
Baker, George F., Jr., **176**
Ball, Lucille, 203, **205**, **216–17**
Balmoral, 7
Balsan, Mme. Jacques (Consuelo Vanderbilt; Duchess of Marlborough), **322**, 323
Baltimore & Ohio Railroad, 59
Bank of America, 24
banking, 150–70
Bardi, The, 156
Barefoot in the Park, 195
Barnato, Barney, 87
Barnum, Phineas T., 212–13, **213**
Baruch, Bernard M., 180
Barzi (family), 153
Bath, marquesses of, 39, 65
Battle Creek Toasted Corn Flake Company, 295
Beale, Mrs. Truxtan, **252–53**
Beard, Miriam, 152
Beatty, Earl, 21
Beaverbrook, Lord, 14, 341–42
Bedford, dukes of, 39
Beebe, Lucius, 19, 56, 82–83, 133, **313**
Beecher, Henry Ward, 62
Beekman (family), 11, 52, 56
Bellamy, Edward, 333–34
Bellini, Giovanni, portrait by, **124**
Belmont (family), 11–12, 18
    August (né Schönberg), 172, 174
    Oliver Hazard Perry, 21, 23, 251, 255
    Mrs., 18
Bendum, Mike, 15
Bennett, Harry, 288–89
Bennett, James Gordon, 216
    James Gordon, Jr., 6, 22, 218–21, 324
Berenson, Bernard, 138, 140
Berk Foundation, David and Minnie, 340
Berlin, Irving, 208, **209**
Bernard, Samuel, 23

Bernhardt, Sarah, 201–2, 224, **225**
Berwind, E. J., 273
    Julia, **252–53**, 273
Beylant, 123
Big Spenders, The (Beebe), 82
Bicker (family), 123–24
Big Bonanza mine, 78–79
Biltmore, 254
Birmingham, Stephen, 174
Bishop's Wife, The, 216
Blue Boy (Gainsborough), 258
Bluhdorn, Charles, 12
Boca Raton, Florida, 57–59
Boiardo, Ruggiero, **232–33**
Bolack, Thomas Felix, 314, **316–17**
Bostwick, Jabez, 94
Boswell, James, 241
Botanic Garden, The (E. Darwin), 238
Botticelli, Sandro, painting by, **155**
Boulton, Matthew, 238–41, **238**
Bourbon, Maria Cristina de (Mrs. Antenor Patino), 88
Boussac, Marcel, 116, **117**
Boyer, Isabella, 261
Bradley, Bill, **334**
Brady, Diamond Jim, 19, 21, **274**, 275
Braque, Georges, 169
Brave New World (Huxley), 284
Brayton, Alice, 229
Breakers, the, 16, 254, **273**
Brevoort (family), 52
Brewster of New York, 17
British East India Company, 125–26, 130
Brooke, James (Rajah), 9
    Sir Charles Vyner, 9
Brookline (Boston), 59
Brown, James J., 76–77
    Mrs. (Molly), 76–77, **77**
Brown, John Y., Jr., 136
Brown, Lancelot "Capability," 65
Brown, Moses, 243–44
Brown University, 244
Brutus, 150
Bryan, William Jennings, 173, 332
Bryant, Marie Hungerford (Mrs. John W. Mackay), 21, 80–81
Buccleuch, Duke of, 39
Buderus, Karl, 163
Buick, David, 289
Burns, Robert, 241
Burroughs, John, **287**
Burton, Richard, 203, **205**
Busch (family), 18
    August A., Jr., **227**
business management, science of, 288–89

Cabot (family), 21, 130
Cagney, James, **204**, 205
Cairo, Illinois, 47
Calixtus III, Pope, 154
Calvert, Cecil, **44**
    George (Lord Baltimore), 44
Campion, John F., 76
Capote, Truman, 319
Captain Fantastic and the Dirt Brown Cowboy, 208

Carborundum Company, 179
Carnegie (family), 12, 101
    Andrew, 11, 13–15, 172, 257, 330–33, **331**,
    332–33, 337, 341–42
Carnegie Foundation, 340
Carousel, 208
Carpenter, Walter, Jr., **266–67**
Carr, Elmendorf L., **252–53**
carriages, 17–18, 238, 261. *See also* coaches;
    surreys; tallyhos
Carter, Robert "King," 44
Cartier, Pierre, 83–85
Caruso, Enrico, **206**, 207
Carver, Roy J., 12
Cash, Johnny, 209
cash registers, 300–304
Castellane, Count Boni de, 21, 255–57
Castlereagh, Lord, 165
Cast Iron Palace, 133
Catalani, Angelica, 203
cattle ranching, 59–62
Catton, Charles, 198
Cavendish, William, 17
Cecil (family), 39
Central Pacific Railroad, 257, 333
cereal industry, 289–95
Cezanne, Paul, painting by, **186**
chain stores, 134–35. *See also* fast-food chains
Chamberlain, Wilt, 210–12
Chaplin, Charlie, 6, 202, **204**, 205
Charles I, of England, 44, 197
Charles II, of England, 39, 44
Charles V, Holy Roman Emperor, 155–56
Charles VI, of France, 156
Charles VII, of France, 153–54
Chateau de Balleroy, 222
Chateau de Saumur, **40**
Chateau de Steen, 198, **199**
Chatsworth, 17
Chetwode, **273**
Chevalier, Maurice, 6
Chevrolet, Louis, 289
Chicago *Daily Tribune*, 281
China, 31, 120, 126–28, **129**
Christian Church, 151–56, 332
Christmas Carol, A (Dickens), 194
Chrysler, Walter, 289
Chung King Foods, 15
Cicero, 10, 38, 150
Clark, Edward, 261
Clark Art Institute, 261
Cleveland, Duchess of, 39
Cleveland, Grover, 172
Cliveden, 53
coaches, **104–5**, 198. *See also* carriages; surreys;
    tallyhos
Coalbrookdale, **236–37**, 241
Coeur, Jacques, 10, 153–54, **153**, 156
Coigny, Mademoiselle de, 17
Colbert, Jean Baptiste, 158
Collier, Peter, 342
Collins, Orvis, 15
Collins Line, 248
Colonna (family), 26
    Marcantonio, 26, **27**
Coltman, Mr. and Mrs. Thomas, 66, **67**
Commoner (Bryan), 173
Computing-Tabulating-Recording Company,
    304

Comstock Lode, 22, 78, 80
Concert, The (Vermeer), 140
conglomerates, 12, 306–7
Conti, Prince de, 160
Conwell, Reverend Russell, 332
Coogan, Jackie, **205**
Coolidge, Calvin, 11, 179
Coolidge, T. Jefferson, 15
Cooper, Douglas, home of, 18, **19**
Cooper, Mrs. Wyatt (Gloria Vanderbilt), **251**
Cooper, Peter, 336–37
Cooperstown, New York, 261
Cooper Union, 336
Copeland, Lammot Du Pont, Sr., **266–67**
    Lammot Du Pont, Jr., 268
Coral Gables, Florida, 57–59, **58**
Corbett, James J. ("Gentlemen Jim"), 210
Cornfeld, Bernie, 180, 224
Corrigan, Laura, 21
Corsair (yacht), 171, 173
cosmetic industry, 304–6
Coward, Noel, 6
Cowper (family), **66**
Cramm, Baron Gottfried von, 135–36, **137**
Crassus, Marcus Licinius, 23, 150–51, **150**
credit system, 159
Crocker, Charles, 257–58, **257**, 333
Croesus, king of Lydia, 150
Crosby, Bing, **205**, 207–8
Cullen, Hugh Roy, **98**, 99, 101
Cunard, Samuel, 130
Cunard Line, 248
Curzon, Lord, 21

Daimler, 18
Dali, Salvador, 198, **200**
Darby, Abraham, 241
Darwin, Dr. Erasmus, 17, 238–39, **238**
Datini, Francesco, 22, 121–22
David (Donatello), **182**
Davies, Joseph E., 291
Davies, Marion, 11, 21, **218**, 219, 222
Davies, Mary, 40
Davis, Arthur Vining, 179
Dawes, Charles G., 22
Day, Thomas, 238
Dean, J. Simpson, **264**
De Beers syndicate, 87–88
Deering, James and William, 259
DeGolyer, Everette Lee, 77
Delacroix, 168
Delano (family), 127
Dempsey, Jack, 210
department stores, 132–34. *See also* chain stores
Derby, Lord, 38
Deterding, Sir Henri, 97
Devonshire, dukes of, 36, 336
Dexter, "Lord" Timothy, 23, 232
diamonds, 86–88
Dickens, Charles, 46–47, 194, **195**, 245
Disney studios, 304
Disraeli, Benjamin, 168
Docker, Lady, 18
Dr. Coles Trust Fund for Ice Cream for the
    Pupils of South Plains and Fanwood, 340
Dodge, Horace, 21, 288–89
    John, 288–89
Doheny, E. L., 59

Dollar, Captain Robert, 130
Domesday Book, 38. *See also* "New Domesday
    Survey" (1873)
Donatello, sculpture by, **182**
Dorr, Dr. John, 340
Dorr Foundation, 340
Douglas, Lewis W., 22
Drake, Sir Francis, 125
Drew, Daniel, 171, 249–54
Duke, Doris, 24, 135
Dumas, Alexandre, 194
Duncan, Isadora, 262
Dunrobin Castle, 41
Du Pont (family), 12, 44, 52, 85, 93, 289, 335
    Alfred, 268
    Alfred Victor, **264**
    Coleman, 268
    Eleuthère Irénée, 262, **263**, 264, 268
    Emile F., **266–67**
    Ethel, **265**
    Eugene, 268
    Eugene E., **266–67**
    F. George, 266, **267**
    Henry A. (Colonel), 264, 268
    Henry Belin, 264, **266–67**
    Henry F., 264, **266–67**, 268
    Irénée, **226**, 227, **265–67**, 268
    Irénée, Jr., 266, **267**
    Lammot, 268
    Mrs. Margaret Osborne, **265**
    Pierre, 268
    Pierre III, **266–67**
    Pierre Samuel, 262–68, **264**
    Polly, 264
    T. Coleman (General), 58
    William, Jr., **266–67**
    Zara, **265**
Durant, William C., 289
Dürer, Albrecht, painting by, **156**, 197
Dutch, the, 42, 122–25, **141–47**
Dutch East India Company, 123–24
Dutch West India Company, 42
Duveen, Sir Joseph, 174, 179, 258

Eastman, George, 295–97, **297**, 298, **299**,
    307, 341
Eastman Dry Plate Company, 296
Eastman Kodak, 208
Easton Neston, **65**
Edgeworth, Richard Lovell, 238–39
Edison, Thomas A., **287**, 296
Edward I, of England, 152
Edward III, of England, 156
Edward, Viscount Lascelles, 68
Electronic Data Processing, 12
Electronic Data Systems, 180
electronics industry, 12, 304
Elizabeth I, of England, 19, **30**, 81
Elizabeth II, of England, 7
Elms, the, **273**
Encore, 20
England, 125
    property ownership in, 38–42, **63–73**
entail, 12, 39, 42, 53
Enterprising Man, The (Collins and Unwalla), 15
Erie Railroad, 249–52
Erpf, Armand G., 231
Esterhazy (family), 6

Everglades Club, 262
Exxon, 304. *See also* Standard Oil
Eyck, Jan Van, 197

Fair, James G., 22, 77–81, **79**
  Birdie (Mrs. William K. Vanderbilt, Jr.),
    81
  Tessie (Mrs. Hermann Oelrichs), 18, 81
Fairbanks, Douglas, 202–3, **204**, 205
Fairfax, Lord, 44–46
Fantasia, 304
Farinelli, 203–7
fast-food chains, 136–37
Fenway Court, 138, **139**, 140
Fenwick, Henry Robertson, 326–27
Ferber, Edna, 99
Ferrières, 170
Ferry, Sandra, 342
Fiddler on the Roof, 24
Field (family), 24, 135
  Ethel (Countess Beatty), 21
  Marshall, 9, 56–57, 120, 133–35
  Marshall II, 24
  Marshall III, 24
Fields, W. C., 214
Filene, Edward A., 133
finance. *See* banking
Firestone, Harvey S., **287**, 289
  Harvey S., Jr., **287**
Firestone Tire and Rubber Company, 287, 289
Fish, Stuyvesant, **270**, 271
  Mrs. Stuyvesant (Mamie), 18, 20, **23**
Fisk, Jim, 24, 171, 180, 249–52
Fiske, Harrison Grey, **278**, 279
  Mrs. (Minnie Maddern), 279
Fitzwilliam, 3rd Earl, 39
Flagler, Henry M., 14, 22, 93–97
Flood, James C., 77–80
Florida East Coast Railway, 94–96
Florida real-estate boom, 57–59, 96–97
Forbes, B. C., 134
  Malcolm, **221**, 222
Forbes (family), 127, 130
  John Murray, 130
  Robert Bennett, 130
Force, Madeleine (Mrs. John Jacob Astor IV),
    50
Ford, Gerald, 336
Ford (family), 12, 335, 341
  Henry, **10**, 11, **12**, 13, 22, 284–89, **286–88**,
    307, 337
  Henry II, **288**, 289, 336
Ford Foundation, 337–40, **338**
Ford, Model A, 288
Ford, Model T, 284–88, **284–85**
Ford Motor Company, 14, 284–85, 288–89
Ford V-8, 289
Foreman, George, 210
Fortune Magazine, 12–13, 59, 89, 307
foundations, 22, 85–86, 336–41. *See also* individual foundations
Fouquet, Nicolas, 157–58, **159**
"Four Hundred," 52, 55
Fowler, Gene, 13, 76
Francis I, of France, 155–56
Franklin, Benjamin, 16, 46
Frazier, Walt, **211**
Frescobaldi (family), 153

Frew, Walter, **176**
Frick, Henry Clay, 18, **256**, 257, 330
Fugger, Anton, 156
  Count Friedrich Karl, **157**
  Jakob, 10, 154–56, **156**

Gabriel, Ralph Henry, 15–16
Gainsborough, Thomas, 258
Gallatin, Mrs. Albert, 52
Gambetta, Léon, 201
Gandhi, Indira, 6
Gangel, Richard, home of, **224**
Gardiner (family)
  Lion, 42–43
  Robert David Lion, 44, **45**
Gardiners Island, 42–44, **45**
Gardner, Erle Stanley, 194–95, **196**
Gardner, John Lowell, 137, 140
  Mrs. Jack (Belle Stewart), 132, 137–40,
    138
Garland, Judy, **192–93**, 194
Garrick, David, 201
Gates, Frederick T., 18, 93
Gehrig, Lou, 210
Geneen, Harold, 12
General Foods Company, 24, 291
General Motors, 14, 268, 289
Generating Inequality (Thurow), 12
George, Henry, 62
George, King, 46
Gerard, James W., **252–53**
Gericke, Wilhelm, 138
Getty, J. Paul, 10, **13**, 41, 89, **92**, 93, 101–2,
    131
Gianini, Amadeo Peter, 24
Giant, 99
Gifford, Walter S., 22
Gilbert, William, 207–8
Gilbert le Gros Veneur (Gilbert the Chief
    Huntsman), 40
Gilded Age, the, **269–81**
Gillette, King, 304–5, **306**
Gimbel, Bernard, 133
Georgione, 123, 140
Girard, Stephen, 170
Glitter and the Gold, The (Consuelo Vanderbilt),
    21
"God Bless America," 208
Goddard, Dr. Robert, 86
Godric of Finchale, 120–21
Goelet (family), 47, 56, 107
  May (Duchess of Roxburghe), **20**, 21
Goes, Hugo van der, painting by, **143**
Golconda, 86
gold, 26, 174. *See also* mining, gold
Gold Hill mining camp, **78–79**
Goldman (family), 174
Goldwyn, Samuel, 202, 215–16
Gore (family), **66**
Gorges, Sir Ferdinando, 44
"Gospel of Wealth" (Carnegie), 331–32, 342
Gould (family), 11–12, 52
  Anna (Countess Boni de Castellane;
    Duchess de Talleyrand-Périgord), 21, 255–
    57
  Frank, 257
  George Jay, **108–9**, 255–57, **256**
  Helen, 257

Jay, 18, 22, 108, 171, 180, 249–52, **254**, 255,
    281, 333, 341
  Jay II, 257
Goya, Francisco José de, painting by, **8**, 9
Grace, William R., 130
Grafton, Duke of, 39
Granose, 290
Grant, Cary, 135, **136**, 137
Grant, Ulysses S., **79**, 81
Grape-Nuts, 290–91
Gray, Gilda, 214
Greatamerica Corporation, 307
Great Atlantic & Pacific Tea Company
    (A.& P.), 134, 136
Great Governing Families of England, The (Townsend), 39
Great Northern Railroad, 333
Green, Edward H., 176
  Mrs. Hetty, 176–77, **177**, 340
  Ned, 177
Greenacres, 202
Green Animals, **228–29**
Greenewalt, Crawford, **266–67**
Greenfield Village, 289
Gregory, Bob, 9
Greville, Charles, 41
Griffith, D. W., 202
Grosvenor (family), 40
  Sir Thomas, 40
Guest, Mrs. Frederick, 314
Guest, Mrs. Winston (Cee Zee), **314**, **322**, 323
Guffey, Colonel J. M., 179
Guggenheim (family), 12, 176, 335
  Meyer, 85, 335
  Peggy, 86, **186**, 191
  Solomon R., 86, **191**
Guggenheim Museum of Contemporary Art,
    86, **191**
Guinness, Mrs. Loel, **323**
Guinness Book of World Records, 7
Gulbenkian, Calouste ("Mr. Five Per Cent"),
    12, 13, **96**, 97–98
  Nubar, 97–98, **97**
Gulbenkian Foundation, 98
Gulf Oil, 89, 179
Gunther, Max, 15
Gwynn, Nell, 39

Habib Sabet, 102
Hadrian's Villa at Tivoli, **18**
Haggard, Godfrey, **252–53**
Haggard, Merle, 209
Haile Selassie, Emperor, 6
Hale & Norcross mine, 78
Hall, Charles Martin, 179
Halsman, Philippe, photograph by, **200**
Hammurabi, Code of, 150
Hancock, John, 17, 130
Handel, George Frederick, 207
Happy Time, The, 208
Harding, Warren G., 179
Hardwick, Elizabeth ("Bess") (Countess of
    Shrewsbury), 15, 17
Hardwick Hall, **15**, 17
Harewood House, 68
Hargreaves, James, 240, 242
Harkness, Stephen V., 94
Harlow, Jean, **308**, 309–10

Harper's Weekly, illustration from, **48**
Harriman, Mrs. J. Borden, **252–53**
Harriman (family), 52
  E. H., 174
  W. Averell, 299
Hartford, George, 120, 134, 136
  George Huntington, 134
  Huntington, 136–37
  John, 120, 134, 136
Harvard, John, **334**
Harvard University, 334
Harvey, William, illustration by, **41**
Haugwitz-Reventlow, Count Kurt von, 135, **136**, 137
Hawksmoor, Nicholas, 65
Hawthorne, Nathaniel, 130
Hearst, George, 82
Hearst, William Randolph, 6, 10, **11**, 13, 16–17, 21, 24, 59, 179, **218**, 219, **220**, 221–22
Hecht, Ben, 216
Hefner, Hugh, 19
Heine, Heinrich, 168
heirs, instructions to, 24, 48–53, 166, 268
Held, Anna, 214
Hell's Angels, 308–10
Henry, Patrick, 46
Henry VIII, of England, 39
Herbert, Victor, 214
Hermes, 209–10
Herodotus, 150
Heth, Joice, 212
Hewlett, William R., 304
Hewlett-Packard Company, 14, 304
Hill, James J., 171, 174, 333
Hillwood, 292, **293–94**, 295
Hirshhorn, Joseph, 88–89, **187**
Hirshhorn Museum, 187
History of the Business Man (Beard), 152
Holbrook, Darius B., 47
Holder, Mrs. Albin, 314
Holmes, Oliver Wendell, 138
Homer, Winslow, painting by, **244**
Homestead Act, 41, 47
Hoover, Herbert, 77, 81, 210
Hope, Bob, 9, 203, **205**, 208
Hope, (Lord) Francis Pelham Clinton, 83
  Henry Philip, 83
Hope Diamond, 82–85, **85**
Hopkins, Mark, 257–58, **257**, 333
Horowitz, David, 342
Horse and Rider (Marini), **190**, 191
horses, 23, 66, **67–69**, **72–73**, **106**, 107, **326–27**
Horton's Tower, **230**, 231
Houghton (family), 335
Hovgard, Carl, home of, 319, **320–21**
Howe, Elias, Jr., 260–61
Hudson, George, 248
Hudson, Joseph L., 133
Hughes, Howard, 10, **13**, 89, 307–12, **308–9**
Hughes Aircraft Company, 310–12
Hughes Medical Foundation, 312
Hughes Tool Company, 308–12
Hugo, Victor, 201
Hull, Lytle, 58
Human Lunar Spectral (Arp), **187**
Humayun, **33**
Hunt, H. L., 10, **12**, 13, 89, 101
  Lamar, 101

N. Bunker, 101
Hunt, Richard Morris, 16, 255
  house designed by, **55**
Hunt, Walter, 260
Huntington, Arabella, 258
  Collis P., 257–58, **257**, 333
  Henry E., 258
Hussey, Obed, 259
Hutton, Barbara, 24, 135–36, **136–37**
Huxley, Aldous, 284

IBEC, 342
IBM. *See* International Business Machines Corporation
Ibuka, Masaru, 6
Ilg, Robert A., 231
I Love Lucy, 203
Importance of Being Earnest, The (Wilde), 40
Inchcape, Earl of, 9
India, 6, 19, 31, 86, 90
Indians, American, 38, **39**, 42, 44
Industrial Revolution, 11, 238ff., 289
Industrial Revolution, The (Ashton), 240
industry. *See* manufacture
inheritance, 39, 135–40, 335–36. *See also* entail; heirs, instructions to; primogeniture
Inheritors, The (Robbins), 196
Insull, Samuel, 180
International Business Machines Corporation, 180, **282–83**, 284, **302–3**, 304
International Harvester Company, 259
invention, 258–61
Investors Overseas Services, 224
Iolanthe railroad car, **111**
Ippolito II d'Este, Cardinal, 234
Iran, 6, 19, 90
Iranistan, 213
Iraq Petroleum Company, 96–97
Irvine, James, 59
Irvine Ranch, 59
Irving, Washington, 47
Isa of Bahrein, Sheik, **100**, 101

Jackson, Hannah (Mrs. Francis Cabot Lowell), **245**
Jackson, Patrick Tracy, 245
Jacobs, Erasmus, 86
Jacobsz, Dirck, painting by, **143**
James, Henry, 132, 138
James I, of England, 42–44, 81
Jardine, Matheson & Co., 127
Jefferson, Thomas, 46–47, 62, 262, **262**, 268, 336
Jennings, Oliver Brewster, 94
jewels, 6, 19, 30–31, 90, **91**
Jews, 152–53, 163, 174
Joan of Arc, 153–54
John, Elton, **16**, 208–9
Johnson, Dr. Samuel, 194, 239
Johnson, Lyndon B., 9
  Mrs. Lady Bird, 9
Johnson, Robert Wood, **13**
Johnston, Alva, 57
Jones, H. Bradley, 319
Jones, John Percival, 22
Jones and Laughlin Steel, 307
Jordan, Eben, 133

Judah, Theodore Dehone, 257–58
Juliana, queen of the Netherlands, 7

Kahn, Otto, 20, 176
Kay, John, 242
Keep, Nigel, 222
Keir, James, 238
Kellogg, Dr. John Harvey, 290–95
  Will K., 290–95, 307
Kennedy, Joseph P., 9, 22, 57
Kentucky Fried Chicken, 136
Kern, Jerome, 209
Keynes, John Maynard, 125
Kidd, Captain William, 43
Kimberley mine, **86–87**, 87–88
King, Reverend Martin Luther, Jr., **334**
King, Captain Richard, 59, 61
King Ranch, 59–62, **60–61**
Kingdon, Edith, 255, **255**
Kinsolving, Mrs. Arthur Lee, Jr., 314, **315**
Kleberg, Richard M, Jr., 61
  Robert, Jr., 59–62, **61**
  Robert Justus, 59, 61
Knickerbocker Trust Company, 176
Kodak, 296, **297–98**
Koppers Company, 179
Kresge (family), 135
Kress (family), 89, 135
Kroc, Ray, 136–37
KTBC-TV, 9
Kuhn (family), 174
Kuhn, Loeb & Company, 174–76

Lady at Her Toilet, A (Ter Borch), **147**
Lamartine, Alphonse, 201
Lambert, Gerard, 305–6
Lambert Pharmacal Company, 305
Land, Edwin H., 297–300
land, 9–10
  absentee owners, 38
  as basis of aristocracy, 38–40, 44
  city real estate, **36–37**, 38, 40, 47–48, 56–57, 81, 134
  eviction from 41, 46, 62
  18th-century English gentry and, **63–73**
  feudal system of tenure, 38, **40**, 42, 44
  Florida boom, 57–59, 96–97
  inheritance laws, 39
  patroonship on Hudson, 42
  permanence of wealth from, 40
  politics and, 38–40
  private-property rights, 38–39, 41, 62
  royal grants, 38–39, 42–44
  Southern plantations, **43**, 44
  speculation, in early U.S., 45–47
  suburbs, 59
Langhorne, Nancy (Lady Astor), **51**, 53
La Paiva, 224
Larcom, Lucy, 245
Lavoisier, Antoine, 268
Law, John, 158–61, **160**
Lawrence, William, 332
Lazarus (family), 135
Leadville Johnny, 76–77
Le Brun, Charles, 158
Lee, Colonel Henry, 21
Lehman, Ernest, 208

Lehman (family), 151, 174–76
    Henry, 120
    Philip, townhouse of, **188–89**
    Robert, 188
Lehr, Harry, **103**, **250**, 251
Leiter, Levi, 133–34
    Mary (Lady Curzon), 21, 134
Le Nôtre, André, 157–58
Leopold II, of Belgium, 82–83
Leo X, Pope, 156
Le Vau, Louis, 158
Levine, Joseph E., 196
Lewis, Joe E., 24
Lewisohn, Adolph, 85
Life Magazine, 26
Lind, Jenny, 213
Linden Towers, 80, **80**
Ling, James, 12, 306–7, **307**
Ling Electric, 307
Ling-Temco Electronics, 307
Ling-Temco-Vought (LTV), 12, 307
Lion, Robert David, 43–44
Listerine, 305
Little, Royal, 12
Livermore, Jesse, 180
Livingston (family), 44, 52
    Robert, 42
Lloyd, Harold, 202, **205**
Loach, R. J. H. de, **287**
Loeb (family), 174–76
    Solomon, 174
    Therese, 174
Lombard, Carole, 222
Lombards, 153
Longest Day, The, 215
Longleat, **64–65**, **70**, 71
Longwood, 268
Longworth, Nicholas, I, 56
Looking Backward (Bellamy), 333–34
Loredano, Doge Leonardo, **124**
Lorillard (family), 56
    Pierre, 59
Louis, Arthur, 12
Louis XIII, of France, 42
Louis XIV, of France, 157–59
Loutherbourg, Philippe de, painting by, **236–37**, 238
Lowell (family), 21
    Abbott Lawrence, **246**, 247–48
    Amy, **246**, 247
    Francis Cabot, 244–45, **245**
        Mrs. (Hannah Jackson), **245**
    James Russell, 138, 247
    Percival, 22, **246**, 247
    Ralph, 246, **247**
Lucas, Andy. *See* Luchich, Anthony F.
Luchich, Anthony F., 179
Ludovica, Infanta Maria, **31**
Ludwig, Daniel K., 10, **13**, 130–32
Lunar Society, 238–39, 241
Lupus, Hugh (Earl of Chester), 40
Luther, Martin, 156
Lykes, Howell Tyson, 314

McAllister, Ward, 52
MacArthur, John D., **13**
McCormick, Cyrus Hall, 15, 258–59, 281, 341
    Robert, 258

    Ruth and John Medill, **281**
McDonald, Richard and Maurice, 136
McDonald's hamburger chain, 136–37
McGonigal, Mary and Kate, 261
McGovern, George, 335
McGraw (family), 335
Mackay, John W., 13, 21, 77–81, **79**, 85
McLean, Edward Beale, 82–85
    Mrs. Evalyn Walsh, **84**, 85. *See also* Walsh, Evalyn
    Vinson Walsh, 82–83, **84**, 85
Macmillan, Harold, 17
McNamara, Robert, 14
Macy, Rowland, 133
Maecenas, Gaius, 150–51
Mann, Sir Horace, **182–83**
Mansfield, Irving, 196
Mansfield, Josie, 252
manufacture, 10–12, 282ff.
Mapleson, J. H., 206
Mar-A-Lago, **291–92**
Marble, Alice, 222
Marble Dry Goods Palace, 132–33
Marble House, 254, **272–73**
Marcantonio the Triumpher, 26
Marchesa railroad car, **111**
Marie de' Medici, 197
Marini, sculpture by, **190**, 191
Marius, 150
Marlborough, Duke of, 20–21, 251, 255
marriage, 39–40, 52
Marsh, Stanley, 223
Martin Chuzzlewit (Dickens), 46, 47
Martin V, Pope, 26
Mason, Captain John, 44
mass production, 284–85
Massys, Quentin, painting by, **148–49**, 150
Mauze, Abby Rockefeller, 89
Maximilian I, Holy Roman Emperor, 155–56
Maxim's, **319**
May, Caroline and Frederick, 218
Mayer, Louis B., 215, **216–17**
Mazarin, Cardinal, 157
Mdivani, "Prince" Alexis, 135, **136**, 137
Medici, the, 151, 156, 182
    Cosimo de', 154, **154**, **181**
    Giovanni di Bicci de', 154
    Lorenzo de', 154, **155**
Medill, Joseph, 281
Mellon (family), 12, 89, 93, 101, 151
    Andrew W., **12**, 13, 18, 89, 177–80, **178**
    Paul, 180, **186**
    Richard B., 177–80
    Richard King, 180
    Thomas, 14, 177
Mendoub, Palais, 222
Mentmore, 170
Merchant of Venice (Shakespeare), 152
Merrick, George E., 57–58
Metro-Goldwyn-Mayer, 215, 217
Metropolitan Museum of Art, 184, **188**
Metropolitan Opera House, 22, 176, **328–29**, 330
Metropolitan Street Railway Company, 9
Middle Ages, 38, **40**, 120–22, **122**
Middle East fortunes, 102. *See also* individual countries

Mikimoto, Kokichi, 310, **311**
Mill, John Stuart, 62
Miller, Johnny, 212
Miller, Marilyn, 214
Mills, Darius Ogden, 18
Milton, 194
mining, 10
    gold, 76–78, 81, 88
    mineral rights, 81
    silver, 77–82, 81, 88, 153
    tin, 88
    uranium, 14, 88–89
Mississippi Bubble, 160–61
Missouri Pacific Railroad, 59
Mi Vida mine, 14
Mizner, Addison and Wilson, 57–58
Molenaer, Jan, painting by, **144–45**
Molière, 158
monasteries, confiscation of land of, 39
Money Changer and His Wife, The, **148–49**, 150
Monitor railroad car, **110**, 111
Monk's Brew. *See* Postum
Monts, Sieur de, 42
Moore, David, 15
Morgan, J. Pierpont, 13–14, 16–17, 23, 52, **112–13**, 151, 170–76, **171–73**, 179, 184
    Junius P., 170
Morgan Library, 17, 173, **184–85**
Morgan the Younger, **176**
Morita, Akio, 6
Morning Bell, The (Homer), **244**
Morris, Lloyd, 53
Morris (family), 44
    Lewis, 42
    Robert, 170
motion-picture industry, 308–12
Muhammad Ali, 210
Mumtaz, Mahal, 33
Munter, William, 124
Murchison, Clint, 99–101
music, 66, 207–9

Namath, Joe, **211**, 212
Nana Opoku Ware II (J. Matthew Poku), 26, **28–29**
Napoleon Bonaparte, 163–65
Nash, Charles W., 289
Nashville, Tennessee, 209
National Bulk Carriers, 130
National Cash Register Company, 300–304
National Gallery (Washington, D.C.), 89, 179, 186
National Institutes of Health, 340–41
National Science Foundation, 340
Nemours, 268
Never Love a Stranger (Robbins), 196
Nevins, Allan, 90
"New Domesday Survey" (1873), 38, 40
New Harmony, 22
New Lanark, 244
Newport, Rhode Island, 16, 23, 52, 76, 103, 218, 254–55, 271, 273, **324–25**, 342, **343**
Newport Casino, **106**, 107, 218, **271**, **324–25**
New York Central Railroad, 171, 249–52
New York City, 48, 56–57
New York *Herald*, 216–18
New York *Journal*, 221
New York Social Register, 11

New York Times, 58
Niarchos, Stavros, 130
  yacht of, **114–15**
Nicholas II, of Russia, and family, **34**
Nickel Plate Railroad, 59
Nicklaus, Jack, 212
Nissen, Greta, 308
Nizam of Hyderabad, **12**, 13
Nobel, Alfred, 334
Nobel Prize, 334, 341
North American Review, 331
Northern Pacific Railroad, 174
North Star (yacht), 252–54
Norton, Charles Eliot, 138–40
Nude Woman, The (Picasso), 201
Nutt, Commodore, 213

O'Brien, William S., 77–80
Occo, Pompejus, **143**
Oelrichs, Hermann, 81
  Mrs. (Tessie Fair), 18, 81
oil, 10, 12, 59–62, **74–75**, 76–77, 81, 89–102
Oklahoma!, 208
Old Battersea House, 222
Oldfield, Barney, **286–87**
Olds, Ransom E., 289
Olympic Airways, 23
Onassis, Aristotle, 23, **115**, 130, **131**
  Mrs. Jacqueline, 20
Once is Not Enough (Susann), 195–96
O'Neill (family), 335
opera singers, 203–7
opium, 126–27
Oppenheimer, Harry, 88
  Sir Ernest, **13**, 88
Origo, Iris, 122
Orr–Lewis, Lady Anne, 227
Orsini, Vicino, 234
Ort, Charles, 57
Our Crowd (Birmingham), 174
Outlaw, The, 310
Owen, Robert, 22, 244

Pacideianus, 209
Pacific Union Club, 80
Packard, David, 14, 304
Packard, James, 289
Paderewski, 138
Page, Walter Hines, 22
Palace Hotel (San Francisco), **313**
Paley, Mrs. William, 20
Palissy, Bernard, 197
Palm Beach, Florida, 16, 262
Palmer, Arnold, **211**, 212
Palmer, Potter, 133
  Mrs. Bertha Honoré, **132**, 133
Panic of 1907, 174, 176, 184
Pao, Y. K., 132
Paramount Studios, 202, 215
Parton, James, 48
Patino, Antenor, 88
  Simon, 88, **89**
patrons of the arts. *See* art, patrons of
patroonship, 42
Patterson, John H., 300–304, **301**
Patti, Adelina, 203–7, **207**
Paulucci, Jeno, 15

Payne, Henry B., 22
  Oliver H., 22, 94
Peabody (family), 12
  George, 170
Peabody Conservatory of Music, **339**
Peale, Rembrandt, painting by, 262, **263**
Pearl, Minnie, 209
Pell (family), 42
Pennock, Herb, 210
Pennsylvania Railroad, 171, 330
Perkins (family), 127
  Thomas Handasyd, 130
Perot, H. Ross, 13, 180
Peruzzi (family), 153, 156
Peterhof, **34–35**
Peter the Great, of Russia, 34
Petrie, Milton J., 12
Petronius, 121
philanthropy, 12, 22, 93, 122, 151, 331–32,
  336–37
Philip IV, of Spain, 197
Philip V, of Spain, 206–7
Philipse, Frederick, 42
Phipps, Henry, 15, 314, 330
"Phiz," illustrations by, **46**
photography, 295–300
Picasso, Pablo, 198–201, **202**
  Mrs. (Jacqueline Roque), 201
Pickfair, 202
Pickford, Mary, 202–3, **204**, 205
Pickle for the Knowing Ones, A (Dexter), 23
Pierce, Webb, 209
Pittsburgh, Pennsylvania, 177, 180
plantations, Southern, **43**, 44
Pliny the Elder, 62
Pliny the Younger, 38
Plutarch, 150
Pocantico Hills, **340**
Poku, J. Matthew (Nana Opoku Ware II), 26,
  28–29
Polaroid, 298–300
political power, 6, 22, 38–40, 150–66, 170, 332
Polk, Frank Lyon, **252–53**
Poole, Ernest, 259
Pope, Alexander, 194
Portsmouth, Duchess of, 39
Post, Charles W., 24, 290–95
  Marjorie Merriweather, 24, 227, 291, **291**,
  292, **293**, 295
Post, Wiley, 310
Post Toasties, 291
Postum, 290–91
Poussin, Nicolas, 157
Pratt, Charles, 94
Priestley, Joseph, 238
primogeniture, 11–12, 39
Promises, Promises, 195
Proper Bostonians, The (Amory), 14
Pullman, George M., 111, 171
Pyne, Mrs. Grafton H., **252–53**

"Quadricycle," 284, **288**
Quesnay, Dr. François, 262

Racine, Jean Baptiste, 194
Radziwill (family), 6
railroads, 59, 166, 171–72, 174, 248–50, 257–

58, 330, 333
  railroad cars, private, 17–18, **110–11**
Ramo, Dr. Simon, 310–12
Reading Room (Newport), 218
real estate. *See* land
rebates, 90–93
Reclining Venus (Titian), **182–83**
Reed, Mrs. Helen Appleton, **322**, 323
Reichenbach, Henry, 296
Reid, Whitelaw, 22
Reksten, Hilmar, 132
Rembrandt, 123–24
Rensselaerswyck, 42
revolution, as peril to wealth, 6, 11, 40
Reynolds, Sir Joshua, 197–98
Rhinelanders, 56
Rhodes, Cecil, 22, **86–87**, 87–88, 334
Rice, Dr. Hamilton, **252–53**
Rich, Morris, 133
Richardson, Elliot, 22
Richardson, Sid, 99–101
Richmond, Duke of, 39
Rickard, Tex, 210
Ringling Bros. and Barnum & Bailey Circus,
  214–15
Ritty, James S., 300
Rives, Constance, **279**
  Natica, **269**
RKO, 310–12
Robbins, Harold, 196, 203
Roberts, Kenneth, 57
Robinson, Edward G., **204**, 205
Robinson, Lota, **270**, 271
Rochester, New York, 297
Rockefeller (family), 12, 44, 52, 85, 89–93, 101,
  136, 335, 342
  David, 93, 180
  John Davison, Sr., **12**, 13–14, 77, 90–93,
  94–95, 288, 330, 333, 335–37, **340**, 342
  John D., Jr., 90–93, 334–35, **340**
  John D. IV ("Jay"), 342
  Laura, 342
  Laurance, Jr., **341**
  Marian, 342
  Marion, 341
  Nelson, 90–93, **340**, 342
  Rodman, **340**, 342
  Sandra (Sandra Ferry), 342
  Steven, 342
  William, 12
  Winthrop, 89
Rockefeller Foundation, 93, 339–41
Rockefeller Institute for Medical Research
  (now Rockefeller University), 93
rock stars, 16
Rodgers, Richard, 208
Rogers, Henry Huddleston, 14, 94
Rolls-Royce, **16**, 18, **116–17**
Roman Empire, 120–21, 126, 150–51
Romanov czardom, 34
Rooney, Mickey, **192–93**, 194, **216–17**
Roosevelt, Franklin D., Jr., 265
Roque, Jacqueline (Mrs. Pablo Picasso), 201
Roscius Gallus, Q., 201
Rosenwald (family), 12
Rossini, Gioacchino Antonio, 207
Rothschild (family), 23, 126, 151
  Alfred de, 24
  Amschel, 165

Anthony, **164–65**
Carl, 165–66
Charlotte, 166
David, **167**
Edmond, 170
Edouard, 170
Ferdinand, 167
Guy de, **167**, 170
Mrs. Hélène, **167**
Hannah, 166
Henri, 170
James, 164–65, 168, 170
Lionel, **164–65**, 166
Lord, 170
Mayer, **164–65**, 170
Mayer Amschel, 162–64, 166
Mrs. Gutele, 163, 168
Nathan, 163–65, **163**, 165–66
Nathaniel, **164–65**
Philippe, **169**, 170
Robert, **168–69**
Salomon, 165–66
Roxburghe, Duke of, **20**, 21
Roy, Harry, 9
Royal Dutch Oil, 97
Royal Poinciana hotel, 96
Rubens, Peter Paul, 140, 197–98
Rubinstein, Helena, **305**, 306
Rubirosa, Porfirio, 135, **137**
Russell, Jane, 310
Russell, Lillian, 21
Russell Sage Foundation, 337, 340
Ruth, Babe, 209, **211**
Ryan (family), 11
Thomas Fortune, 9, 18

Sachs (family), 174
Sadymatte, 150
Safety Razor Company, 306
Sage (family), 12
Russell, 24, 337–40, **337**
Mrs. Olivia, **337**
St. Albans, Duke of, 39
St. Loe, Lord, 17
salesmanship, 300–301
Sallust, 201
Samuel, Marcus (Viscount Bearsted), 97
Sandow the Strong Man, 214
Sandringham, 7
Sanitas Food Company, 290–95
San Simeon, **4–5**, 6, 17, **219**, 221–22
Santa Gertrudis cattle, 59–62, **60–61**
Saratoga, 275
Sarawak, White Rajahs of, 7–9
Sargent, John Singer, 138–40
Sason Ben Saleh, 126
Sassoon (family), 125–27
Alfred, 127
Mrs. (Theresa Thornycroft), 127
David, 126–27, **126**
Elias, 127
Philip, 127
Sassoon David ("S.D."), **126**, 127
Siegfried, 127
Sybil, 127
Victor, 127, **127**
Saturday Evening Post, 57
Satyricon, 121

Saudi Arabia, 6–7
Schermerhorn (family), 56
Caroline Webster (Mrs. William Back-house Astor, Jr.), 48, **49**, 50, **51**, 52–53, 55, **103**, 174
Schiff, Jacob, 174–76, **176**
Schriftgeisser, Karl, 85
Schwab, Charles M., 6, 18
Scott, Thomas A., 330
Sedgwick, Ellery, 138
Seligman (family), 174
Joseph, 120
Selim Habib, 83
"Sesame Street," 339
Shah Jehan, 33
Shaker Heights, Ohio, 59
Shakespeare, 152
Shapiro, Irving, 268
Sharon, William, 22, 78
Sharp, Hugh R., Jr., **266–67**
Shell Oil, 97
shipping, 170, 244
Shoemaker, Willie, 210
showmen, 212–16
Shrewsbury, Earl of, 17
Siddons, Mrs., 201
silver. *See* mining, silver
Simon, Neil, 195, **197**, 222
Singer (family), 11
Isaac, 259–62, **260**
Mrs. Isabella, **260**, 261
Paris, 58, 262
Winaretta, 261
Singh, Maharajah Gulab, **31**
Skibo Castle, **333**
Slater, Samuel, 243–44
Sloan, Alfred P., Jr., 289
Small Business Administration, 15
Smith, Adam, 239, 332
Smith, Alva (Mrs. William K. Vanderbilt), **250**, 251
Smith, James, 6
Smithson, James, **334**
Smithsonian Institution, 334
social conscience, 56, 247
social position, 21
Sony, 6
Sorel, Agnes, 154
Sound of Music, The, 208
South Africa, 86–88
Southern Pacific Company, 258
South Improvement Company, 90, 94
South Pacific, 208
Spencer, Herbert, 62
Sponsler, Mary Ann, 261
sports. *See* athletes
Sprang, Joseph, **306**
"Spruce Goose" flying boat, 310
squares (plazas), 40, **41**
Standard Oil Company, 14, 22, 90–97, 337
Stanford, Leland, 257–58, **257**, 333
Stanford University, 258
Star of the East diamond, 82
Starr, Roger, 41
steel industry, 330, 333
Steen, Charles A., 14, 22
Steichen, Edward, photograph by, **172–73**
Stephenson, George and Robert, 248
Stern, Leonard, 12

Stevens (family), 336
Stewart (family), 52
Stewart, Alexander Turney, 47, 132–33
Stewart, Belle (Mrs. Jack Gardner), 132, 137–40, **138**
David, 137
Stewart, William Morris, 22
Stokowski, Leopold, 251
Stotesbury (family), 11
Mrs. Edward T., 20
Stratton, Charles S. (General Tom Thumb), 213, **213**
Straus, Nathan, 133
Strauss, Lewis, 299
Stravinsky, Igor, 207
Stroganov (family), 6
Strong, Henry, 296
Strong, Kate, **279**
Strutt, Jedediah, 243
Stubbs, George, paintings by, **63**, **72–73**
Studebaker, Clement, 289
Stuyvesant (family), 11
suburbs, 59
Sulla, 150
Sullivan, Arthur, 207–8
Sullivan, John L., 210
Summa Corporation, 312
surreys, **106**, 107. *See also* carriages; coaches; tallyhos
Survivors, The (Robbins), 196
Susann, Jacqueline, 195–96
Sutherland, Duke of, 40–41
Sutton Place, **92**, 93, 102
Swanberg, W. A., 221
Swanson, Gloria, 202, **204**, 205
Swell Hogan, 308

Taj Mahal, **32–33**
Talleyrand-Périgord, Duc de, 21, 257
Duchess de, 21, 255–57
tallyhos, 17, **107**. *See also* carriages; coaches; surreys
Tavernier, 83
taxes, 6, 24, 40–41, 335–36
Taylor, Elizabeth, 203, **205**
Temco Electronics, 307
Temple, Shirley, **204**, 205
Temple, Sir William, 124
Ter Borch, Gerard, painting by, **147**
Terry, Ellen, 140
Tetzel, John, 156
Texas oil millionaires, 98–101
textile industry, 240–48
Thimonnier, Barthélemy, 259–60
Thomson, Lord Roy, **221**, 222
Thornton, Charles B., 310–12
Thornycroft, Theresa (Mrs. Alfred Sassoon), 127
Thumb, General Tom (Charles S. Stratton), 213, **213**
Thurow, Lester C., 12
Thynne, Sir John, 65
Tide Water Associated Oil Company, 101
Tilden, Bill, 222
Timber Line, 76
Times (London), 222, 336
Titanic, 50, 76–77
Titian, 123, 140, 182, 197

titles, acquisition of, 21, 39–40
Todd, Sarah (Mrs. William Backhouse Astor), 52
Tom Thumb locomotive, 336
Tonight show, 208
Topridge, Camp, **292**
Townsend, F. M. L., 39
trade, 10, 120ff, **125**, **128–29**, 150–56, 170
    with the East, **118–21**, 120, 123, 126–28, 153
Transcontinental and Western Airways. *See* Trans World Airways (TWA)
Trans World Airways (TWA), 310–12
Trevithick, Richard, 248
Trident Press, 196
Troubetzkoy, Prince Igor, 135, **137**
trust law, 247
Tunney, Gene, 210
Turgot, Anne Robert Jacques, 262
Tutankhamen, Pharaoh, 25
Tuxedo Park, 59, 275
Twain, Mark, 194, 332
20th Century Fox, 208, 215
Tz'u Hsi, Chinese Dowager Empress, 231

Uihlein (family), 335
Union Pacific Railroad, 174
United Artists, 202
United Auto Workers, 289
United Fruit Company, 15
United States Steel Corporation, 6, 172
U.S. Treasury, 172
University of Rochester, 297
Unwalla, Darab, 15
Uppark, **71**
uranium boom. *See* mining, uranium

Valley of the Dolls (Susann), 195–96
Van Alen, James H., 324
Vanderbilt (family), 11, 21, 107, 341
    Alfred Gwynne I, **106**, 107
    Alfred Gwynne II, **251**
        Mrs., **250**, 251
    Consuelo (Duchess of Marlborough; Mme. Jacques Balsan), **20**, 21, **250**, 251, **322**, 323
    Cornelius I (Commodore), 18, 47, 171, 248–54, **248**
        Mrs., 21
    Cornelius II, 273
        Mrs., **279**
    Cornelius Jeremiah, 254
    George, 254
    George Washington II, 254–55
    Gertrude (Mrs. Harry Payne Whitney), 322
    Gloria (Mrs. Wyatt Cooper), **251**
    Harold, **250**, 251
    Mrs. Cornelius III, **252–53**, 255
    Reginald, **250**, 251
    William Henry, 94, 107, 254
    William Henry III, **250**, 251
    William Kissam, 18, 52, 254, 273, **274**, 275, 335
        Mrs. (Alva Smith), 21, **250**, 251, 255, 273, 279, **279**
    William K., Jr., 81, **250**, 251

    Mrs. (Birdie Fair), 81
Vanderbilt Cup Races, 18
Van Rensselaer (family), 11, **42**
    Kiliaen, 42
    Mrs. John King, 52
Van Sweringen, Mantis J. and Oris P., 59
Vatel, 158
Vaux-le-Vicomte, 157–58, **158–59**
Venice, 120, 122–24, 152–53, 157
Vermeer, Jan, 124, 140, 147
    paintings by, **141, 146**
Veronese, Paolo, 123, 197
Versailles, 16, 158, 221
Very Very Rich and How They Got That Way, The (Gunther), 15
Vesco, Robert, 180
Villa Artemis, **314**
Villa d'Este at Tivoli, **234–35**
Villa Orsini at Bomarzo, **234**
Vinh, Doan, 136, **137**
Virginia aristocrats, 44
Virginia City, Nevada, 78–80, **79**
Vizcaya, **259**
Voltaire, 194, **194**

Waddeson Manor, **166–67**
Wales, Prince of (future Edward VII), 201
Wales, Prince of (later George IV), 72
Walker, Samuel and Aaron, 240–41
Wall, Berry, 19
Wall, Joseph Frazier, 332
Wall Street, 174, 176, 180
Walsh, Evalyn (Mrs. Edward Beale McLean), 82–85
    Tom, 81–82, **82**, 133
        Mrs. **83**
    Vinson, 82
Walters, Lucy, 39
Wanamaker, John, 133
war, 6, 11
Warburg (family), 174
    James P., 299
Warner, Jack, 6
Warren, Lavinia, **213**
Washington, George, 44–46, 130, 170
Watson, Thomas J., **302–3**, 304
    Thomas, Jr., **303**
Watt, James, 238, **238–39**, 240–41, 248
Wedgwood, Josiah, 63, 238, **238**, 239–41
Wellington, Duke of, 164–65
Wells, W. Storrs, 273
Wendel, Ella, 56, **56**
    John, 56
    Rebecca, 56
Wertheim (family), 174
West, James Marion, 22
    James Marion, Jr. ("Silver Dollar" Jim), 98–99, **99**
Westminster, Duke of, 9, 40
West Shore Railroad, 171
West Virginia Wesleyan College, 342
whims of very rich, 22–24, **223–235**
White, Mrs. Ellen, 289–90
White, Stanford, 16, 218
"White Christmas," 208
Whitehouse, J. Norman de R., **252–53**
Whitney, John Hay, 22
    Mrs. Harry Payne (Gertrude Vanderbilt),

322
    Richard, 180
    William C., 9, **274**, 275
Widener, Peter Arrell Brown, 18, 89, 179
Wilde, Oscar, 40
Wilhelmina, queen of the Netherlands, 7
William, Duke of Normandy, 38
William of Hesse, Prince, 163–65
William the Conqueror, 40
Williams, Mrs. Harrison, 20
Williams, Ted, 210
Willing (family), 170
    Ava (Mrs. John Jacob Astor IV; Lady Ribblesdale), 50, **51**
Wilson, Charles E., 14
Wilson, Richard T., **106**, 107
Wilson, Woodrow, 18, 108
Wilson and Company, 307
Winston, Harry, 85
Winterthur, **264**, 268
Wise, Robert, 208
Witte, Emmanuel de, painting by, **142**, 143
Wooldridge, Dr. Dean, 310–12
Woolworth, Frank, 120, 134–35
Woolworth Building, **135**
Wren, Sir Christopher, 222
Wright, Frank Lloyd, museum designed by, **191**
Wright, Joseph, 66
    painting by, **67**

Yachts, 17–18, 21, **112–15**, 173
Yohe, May, 83
Young, Robert, 99

Zanuck, Darryl F., 6, 215
Zemurray, Samuel, 15
Ziegfeld, Florenz, 214–15
Zoffany, Johann, painting by, **182–83**
Zoonomia, or the Laws of Organic Life (E. Darwin), 238